O9-ABE-776

CONTEMPORARY EVANGELICAL THOUGHT

CONTEMPORARY EVANGELICAL THOUGHT

ANDREW W. BLACKWOOD
CARL F. H. HENRY
EARLE E. CAIRNS
DIRK JELLEMA
GORDON HADDON CLARK
HAROLD KUHN
FRANK E. GAEBELEIN
ROGER NICOLE
EVERETT F. HARRISON
EDWARD JOSEPH YOUNG

Edited by

CARL F. H. HENRY

Channel Press · Great Neck · New York

First Printing

LIBRARY OF CONGRESS
CATALOGUE CARD NUMBER: 57-7630

PRINTED IN THE UNITED STATES OF AMERICA
BY THE HADDON CRAFTSMEN, INC., SCRANTON, PENNSYLVANIA

CONTENTS

PREFACE

THE HALF century just ended is memorable for theological neglect and failure. Respected thinkers scorned biblical Christianity. In its place they championed the secular contemporary gods of liberalism.

With the recent collapse of these man-made alternatives to evangelical Christianity has come, however, a new day. Historic Christian theism now holds a fresh relevance for our tired and disillusioned age. Rediscovery of evangelical truth has begun.

Because liberalism dominated the religious movements, especially education and publication, the between-the-wars generation little sensed the basic Christian teachings hanging so perilously in the balances. With the intellectual giants of the age conspicuously devoted to a compromising theology, the uninformed or misinformed masses found it difficult to discern the dangers of the prevailing thought patterns.

True, evangelical forces were unimpressive in their literary contributions during those years. They failed woefully in baring the weaknesses of the liberal compromise. The public decline and collapse of liberal theology came slowly; actual desertion by theological strategists came even grudgingly.

It would be grossly incorrect, however, to credit the evangelical movement with no contribution whatever to the decline and fall of liberalism. Its analysis of liberalism's weakness, and by contrast its exhibition of biblical Christianity's strength, hastened the dawning of a new day. Despite its limited intellectual leadership and financial means, the conservative wing inherited by default the spiritual task of evangelism and missions neglected by the organized church. On front after front the evangelical movement had to contend against sub-Christian and anti-Christian bias. Holding fast to the Gospel proclamation, both on mission fields abroad and in pulpits at home, evangelical Protestantism sounded the only summons to Christ as the Redeemer from sin.

In spite of its sparse and sometimes ineffective impact, evangelical literature was nevertheless present and significant. Its sturdy defense of Christian convictions, and the production of at least a core of material, struck a telling blow even as liberalism was reaching its full power. This evangelical witness carried forward the virile literary inheritance of a past which reached back through the Reformation even to the apostolic age. Evangelicals continued to emphasize the inextricable relationship between the fate of the Bible and the fate of Christianity. Interestingly enough, even the newer mediating theology of our day is returning to this awareness.

Today the forces of evil threaten almost all the citadels of Christianity. The world about us lies confused, uncertain and apprehensive. Nothing is so much needed as an enduring perspective to correct and maintain the focus and range of spiritual sights.

Just now the American mind is reappraising its bias against traditional religion and the implicit disdain for such religious phrases as "contemporary evangelical thought." While evangelical missions and evangelism were tolerated in the forepart of the twentieth century, the term "evangelical" was held in derision as an anti-intellectualistic shadow from the past. "Evangelical thought," moreover, was regarded as an incongruous association of ideas. And "*contemporary* evangelical thought" even more so! Did not all genuine scholarship require the adjective "liberal"? Could any viewpoint other than modernism be considered relevant?

Today the climate of the times is changing. The fortunes of liberalism rather than of evangelicalism are nailed more and more to the mast of anti-intellectualism. Furthermore, liberalism is now diagnosed as both socially and academically irrelevant.

The present volume has two aims: first, to sketch the evangelical contribution in the present century of theological stress, and, second, to clarify present conservative thought on some of the crucial centers of Christian concern.

The contributors have made more than merely an objective survey. As respected participants in the theological enterprise they have injected their personal convictions as well. While their agreements are not absolute, concord far outweighs their differences. With impressive unanimity the writers discuss in a worthy way questions of great religious interest and importance. Those cherished evangelical convictions which form a part of the religious tradition of the West supply primarily the foundation of these stimulating chapters. The century's upheavals and troubles are traced to the depreciation of these great Christian verities. The writers are alert to the partial rediscovery of these great truths, and to the related new interest in the neglected past. They emphasize, likewise, what the evangelical heritage offers for this hour of divided loyalties. They discuss and evaluate current evangelical contributions, indicating areas both of achievement and of neglect. Where the literature is abundant, some of the writers have ventured to handle their subjects with biographical fullness; where it is limited, the essayists have dealt rather with theological ideas and with the relevant tensions. We are certain that readers will endorse the conviction that the ten articles in this volume, as representative of conservative Christian thought, grapple in an enduring way with the questions of supreme spiritual significance.

With some of the subjects treated I have no expert acquaintance. A few, at least in certain sections, I would have handled somewhat differently. The essay on science and religion fell to me by way of default rather than of preference. Those to whom I turned for such a chapter were precluded from participation because of prior commitments. Since no compilation of this kind would appear reasonably complete without such a chapter, I ventured to supply this treatment myself. It suggests the direction of my own thought for a contemplated larger work on the concord of Christianity with science.

It has been a personal pleasure to coordinate these writings. The contributors have made available, I feel, a survey and perspective of evangelical theological effort much needed in our decade. Special appreciation is due Evangelical Books for assuring a wide readership from the outset.

CARL F. H. HENRY

Fuller Theological Seminary
Pasadena, California

THE OLD TESTAMENT

Edward J. Young

Edward J. Young has pursued his interest in the Old Testament and in the Hebrew language in both the Old and the New Worlds. He holds a Ph.D. degree from Dropsie College, but his studies were followed in Newman School of Missions in Jerusalem, Centro de Estudios Historicos in Madrid and University of Leipzig, as well as on American campuses. He has written The Prophecy of Daniel *(1949),* Introduction to the Old Testament *(1949),* Studies in Isaiah *(1954), and* Arabic for Beginners *(1949).*

1. *Edward J. Young:*

THE OLD TESTAMENT

THE OLD Testament is the Word of God. It is a message, a revelation to us from none other than God Himself. Without it much in the New Testament would not be understandable. The Old Testament provides the proper background for the interpretation of the New. It tells how God created the world, how man fell into sin and how God announced to man His intention to save him and to form a people for Himself. By means of type and prophecy, the Old Testament points forward to the One whom God was to send to save mankind, and in Jesus Christ, the Old Testament promises received their fulfillment.

The Old Testament is needed today for many reasons. Among them is the fact that the Old Testament makes so clear the will of God for mankind. In simple language it tells what is right and what is wrong. It makes clear that punishment will always follow wrongdoing, and that even those chosen of God may expect to be punished if they go astray. Man cannot follow the path of expediency; he must do that which is right. This much needed lesson of the present day is emphasized in the Old Testament.

If the Old Testament is not what it claims to be, we are robbed of an authoritative revelation about the creation of heaven and earth, of the origin of sin in the world, and of the promises that God will deliver man from his sin. If the Old Testament must be deserted, then Christianity is weakened at its foundations. Indeed, if the Old Testament is nothing more than a human document, and not a special revelation of God, it follows logically that the New Testament is also but a human document. If the Old Testament is to be abandoned, it is not all that must be abandoned. We shall soon make the discovery that we are also abandoning, and must abandon, the New Testament as well.

I. THE ASCENDANCY OF THE WELLHAUSEN SCHOOL

To understand and evaluate the attitudes toward the Old Testament which prevail today, it would be well to consider the background which has given rise to these attitudes. As throughout the long history of the church, so also at the present there are those who believe that the Old Testament is the Word of God, trustworthy and inerrant. Those who hold this position are believers in Jesus Christ, and in their attitude toward the Old Testament they are simply following Him. Jesus Christ Himself looked upon the Old Testament as do many Bible-believing Christians of the present. For Him as for them it is the Word of God, completely authoritative in all of its utterances and commands.

It goes without saying that this high view of the Scriptures of the Old Testament has not met with universal acceptance. At the beginning of this century there was dominant an attitude toward the Old Testament which was diametrically opposed to that of Jesus Christ Himself. This attitude received great impetus through the writings of a professor at Göttingen, Julius Wellhausen, who published in 1883 a history of Israel in which he popularized views which were then gaining ascendancy in scholarly circles. These views had respect both to the composition of the biblical books and also to the religious and historical development of the Hebrews.

The first five books of the Bible, commonly known as the Pentateuch, have traditionally been regarded as the work of Moses, the great lawgiver of Israel. This tradition is well founded, and rests in part upon statements in the New Testament itself. Overwhelmingly cogent are the arguments which may be marshalled in its defense. To Wellhausen, however, these arguments had little or no weight. He defended an entirely different conception of the authorship of the Pentateuch. Not only was the Pentateuch *not* the work of Moses, he maintained, but it was not even the work of one man nor the product of one mind. Its earliest parts came from two quite distinct documents, he insisted, and in accordance with the practice of his time, Wellhausen labeled them "J" and "E" (J standing for Jehovah, hence, the Jehovist document, and E for Elohim, the Hebrew word for "god"). These two documents, independent of one another in their origin, he thought to have come from a time considerably later than that of Moses; and from these two, he theorized, the Jehovist author compiled a work, principally narrative in character, and thus the two distinct documents were in effect brought together.

Wellhausen then went a step further: The book of Deuteronomy—the last book of the Pentateuch—not only was not composed by Moses, but did not appear until after the combined work of J and E. In the year 622 B.C., the book of the Law was discovered in the temple and, according to Wellhausen, it was Deuteronomy, or part of it, that was found at this time, and that was produced at this time. As a result of its discovery, there occurred a "Deuteronomic" reform, carried out by King Josiah.

The Pentateuch also contains many legal and statistical sections, which were regarded as priestly in character. Before the time of Wellhausen, it had often been asserted that these constituted the earliest portion of the Pentateuch. Wellhausen, however, threw in his opinion with those who considered these sections (commonly designated as P, i.e., priestly) the latest parts of the Pentateuch. They were composed, it was maintained, largely by Ezra. Then, finally, the entire Pentateuch was worked over and edited by a redactor.

This attitude toward the composition of the Pentateuchal books went hand in hand with a particular view of the history of Israel and of its religious institutions—one we might call the "development theory of Israel's religion." Briefly we may say that Wellhausen gave impetus to the view that originally Israel might erect an altar and sacrifice wherever she wished. The religious beginnings of Israel were essentially similar to those of other nations, according to this explanation. As Israel progressed, her conception of God developed. Having passed through such stages as animatism, animism, polydemonism, totemism, henotheism, and then others, Israel finally obtained a monotheistic conception of God. A great change of far-reaching consequence, according to Wellhausen, took place with the discovery of the book of Deuteronomy in the temple. As Josiah read this law, he immediately proceeded to enjoin the reforms which it commanded. As a result, from this time, only one legitimate place for sacrifice was recognized, namely the temple at Jerusalem. Centralization of the religious cult became a watchword with Wellhausen and those who shared his views. Only later, presumably as a result of growth and development, did the pure monotheism of the second part of Isaiah come to be Israel's possession.

We are far from claiming that we have given an adequate representation of Wellhausen's view. All that we have sought to do is to set forth some of his principal tenets. We believe that enough has been presented, however, to enable the reader to appreciate the fact that the reconstruction of Israel's history proposed by Julius Wellhausen, and the picture of that history offered in the Bible itself, are poles apart. In fact, they are mutually exclusive conceptions. If the Bible is correct, Wellhausen is wrong; and if Wellhausen is correct, the Bible most certainly is in error. A man may hold to one or the other of these two conflicting positions; he cannot possibly support both. At the turn of the century Wellhausen and his school occupied the dominant position in Old Testament studies. Influential as it was, however, the viewpoint of this school was not universally accepted; it was, in fact, rejected even by some scholars who themselves did not hold to the infallibility of Scripture.

II. EARLIER EVANGELICAL OPPOSITION TO WELLHAUSEN

It must not be thought that those who accepted the Bible at face value allowed the views of Wellhausen to pass unchallenged. From the vantage point of historic supernatural redemptive Christianity, powerful voices were raised in defense of the Bible. There were those who were well aware of the implications of the newer position, who clearly saw that in its very essence it was hostile to the Christian faith—a fact, incidentally, which Wellhausen himself, brilliant man that he was, seems to have recognized.

In America the opposition to the newer critical views was carried on most ably by the late William Henry Green. The rich heritage of earlier German conservative theologians was Green's, and in addition he had been a close associate of Joseph Addison Alexander, Charles Hodge and some of the other defenders of the faith at Princeton. Green was a master of the Hebrew language and of the literature of Old Testament scholarship. He served as a forerunner of attempts made during this present century to stem the tide of destructive criticism.

Perhaps the strongest and most consistent voice raised during the present century, a voice which now, alas, has been hushed, was the *Princeton Theological Review*. This scholarly magazine carried articles in exposition and defense of the historic faith of the church, articles which for thoroughness and scolarly ability matched anything that the advocates of a destructive criticism could produce. These articles dealt with attacks on the Bible both generally and specifically. Equally important were the full reviews of books which the *Review* regularly published. Unfortunately, it has been discontinued, and consequently a powerful voice in defense of the historic Christian faith has been silenced.

Among prominent defenders of the biblical view of the Old Testament during the second decade of the present century the name of Robert Dick Wilson stands out pre-eminently. Wilson followed in the steps of his predecessor, William Henry Green, and sought to carry on the same position of intelligent loyalty to the Bible. His earliest writings were grammatical, but he soon plunged into what turned out to be a lifelong defense of the book of Daniel. This book had proved to be a line of demarcation between conservatives and those who did not regard the Scriptures as infallible. Throughout his life Wilson sought to defend the book from the charges that had been made against it. To his work he brought many rich gifts, and among them was a profound knowledge of the ancient Semitic languages. He considered one by one the charges which had been raised against the integrity and trustworthiness of Daniel, and then presented his reply, a reply which was accompanied by an immense erudition and learning. Any serious student of the book of Daniel will be compelled to take account of Wilson's writings.

In Germany itself there appeared a most capable and able defender of the faith in the person of Wilhelm Möller. Beginning as an adherent of the Wellhausen school, Möller made a special study of the question of the origin of Deuteronomy, and it was this study which convinced him of the untenability of the dominant critical position. Realizing that Wellhausen's position was hostile to the well-being of the Christian faith, Möller became an ardent champion of that view of the Old Testament which the Lord Jesus Christ Himself had espoused.

One of his earlier works was translated into English under the title *Are the Critics Right?* A somewhat short work, it presents nonetheless a cogent refutation of the major tenets of the school of Wellhausen. It is my opinion that Möller is particularly effective in discussing the origin of Deuteronomy. It was evidently this question which had preyed most heavily on his mind, and here his discussion is most incisive. Equally valuable, however, is his consideration of other peculiar tenets which were being advocated in his day. From his able pen there came a veritable stream of books and pamphlets. We note in particular his *Introduction to the Old Testament* and his *Biblical Theology of the Old Testament;* it is unfortunate that these works have not been translated into English.

Those who have written in defense of the biblical view of the Old Testament have never been many in number. This is not to say that there are not and have not been many competent scholars who hold and have held to the absolute authority of Holy Scripture. Yet, those who have engaged in scholarly writing have not been in the majority. On the other hand, the "critical"[1] views have had many and able representatives. This might be a cause for discouragement, but it need not be. Truth is not counted by majorities. The Word of God will stand, despite whatever attacks have been made upon it. In the light of the fact that the majority of scholarly opinion so vigorously embraced the essential tenets of the Wellhausen theory, it is most remarkable to note the subsequent history of that theory.

III. WELLHAUSEN'S THEORY AND THE PRESENT

It must not be thought that the ideas of Wellhausen stood out alone and isolated. They fitted the prevailing climate of opinion quite well. That climate of opinion, like the one which prevails today, was actually hostile to supernatural redemptive Christianity. What Wellhausen and others taught in the field of Old Testament had parallels elsewhere. At the time when the development theory of Israel's religion was dominant, an evolutionary view of life and the world was also reigning. There

[1] In this essay the word critical (in quotation marks) has reference to those who, rejecting the infallibility of Scripture, assume unaided human reason a capable judge of Scripture and so submit the Scriptures to their own judgment.

is no denying that the life and writings of Charles Darwin had a tremendous effect upon the thinking of the time. Indeed, as the foundation upon which the complex ideas of the time rested, there stood Darwin's theory of evolution. In the field of philosophy Hegel had exercised great influence, and this fact, in our opinion, made itself felt in the general reconstruction of Israel's history presented by Wellhausen. In the field of New Testament studies a parallel may be found in the influence of Adolf Harnack, with his purely human historical Jesus. In theology the views of Albrecht Ritschl were prominent, and from them has come that popular phenomenon which is generally called Modernism, a phenomenon which has wrought incalculable harm in the church of the living God. Such then was the complex of ideas and views which was in ascendancy at the beginning of the present century.

Now the climate of opinion is quite different; a number of things happened to cause significant shifts in thought. For one, the first World War shattered the then widely-prevailing confidence in human goodness and in human power. Man was not a being grandly progressing toward some utopia of his own devising, but a creature who could engage in most vicious activity. The old idea of progress was suffering severe setbacks. With respect to the Old Testament it had been maintained that the Israelites had progressed from the simpler to the more complex and highly developed forms of religion. That view, however, came into serious question. There was something radically wrong with a creature who, evolving toward the better throughout the years, could nevertheless engage in anything so horrible as the first World War.

Other factors conspired against the easy-going conception of human goodness which was reigning as this century began. Most important of these were the discoveries of archaeology. The present century has been *par excellence* a century of discovery and excavation, and the results of this activity have greatly affected some of the views that were earlier entertained by scholars. As a result of these two causes and others as well, there has come to pass quite an important shift in opinion on the part of the scholarly world. The influence of the Danish philosopher and author Kierkegaard is more and more making itself felt, and the older views of the Ritschlian theology are no longer dominant.

In the field of theology the writings of Karl Barth and Emil Brunner, together with others who share their essential position, are now in the ascendancy. In biblical studies the schools of form-criticism are wielding tremendous influence. A great shift has come about, and one of the characteristics of this shift is that today biblical language is employed in setting forth the newer views. That these newer views are not to be identified with evangelical Christianity will soon become obvious to any who will take the trouble to study them.

Our purpose however is not to examine these newer views save as they apply to the Old Testament. At several points the positions of Wellhausen have had to be modified. For example, it was a basic tenet of the older view that the book of Genesis could not be relied upon to give an accurate picture of the period of the patriarchs. It did, this theory held, give a correct picture of the time in which it was composed (i.e., several hundred years *after* the time of the patriarchs), but since it was composed so long after the patriarchs had lived, it could not be relied upon in what it said about them.

Archaeology has caused this opinion to be greatly modified. The code of Hammurabi, for example, which was discovered in the winter of 1901-02, has cast some light upon Genesis. More important, however, were the discoveries which were made at Yorgan Tepa, the ancient city of Nuzi, in Mesopotamia. These remarkable texts have cast considerable light on the background of Genesis, and they have been assisted in this by the texts which were discovered at Tell el-Hariri, the ancient Mari. It is now rather generally recognized that the picture of the patriarchs given in Genesis is true to fact. This is not to say that modern scholars acknowledge the actual historicity of the patriarchs themselves; they do, however, admit that the picture of the background given in Genesis is correct. Were Julius Wellhausen living today he would doubtless modify his statements concerning Genesis.

In defense of Wellhausen it might conceivably be said that he was simply a child of his times, that he had to work with the best information available to him. Such a defense will not impress the humble Christian believer. According to the Word of God itself, no one need be merely "a child of his times." Rather, all are commanded to live under the light of eternity. God Himself had already spoken to us concerning the period of the patriarchs. Therefore, men like Green and Wilson, and others who followed them, were far more scientific in maintaining the trustworthiness of Genesis than was Wellhausen, who, rejecting the clear revelation of God, simply relied upon human wisdom. Thus it was to be expected that the discoveries of archaeology would prove him to be wrong on this point. We may well anticipate that at other points also, where the discoveries of archaeology are relevant, they will speak in defense of the Scriptures.

IV. THE PERIOD BETWEEN THE WARS

During the period between the two great World Wars, Robert Dick Wilson stands foremost as a leading defender of the Old Testament. Of importance also was John H. Raven, author of the *Introduction to the Old Testament,* first published in 1906. This work was thoroughly faithful to the Bible. Dr. Raven, a minister in the Reformed Church of America, was a most competent scholar and a man of unquestioned loyalty and devotion to the Scriptures; his book has been used as a text in many theological seminaries and Bible institutes, and there is no doubt that it has proved to be of great help to those who were studying to preach the Gospel. It has been of great blessing to the Church of Christ.

During this period Oswald T. Allis made some significant contributions in his scholarly articles which appeared in the *Princeton Theological Review,* of which he was the editor. With a keen insight into the nature of modern thought, Dr. Allis reviewed much of the newer literature and wrote several scholarly articles which have served as a preparation for his later books. Mention must also be made of the appearance in 1929 of the complete *International Standard Bible Encyclopaedia,* a work executed under the editorship of the late James Orr, a Scottish theologian who himself had written a volume in defense of the Old Testament (1906). Into this work the best of conservative scholarship was concentrated. Scholarly ministers have found genuine aid in this encyclopaedia in the study of the Scriptures. Save for a few places, the work is entirely loyal to the Bible. Its appearance was a crowning achievement for Biblical scholarship, and a competent and up-to-date revision of this work would be a great boon to the present day church.

Mention must also be made of the scholarly work of Melvin Grove Kyle. Dr. Kyle was primarily an archaeologist, and played a prominent part in the excavation of Kirjath-Sepher. He had the ability of popularizing his studies, and has left several volumes which are of genuine interest to the layman. Among these were *Moses and the Monuments* (1920), and *The Problem of the Pentateuch* (1920). In addition to his archaeological work Dr. Kyle was an expert Hebrew scholar, and the fruit of his studies may be found in the *International Standard Bible Encyclopaedia,* a work in which he took a prominent part.

Perhaps it is apposite to ask at this point why there was such a dearth of conservative scholarship in the period between the two world wars, and particularly during the Twenties. The question is difficult to answer. In this period the struggle between modernism and historic Christianity was at its peak in many of the evangelical denominations of America, and without doubt this struggle engaged the time and energies of many scholars. Yet this situation alone cannot be blamed for the dearth of conservative scholarship. It is a well-known fact that some of the greatest discoveries of biblical truth are made in times of conflict. Such was the case, for example, at the period of the Reformation. In the throes of conflict Luther brought forth the scriptural teaching on justification by faith. So it will always be. The conflict between faith and unbelief in the churches did indeed occupy the energies of men, but one cannot charge the dearth of conservative scholarship in the period of the Twenties to this fact alone.

One reason why the decade of the Thirties appeared so barren as far as evangelical scholarship is concerned is to be found in the fact that Princeton Theological Seminary faltered. Ever since its founding in 1812, this institution had been a bulwark of faith in the Bible as the inspired, inerrant, infallible Word of God. The influence of this great school was by no means confined to the Presbyterian Church. Rather, it extended itself wherever the Word of God was loved and believed. But the end of the old Princeton, with its devotion to the high view of the Bible, is without a doubt one of the principal reasons why the Thirties saw such a dearth of evangelical scholarship in the field of Old Testament.

V. A RESURGENCE OF EVANGELICAL SCHOLARSHIP

The decade of the Forties, however, witnessed a resurgence of genuine scholarship among Bible-believing Christians. Here again mention must be made of the writings of Oswald T. Allis. As has been pointed out, Dr. Allis had already written many scholarly and learned articles; in the Forties, however, his first book appeared under the title *The Five Books of Moses.* In this work the author made a frontal attack upon the Wellhausen theory, a position then still widely held. In a second edition he gave some consideration to modern outgrowths of that theory.

This work is truly significant; it is a cogent presentation of those views of the Pentateuch which are hostile to supernatural Christianity, contrasting them with the biblical view. The author then makes an exhaustive study of the so-called "documentary hypothesis of the Pentateuch," the hypothesis which maintains that the Pentateuch is not the work of one man, Moses, but that rather it is a compilation made from various previously existing documents.

The history of this documentary hypothesis is quite interesting. It received one of its first expressions in the writings of French physician Jean Astruc (1753). He was quite satisfied with the results of his work and felt that he had solved some of the difficulties in the book of Genesis. Astruc confined his study to Genesis and to the first two chapters of Exodus. Others who followed after him carried the theory farther, until at last it was applied to the entire Pentateuch. It soon became apparent that the usage of the divine names, Jehovah and Elohim, which was the original criterion employed, was not at all sufficient. There was another complication resulting from the fact that at one time a certain document was regarded as the earliest, and at another time, still another. What is so striking about the application which Wellhausen made of this theory is that he took the document which before his time had generally been regarded as the earliest, and declared it to be the latest.

Into all of this Dr. Allis enters and brings to bear not only his keen mind but also his recognized erudition, and best of all, his humble devotion to the Word of God. He points out the tremendous difficulties which the documentary theory creates, and shows its weaknesses and inconsistencies. More than that, however, he advances positive and strong arguments for believing that Moses was the author of the Pentateuch.

Of particular value is the treatment accorded the so-called "development hypothesis." This must be distinguished from the documentary hypothesis which we have just considered. The development hypothesis may be regarded as the particular contribution (if it can be called "a contribution") of Wellhausen and his school. As we have already pointed out, the theory posits the gradual development of Israel's distinctive religious ideas and institutions. Is this theory, however, taught in the pages of the Bible itself? That question is answered firmly in the negative by Allis. One who reads this section of the book will be strengthened in faith. He will see not only the tremendous weakness in the development hypothesis, but he will also see that the biblical picture of Israel's religion is the true one.

Finally, Allis's *The Five Books of Moses* constituted a vigorous challenge to naturalistic interpretations of the religion of Israel, and a powerful defense of the position that Israel's religion is a divine revelation. Valuable and useful is the discussion, for example, of the relationship between the Pentateuch and archaeology, and the question of the ultimate issues involved. The author writes as a believer and as one facing an enemy that threatens the well-being of the Church. It may safely be said that the arguments marshalled in this book constitute a powerful refutation of the position of negative and destructive criticism. Widely used in conservative circles, it is an admirable text and introduction to the subject.

The first edition of Allis's book appeared in 1943, and was followed in 1949 by a second, a volume enlarged by the inclusion of more material and by more extended treatment of modern developments. Notable among these is the examination of modern form criticism as it applies to the Pentateuch. Evangelicals may indeed be grateful that God has raised up such a strong witness for their position.

Two years after the appearance of *The Five Books of Moses,* Allis published another book, one dealing with quite a different type of subject. This second work bore the title *Prophecy and the Church.* It presents a vast amount of positive scriptural interpretation and ventures a refutation of the position that the Church of Christ is a parenthesis in God's dealings with His people Israel. The appearance of this work made it perfectly clear that exegetical theology had by no means died out among evangelicals. The volume naturally produced an immense amount of discussion. Many evangelicals do not share the position of Allis, but, in the writer's opinion, they have produced no satisfactory answer to him.

In 1950 Allis published another book, this time returning to critical problems. One of the battlegrounds between faith and unbelief is the question of the authorship of Isaiah. According to the New Testament, which quotes from and refers to Isaiah more than to any other book of the Old Testament, the author of the book was the eighth century prophet, Isaiah. For nearly two hundred years, however, a certain class of critic has disregarded the clear statements of the New Testament and has maintained that the book is the work of at least two or more authors. In *The Unity of Isaiah* Allis makes a powerful defense of the New Testament view of the book's authorship.

There is much in this work that is valuable. For example, the second chapter contains very helpful information on the subject of true prophecy. It is, however, in discussion of the Cyrus prophecy (Isaiah 44:24-28) that the book makes the greatest thrust. By means of a most thorough and careful study of this prophecy, Allis points out that the passage sets forth Cyrus as one who will come in the distant future. The force of this argument for the question of the authorship of the prophecy has not been sufficiently recognized, nor has the book received a satisfactory reply from those who do not share its basic position.

It will be seen then that during the Forties Oswald T. Allis was the pioneer among conservative Old Testament scholars. His voice gave much encouragement to those who were preparing themselves to teach and to preach the Gospel. With the passing of the years, the works he has written have not lost their timeliness and value. They must be consulted by all who are seriously interested in the matters of which they treat. In them the evangelical world, as far as the field of Old Testament is concerned, has found a strong voice.

During the decade of the Forties another encouraging sign was the appearance of a number of reprints of former classical works in the field of Old Testament, as well as in other fields. The pioneer in this venture was the publishing house of Eerdmans, which in 1947 began to reprint the commentaries of John Calvin. In 1948 appeared Calvin's commentary on Isaiah. The publication of these works proved a great boon to conservative scholarship and to evangelical believers generally.

In this work of reprinting former books, several evangelical publishers took part. From the Old Testament field and standpoint we mention in particular the printing of the commentaries of Calvin, Barnes, Keil and Delitzsch, and the works of Joseph Addison Alexander. Keil and Delitzsch represented the best of nineteenth century exegetical theology. Their commentaries contain translations of the text and philosophical and exegetical discussions. They are, therefore, of the utmost value to serious students of the Bible. Since they are scholarly works, one who would use them to best advantage must have a knowledge of the original languages of the Scriptures.

A word should also be said about the commentaries of Joseph Addison Alexander. America may ever be proud of such an exegete. His works exhibit the same staunch devotion to the Bible that is found in the writings of Keil and Hengstenberg of Germany. Alexander possessed a deep insight into the Hebrew language, and his work is replete with helpful remarks on the structure of the Hebrew sentences. It is also profoundly loyal to the Scriptures, and hence forms a valuable combination. The reprints include both the commentary on the Psalms and on Isaiah. The publication of these books is a boon to the evangelical world.

Fine as reprints are, and necessary as they are, they are no substitute for patient present-day research. No serious student of the Old Testament can afford to be without Calvin and Alexander. At the same time, the man who relies upon them exclusively and who does not work on his own is not likely to engage in fruitful scholarship. There is need for a resurgence among evangelical believers of true scholarly activity. The majority engaged in the field of scholarship is without a doubt today on the side of those who do not accept the absolute trustworthiness of the Scriptures and the doctrines of evangelical Christianity. This, however, is no excuse for the lethargy which seems to have crept over the believing world.

In the Lutheran Church two names have been particularly prominent. Alexander Heidel has done excellent work in the cuneiform languages. In his *The Babylonian Genesis* (1942) he presented an up-to-date translation of the cuneiform document, which has been regarded as an account of creation. He includes a valuable discussion of the relationship of this document to Genesis, a discussion in which the uniqueness of Genesis is defended. A second work, *The Gilgamesh Epic and Old Testament Parallels* (1946), reveals the same scholarly qualities of the first, and is a useful book of reference for the serious Old Testament student.

H. C. Leupold of Capitol University Seminary has distinguished himself by his excellent commentaries on various books of the Old Testament. His work is scholarly, but he has the ability of stating profound truths accurately and clearly in simple language. A devotion to the absolute trustworthiness of Scripture is manifest in whatever he writes. Excellent indeed is his commentary on Genesis. The same may be said of his later works on Daniel and Ecclesiastes. Here is exegetical scholarship of a high order, coupled with humble devotion to the Word of God. No serious student of Scripture can afford to neglect what Leupold has written.

In *The Prophecy of Daniel* (1949) the writer of these words sought to offer a positive interpretation of the prophecy, and also to point out some of the weaknesses in the critical position. In *An Introduction to the Old Testament* (1949) an attempt was made to provide students with a discussion of the Old Testament books from the standpoint of historic orthodox Protestantism. *Isaiah Fifty Three* (1952) is a devotional and expository study intended to present a biblical interpretation of the passage. In *Arabic for Beginners* (1950) the writer sought to make accessible to theological students a reading knowledge of the Arabic language. *My Servants The Prophets* (1952) attempted to point out the uniqueness of Old Testament prophecy. *The Messianiac Prophecies of Daniel* (1954) is a popular survey of the teaching of Daniel, and *Studies in Isaiah* (1954) contains several articles dealing with various controverted points in the study of Isaiah. In particular it seeks to present a defense of the Messianic interpretation of Isaiah 7:14 (insisting that the correct translation of the disputed word in this verse is "virgin"), and also of the Messianic interpretation of the Servant of the Lord in the latter chapters of Isaiah.

At the present time there appears to be an upsurge of scholarly activity among evangelicals. Joseph P. Free of Wheaton College has published a useful handbook on the subject of archaeology. This work is intended to popularize the results of the science, and serves as a helpful introduction for the layman. Dr. Free has also engaged in the excavation of Dothan in Palestine, and the results of his activity appear in the *Bulletin of the American Schools of Oriental Research.* Dr. James A. Kelso of Pittsburgh-Xenia Seminary is also an evangelical scholar. He is a first-rate archaeologist, whose articles also have appeared in the above-mentioned *Bulletin* and in the *Journal of Biblical Literature.* One of the most recent of these (September, 1955) is an article on the archaeology of the monastery at Qumran.

Of particular significance are the writings of Merrill T. Unger of Dallas Theological Seminary. Among these we note his *Introductory Guide to the Old Testament* (1951), a work dealing both with the subjects of special and of general introduction. It discusses such questions as the inspiration of the Scriptures, the languages in which the books were written, the canon and the text of the Bible and the Apocrypha, as well as the particular questions of introduction which apply to each individual book. An outline of the individual books is included so that the work becomes a useful guide to the student. This volume serves as a good, handy introduction to this subject.

In the writer's opinion the most significant of Dr. Unger's works is his *Archaeology and the Bible* (1954). Archaeology is discussed in its relation to the Bible, and in the course of the discussion many of the complex problems raised by the study of archaeology are competently handled. As a practical handbook to archaeological study the book is indeed admirable.

Perhaps one reason why so few enter the field of Old Testament studies is the fact that the Hebrew language is apparently one of the most difficult of languages for an English-speaking person to learn. It is true that a reading knowledge of Hebrew prose can be obtained in a fairly short time by anyone who diligently applies himself to the matter; yet when one seeks to go on to a mastery of the subject he encounters many difficulties. Thus the question of how to impart instruction in Hebrew is one which must occupy the energies and attention of all who are interested in the subject.

In the study of Hebrew there are at least three points at which difficulty obtrudes itself. In the first place the language is written and read from right to left, and while this is not necessarily a great obstacle, it is a point that at first constitutes a complexity. In the second place, the vocabulary is strange; and while the vocabulary of the Old Testament is not nearly so large as that required for a reading knowledge of Latin or of classical Greek, it is a vocabulary which consists of strange sounds, and there is little with which one may compare it. For example, when the student is told that the root *qatal* means "to kill" (grammarians seem to think that the word "to kill" is a useful one to use as a Hebrew paradigm) there is nothing in English with which the word may be compared. Consequently, the vocabulary of Hebrew, while not as large as that required for a reading knowledge of many other languages, is nevertheless discouraging.

And in the third place, the Hebrew alphabet causes difficulty. There are only twenty-two consonants, but five of these have two different forms. Originally the language was written with consonants alone. A series of marks, for the purpose of indicating the vowel sounds, was later introduced. The Bible as we now have it is printed with consonants and "pointed" with the vowel points. As one reads, his eye must be concentrated not only upon the line itself, but, since some of the vowel points are written above the line and some below, he must also note what is above and what is below. Moreover, some of the points are inserted into the bosom of the letter itself. In reading Hebrew, therefore, the eye must study three lines.

Anything that can be done to make this difficult language more accessible to English-speaking people will be a boon. R. Laird Harris of Faith Theological Seminary has published a very useful little introduction to the language. The work is characterized by its succinct statement of grammatical principles. Only that which is essential to the impartation of a reading knowledge of the language is included. However, the principles of the language are clearly stated, and there are abundant exercises.

There are different theories as to the best method of learning to read a language. Dr. Harris embraces the traditional method of first presenting the grammar and then offering exercises which illustrate the particular grammatical points in question. Thus the student who uses this book will read a number of sentences for translation from Hebrew to English as well as a number for translation from English to Hebrew. For those who prefer this method, it can safely be said that this small book by Dr. Harris is one of the best. He who works through it faithfully will find himself in possession of the rudiments of Hebrew grammar, and further progress in the language will not be unduly difficult.

Another Hebrew grammar produced by an evangelical scholar is *A Grammar of the Hebrew Language* (1951), written by G. Douglas Young. This book follows quite a different method from that employed in Dr. Harris's grammar. In it the learner is plunged with both feet, as it were, into the center of the language itself. He begins immediately to read from the biblical book of Ruth. A knowledge of the alphabet is not immediately necessary, for the text is presented in transcription. Thus, the student reads quite an amount of Hebrew and learns the essential features of the language before he actually comes to grips with the alphabet itself.

Opinions differ as to whether or not this is a wise procedure. Those who have taught Hebrew know that the alphabet is indeed difficult for American young men who come to the study of the language with little or no linguistic background. There is much to be said for the usage of a simplified system of transcription. The Turkish language, for example, is now written in Latin characters, and say what one will, it is far easier to read than it was when written in the old Arabic characters. Scholars may scoff at any device so simple as transcription, but, be that as it may, Dr. Young may be the pioneer in simplifying the study of Hebrew.

The great contribution of Dr. Young's grammar, however, lies in its description of the language itself—a factor of importance which has not always been recognized. In time, however, Hebrew study will without question proceed upon the lines of the description of the language found in his book. There are in the Semitic languages three basic vowels, *a, i,* and *u.* In Hebrew these vowels appear both as long and short. When they are short they may change depending upon the type of syllable in which they occur and their proximity to the accent of the word. This is a phenomenon which runs through the entirety of the language. Its significance is not generally recognized, and the present work has the merit of being the first, so far as this writer knows, of bringing out and carrying through with some consistency this important principle. The inclusion of exercises would greatly enhance its usefulness. It must be said in all fairness, however, that it was not the intention of the author to include such exercises. His plan is to plunge the beginner into the reading of texts at the start, and have him learn the rudiments of the language from the text itself.

Dr. Young has carried on his grammatical studies in other fields also. He has made a study of the poetry of Ras esh-Schamra which is most helpful. As is now well-known, a famous discovery was made in 1929 on the Syrian Coast, north of Beirut, at a place which bears the modern name of Ras esh-Schamra (fennelhead). Here many old texts, written in a cuneiform alphabetic script, were brought to light. Upon translation these texts were found to contain much that resembled the Bible. The texts themselves presented mythological poems, but the style and vocabulary bore many points of contact with the language of the Scriptures. Dr. Young engaged in a careful study of the poetry and made the discovery that it contains no consistent type of metre. This is important in view of the claims of some that there is metre in the poetry of the Bible, and that the present text of the Bible, not fitting this metre, often stands in need of correction. Other scholarly articles have also appeared from Dr. Young's pen.

Allan A. MacRae has contributed part of the volume *Nuzi Personal Names.* Martin Wyngaarden of Calvin Theological Seminary has written a work on *The Scope of Spiritualization in Prophecy,* which has just appeared as a reprint. A useful guide to the literature introductory to the study of the various Semitic languages, *A Basic Semitic Bibliography,* was published by William S. LaSor of Fuller Theological Seminary. In the field of biblical interpretation, Charles Feinberg has written a popular exposition of the prophecy of Zechariah.

Attention must be called to the Inter-Varsity Fellowship of England, which has published several most helpful works. At present it is engaged in the publication of popular commentaries which should prove to be of great interest to students of the Bible. A one-volume commentary on the entire Bible, representing the combined effort of some fifty evangelical scholars, has recently appeared. Among these contributors may be mentioned J. Stafford Wright, who has also written a most useful booklet on the question of the date of Ezra's return to Jerusalem. William J. Martin of the University of Liverpool is one of the most competent of evangelical Old Testament scholars, as may be seen from his lecture "The Dead Sea Scroll of Isaiah."

In the United States a hopeful sign is the establishment of the Evangelical Theological Society. This organization has adopted as its standard the statement, "The Bible alone and the Bible in its entirety, is the Word of God written and therefore inerrant in the autographs." In this doctrinal statement the Society has gone to the heart of the matter as far as the Bible is concerned. The Society should prove of great help for the mutual encouragement of those who believe in its doctrinal position. At its various meetings some competent papers have already been presented, and these are now available in mimeographed form. If the Society continues to uphold the standards with which it has begun, it will prove to be of continued help and support to the conservative position.

Two prominent members of the Society have published useful works in the field of Old Testament. J. Barton Payne has written a helpful handbook for the study of Old Testament history. This little work is written in popular style and is designed for use in the classroom. Robert Culver has written a premillennial interpretation of the prophecy of Daniel in which he has seriously tackled the difficult exegetical questions of the book. We hope that more will be coming forth from his pen.

When we turn our eyes to the Netherlands, we discover that much productive activity has been carried on. One of the most prominent of conservative Old Testament scholars is G. Ch. Aalders. Over the years Aalders has produced a number of works in defense of the integrity of the Scriptures, for the most part of an exegetical nature. Aalders has contributed to different series of commentaries, and has exerted a wholesome influence; one of his works in particular calls for mention. It is a thorough discussion of the first three chapters of Genesis, and in it he contrasts the biblical account of creation with the Babylonian and with other accounts. Aalders engages in a most thorough exposition of the passages and discusses the many questions involved in their study. One can only be amazed at the profundity of insight and exegetical ability displayed in this work.

It is as an exegete that Aalders stands out particularly. He has contributed volumes to the series known as the *Korte Verklaring,* i.e., the Short Exposition, and he has already written the volumes on the Song of Songs, Ecclesiastes and a first volume on Ezekiel for a larger series of commentaries. These works are written in Dutch, and consequently are accessible only to a limited number of readers. It would be a boon to scholarship generally if they could be translated into English. Aalders is a thorough scholar and is perfectly at home not only with the original language of the Old Testament but also with the cognate Semitic languages, and with the vast literature which has been produced upon the Biblical books which he discusses.

In his writings Aalders is loyal to the position that the Scriptures are the inspired and infallible Word of God. At the same time he sometimes departs from traditional views of the dates and authorship of the Old Testament books, as may be seen in his little work—in many respects an admirable book—*A Short Introduction to the Pentateuch* (English title). This writer has sometimes been troubled by Aalders' willingness to depart from traditional positions, particularly where such departure does not appear to be necessary. It is possible that a student of Aalders might go on from where Aalders left off to positions which are in themselves not consonant with the absolute trustworthiness of the Scriptures.

Among Dutch scholars mention must also be made of W. H. Gispen, who has impressed many with his scholarly work. Gispen has written a commentary on Leviticus which is nothing short of admirable. It consists of a careful discussion of the Hebrew text of Leviticus, a discussion of differing interpretations and an exposition of the text itself. It is certainly a model commentary.

The series known as the *Korte Verklaring* is a set of popular commentaries upon the books of the Bible. It is indeed a sign for encouragement that Inter-Varsity of England is beginning the preparation of a somewhat similar series in English. There is always a dearth of good commentaries upon the books of the Old Testament and the Dutch scholars have gone a great way toward supplying a satisfactory series.

There exist, then, signs of a renaissance of evangelical scholarship. To the writer it is a hopeful sign that in this country many young men are beginning to publish the fruits of their studies. Many of the younger evangelical students have had the privilege of sitting at the feet of an inspiring Jewish scholar, Cyrus H. Gordon. Dr. Gordon, a master of the cuneiform languages, has given to numerous young evangelicals the tools necessary for advanced research. It is particularly encouraging to note the uses to which a scholar such as G. Douglas Young is putting this training.

In the brief survey of evangelical scholarship just given, it has of course been impossible to include every name. Many competent scholars do little or no writing at all, and it has been possible to include only the names of those who have published books. It may seem to the reader that the list is small indeed. If the Old Testament is the Word of God, the question may be asked, why have those who thus believe in the Old Testament not written more? Why have they not entered vigorously into the written defense and exposition of the Old Testament? These are deserving questions and they call for an answer.

VI. MODERN THEOLOGY AND THE SCRIPTURAL POSITION

Before an attempt is made to answer the questions just raised, it will first be necessary to contrast the biblical view of the Old Testament with that which is in vogue today with modern scholarship. The Bible itself has much to say about its own nature and character, and he who would be true to the Bible will seek to follow it wherever it leads. If the Bible speaks of the authorship of any of its own books, that is sufficient for the true believer. That very fact, in itself, settles the issue. If the Bible is the Word of God, the Bible, when it speaks, must be heard and obeyed.

The Lord Jesus Christ regarded the Scriptures as possessing an authority so great that they could not be broken (John 10:35). In other words, when the Old Testament speaks, it speaks with an indefectible authority. This attitude of the Lord has also been the traditional attitude of the Christian Church and it is that of Bible believers today. If this be correct, the Old Testament is to be regarded as a preparation for the coming of the Christ. It relates the creation of the heaven and the earth, the temptation and fall of man into sin, and the necessity for redemption to be accomplished by God if man is to be saved. The Old

Testament prophesies the coming of One Who should deliver fallen man from his sin and from its consequences. This coming One is the Messiah, the Anointed One of God. Toward Him all prophecy of the Old Testament points; indeed, in a certain sense the entire Old Testament is itself prophetical, pointing forward to the coming of the Messiah.

It is of course true that the Old Testament speaks of much that is ancillary to this great central message of redemption. And whenever it speaks, it is with authority. The Old Testament treats, for example, of the subject of creation, and what it says is perfectly true and in accord with fact. It is not a textbook upon the subject of science and astronomy, yet whatever it states on these subjects is itself true. It may not be a textbook of science, but it certainly is a textbook of strategic importance for the *philosophy* of science, for its ultimate author is none other than God Himself.

The question which arises, of course, is whether this view of the Old Testament can be maintained upon the basis of a "critical" position? To this we must answer that consistently it cannot. The nineteenth century witnessed a tremendous amount of such "critical" activity. Much thought and attention were devoted to the question of identifying the supposed documents which were thought to compose the Pentateuch. To the study of the origin and the composition of the individual books of the Old Testament an immense amount of study was devoted. At the same time the message of the Old Testament, as the advocates of these "critical" methods are now themselves acknowledging, was greatly neglected. Biblical theology—the study of the progress of God's self-revelation of Himself in the pages of the Bible—was, during the nineteenth century and the early part of this century, greatly neglected.

At the present time there is a shift in emphasis upon the part of those who, while not accepting the infallibility of Scripture, are nevertheless engaged in its study. There is recognition of the importance of the study of the content of the Bible as well as the question of its origin. Consequently, there has indeed been a renaissance of what is called (erroneously, this writer believes) "biblical" theology. An attempt is being made to preserve the "gains" of the study of the nineteenth and early part of the twentieth centuries and to combine them with a study of the contents of the Bible.

A superficial observation may be passed upon this procedure, namely that it is a most inconsistent one. When men accept the position of Wellhausen respecting the date and origin of the books of the Old Testament, how can they arrive at a truly biblical theology? If the Pentateuch is not the work of Moses, but rather a compilation of conflicting documents which are not infallible in their statements, how can a trustworthy picture of the early history of Israel be derived therefrom? If the book of Isaiah is not the work of the great eighth century prophet, but rather is a compilation of oracles written by a number of authors under differing circumstances and conditions over a period of many years, how can we derive therefrom any dependable picture of the Messiah? It is true that we can learn what certain people—who they were, we do not necessarily know—thought about the Messiah, but can we possess any assurance that they were correct in their beliefs?

The emphasis today upon "biblical" theology is in reality a confession of the barrenness of the purely "critical" methods of the last century. At the same time the conclusions which now go under the name of "biblical" theology do not logically follow from the methods of study employed by those who refuse to accept the Bible as infallible. If one begins with the presupposition that the unaided mind of man is capable of submitting the Word of God to its own judgment, and so placing itself above the plain statement of that Word, one cannot conclude with the teachings of an evangelical Christianity. And this brings us to the heart of the matter.

Is there after all, on the part of the scholarly world, a real revival of the acceptance of the teachings of the Bible? We believe there is not. We hear much today about God's wondrous acts for the salvation of mankind. Some questions, however, must promptly be raised. Do the modern scholars mean by these things that which Bible-believing Christians have meant by them? The answer, we think, is again in the negative.

One example will suffice. It has been said that in faith we may believe that Jesus Christ is the Servant of the Lord of Isaiah Fifty-Three. As scientific students, however, we cannot come to any such conclusion. As scientific students we shall have to admit that Isaiah Fifty-Three was simply the prophetic remodeling of an old poem in which certain ideas were embodied. It looked toward the future, but its writers did not intend it as a prophecy of Jesus Christ. Is it therefore a great gain to be told that in faith we may believe that Isaiah Fifty-Three is a prophecy of Jesus Christ? Underlying this type of statement, so common today, lurks that old distinction which Immanuel Kant brought to the fore between the phenomenal realm (that which we know with our senses) and the noumenal (the invisible). To say that in the realm of faith we may declare that Jesus Christ is the Servant of Isaiah Fifty-Three is in effect to say that only in the realm of the noumenal (that which is beyond us and really unknown to us) is He the Servant. In the everyday practical realm, the phenomenal, the realm with which we have acquaintance, the realm in which our scholarly activity is to be carried on, Jesus Christ is not the Servant at all.

When we talk of the realm of faith we may employ Christian and orthodox terminology to our heart's desire, and it is precisely that which many are doing today. As a result some evangelical scholars have been deceived by the nature of "critical" Old Testament study. There is much talk about a return to orthodoxy. In reality, however, there is no such return at all. If Jesus Christ is the Servant of the Lord of Isaiah Fifty Three, He is that Servant as a matter of actual fact. He cannot both be and not be that Servant. And if the prophecy did not envision Him and predict Him, then, no matter how much we may wish it, He is not that Servant. He either is or He is not the Servant. There is no middle ground. It is no comfort to be told that He actually is not the Servant, but that in the realm of faith we may believe Him to be the Servant.

Here is the point at which evangelical scholarship must challenge the thinking of the day. In more clear-cut fashion than hitherto, evangelical scholarship must come to grips with the nature of modern thought. The greatest mistake that present-day evangelical scholarship can make is to become confused as to the nature of modern thought, and to conclude that modern thought, since it now employs Christian terminology, has suddenly become Christian. It has done nothing of the sort. Evangelicals working in the Old Testament field must learn to penetrate to the philosophical basis upon which modern thought rests. It is founded upon a non-Christian dualism, and when it presumes to proclaim the great Christian verities, telling us that they are in the realm of faith, or *Urgeschichte,* this is but another way of relegating the realities of the Christian faith to the old area of myth and legend and unreality. In simple language, these verities of the Christian faith are thereby treated as not verities at all. If it is only in the dimension of faith, or *Urgeschichte,* or supra-history, that Jesus Christ is the Servant of the Lord, then the conclusion is inescapable that Jesus Christ is not the Servant of the Lord at all. The great crying need for modern evangelical scholarship in the field of Old Testament is to come to grips with the basic thought of modern unbelief and to assert with great vigor and in utter dependence upon the Spirit of God, the true and genuine historical basis of the Christian faith.

VII. THE DIFFICULTIES OF EVANGELICAL SCHOLARSHIP

The testimony of the Bible to itself, and the position, therefore, which a consistent evangelical scholar would wish to maintain, is that the events recorded in the Old Testament actually occurred. Far from denying or hiding the historicity of these events, the consistent evangelical scholar would glory in their historicity. God, who made the heaven and the earth, did, as a matter of fact, enter this world and perform wondrous miracles for the salvation of man. The covenant which was ratified at Sinai is not a mere idea to be discussed, but something that actually occurred. There is a Mount Sinai; there was a Moses and a people of Israel. God did come down upon the mount in wondrous fashion. These great events are historical; they took place here upon this earth in precisely the manner that the Old Testament says they did. And herein lies the relevance of the biblical position to the present day. Men of today need to hear not the proclamation of eternal ideas but rather the announcement that something has been done to deliver them from their sins. Eternal truth in itself can only heighten the guilt of man and so bring despair. But hope is found in the announcement that in that faraway land of Palestine something was done to save the sinner.

God grant that the evangelical scholarship of our day may rise to the challenge that faces it! During the last century men like Joseph Addison Alexander and William Henry Green did not fear to take up the cudgels for full truthfulness of the Scriptures. They were well aware of the nature of the unbelieving thought of their day. In Germany, Hengstenberg and Keil and Delitzsch did the same. They saw the danger of rationalism and of mediating, compromising positions. Can we today also rise to the challenge? Can we come to grips with contemporary thought and point out its error?

But the task of the evangelical scholar must not be merely negative. There is much positive work to be done. There are commentaries to be written, and many projects remain to be carried out. The work of men such as Free and Kelso in archaeology, for example, is most important. As we face the challenge that lies before us we may return to the questions which were raised earlier. Why have not Old Testament scholars written more, and why have they not been more vigorous in their work?

In answer to these questions several points need be stressed. In the first place there are peculiar qualifications which are necessary for a competent Christian Old Testament scholar today. First and foremost among these is a proper doctrinal training. Much evangelical writing has been superficial and ineffective because of a lack of doctrinal knowledge. The man who is immersed in the fine points of Hebrew grammar needs to see the whole picture. He must realize the true nature of the Old Testament as a preparation for the New. We who labor in the field of the Old Testament need ever to keep reading in systematic and in biblical theology. If we neglect the works of the masters of systematic theology such as Hodge, Sheed, Dabney, Thornwell, Kuyper, Bavinck and Warfield, we cannot expect to understand the Old Testament in its relation to the New. We must not relegate systematic theology to the limbo of the unimportant, but must continue our study thereof.

There is a second reason which weighs a great deal with this writer; it is the previously discussed difficulty of the Hebrew language. At this point the Jewish scholars have a tremendous advantage. They begin the study of Hebrew as children and learn the Hebrew Bible as we learn our English Bible. If anything, their knowledge far surpasses ours. We who would work in the field of the Old Testament must acquire a mastery of Hebrew. This is not an easy task. It requires constant study and application. There is, however, a method which can be suggested, and which is most helpful. It is the practice of reading daily a portion of the Hebrew Bible.

One of the great weaknesses of Gentile Old Testament scholarship is that it depends too much upon dictionaries. One can tell that some scholars do not actually have the feel of the Hebrew, but take each passage as it comes and examine and then discuss it with the aid of the dictionary. By this method it is impossible to acquire a satisfactory knowledge of the language. The usage of a dictionary, important as it is in certain circumstances, is not sufficient to give to a student the feeling that is requisite for a proper understanding of the language.

There is only one method, it would seem, by which this feeling for a language such as Hebrew can be acquired. And that is by means of constant reading in the language. It would be a good idea if Old Testament scholars would make a practice of reading aloud several verses of the Hebrew Old Testament each day. The reading should be done slowly and thoughtfully. If a good translation is at hand, the reader can immediately check on the meaning of unfamiliar words. Above all the reading should be performed aloud. If this is done faithfully, day in and day out, it will soon result in a genuine feeling for the language. The rhythm and music of the Hebrew will, in a surprisingly short time, make themselves known to the one who diligently reads from the Hebrew Bible each day.

One who would do satisfactory work in the field of Old Testament must also possess an adequate knowledge of the cognate languages of Hebrew. This involves, of course, some familiarity with Aramaic, Syriac, Arabic, the various cuneiform languages, Ethiopic and also Egyptian. It is in the nature of the case impossible for one man to be a master of each of these languages, but he should have sufficient knowledge so that he can follow learned articles which make reference to these languages. If possible, he should attempt at least one year's study of each. It may seem to some that such knowledge is unnecessary. Did not the great master exegetes of the nineteenth century write without a knowledge of so many languages? True enough, but since their times many remarkable discoveries have been made, and these discoveries often bring to light documents written in the cognate languages. To deny oneself access to this material is to shut oneself off from much new light which recent discovery has cast upon the Bible.

And this brings us to the point that one must keep abreast as best as he is able with the progress of discovery and excavation. Patently, it is practically impossible for every scholar to have a firsthand acquaintance with excavation, but it is surely incumbent upon one who wishes to do justice to his field to keep up with the written reports of excavation. Furthermore, the new excavations have brought to light a great amount of material which is crying for study. Bible-believing scholars cannot afford to neglect such material.

From what has been said it is evident that the specialist in Old Testament must be a linguist. His linguistic attainments, however, must not be confined to a study of the ancient languages. Without Latin, Greek and Hebrew he will accomplish little solid work; but even more, there are modern languages, also, a reading knowledge of which must be mastered. Modern scholarly output is by no means confined to English. A man who cannot read German fluently simply cannot keep abreast of much extremely valuable material. In addition to German, writings in French, Spanish and Italian are also of great importance. And today, with the ascendancy of scholarly study in the Scandinavian countries, a good reading knowledge of at least Swedish is almost a necessity. To this must be added the fact that important material is also appearing in Turkish and in Modern Hebrew.

These, then, are some of the reasons why so few conservative men have devoted themselves to the important field of Old Testament and why so few have produced scholarly work. The field is difficult, and its demands are most taxing. There simply is not room for the man who will not pay the price of patient study and toil. It may be that one reason for the meager output of conservatives has been laziness. In this respect some of the "critical" scholars put us to shame. One can but be amazed at the industry and diligence that have been displayed by some of the liberal scholars. They are not afraid of hard work.

VIII. THE CONTRIBUTION OF EVANGELICAL SCHOLARSHIP

What contribution must evangelical scholars make today? May it not be said that there already exist sufficiently good commentaries? Has not the theory of Wellhausen already been satisfactorily answered? Has not archaeology already demonstrated the untenability of many "critical" theories? Would it not be better if we simply spent our time in preaching the Gospel?

Such questions are often heard. They represent a plausible reasoning; plausible indeed, but utterly false. It is true that truth does not change; it is true that there is an abiding message of the Bible. Through our research we shall not discover the Bible to be a book different from our forefathers' conclusions regarding it. Our scholarship will not tell us that there is a new way of salvation, nor that Christianity is something different from what men like Luther and Calvin thought it to be. Truth does not change. The purpose of evangelical Old Testament scholarship is not at all to discover new things. If men ask what contribution can be made, the answer is that the greatest possible contribution of a Bible-believing scholarship is to expound the Holy Scriptures, to bring forth new light from them, to illustrate them and to point out their trustworthiness.

Is there not a danger, it is sometimes asked, that such scholarship will discover things that will overthrow the historic Christian faith? The answer is, of course, that such is not the case. After all, God has given us the Bible; it is His own "God-breathed" word. God also is the Creator of heaven and earth. Everything created, therefore, must testify of Him. The more we study archaeology, for example, the better we will understand the setting in which the great events of biblical history occurred. We need not fear truth; rather we should earnestly seek it wherever it may be found. Scholarly study of the Bible, if conducted on Christian-theistic principles, can only result in a deeper understanding of the Holy Word of God.

What contribution, then, is there for evangelical scholarship of today to make? In the first place there is the necessity for a deeper understanding of the truth of the Word of God. This can only be obtained in one way—through patient and sympathetic exegetical study and research. There is a tremendous need for exegetical works upon the books of the Old Testament. It will not do to say that we have Keil and Delitzsch and that, therefore, nothing more is needed. Great as are these works, and they *are* great works, they are not sufficient to meet the needs of the Church of Christ for today. They must be equaled in quality by commentaries produced by men who have come to grips with modern thought, and who are capable of searching the Scriptures. Today much more is known about Hebrew than when Keil and Delitzsch wrote. There must therefore be that same patient study of the Hebrew words of each verse which characterized the works of the great nineteenth century masters.

It is the evangelical who will bring out the meaning of the Scriptures. He is not going to spend his time emending the text or seeking to identify the various supposed documents of which that text is composed. Rather, he will seek to understand what the writer is saying. To do this he will come to grips with the question of the meaning of the Hebrew words, and he will call upon the resources of the many cognate languages and also of archaeology. What a wealth of material stands ready to assist him! It is not material, however, which is always easily accessible. For example, he may have to work patiently through the Mari texts for illustrations of certain grammatical principles, or for illustrations of particular matters mentioned in the Old Testament.

Great and varied indeed is the amount of illustrative material that stands ready for the usage of the evangelical scholar of today. Great as it is and varied as it is, however, there is one thing for which it cannot now and never can be a substitute, namely, the indwelling of the Spirit of God. In the last analysis, only the man who is born of God, who has been regenerated by the Holy Spirit and so is Spirit taught, can bring out the deep things of the Word which God has given. No amount of patience and diligence of research can ever take the place of the gift of God's Holy Spirit. One sometimes receives the impression that the reason some of the reputed "return" to biblical theology is so barren is that it is being conducted by men who give little evidence of having submitted their minds to the Spirit of God. It is, then, the regenerate man who can bring forth the deep things of Scripture. How great is his sin if he neglects to do this!

In seeking to expound the Scriptures the evangelical has the great opportunity of bringing forth illustrative material. One example will suffice. There has been much insistence, lately, that the famous passage Isaiah 7:14 is not a direct prophecy of the virgin birth of Christ, and that the word *almah,* which it contains, should be translated merely as "young woman." If, in reply to this assertion, the evangelical were simply to rely upon the arguments which were employed by the scholars of the last century, his case would lose greatly in force. Now, however, he may appeal to the usage made upon the remarkable texts found in 1929 at Ras Schamra. There he discovers an employment of the word similar to that of Isaiah's. He discovers that on these texts the word is used of an unmarried woman. He also discovers that on certain Aramaic incantation bowls, the corresponding form of the Hebrew word *bethulah* is used of a married woman. Thus, he has reassurance that the traditional translation "virgin" is to be preferred over "young woman." The illustrative material is at hand; it must however be studied, and be studied by those who believe the Bible to be the infallible Word of God.

It cannot be stressed too strongly that one of the most important contributions that the evangelical can make today is that of engaging in the defense of the Bible. Attacks upon the trustworthiness of Scripture did not cease with the passing of the nineteenth century; if anything, they are being made with even greater force today. And they must be answered. They cannot be answered, however, by name-calling. It is most unfortunate that there have been evangelicals who have thought that a few remarks about "higher critics" dispose of the question. The evangelical must exhibit love in his defense of the Bible. Many of the men whose positions he opposes are men of high quality and deep sincerity. He may disagree *toto coelo* with their position, but he may love and admire them personally. If the evangelical ceases to act like a gentleman, he brings harm to the cause of Christ.

If the evangelical will make sharp the contrast which exists between modern thought and historic Christianity he will be rendering a great service. He must meet the attacks that are constantly being made upon the Bible. To do this he needs all the resources of his learning, but he needs above all the Spirit of the living God. To take a clear-cut and positive stand upon the side of evangelical Christianity will doubtless separate the true evangelical from some, but it is the only way in which the cause of truth can progress. The evangelical scholar need not be ashamed. Great is his heritage. He stands in the line of men such as Hengstenberg, Keil, Alexander, Green and Wilson. Like them he must set the Christian position sharply over against modern thought. When he has done this, and when he has expounded the Christian position to the best of his ability, then and then only has his responsibility been discharged. Then will the Spirit of God honor the stand that has been taken for His infallible Word.

THE NEW TESTAMENT

Everett F. Harrison

Everett F. Harrison holds a Ph.D. degree from the University of Pennsylvania. He has had missionary and pastoral experience, but his ministry has been for the most part devoted to theological education—thirteen years at Dallas Theological Seminary, and the past nine years as professor of New Testament at Fuller Theological Seminary, where he was a member of the charter faculty (1947). He is author of The Son of God Among the Sons of Men.

2. *Everett F. Harrison:*

THE NEW TESTAMENT

BEGINNING a series of special lectures, A. T. Robertson on one occasion held up a copy of the Greek New Testament and declared, "This is our most precious possession."

If this be so, and we heartily concur that it is, then the determination of the original text of the New Testament is of such importance that it affords a natural starting point for our investigation of the present situation. However much scholars may diverge in their interpretation of Scripture, they confess themselves bound by the text as their starting point, and are ready to accept the wording which is established on scientific grounds. Men may reasonably debate individual problems of text involving variant readings, or readings which give the appearance of being corrupt, but when one is guilty of setting the text aside because it conflicts with his notions of what the text ought to say, he proclaims his irresponsibility as a scholar and invites suspicion of his conclusions.

I. PROGRESS IN TEXTUAL CRITICISM

What advance has been made in recent times in the field of textual criticism? The labors of Westcott and Hort, consummated in the latter part of the nineteenth century, clearly marked an epoch. From that time the doom of the *Textus Receptus* was sealed. This text, which underlies the King James Version, was built upon the great mass of manuscripts which had accumulated in the libraries of Europe and which were studied with new interest in the days of the Reformation. Most of these manuscripts were late, and reflected a type of text which Westcott and Hort called Syrian. By the genealogical method these scholars showed the dependence of these manuscripts on a type of text which was not truly ancient but which originated in the fourth century as the result of an effort to standardize the text. The need for revision arose because of repeated copyings of the text in widely separated areas without any centralized control, resulting in numerous variants. The positive contribution of Westcott and Hort was the discovery of certain text types which preceded the Syrian revision. Often their readings were combined in the text which stems from that revision. Of these pre-Syrian strains, the Western was judged to be least reliable, largely because of its tendency to admit glosses and traditional material. The Alexandrian type was reasonably accurate but tended to make corrections of a minor nature for the sake of smoother grammatical construction. The third type was called Neutral, since it seemed to avoid both these tendencies. The distinctive readings of manuscripts representing this type commended themselves to Westcott and Hort as being in accord with the thought and style of the various Biblical writers and as being unlikely to contain scribal alteration.

The presence of both Western and Neutral types in support of a reading gave assurance that this reading was the original. If these two types presented competing readings, however, the nod was given to the Neutral except for certain places where the Western was obviously shorter and superior, reversing its usual tendency. Westcott and Hort gave the world two volumes, one a text of the Greek New Testament, the other an explanation of the principles on which the text was formulated, together with a discussion of certain passages which present problems to the textual critic.

Various objections have been raised against the work of these men in subsequent years. Their devotion to Neutral witnesses was sometimes carried to an extreme, quite contrary to the best sense of a passage. Conversely, they gave too little credit to Western readings. This prejudice is pointed up by the fact that they chose the terminology "Western non-interpolation" for those instances in which the Western text was shorter and superior to the Neutral, instead of calling them by the term "Neutral interpolation." Apparently they were concerned to safeguard the prestige of the Neutral text. They failed to see as clearly as later investigators have that the Neutral type is itself the result of revision, and has not come down from its source with the degree of purity which they ascribed to it. Furthermore, their genealogical method, despite its great utility in unseating the *Textus Receptus* from its long domination, was not serviceable in getting back of the second century, when the divergencies between Neutral and Western were already in existence. It could not furnish criteria for a decision between two lines of textual descent both of which are ancient.

It is probable, too, that Westcott and Hort underestimated the degree to which scribal alterations have affected the text. J. Rendel Harris was credited with the caustic remark that to Hort the scribes were all angels. A recent work by C. S. C. Williams, *Alterations to the Text of the Synoptic Gospels and Acts* (1951), attempts to show that certain texts were altered for doctrinal reasons. Yet, even if all his contentions are admitted at their face value, the amount of such alteration is not large.

New names have been suggested for the text types isolated by Westcott and Hort. Instead of Syrian we now hear of Koine (von Soden's term) or Byzantine. Because the word Neutral is not altogether satisfactory, the term Alexandrian is commonly used, the name being given on the basis of the assumed origin of this text type in the city of Alexandria. Or it is called Hesychian, after Hesychius, who was active in textual study and revision in this Egyptian city about 300 A.D. The designation Western has been felt to be particularly inappropriate for the conglomeration of manuscripts from various parts of the Mediterranean world which formerly were grouped into this category. However, it is still serviceable for those which are truly Western, such as Codex Bezae, the Old Latin Version, and certain patristic writers of North Africa, Italy, and southern Gaul.

A new text type has gradually won recognition, the Caesarean. Its isolation came in stages, through the researches of W. H. Ferrar, then Kirsopp Lake, both of whom found certain minuscule manuscripts with common affinities which did not fit the recognized text types. The Koridethi Gospels were later added to these. B. H. Streeter sought to fix this type with greater precision, noting that it stood roughly between the old Neutral and Western texts in its character, differing from both sufficiently to warrant a separate classification. The Chester Beatty Papyri, discovered in the 1930s, fell somewhat into this pattern also, especially in Mark. In the Pauline Epistles the Neutral type is quite strongly attested by these papyri. The term Caesarean now appears to be somewhat of a misnomer, however, since these papyri were discovered in Egypt and bear witness to the use of this so-called Caesarean type of text before its use by Origen at Caesarea. Some scholars are hesitant to admit that the manuscripts which contain this type of text possess sufficient homogeneity to warrant the practice of speaking of the Caesarean text. Further study is needed to clarify this issue.

The researches of G. Zuntz have convinced him of the great importance of the Chester Beatty Papyrus of the Pauline Epistles (P^{46}). As a rule P^{46} strengthens and confirms the testimony of the Neutral witnesses, but he thinks that it can be right when found with a single Western witness in opposition to all the rest of the manuscript tradition.

In general the discovery of new materials, and the study of materials already to hand but never fully examined, has tended to make more difficult the assignment of all our witnesses to a few well-defined text types. A direct result of this is a decreased confidence in the process of attempted settlement of disputed readings on the basis of the testimony of the text types as the finally conclusive factor. More weight is being given to decisions reached on the basis of the merits of distinctive readings in individual passages, with due consideration of all the factors involved, rather than to decisions reached by reliance on the guidance of text types almost exclusively. In other words, this means that internal criticism is being given a larger place proportionately than was true a few decades ago. For a good statement of the present situation, one may consult the last two chapters of F. G. Kenyon's book, *The Text of the Greek Bible* (1937). A. T. Robertson's *Introduction to the Textual Criticism of the New Testament* (1925) is still useful but needs revision in the light of recent discoveries and the trends noted in the preceding paragraphs. Dr. B. M. Metzger of Princeton Theological Seminary would be an ideal man for this task.

In most of our schools the printed Greek text in use is that edited by Nestle. This work is revised every few years and has now gone through more than a score of editions. Its critical apparatus includes the newer materials which have come to light in recent years. A few changes in the text are made from time to time by the editor and his advisers on the basis of scholarly opinion which is communicated to them, but on the whole the Greek text most widely distributed today may be said to have reached a fairly settled state.

The disadvantage of the critical apparatus provided in Nestle is its brevity. In 1945 a group of American scholars made a move to create a new critical apparatus, not simply combining the results of the work of Tischendorf, von Soden, Legg, and others, but considering afresh the vast accumulation of materials, including the collation of new manuscripts and manuscripts heretofore not closely examined. This has grown until it is now an international project, centering in Chicago. Some years will elapse before this huge task can be completed. Reports indicate that the *Textus Receptus* will be used as the basis of the work, not however as an endorsement of this outmoded text, but for the sake of convenience. The theory is that the best text will be seen and appreciated to better advantage as it is thrown over against a text which differs substantially from it. This is an application of the silhouette principle.

So the effort to attain the correct text, that which most closely approximates the original, goes on. One should not allow himself to be dismayed by the claims made from time to time that there are literally tens of thousands of variations in our manuscripts. The more the manuscripts increase (the number is already enormous) the greater will be the sum total of the variations. This is inevitable. But it should be clearly recognized that these are usually minor in nature, consisting in differences of spelling, the presence or absence of the definite article, synonymous words, words which closely resemble one another in form and therefore are easily substituted by a copyist, and other variants of this general sort.

Actually there is far more agreement than disagreement between the *Textus Receptus* and the improved text of our times.

The next step after the settlement of the text is its translation into English. Lively interest continues in this area. The most notable contribution on the American scene is the appearance of the Revised Standard Version, the New Testament portion of which has been in the hands of the public about ten years. Some prejudice has been aroused by the complaint that the scholars involved were almost entirely liberal in their theological outlook. This fact should not prevent an objective appraisal or a real appreciation of their work. The elimination of "thee" and "thou" except in prayer has troubled some readers. Those who were accustomed only to the King James Version were shocked to discover that whole verses or even paragraphs were lacking in the new version. If the Christian public had been kept better informed over the years on the science of textual criticism, no such shock would have been felt. The simple fact is that the King James Version rests on the *Textus Receptus,* which has since been superseded by the discovery of better manuscripts and a growing appreciation of the principles upon which the text should be established.

That there are many decided gains in the new version is undeniable. Its avoidance of obsolete or stilted language, its care in the rendering of tenses, its judicious division of the text into paragraphs, are some of the areas of achievement. Now and then its translations reflect the views of "advanced" scholarship, as in the rendering, "elemental spirits of the universe" in place of the traditional "elements of the world." It is doubtful that Paul's expression would have been understood as "elemental spirits" in his day, whatever may have been the case in the following century. Certainly the concept of universe is almost totally absent from Paul, as is true of those who worked from a Semitic background.

Another instance of daring by the translators is their rendering of I Corinthians 7:36-38, following Lake and others. It is precarious to argue from Paul's preference for the unmarried state to the conclusion that he endorses an indefinite engagement or a so-called spiritual marriage. In I Corinthians 9:10 the text is altered in accordance with the conjecture of Bois, and the key word *pantos* is rendered "entirely," committing Paul to a position which ignores the literal force of the Old Testament passage which he quotes in favor of the allegorical. Far more important than this one reference is the hermeneutical approach toward the Old Testament which is thus foisted upon Paul. But such questionable items are not so numerous as to blind us to the general excellence of the version. The translators themselves recognize that their work is not finally definitive and they seem open to suggestion and correction.

Of the recent translations by individuals, those by Williams and Phillips have won wide acclaim. The latter is popular among young people. It is racy and far removed at times from a literal rendering. Evidently the author has been concerned above all with making the message of the New Testament meaningful to a generation which has been tragically ignorant of its contents.

II. THE DEAD SEA SCROLLS AND THEIR IMPORTANCE

Of all the discoveries relating to the Scriptures and the Christian movement that have occurred in modern times the most exciting and significant have been those taking place for the past ten years along the northwest side of the Dead Sea. A series of caves have yielded up scores of manuscripts as well as such customary artifacts as coins and pottery. The actual headquarters of the group responsible for the deposit of these materials has been unearthed at Qumran. Here the members of the group studied the Law intensively and maintained a communal type of life. Manuscripts both biblical and otherwise have been found in unexpected profusion. Among the biblical items the scroll of Isaiah is the largest single find, but fragments of most of the books of the Old Testament have been located.

From one of the documents prepared by the group, now known as the Manual of Discipline, it has been possible to identify the sect with the group which produced the Damascus document, which had been known and studied for some decades. Both writings make mention of a Teacher of Righteousness as the central figure in their society, and identify the group as members of the New Covenant, with the study of the Law as their chief occupation. It is widely held that this society belonged to the Essenes or at any rate was closely affiliated with them. This conclusion is reached on the grounds of similarities in beliefs and practices of the sect when compared with what we know of the Essenes from ancient sources. It is also predicated on the supposition that a territory as restricted as this would not be likely to harbor two diverse groups. The activity of the sect in this area seems to have ranged from Maccabean times, or somewhat before, down to the Jewish revolt against Rome which culminated in the destruction of Jerusalem in 70 A.D.

It is necessary, then, to investigate the possible bearing of this community and its literature upon Christian origins. The points of special connection or possible connection are John the Baptist and his ministry, the person and position of Jesus, the factors underlying the composition of the Fourth Gospel, and the nature of the early Church. These matters can only be touched upon here with the greatest brevity.

The possibility of contact between John and the Qumran community lies in the fact that according to Luke 1:80 he was in the deserts until the time of his showing to Israel. His catechetical instruction to inquirers seems to have some similarity to ideas found in the scrolls, namely, his counsel of non-violence to the soldiers and his encouragement to the people generally to share their goods with one another. But to offset this, certain differences are observable. Absent from John's instruction are exacting rules and regulations such as the sect practiced, including a probation period for new members, as well as the principle of separation from the society of the world about them.

W. H. Brownlee has conjectured that the points of agreement may be due to John's residence for some time among this group, and the disagreements may be attributed to his dissatisfaction with some features of the movement, particularly its withdrawal from society and its lack of vigorous propaganda directed toward the nation. The ablutions of the sect have suggested to some minds the notion that John's baptizing activity owed its inspiration to his contact with this group. Yet the once-for-all characer of John's baptism seems to have no counterpart in the Qumran literature. Finally, John was a Nazirite, whereas the sect had new wine at their meals. Some connection between John and this group may be allowed, but the differences have to be accounted for.

What about Jesus of Nazareth? Do the scrolls throw any light upon Him? Dupont-Sommer thinks so. He has developed a theory that the Teacher of Righteousness (or Master of Justice) furnished a prototype of the Christian Messiah. His effort is directed to finding in historical conditions before the Christian era a development which explains the Suffering-Servant motif in the life of Jesus. Before Dupont-Sommer, the proposal had been made by Schechter that at least some Essenes thought that their great leader would come to life again. In seeking an identification of the Teacher of Righteousness with a historical figure, the French scholar favors Onias, a pious man who was killed in the struggle between the forces of Aristobolus and Hyrcanus just prior to the coming of the Romans into the control of Palestine in 63 B.C. He has suggested that the death of this man produced a literature among his followers which later became incorporated into the canonical Scriptures, thus accounting for the Servant of Jehovah passages. But was Onias a man of the Essene type? Did he have followers? We have no information which leads to an affirmative answer. Furthermore, as H. Rowley has pointed out, it is futile to suppose that the Jews, the very ones who instigated the death of Onias, would adopt the writings of his followers and insert them into their Scriptures.

The extravagant claims advanced by Dupont-Sommer as to the similarities between the Teacher of Righteousness and Jesus of Nazareth are not sustained by the documents, particularly the assertion that the former is also the Elect, the Messiah, and the Redeemer of the world. Too much is read into the testimony of the scrolls in order to find such parallels. It appears that Dupont-Sommer is modifying his position in the direction of a more conservative outlook, but meanwhile popularizers are heralding the unjustifiable conclusion that the Dead Sea Scrolls have demonstrated that there is nothing unique in Christianity.

Whereas the Qumran group had its theology strongly tinctured by legalism, the entire testimony of the New Testament concerning the way of salvation in Jesus Christ grounds it on grace, something to be received by faith. The Teacher of Righteousness is no real counterpart to our Lord, who remains *sui generis*.

As to the bearing of the scrolls on our understanding of the Gospel of John, we have the benefit of a study by W. F. Albright which has just appeared as part of the *festschrift* volume in honor of C. H. Dodd. He concludes that there are at least four major areas in which John differs widely from the position of the Essenic groups: the doctrine of a suffering (and not simply a reigning) Messiah, the mission of Christ as inclusive of the world and not simply of the elect in its saving purpose, the healing ministry of Christ upon the bodies and souls of men rather than a sanctifying of His immediate followers, and Christ's emphasis upon the message of love and not simply of righteousness.

Professor Lucretta Mowry of Wellesley believes that John borrowed his system of ethical dualism from the Essenes but gave it a theological rather than a metaphysical turn. She sees also an apologetic element in the Gospel of John directed against the extreme ritualism of the Essenes and their dependence upon the Law (John 2, 3, and 5 especially). We may learn something here, but at the same time the interpreter of John should beware of efforts to find subtle undertones pervading the Gospel to an extent that beclouds the simplicity of its message. Dualism is such a common thing in many religions that we ought to have definite proof that John is depending on Iranian thought or proto-Gnostic ideas before making his contrast between light and darkness a necessary reflection of such sources.

In the area of the beginnings of the Church, our attention is drawn to the fact that the community of goods practiced for a time among the disciples in Jerusalem may well have its provenance in the Essenic regulations, although an appreciable difference remains, due to the fact that Christians did this voluntarily and not as a matter of cultic regulation. Some connection of the Christian sacraments has also been sought in the Essene practice of pronouncing a blessing on bread and wine. But the use of these particular elements is of secondary importance. When we inquire as to the significance behind the two observances, it is difficult to find any anticipation of the Christian institution.

A theory of the influence of the Qumran group upon early Christianity through the Hellenists has been worked out by Oscar Cullmann, who finds that the point of special similarity is the rejection of temple worship. The Qumran sect had a strong priestly composition (cf. Acts 6:7) but it probably shared the Essene dissatisfaction with the temple and its worship. Cullmann seizes upon the martyrdom of Stephen, the ringleader of the Hellenists, as evidence that he and his group disowned the temple in a way not shared by the apostles and their followers, since the latter group was not involved in the persecution which ensued. This iconoclasm of Stephen is traced to Essene or Qumran background. Cullmann goes further than the evidence warrants, however, when he maintains that Stephen found the culmination of Israel's disobedience in the construction of the temple under Solomon. Stephen's accusers, we grant, charged him with speaking words against the holy place, but he himself in his address did not attribute disobedience to Solomon for building the temple any more than to David for cherishing a desire to build it. His complaint rather was that Israel's devotion to the temple had become a static thing. The nation was not prepared to welcome fresh revelation from God, particularly as this was presented in the claims of Jesus, One greater than the temple.

Speaking generally, the discovery of the Dead Sea Scrolls is bound to increase our appreciation of the complexity of the Judaism out of which Christianity sprang. The previously known literature of the period, the Apocrypha and Pseudepigrapha, is being searched more carefully than ever in order to get a clearer picture of this epoch. Evangelicals should be stimulated by these finds to take a larger place in such investigations than they have in the past.

As a means of becoming at home in this newly discovered literature, one can do no better than consult Millar Burrows's volume, *The Dead Sea Scrolls* (1955). The author's treatment is objective and well balanced, an antidote to the welter of speculation which is rife today on certain aspects of these materials. His conclusions are remarkably restrained, as attested by such a statement as this: "It is not necessary to suppose that any of the writers of the New Testament had ever heard of the particular sect that produced the Dead Sea Scrolls, and I see no definite evidence that they had" (pp. 342, 343). Or this: "After studying the Dead Sea Scrolls for seven years, I do not find my understanding of the New Testament substantially affected" (p. 343). Or this: "Perhaps the best thing the Dead Sea Scrolls can do for us is to make us appreciate our Bible all the more by contrast" p. 343).

III. THE HISTORICAL FOUNDATIONS OF CHRISTIANITY

Half a century or more ago liberalism was riding high, feeling that it had achieved notable success in its quest for the historical Jesus. Harnack's famous lectures under the title, *What is Christianity,* delivered in the University of Berlin during the year 1899-1900, epitomized the liberal position. Jesus was a prophetic figure with a great message for the world, but the supernatural aura with which the Gospels surround Him is due to the progressively developing Christology of His followers. Criticism must strip away this interpretative element. It did so by quietly removing from the text, as later accretions, anything attributed to Jesus which rose above the level of possibility for a human figure. It was felt that in Mark's Gospel the real Jesus appears most clearly, with a minimum of theologizing. The liberal approach received a jolt when W. Wrede made it appear that Mark, so far from being a relatively pure historical account of this human Jesus, was actually permeated with Christological elements quite uncongenial to the assumptions of the liberal picture. Within more recent years C. H. Dodd, in an important book entitled *History and the Gospel* (1938), has clearly shown that for the Evangelists the historical and theological elements interpenetrated one another in such a way that they could not be sundered. These men did not know an untheological Jesus, but One who, whether as teacher or miracle worker, was a supernatural person with a consciousness of having come from God and sustaining a unique relation to Him.

Following World War I a new approach to the study of the Gospels began to take shape in the hands of certain German scholars. To it has been given the name Form Criticism. It was felt that the period between the life of Jesus and the emergence of our written Gospels held the key to a better understanding of the Gospel materials. Why were some things incorporated into the records and others omitted? In this oral period, when the Gospel traditions were taking fixed form, the Church was growing. Form criticism suggested that the needs and interests of the Church determined the elements which survived and passed into the Gospels as we know them. The study of the Gospels seemed to disclose the presence of certain literary patterns which were observable also in the folk literature of many peoples in ancient times. Pronouncement stories, parables, myths, legends—these were some of the "forms." The critics recognized too the importance of the passion narrative. They posited that the Gospels are really mirrors in which the history of the Church's life is reflected. Some went so far as to suggest that the tradition regarding Jesus was altered to make it fit the beliefs and practices of the early Church.

This approach minimizes the importance of Jesus for Christian beginnings. It supposes that the early Church had no interest in the life of Christ for its own sake, but appropriated to itself only what was germane to its own life. This is incredible psychologically. In order to establish the Church Jesus must have been a towering figure and must have made an impression on His followers quite beyond that of a mere prophet or wonder worker. In the very nature of the case the first Christians must have had a lively interest in gathering and retaining every bit of information available about Him. The prologue of Luke's Gospel bears witness to this very activity. Even before the composition of our canonical Gospels others were composed, and Luke informs us that these accounts, no less than his own, dealt with the things which had been fulfilled in connection with the life of Christ (not with ideas and practices of the early Church).

Furthermore, the teaching of converts began immediately after Pentecost. What then was taught? The Church had as yet no history, no conflicts. It must have taught the things concerning Jesus Christ which the apostles and others were able to recall from personal knowledge. No other conclusion is possible. But this conclusion undermines the very thesis of form criticism, for we dare not assume that when our written Gospels were published they represented a departure from the oral tradition. They must have been at one with this teaching. This was the justification for putting it into written form. In fact, if the written form represented a deviation from the oral teaching, it would have brought on serious controversy within the Church. Of such controversy we have no record or hint.

Form critics have handled the miracles of Jesus in a way which is thoroughly unpalatable to the Christian consciousness. They have labeled them "tales," and have sought to link them with accounts of Rabbinic healings and with reports of the therapeutic activities connected with healing cults in the Hellenistic world. According to Dibelius and Bultmann, the purpose of the miracle stories in the Gospels is to present Jesus as a wonder worker. The miracles are demonstrations of His power and the report of them is calculated to show the superiority of Jesus to other wonder workers. There is no particular connection with the character of Jesus nor with the ethical and redemptive elements of His message. To this position L. J. McGinley has brought a potent rebuttal based upon a survey of the Rabbinic and Hellenistic miracle stories in comparison with the Gospel accounts. He concludes that the great difference between the Synoptic tradition and the Rabbinic and Hellenistic healing stories is in their "historical and spiritual tone." The reason back of this is that the Synoptic tradition "was not a compilation of popular anecdotes, evolving over a long period of time, careless of the reality of the fact" (*Form-Criticism of the Synoptic Healing Narratives,* (1944, p. 153). In writing his book, *The Miracle Stories of the Gospels* (1941), Alan Richardson has had the Form critics in mind also, and has shown that the miracles cannot be construed simply as wonders, but are a definite part of the mission and message of Jesus. Readers of the Gospels are well aware of the demand for faith in Jesus in connection with the miracles. Such demand is quite foreign to the alleged parallels of a Jewish or Hellenistic sort.

The mood of the present hour is certainly more friendly to the evangelical position than was the case when form criticism was at its height. This has created embarrassment for some who took a rather negative position on the historical value of the Gospels and now feel the necessity of excusing their mistake with as good grace as possible. An outstanding example is R. H. Lightfoot's declaration in *History and Interpretation in the Gospels* (1935) that "the form of the earthly no less than of the heavenly Christ is for the most part hidden from us. For all the inestimable value of the gospels, they yield us little more than a whisper of his voice; we trace in them but the outskirts of his ways" (p. 225). In a later book, *The Gospel Message of St. Mark* (1950), the author takes pains to explain that his statement was virtually a quotation from Job 26:14, and that his own point was that of Job, to emphasize the contrast between the comparatively small knowledge available to man and the far greater portion which lies beyond his ken. If this were all that Lightfoot intended, it would amount to no more than a restatement of John 20:30; 21:25. But one cannot help wondering if this is actually the force of the original statement by Lightfoot. Form criticism would have us believe that the information in the Gospels, for the most part, does not permit us to know Jesus as He was but only as the Church has presented Him. We are left with the impression that the difference between the two items is very considerable.

It is not altogether surprising, in view of assaults on the integrity of the Gospel narratives, that some evangelicals should be suspicious of any critical approach to the documents, whether from the standpoint of form criticism or of the source criticism which preceded it. All schools of thought have to deal with the same material. Some account must be given of the similarities as well as the differences in the records of the Evangelists. But there is no reasonable ground for fear that verbal inspiration is endangered when it is granted that some of the Gospel writers drew upon previously existing accounts. A somewhat similar process is discernible in the Old Testament, where the compiler of the Chronicles made large use of the annals of the books of Kings. Our Lord and the early Church accepted both sections as Scripture. If the evidence points to Mark as the basic Gospel, with Matthew and Luke making liberal use of its materials but supplying additional data from their own recollections or researches, there should be no antecedent objection to this methodology.

One of the leading form critics of our time has been Rudolf Bultmann, whose radicalism is well known. He advocates that various layers of tradition can be discerned in the Gospel materials. The oldest is probably traceable to Jesus in some sense, but it is impossible to be sure. He commits himself to the proposition that "there is a possibility that the contents of this oldest layer are also the result of a complicated historical process which we can no longer trace" (*Jesus and the Word,* 1930, p. 13). This skepticism has continued to dominate Bultmann's work as he has moved into other areas of approach to the New Testament. One of these is *Gnosis.* Pursuing much the same line as Reitzenstein before him, he has sought to show a considerable degree of Gnostic influence upon the

New Testament by comparison with the Mandean-Iranian literature. But much of it is too late to have affected New Testament writers, and there is the further difficulty that the use of similar or even identical language does not necessarily connote identity of thought patterns. The inability to demonstrate dependence of the New Testament upon these materials besets Bultmann's work just as it did that of Reitzenstein. Study of the Dead Sea Scrolls is showing that one does not need to look beyond Judaism for the reputed Gnostic influence upon John and other biblical writers. Albright remarks:

> Perhaps the most important service of the Dead Sea Scrolls will be the demonstration which may be brought from them that John, the Synoptics, St. Paul, and various other books draw from a common reservoir of terminology and ideas which were well known to the Essenes and presumably familiar also to other Jewish sects of the period—(*The Background of the New Testament and its Eschatology*. Studies in honour of C. H. Dodd, ed. by Davies and Daube, 1956, p. 169).

More than one scholar has pointed out that whereas Gnostic dualism was physically based, that of John's Gospel is ethical in nature. Albright summarizes the effect of the new information from the Dead Sea area on the subject of *Gnosis* with the categorical statement, "There is . . . less evidence than ever to support the claims of Gnostic influence on Paul and John" (p. 170).

A decisive point in Bultmann's career came with his decision to attend the lectures of the philosopher Heidegger, which he did for a year, even though he himself was a professor in the university. This influence began to permeate Bultmann's work and to shape his thinking along the lines which were to make him such a controversial figure. While he did not succumb to the atheism of Heidegger, but continued to insist on faith in God and obedience to the Christian message, nevertheless his own approach to the New Testament took on a decidedly existential character. He began to advocate that the biblical materials can only be understood aright when it is perceived that they are placed on a mythological framework. Myth sets forth man's hopes and fears, his dependence upon the powers of the universe which surrounds him. Man hereby expresses his own sense of inadequacy and his own insecurity. The real thrust of mythology, though it deal with the divine and the demonic, is nevertheless man-centered. What cannot be put into anthropological terms is not actual, according to Bultmann's way of thinking. Such important elements of the Christian proclamation as the pre-existence of Christ, His miracles, and even His resurrection, come under the category of myth. Bultmann makes the whole compass of Christian doctrine to be set forth in the language of mythology, the origin of which he thinks can easily be traced to the mythology of the

Jewish Apocalyptic and to the redemption myths of Gnosticism. He thinks that we cannot expect modern man with his scientifically ordered world view to accept the Christian message as long as it is thus tied to a mythical world view. The whole structure must be demythologized to make the Gospel pertinent to the viewpoint of modern man. What ancient man tried to say through mythology we must say through existential presentation.

Wilhelm Herrmann also strongly influenced Bultmann by his insistence that the Church could not expect to win thinking men to its banner by the presentation of dogma as the necessary condition for faith. It must demand only sincerity and love. From Herrmann came also Bultmann's subjective view of faith, which so closely integrates with his Existentialism. Faith is more the way to self-understanding than the way to God.

No doubt Bultmann is deeply convinced in his own mind that the Church must give up the world view which he thinks is presupposed in the Scriptures if it is to win modern man. We must not forget that Strauss also felt that he had a mission to make the life of Jesus intelligible to his day by applying the category of myth to much which the Gospels presented as historical fact. It is far from proven that these concessions to the modern viewpoint have been successful in removing barriers which keep men from becoming Christians. Some have intellectual difficulties, to be sure, but the real barrier has always been man's sin and self-sufficiency. Furthermore, what is accomplished if men find the way to Christ made easy only to discover in the end a warped and shrunken Christ?

A protest is properly raised against Bultmann's highhandedness in dealing with the text. Not long ago the editor of *The Expository Times* (January, 1956), took him to task for treating as interpolations passages in John which he found intractable in connection with his own viewpoint. Men of less prominence would be sharply criticized for such tactics. Why should Bultmann be excused simply because he has attained to reputation as a critic?

Bultmann's appeal to the student mind in Germany has been strong indeed. That appeal may be attributed more to his method than to anything else. The Germans are traditionally devotees of method. Bultmann's is a combination of several elements, the Form Criticism approach which forces us to see Jesus almost solely through the eyes of the Church, his demythologizing, his peculiar eschatological emphasis (judgment and kingdom are not future, but realized; that is, already here), and his existential approach to hermeneutics. Anything in the Gospel records which goes beyond the reach of existential treatment is for Bultmann rendered irrelevant. Thus we see how far he has departed from the biblical orientation, which is God-centered and Christ-centered.

One of the tragic aspects of this development of our times is that

Bultmannism is being treated in British and American circles largely as an academic matter. In Germany, however, men realize that it is a life-and-death struggle for the historical truth of the Gospel. When the venerable Karl Heim was accorded public honors at Tuebingen on the occasion of his eightieth birthday, with the province and the nation taking note of it as well as the local community, this great soul took the opportunity to address the people in solemn warning against the views of Bultmann and his disciples which were threatening the very foundations of the Christian faith. Evangelical students from America now living in Germany bear testimony to the fact that the German young people who have espoused Bultmannism give no evidence of that bright, warm spiritual life which New Testament Christianity everywhere produces. Instead, there reigns in its place an arid intellectualism. Men are known by their fruits. The same is true of systems of thought.

Some real gold does shine through the dross of this scholar's work, as for example his insight into Paul's teaching on justification. He meets the claim that Paul's doctrine of forensic righteousness is unsound because the justified man is still actually a sinner by showing that the teaching simply relates to the truth of the establishment of right relations with God. The conduct of the Christian belongs to a different category. Then, too, it is acknowledged on all sides that Bultmann has the courage to grapple with big problems and does so in a forthright way. In the long run this will work out for good to the Church, since evangelicals will be compelled to state their own position more clearly with reference to modern tensions, including the very issues raised by this scholar.

Several New Testament men in Germany are standing courageously against the tide of Bultmannism, notably O. Michel, E. Stauffer, J. Jeremias, and K. H. Rengstorf. In these men the influence of Adolph Schlatter may be traced in varying degrees. The latter part of Schlatter's life was spent as Tuebingen, where he was eminently successful both as lecturer and writer. One of the unfortunate effects of World War I was the cutting of communications between German scholarship and that of the Allied countries. Included in this loss was the neglect of Schlatter by scholars abroad. Even to this day few of his works have been translated into English. Ways and means should be found of cutting down the time lag between Continental scholarship and our own. Often it happens that men are dead or advanced in age before their work becomes generally known across the water.

IV. INDIVIDUAL CONTRIBUTIONS

No conservative New Testament scholar on American soil has been as prolific in our generation as A. T. Robertson. His major interest was in grammatical studies, which resulted in the publishing of several grammars, notably the ponderous tome, *A Grammar of the Greek New*

Testament in the Light of Historical Research (1914), which has since passed through several editions. It stresses the newer approach to the language of the New Testament associated with the researches of Deissmann, champions the eight-case system for the study of the noun, and underscores the importance of kind of action (as distinct from time of action) in the verb. Several smaller grammars written by others have shown their dependence upon Robertson. In his commentaries, Lenski is in the habit of making rather frequent reference to pertinent sections of the large grammar. As a sample of Robertson's critical labors, mention should be made of *Luke the Historian in the Light of Research* (1920). In quite a different sphere still is the six-volume work entitled *Word Pictures in the New Testament* (1930-1933). These are more grammatical and less theological in their emphasis than Marvin Vincent's *Word Studies in the New Testament* (1887-1900). The latter, a four-volume work, has recently been reissued. Kenneth Wuest of Moody has made a specialty of word studies and has produced several volumes designed particularly for Christian workers who are unfamiliar with the Greek language.

If we may glance back momentarily to the area of grammatical studies, the best intermediate grammar available today has been prepared by two conservatives, H. E. Dana and J. R. Mantey, *A Manual Grammar of the Greek New Testament* (1927). It stands in need of revision at some points, and it would be a great service to students if this could be done in the near future. C. F. D. Moule of Cambridge has recently published a work along somewhat the same lines, *An Idiom-Book of New Testament Greek* (1953). It is not quite as well adapted for class use as Dana and Mantey.

J. Gresham Machen has been the most commanding figure in conservative New Testament studies in America in recent years. Associated with Princeton Theological Seminary and then with Westminster, he exercised wide influence both by his classroom teaching and by his writings. Those who had the privilege of sitting under his instruction bear testimony to his keenness of mind, his success in imparting his material, and his unswerving devotion to the truth of the Gospel. The apologetic emphasis was strong in all his work. He was patient with doubt, for he himself had felt its gnawings during his student days. But his indignation was stirred by those who supinely accepted the dicta of liberalism and refused to subject themselves to the stern discipline of patient research into the questions at issue. Above all he deplored the dishonesty of those who continue to use the phraseology of evangelical Christianity in their ministry in order to assure their constituents that they are on the right side theologically, but all the while subtly engage in tearing down the faith once delivered to the saints. We are fortunate in having N. B. Stonehouse's biography of Machen, a rewarding book for ministers and theological students especially, but highly instructive for laymen as well.

Of supreme concern to Machen was the historical criticism of the New Testament. In the field of the study of the Gospels, his great contribution was the definitive work, *The Virgin Birth of Christ* (1930), an exhaustive treatment of this subject. But he is likely to be remembered by future generations more particularly for his contribution to Pauline studies, *The Origin of Paul's Religion* (1923), in which he outlined the background of Paul and his relation to Jesus, showing the importance of the position of Paul for Christian origins. The most distinctive part of the book is the presentation of the various non-supernaturalistic approaches to Paul's theology, namely, liberalism, Jewish apocalyptic, and the comparative religion school with its claim of dependence upon pagan mystery cults.

Here Machen is at his best, allowing leading spokesmen for these viewpoints to state their case, then proceeding to expose weaknesses and fallacies in their positions. The book has been criticized on the ground that it does not include an adequate exposition of Machen's own position, the historic, traditional, supernaturalistic view. No doubt this objection is valid, although Machen himself probably felt that the view was sufficiently well known, having been held and maintained in the Church for centuries, so as not to require the same critical presentation as was necessary for the others. Limitations of space may very well have been a factor also.

As Machen's successor at Westminster, Stonehouse has ably carried on in the spirit of his teacher and friend, with similar ideals and objectives. *The Witness of Matthew and Mark to Christ* (1944) is a solid contribution which goes far toward offsetting the modern tendency to depreciate Matthew as palpably inferior to Mark in its testimony to the career of Jesus. Instead of contenting himself with source criticism, Stonehouse tackles the larger interests, such as the Messianic consciousness of Jesus. In *The Witness of Luke to Christ* (1951), the same general pattern is followed, presenting the major contribution and emphases of the book as disclosed by exegesis, along with considerable attention to recent critical approaches to the book, in particular the point of view set forth by R. H. Lightfoot in his *Locality and Doctrine in the Gospels* (1938). Stonehouse is also editor of the *New International Commentary on the New Testament,* which is approximately at the half-way mark in its schedule of publication. Though the volumes are not of uniform excellence, they are highly serviceable. The work of F. F. Bruce on the Acts stands out in this series. Most of the contributors are men of the Reformed tradition.

An associate of Machen for many years at Princeton was Geerhardus Vos, a man who attained top rank in the field of biblical theology. His mimeographed notes on this subject were finally made available in book form. Unfortunately the study was not carried to the end of the New Testament, although this lack was somewhat compensated for by the publishing of his *Pauline Eschatology* (1930). His other great work is *The Self-Disclosure of Jesus* (1926), which bears the sub-title, *The Modern Debate about the Messianic Consciousness.* The strength of Vos's work lay in the solid exegetical foundation which he provided for his conclusions. One present need is for such revision of Vos as will suffice to bring it up-to-date, including a vigorous critique of the views of Rudolf Otto and of T. W. Manson on the "Son of man" problem.

George E. Ladd of Fuller Seminary is intensely interested in these very fields, and has already produced a useful volume, *Crucial Questions about the Kingdom of God* (1952). In due time a more elaborate work in the same area may be expected from his pen.

In the latter part of his life, Henry C. Thiessen of Wheaton College was absorbed in studies which resulted in a widely-used text book, *Introduction to the New Testament* (1943). It is unfortunate that so little use is made in this book of the findings of Continental scholarship. A few issues which represent critical areas of tension in current discussion have arisen since the book was published. Consequently, one of the crucial needs of the hour is a thorough volume on New Testament introduction which will deal comprehensively with all the major issues. The reprinting of Zahn's monumental work is of great assistance, but certain modern problems are not included because of their recent emergence.

Merrill C. Tenney of Wheaton has moved to supply the need for this coverage with special reference to the college student in his volume, *The New Testament: A Survey* (1953). Critical problems are touched upon, but more lightly than is desirable for the seminary student. One of the best features of the book is the introductory portion of over a hundred pages devoted to the background for the New Testament. Tenney has also made a helpful contribution in another area of personal interest to himself, namely, the inductive approach to Bible study. His works on Galatians and on John bear witness to the varied riches which may be uncovered in many books of the Bible with the help of this method.

It is not often that a man attempts to comment on the entire New Testament, much less the whole Bible. Lenski attempted it some years ago, and his work has proved stimulating and generally satisfactory to many students. He wrote out of a Lutheran background. Now William Hendriksen is undertaking a similar project, with two volumes on John and one on Thessalonians so far in print. They should have a favorable reception by Bible students. Incidentally, it is too bad that Moorehead's series of studies on the New Testament have not been reprinted in their entirety. Many treasures are stored away in these unpretentious volumes.

The study of John's Gospel continues to have its fascination. H. P. V.

Nunn in his book, *The Authorship of the Fourth Gospel* (1952,) has made out a strong case for the traditional position. Stauffer of Erlangen continues to uphold this view. His *New Testament Theology* (English translation, 1955), despite a few doubtful positions, is probably the best such work available. Sir Frederic Kenyon in *The Bible and Modern Scholarship* (1948) has pointed out that archaeological evidence (the discovery of fragments of the Gospel dating from the first half of the second century) has removed the objection that the Gospel dates from a period later than the lifetime of John the son of Zebedee. Albright's discussion of John in the light of the recent discoveries in Palestine comes out squarely for the traditional dating of the Gospel before the close of the first century. He is not prepared to commit himself on the question of authorship beyond the insistence that the writing preserves the memoirs of the Apostle John. Albright is particularly helpful in maintaining that there is no basic cleavage between John and the Synoptics, such as a radical criticism has often asserted. The many-sidedness of Jesus and His teaching is attested by the two strains of tradition, the Synoptic and the Johannine. Tenney's volume, *John: The Gospel of Belief* (1948) unfolds the message of the book through a careful study of its literary structure. Sir Edwyn Hoskyns' approach to John might be called a theological commentary, *The Fourth Gospel,* (1940). It has many insights of value for the serious student of this pivotal book which has challenged so many of the best minds on British soil. Dodd's work, *The Interpretation of the Fourth Gospel* (1953) is not a commentary but rather a treatment of some of the principal themes, especially in the light of the thought environment out of which the book presumably sprang. Dodd thinks that the evidence of the Gospel, especially the knowledge of the Torah disclosed therein, warrants the conclusion that the writer was a Jew, but he feels that Acts 4:13 militates against identifying him with John the son of Zebedee, for the latter was unschooled and unskilled in such matters. May we not say, however, that the very success of John (as of Peter also) in presenting the Christian message to such an august body as the Sanhedrin shows the inadequacy of the estimation of the two apostles entertained by the Jewish leaders? The situation depicted in this chapter is itself a stage on the road of John's progress toward that goal of personal development which would fit him to write such a production as the Fourth Gospel.

C. K. Barrett in *The Gospel According to St. John* (1955) holds that the writer may have been the pupil of the Apostle John, a view rather widely held today. He contends that a great deal of the material in John is the amplification of items contained already in the Synoptic tradition, so that for the careful student the impression of almost total disparity between John and the Synoptics is appreciably lessened.

This book by Barrett may well become the most used Greek commentary on the Fourth Gospel.

Many things are at stake in the debate on the authenticity or at any rate the accuracy of John's Gospel. One is the discernment of the early Church. Was the Church at fault in receiving this writing on a par with the Synoptics when it differed so materially from them in its contents and in its presentation of Christ? Again, this Gospel holds a crucial place in the development of creed. Insistence on belief in Jesus as the Christ, the Son of God, pervades the book. E. F. Scott in *The Lord's Prayer* (1951) claims that Jesus did not require propositional assent, but only the repetition of this prayer. But John stands between the Synoptics and the creedal formulations of the early Church as a protest against the notion that one can "follow" Jesus apart from deep conviction as to His divine person. Further, John is a pivotal book inasmuch as it reflects the actual course of the history of Christianity in the first century. It deserves to be studied as a companion to the Acts. Whereas the Synoptics emphasize the mission of Jesus to the lost sheep of the house of Israel, John not only gives us a recital of the mission to Samaria (chapter 4; cf. Acts 8), but also Jesus' contact with the Greeks (John 12), in line with the carrying of the message to the Gentile world as sketched in Acts. Still further, he goes on to emphasize the "whosoever" of the Gospel appeal, which is agreeable to Paul's teaching on the obliteration of distinctions in Christ, whether Jew or Greek, male or female, bond or free.

For the investigation of the historical questions pertaining to the apostolic age, we are greatly indebted to Sir William Ramsay, who wrote a veritable library on Luke and Paul and the earlier phases of the history of the Church. His work has been the more appreciated because in his student days he was prejudiced against the reliability of Acts and came to a favorable judgment on this work only after personal investigation on the soil of Asia Minor. He found that Acts could not possibly have been compiled in the second century, but must have been written by someone intimately acquainted with the geography, history, and customs of the regions in which Paul's missionary labors were carried on.

Among more recent writers in the same general field of study F. F. Bruce deserves special mention. In addition to his two commentaries on Acts, one based on the Greek text, the other on the English, he has written three brief but meaty volumes on the history of the early Church. College students in particular have reason to be grateful for the help given to them in Bruce's slender volume, *Are the New Testament Documents Reliable?* (1943.) Not quite so well known but equally helpful is his work entitled *The Books and the Parchments* (1950), which gives the necessary background material for an appreciation of the legacy we have in our Bible.

Olaf Moe's two volumes on *The Apostle Paul* (English translations 1950, 1954) have taken their place in the foremost rank of works on this subject. One deals with the Apostle's life and labors, the other with his teaching. With very minor exceptions, these studies are a faithful presentation of the biblical materials on Paul. They are suitable for textbook use as well as for general reading. Many students of Paul have found help and guidance also from *A Man in Christ* (1935) by James S. Stewart of Edinburgh.

One of the most hotly debated areas of New Testament study is the Pastoral Epistles. While the majority of scholars in our time deny them to Paul, E. K. Simpson in his book *The Pastoral Epistles* (1954) stoutly defends their Pauline authorship and furnishes a valuable commentary on these books, especially from the standpoint of the lexicography. Some moderns are of the opinion that authorship is unimportant here and that undue concern over it may serve to hinder the unbiased study of the epistles in question in the effort to fit them into the proper niche in the development of the Church. But can we be satisfied with the assertion that someone wrote these letters in the name of Paul with no intent to deceive but only to give expression to genuinely Pauline sentiments? After all, we find it a bit difficult to accept the dictum that there was no intent to deceive and that the Church could properly regard them as "Pauline." Did not the early Church discipline the presbyter who penned the *Acts of Paul and Thecla* despite his protestations that he did it only out of love for the Apostle? More work needs to be done on the Pastorals, especially to sift the argument that the vocabulary precludes Pauline authorship.

Christianity came into a world already replete with religions, religious ideas, and vocabulary and practices. Some students have been greatly impressed with the similarity between these religions, especially those known as mystery religions, and Christianity. They are able to point to the use of the same terms in many cases. It is easy to assume identity of meaning and then argue to the dependence of Christianity upon these pagan faiths. One of the finest books in this field, written more than forty years ago, is H. A. A. Kennedy's *St. Paul and the Mystery Religions* (1913). A review of this whole area of study and a judicious appraisal of the principles which should guide in it are given in highly condensed form by B. M. Metzger in the *Harvard Theological Review* for January, 1955.

Several men have made important contributions to New Testament research in our time who are not fully conservative in their point of view. Sharing in what has been called the new biblicism, they have been active in drawing out the message of the New Testament while resisting the full claims of apostolic authority. If something in the teaching of Paul, for example, seems unacceptable in view of the modern outlook in the philosophy of religion or in psychology, they do not hesitate to reject it. We can only accept with gratitude the positive results of the labor of such men while deploring their unwillingness to rest completely upon the authority of the Word of God.

Dodd has been a prolific writer whose influence on New Testament studies has been immense. One of his best contributions has been in the field of the *kerygma,* or Gospel message. His book, *The Apostolic Preaching and its Developments* (1936) shows conclusively that the same basic ingredients of the *kerygma* appear in the sermonic material of the book of Acts, in the Gospels (especially in the outline of Mark), and in the epistles. This emphasis on a unified message has helped to re-establish on secure foundations the possibility of a true biblical theology of the New Testament as opposed to a fragmentary approach through the study of the various writers of the New Testament and their somewhat varying terminology. A. M. Hunter's *The Message of the New Testament* (1944) has stressed this unity in diversity throughout the various portions of the New Testament.

Of a more controversial nature is the thesis of Dodd connected with realized eschatology. The whole subject has quite a history. In the older liberalism of Harnack the eschatological element in the teaching of Jesus was treated as of minor importance. It was more of an embarrassment to the interpreter than anything else. But along came Albert Schweitzer to insist that eschatology was at the very center of the consciousness and teaching of Jesus. The Master fully expected to return shortly and inaugurate His kingdom. Schweitzer placed great emphasis on such a verse as Matthew 10:23 and minimized or ruled out other data which pointed to a rather lengthy period before the return of the Lord. Dodd's position is set forth in his own statement, "For the New Testament writers in general, the *eschaton* has entered history; the hidden rule of God has been revealed; the Age to Come has come." The apostolic Church indeed expected the Lord to return soon. With the passing of time its calculation was proved to be erroneous, but instead of giving way to despair, the Church gradually came to understand that the thing it looked for had already happened. The coming of Christ had occurred. In John's Gospel, for example, we have the coming of Christ affirmed in this framework. Dodd has emphasized a great truth but has done so at the cost of sacrificing any future coming of Christ in a definite historical sense. Yet the New Testament writers cling to this as surely as they cling to the truth that the new age has already penetrated the present.

In another direction Dodd has placed us in debt, namely, in his study of the early Christian use of the Old Testament. The results are set down in his book, *According to the Scriptures* (1952), in which the writer unfolds a hermeneutical pattern common to the apostolic preaching and teaching. Themes are handled in much the same way in the various New Testament books. What influence has been at work to produce this common outlook on the Old Testament? Dodd is willing to grant that it is due ultimately to the teaching of Christ Himself, but he introduces an unnecessary reservation by saying, "That He formally set before them a comprehensive scheme of biblical interpretation, after the manner of Luke 24:25-27, 44-45, we may well hesitate to believe" (p. 110). The Scriptures trace this new appreciation of the Old Testament and especially of the presentation of the Messiah contained therein to the period following the resurrection. The fruits of this instruction from the Lord appear almost immediately, at Pentecost, whereas they are not observable in the period before the Passion. Therefore we are warranted in holding that it was the risen Christ who gave this instruction. We can go further and say that the Christian interpretation of the Old Testament is a strong indication of the actuality of Christ's bodily resurrection and of His ministry among the apostles in the post-resurrection period.

Another valuable treatise by Dodd is *The Bible and the Greeks* (1935), now available again after being out of print for several years. Of special importance is the study undertaken therein under the heading of Atonement. Dodd's contention is that the translators of the Septuagint, in using *hilaskesthai* and its derivatives to render the Hebrew root *kipper,* did not attach to the word the classical sense of propitiation but rather gave it the force of expiation. While he admits faint traces here and there of the idea of appeasement of divine wrath, he thinks that where the subject is a human being, the idea expressed by the verb is simply one of expiation, and where the subject is divine the thought expressed by the verb is forgiveness. The Revised Standard Version was influenced by Dodd's conclusions, adopting *expiation* as the rendering for *hilasterion* in Romans 3:25.

An answer to Dodd has appeared in Leon Morris's book, *The Apostolic Preaching of the Cross* (1955). His basic objection, which appears to be well-founded, is that Dodd has ignored the context wherein the terms for propitiation appear, both in the Old Testament and in the New. These contexts disclose the anger of God at sin as the substratum of the terms used, therefore the idea of propitiation should not be regarded as deleted from these passages. Morris's point in regard to Romans 3:25 is that Paul has given prominence to the wrath of God in 1:18—3:20 as well as to the theme of divine judgment. Now, as the Apostle passes to the second main section of the book and unfolds God's provision of righteousness for sinful man, there is every expectation that the teaching will include the item of appeasement of the wrath of

God. Yet, if this element be excluded from *hilasterion* in 3:25, no place is found for this emphasis at all.

By way of conclusion, it should be frankly stated that conservative scholarship labors within bounds which are erected by its views of revelation and Scripture. It does not feel free, nor does it have the inclination, to make the daring hypotheses which some have made in the past who have approached the text in a spirit of scientific curiosity, applying only the devices of research guided by reason. Conservatives confess that they cannot view this collection of sacred literature as they would view any other. Their own lives are searched as they peruse the contents of this Book. They must bow before its authority. It should be emphasized that this attitude of reverence is not something merely traditional. Rather it is self-imposed. It is a burden, if burden it be, which is voluntarily assumed. The writings of these scholars may lack in novelty. But when one looks back over the years to note how many theories which once drew the plaudits of the world are now but discarded relics along the highway of human knowledge, it becomes apparent that novelty is no criterion of worth nor even necessarily of progress. One does well to remember that the great mass of literature which has grown up around the New Testament is concerned with the books of Scripture themselves far more than with the vagaries of critics. The New Testament stands out high above all the works which have been written about it. It is this New Testament which conservatives accept and seek to expound.

Our task is basically twofold: to defend the Gospel which is here set forth against the attacks of unbelief and misrepresentation, and also to explore the riches of the Word in the light of the ever-increasing light which is being thrown upon it by our expanding knowledge of the times in which Christianity took its rise and the language in which the message is conveyed. The tools for this study are constantly being augmented, so that the task is easier to fulfill and its performance the more thrilling.

Presumably there will always be those who approach the New Testament professionally. It means little more to them than the heavens to the astronomer or the earth to the geologist. But it is our persuasion that we cannot really understand the New Testament if we approach it merely as historians, indifferent to the claims of Christ and His Gospel upon our own lives.

With the words of Floyd Filson we find ourselves in hearty accord: "I hold that we cannot complete the task of scholarship without working into our picture a personal response for or against the New Testament explanation." The Christian evangel was originally a challenge to faith. We lose immeasurably if we make it merely a theater of discussion and debate.

THEOLOGY

Roger Nicole

Roger Nicole holds the Licence D'enseignement ès Lettres Classiques *(M.A.) from the Sorbornne (Paris), a Th.D. from Gordon Divinity School, and is a candidate for the Ph.D. degree at Harvard Divinity School. He is a charter member of the Evangelical Theological Society, and served as its president in 1956. He has delivered annual lectureships at Western Conservative Baptist Theological Seminary, Conservative Baptist Seminary in Denver, and Central Baptist Seminary, Toronto. Since 1945 he has served as professor of theology at Gordon Divinity School. At present he is engaged in the preparation of a volume on the doctrine of the atonement.*

3. Roger Nicole:

THEOLOGY

ANYONE WHO undertakes a history of evangelical theology between 1890 and 1956 will normally expect to expose himself to questions and perhaps criticisms in a number of respects. For the precise limits of the relevant material to be considered are certainly a matter of opinion, and may easily be subject to debate. The writer is aware that he has decided a number of issues in a manner some persons are likely to dispute. It may be wise to state some of these controversial areas from the very start.

First—the meaning of "evangelical" is clearly not the same for all people. Some refer that adjective broadly to the Protestant view as contrasted particularly with the Roman Catholic position. Others take it as representing only one segment of Protestantism, the more conservative segment, in contrast with the liberal or modernist approach. In this connotation, the term evangelical would still include everything from neo-orthodoxy to extreme fundamentalism. Others employ the term to characterize a small group who agree on doctrinal issues in almost every particular, and would deny that characterization to anyone but those who are most closely akin to themselves.

In our use, the term evangelical falls in inclusiveness between the second and the third of these meanings. It applies to those people and groups who maintain the historic Christian faith in the tradition of the great formulations of the Christian Church from the Protestant point of view, and in a spirit of determined loyalty to the Bible as the written revelation of God. Especially in connection with the attitude toward the Bible a line of discrimination is drawn between neo-orthodoxy and evangelicalism. In view of this fact, the development of neo-orthodox theology will not be considered. Even where people agree on the meaning of evangelical, their appraisal of the position of individual theologians may differ: both the inclusion and the omission of certain names will perhaps surprise, but, it is hoped, not shock the informed.

Second—the word "theology" also is susceptible of various meanings. It may refer to the whole area of religious study. It may, in a more limited sense, apply to that part of this study in which a systematic presentation is given of the doctrine and the ethics of the Christian faith. In a more limited sense still, it may refer to the study of the doctrinal tenets of the faith, while Christian ethics deals with their application to conduct and life, and Christian apologetics with the vindication of the Christian position. Finally, theology may refer merely to the particular *locus* of dogmatics in which the being of God is the object of special attention. In this paper, theology will be construed to mean mainly dogmatics, in accord with the third definition.

Even with this clarification firmly in mind, it will be difficult at times to determine whether a particular work or a particular person properly fits that category. The interrelationships of the various branches of theological study are abundant, and judgments may differ as to the nature of the contribution made by many who have labored in more than one field.

Third—the dates suggested, 1890 to 1956, are also somewhat open to question. History does not find itself bound to operate according to neat calendar specifications. Overlapping, gradual beginnings and gradual extinctions are probably more frequent than sudden crisis-like events, for which a date and a place can readily be assigned. The date 1956, of course, may find its justification in the time of composition of the paper, but it should be well understood that the writer cannot claim to have a fully adequate coverage of everything of significance in the very recent past. Even if he did, perspective would be lacking to render a judgment with complete assurance.

The date 1890 is subject to much more question. It is preferred to 1900 because it represents, more than the latter, a basic turn in the approach to dogmatic theology, especially in the Anglo-Saxon world. That date marks approximately the beginning of the very wide inroads of biblical criticism upon doctrinal conceptions. This is almost the date which J. S. Lawton chose as the starting point of his historical review of Christology in Anglo-Saxon lands (J. S. Lawton, *Conflict in Christology. A Study of British and American Christology from 1889-1914* [1947]). The same date marks also the practically complete dominance of Ritschlianism in Germany and surrounding lands. It represents a focal point in the Calvinistic revival in the Netherlands. Thus, that date may be justified, not indeed as a hard-and-fast determination, but as an approximate chronological location, and as a general starting point for the present study.

Fourth—even when all critical decisions have been taken on the issues just mentioned, the division of the material still presents a delicate problem. There might be advantages in discussing the subject geographically, examining the theological movement throughout the whole period in each country or region separately. The difficulty with this approach is that interrelationships between countries have been increasingly important, and that this type of division may lead one to undervalue these. Another principle of division might be the chronological one, according to which the whole theological movement would be examined throughout the world in successive smaller periods. The problem with this approach would be that dividing lines in one area may not correspond to those found in another, and the continuity of development and influence in particular countries or groups would be constantly broken up for the sake of chronological sequence. A third principle of division might be called the topological one, in which certain *loci* of systematic theology would be considered separately in the historical development of their treatment. This would tend to fragmentize the presentation still more. A final principle which might be employed is the denominational one, in which the movement of theology within particular religious groups might be studied. This approach has merit even in the period under consideration, although it must be noted that frequently within that period, even in evangelical circles, the denominational lines were less clearly drawn out than was the case in earlier ages. This paper will adopt primarily a geographical division, and under the United States, which for obvious reasons will receive more extended attention, will subdivide the material with reference to denominations or to particular religious groups.

I. GERMANY AND GERMAN-SPEAKING COUNTRIES

At the turn of the 1890s the situation in Germany from the viewpoint of evangelical theology was far from satisfactory. The Ritschlian theology had very largely taken over the learned institutions of the whole country. Even those who opposed this point of view seldom did so from the standpoint of belief in the full authority of the Scriptures and in the fundamentals of the Christian faith. Men who held to these positions were scorned as obscurantists, unworthy of consideration by those who had a scientific training. They were excluded from professorial chairs in the seminaries. "Repristination," says Horst Stephan, "it was proved, could not be carried on" (*Geschichte der evangelischen Theologie seit dem deutschen Idealismus,* p. 240). Generally their approach to the Bible was stigmatized as mechanical, and the doctrine of inerrancy was confused with a belief in mechanical dictation. Under those circumstances it took great courage to maintain the evangelical position, and it is not surprising that only a few works of scientific value maintained an uncompromising defense of the conservative faith. The following, however, may here be mentioned.

W. Rohnert (1837-1902) was a Lutheran pastor who at the turn of the 1890s wrote a work on inspiration in which he advocated the old Lutheran doctrine of the plenary inspiration of the Scriptures. He also wrote short works on *The Means of Grace* (1886) and on *Eschatology* (1902). A *Lutheran Dogmatics* by him appeared in the very year of his death (1902). This man was greatly gifted in the simple and clear expression of his beliefs. His presentation of the doctrine of inspiration is one of the best historical summaries on the subject.

Wilhelm Koelling (1836-1903) exercised his ministry most in Silesia. He wrote a work on the Person of the Holy Spirit (*Pneumatologie,* 1894), another on the *Doctrine of Inspiration* (1891) and a large work concerning the Substitutionary Satisfaction of Christ (1896, 1899).

Beside these men, any mention of upholders of a conservative view of the Scriptures must include the names of E. Haack, Otto Holtzheuer (1836-1906), K. F. Noesgen (1835-1913), and J. H. Ziese.

From the Reformed Church the name of Eduard Boehl (1836-1903) needs to be mentioned. He wrote a large *Dogmatics* (1887), a work about *The Incarnation of the Divine Word* (1884) and another concerning *Justification Through Faith* (1890, English translation, 1946). This same author dealt also in two volumes with the Christology of the Old Testament and the question of the quotations of the Old Testament in the New. He engaged in some controversy with Abraham Kuyper of the Netherlands on the subject of the conditions of our Lord's life on earth. In spite of his recognized departure from the traditional Reformed faith in this respect (in part due to the influence of Kohlbruegge), he must be reckoned a stanch supporter of the conservative position.

The name of F. Bettex might be suggested as that of a conservative scholar who had scientific training and theological insight. In the same context we may mention also the name of Helmut Echternach, who in 1937 in a pamphlet entitled *It Is Written* advocated an extreme view that Luther's German translation of the Bible is authoritative in the field of church dogmatics.

From the circles of the Plymouth Brethren came Erich Sauer, principal of the Bible school at Wiedenest near Cologne. He manifests a thorough knowledge of the Scriptures joined with real philosophical insight. His pen has been fertile. Already he has penned volumes on *The Nobility of Man, The Dawn of World Redemption, The Triumph of the Crucified, From Eternity to Eternity,* and *In the Arena of Faith.* The latter four titles have been translated into English and have met with singular favor in conservative circles in the United States.

This brief survey of conservative effort in Germany would be incomplete without mention of at least the names of two theologians of great ability who held very conservative positions, without however advocating the doctrine of the plenary inspiration of the Scriptures. Adolf Schlatter (1852-1938) was a New Testament scholar of wide repute, who devoted considerable attention also to the study of systematic theology and the doctrine of the early Church. His commentaries on the New Testament show great respect for Scripture. One of his works, *The Church in the New Testament Period,* has just been translated for 1956 publication. Paul Feine (1859-1933) was predominantly a New Testament scholar. His work on *New Testament Theology* (1910, 6th ed. 1934) takes a very conservative position, bolstered by a thorough acquaintance with the whole New Testament field and its literature. Both these scholars supplied a source of great encouragement to conservative theologians, even though they did not share in every respect their doctrinal position.

II. THE NETHERLANDS

In many respects the situation in the Netherlands resembles that in Germany. This country is characterized by the same taste for scholarship so marked in its great neighbor. In some cases, in fact, Dutch scholarship is better rounded than the German, because of its cognizance of theological effort in English-speaking, French-speaking and German-speaking countries, as well as of that carried on at home. As in Germany, so in the Netherlands the rise of liberalism exercised a very strong influence, particularly upon the State Church. To a large extent, consequently, the conservative position was frequently viewed as lacking the support of competent scholarship, and therefore as deserving of little attention from informed people. Because of the inroads of modernistic teaching into the seminaries and into the pulpits of the whole country, two great movements of secession from the State Church were begun in the course of the nineteenth century: the *Afscheiding* (1837) and the *Doleantie* (1886). Under the able leadership of Abraham Kuyper and Herman Bavinck these movements prospered greatly, and united in 1892 under the name of *Gereformeerde Kerken. Gereformeerd* and *Hervormd* both mean Reformed. The latter applies to the State Church, the former is used by the Free Church. Since there is only one adjective in English to render both, translation is difficult and sometimes confusing.

In one respect at least the situation in Holland was markedly different. While in Germany the conservative side had been left without any leader of impressive caliber, in the Netherlands, on the contrary, there arose especially two men of outstanding ability: Abraham Kuyper and Herman Bavinck. Their scholarship and competence could not possibly be denied, and they exercised far-reaching influence, stimulating a whole galaxy of young scholars who walked in their steps.

Kuyper (1837-1920) was trained in liberal circles, having studied at the University of Leiden, where he fell strongly under the influence of the Hegelian J. H. Scholten. In the course of his first pastorate at Beesd he was definitely impressed by the strength which the old Reformed faith gave to some of his unlearned but stalwart parishoners. Under this influence he was led to reconsider the foundations of his own theology and he embraced heartily the evangelical faith, such as had been established at the time of the Reformation. Later on he was called to a large pastorate in Utrecht. After some time there, he was led to launch out into greater areas of responsibility and influence, particularly in connection with the publication of two periodicals, one a weekly, *De Heraut* (since 1872), and the other a daily paper, *De Standaard* (since 1878). Under his guiding influence, the Free University of Amsterdam was founded in 1880, dedicated to the advancement of knowledge on Reformed principles, and emphatically committed to the upholding of the standards of the Reformed Church (Belgic Confession, Heidelberg Catechism, Canons of the Synod of Dordt). Through all these undertakings he achieved great eminence, and his influence was felt even to the extent of developing a political party which obtained the majority in the Parliament. In 1901 Kuyper was appointed Prime Minister of the Netherlands.

For the present discussion the area of particular interest is the theological achievements of Abraham Kuyper, which came to fullness in the period under consideration. During that time he developed his theological lectures in the field of systematic theology at the Free University of Amsterdam. While these were not published in a finished form, the class notes of students were privately edited, and appeared in five large volumes entitled *Dictations in Dogmatics (Dictaten Dogmatiek,* 1910). In the course of publication of *De Heraut* he wrote a series of important articles on subjects of theological significance. Later republished in book form, they often represent tremendous monographs on the several themes. Among these may be mentioned his three volumes on *Common Grace* (1905), three volumes on the *Kingship of Christ* (1911-13), and his Commentary on the Heidelberg Catechism in four volumes (1896-97), which represents perhaps the most authentic presentation of Kuyper's views of the Christian faith as a whole. Toward the end of his life he also wrote extensively on eschatological subjects. The work appeared posthumously in four volumes under the title *About the Consummation* (1920). One of the most famous works of Kuyper is his Stone lectures on *Calvinism* delivered in 1898 at Princeton Theological Seminary. They represent in a remarkable way the breadth of view of this man, a proved master not merely in theology but in other areas of human endeavor. One should mention also his *Encyclopedia of Sacred Theology* (1894), which appeared in three volumes in the Netherlands and which represents perhaps the best example of scholarly work on his part, since it was not designed to be a series of magazine articles but rather was meant to introduce the seminary student to the whole field of theology. This work has been in part translated into English by J. H. Vries, (1895, reprint 1955). An earlier treatise on *The Work of the Holy Spirit* was also translated (1890). It had been published just prior to the period with which we start our discussion of the history of evangelical theology. The above list fails to mention a multitude of pamphlets, printed addresses and devotional writings.

The genius of Kuyper impressed in a remarkable fashion many men of high achievements. His influence was felt widely not only in his own circles but even in other groups. At the Free University of Amsterdam many flocked to receive his teaching and to benefit by the instruction of the faculty he had gathered around himself. Kuyper is remarkable in his theological endeavors for the strength of his Calvinism and his whole-hearted allegiance to the standards of the Reformed Church. On a number of points Kuyper developed original positions which have not always been followed in Calvinistic circles. Among these may be mentioned supralapsarianism, the doctrine of justification from eternity, and the doctrine of the presumptive regeneration of the children born in the covenant.

Herman Bavinck (1854-1921), who was for many years associated with Kuyper and succeeded him in the chair of dogmatics at the Free University of Amsterdam, was a genius of another sort. He too in his early training had contact with liberal theology, having attended the University of Leiden and having been there under the influence particularly of A. Kuenen, for whom he had great personal attachment. Nevertheless, he never upheld modernistic views. He entered the ministry in the group of the *Afscheiding* in which his father had been active and where after short pastorates he became professor at the Theological Seminary of Kampen. One of his earliest works was the re-edition of the treatise on Christian doctrine prepared by some of the seventeenth century professors of Leiden titled *Synopsis Purioris Theologiae* (1880). The work for which he is particularly remembered is his large *Reformed Dogmatics (Gereformeerde Dogmatiek)* in four volumes, whose first edition appeared between 1895 and 1901, and which was published in a second greatly enlarged edition between 1906 and 1911. In this work of great balance and thorough Reformed conviction, Bavinck manifested to the utmost his remarkable qualities as an exegete, as a church historian, and as a dogmatician. Each doctrine is considered in its biblical foundations, in its historic development, and in its interrelation with other doctrines. This work is characterized throughout by thorough research, sane judgment, clarity of expression, and extensive biblical investigation. Bavinck proved himself well acquainted not only with the past history of theology, but also with contemporary currents, and he exhibited admirable scholarship in his handling of the whole material. It may be doubted whether there ever appeared a work on systematic theology that for the thoroughness and balance of treatment can be rated superior to that which Bavinck produced. Unfortunately only the second volume of this work is available in English under the title of *The Doctrine of God* (1951). In 1907 Bavinck published an abridged study of Christian doctrine entitled *Magnalia Dei,* a work now being translated and scheduled for 1956 publication under the title *Our Reasonable Faith.* Toward the end of his life Bavinck turned his particular attention toward the problems of Christian education, and wrote a number of volumes in that field. In addition to these works he wrote many other studies. Among the more important are his book on *Calling and Regeneration* (1902), his short work on *The Assurance of Faith* (1901), and his Stone lectures on *The Philosophy of Revelation* (1908). Bavinck died in 1921 less than eight months after Kuyper.

Bavinck and Kuyper did not remain alone in their work and in their stalwart championing of the evangelical position. They gathered around themselves a large group of men of ability who shared their Reformed view. The movement has continued even to this day. The names and achievements of all who have published valuable material in Christian doctrine from this viewpoint would be a long list. A few names and a brief mention of the work of each will have to be sufficient.

One of Kuyper's early associates was Wilhelm Geesink (1854-1929). His work is most remarkable in the area of Reformed ethics, but in a large four-volume work on the *Ordinances of the Lord* (1907, 1908) he touched many dogmatic subjects. Two of Abraham Kuyper's sons, H. H. Kuyper and Abraham Kuyper, Jr., were distinguished theologians. The former wrote a volume about the *Covenant* (1907), and an important study about *Evolution and Revelation* (1903). The latter wrote a number of works, including *Knowledge of God* (1907), *Image of God in Man* (1929), *the Covenant* (1906, 1908), *Theodicy* (1931), *Sanctification and Glorification* (1935), and many devotional studies. These two men, in the main, followed closely the thought of their father. The successor of Bavinck at Amsterdam was Valentine Hepp (1879-1950) who wrote about the *Antichrist* (1919), a work on the *Testimony of the Holy Spirit* (1914), and also his Stone lectures on *Calvinism and the Philosophy of Nature* (1930). A. G. Honig (1864-1940) succeeded Bavinck in his chair of dogmatics at Kampen. He is the author of a *Reformed Dogmatics* in one volume published in 1938, and of a number of shorter treatises on theological subjects. Many men who came to study at the Free University of

Amsterdam produced helpful contributions in systematic theology, among them J. Jansen, W. L. Joubert, P. A. E. Sillevis Smit, J. C. Ubbink, C. N. Impeta, B. B. Keet, T. Brinkman, J. Thijs, S. P. Dee, C. Koppenaal, L. Van der Zanden, H. J. Westerink, H. J. Jager, P. J. Richel, P. Van der Spek, G. E. Meuleman. An increasing influence of the Free University is observable upon students from South Africa (J. J. Mueller, A. B. du Preez, B. J. de Klerk, F. J. M. Potgieter, D. Kempff, J. L. de Villiers, J. A. Heyns), and from the United States (Y. P. de Jong, H. H. Meeter, W. Burggraaf, H. Kuiper, R. Bronkema, R. J. Danhof, W. H. Rutgers, F. H. Klooster, L. Smedes, E. H. Palmer, A. de Jong, R. A. Killen) to mention only those predominantly interested in dogmatics.

S. Greijdanus (1871-1943), known mainly as a New Testament scholar, has published theological studies concerning the *Incarnation* (1903) and also the *Doctrine of Imputation.* F. W. Grosheide, also a New Testament scholar primarily, has written concerning the New Testament canon (1935) and on the *Expectation of the Second Coming of Christ* (1907). G. Ch. Aalders (1880-), primarily an Old Testament scholar, has contributed important works on the *Covenant* (1939) and on *Divine Revelation in Genesis One Through Three* (1932). Klaas Schilder (1890-1953), perhaps best known for his trilogy upon the sufferings of our Lord, was professor of dogmatics at Kampen and wrote on the doctrine of *Heaven* (1935) and of *Hell* (1932). His particular views were most clearly expounded in his unfinished commentary on the Heidelberg Catechism which appeared in four volumes (1947-1951). Schilder was a controversial figure, and led a section of the church into a schism which caused great difficulties in the 1940s. But these ecclesiastical problems cannot in any way becloud his true claim to recognition as a conservative theologian of uncommon ability.

Klass Dijk (1885-) is another writer who produced extensively in the field of dogmatics. He wrote his doctoral thesis on *Infra- and Supra-Lapsarianism* (1912). Subsequently he published books concerning the *Scripture* (1931), the *Providence of God* (1927), *Predestination* (1924), and *The Reign of a Thousand Years* (1933). More recently he issued in three small volumes a treatise on *Eschatology* (1951-53).

D. J. de Groot in his doctoral thesis discussed Calvin's view of Scripture, maintaining that Calvin held to the inerrancy of the Bible. Later de Groot wrote an important monograph on the *New Birth.* A. D. R. Polman (1897-), presently professor of dogmatics at Kampen, wrote an important thesis dealing with the doctrine of *Predestination in Augustine, Thomas Aquinas, and Calvin* (1936). He has published a four-volume work, well-documented, upon the Belgic Confession of Faith (1949-1953), and is presently engaged in the elaboration of a four-volume work about Augustine's theology.

Without a doubt, however, the most impressive living theologian of the Netherlands in the field of dogmatics is Gerrit C. Berkouwer (1903-). This scholar, who holds the chair of systematic theology at Free University of Amsterdam, is a worthy successor to Kuyper and Bavinck. He is presently engaged in putting in print a systematic theology of nineteen volumes, nine of which have appeared since 1949. The volumes already available deal with *Justification* (1949), *Sanctification* (1949), *Perseverance* (1949), *The Providence of God* (1950), *General Revelation* (1951), the *Person of Christ* (1952), the *Work of Christ* (1953), the *Sacraments* (1954) and *Election* (1955). Five of these have now been in part translated into English. Unfortunately, some of the scholarly apparatus which greatly enhances the Dutch publication has been omitted in English, so that references to original sources are not always available in the translations. In addition, Berkouwer has produced several other volumes of significance for dogmatic theology. His doctoral dissertation dealt with *Faith and Revelation in the Recent German Theology* (1932), and in 1938 he approached somewhat the same problem in a monograph on *The Problem of Scriptural Criticism*. He has given particular attention to the theology of Karl Barth, having written an important book about him in 1936, another concerning *Barth's View on Infant Baptism* in 1947, and more recently in 1954 a large monograph entitled *The Triumph of Grace in the Theology of Karl Barth*. This latter volume has just been translated into English. Berkouwer, furthermore, is a specialist in the realm of Roman Catholic dogma, and has written two large volumes dealing with this aspect of the field. Finally, in a series of lectures delivered in the United States, he has given a brief general orientation to present-day problems under the title *Modern Uncertainty and the Christian Faith* (1953). Berkouwer's work is characterized throughout by a profound respect for Scripture, a fresh investigation of scriptural foundations, a careful positionizing of historical currents, a thorough acquaintance with the primary sources of present day theology, and a wholehearted allegiance to the traditional Reformed faith. While he has benefited much by the labors of Kuyper and especially Bavinck, he is in no wise enslaved to them. His vigorous and scholarly presentation of the field of theology has caused even those who disagree with him to recognize his consummate ability.

One cannot conclude this brief review without naming at least the following men who belonged to the same movement: T. Hoekstra, G. Doekes, W. A. Wiersinga, A. M. Diermanse, T. G. Feenstra, E. Smilde, and the premillenarian A. M. Berkhoff. All have published works dealing with doctrinal subjects.

As a scholarly organ of evangelical theology it is good to mention in closing the learned journal *Gereformeerd Theologisch Tijdschrift*, which was founded in 1900 and is being published until this day.

III. FRANCE AND FRENCH-SPEAKING COUNTRIES

At the turn of the 1890s the situation in France and in French-speaking countries was not particularly auspicious for conservative theology. True, some men like Frédéric Godet (1812-1900), A. Grétillat, A. Berthoud, and E. Doumergue were standing in stanch defense of many of the dogmas acknowledged by the Reformed churches. But some of these approved substantial alterations of traditional positions, and none would commit himself to the plenary inspiration of the Scriptures. In the period under consideration therefore, especially in its beginnings, men of scientific stature who held to the view represented in an earlier age by Louis Gaussen, J. H. Merle d'Aubigne and Agénor de Gasparin were almost completely lacking. A marked exception is Auguste Lecerf (1872-1943). By a direct approach to the theology of Calvin, and from that to the Scriptures, this scholar was led to embrace a thoroughgoing Reformed position, which he then represented at the theological faculty of Paris. Naturally at first he could not be established in the chair of dogmatics, his main interest, for his position was too far different from that of his colleagues. He taught English there, but even in that way he managed to exercise a strong influence upon a number of the students. Only in his later years he finally became professor of dogmatics at the Free Theological Faculty. From his pen we have a short thesis on *Determinism and Responsibility in the System of Calvin* and his *Introduction to Reformed Dogmatics* (1931-1938) which appeared in English in 1949. In this last volume, which provokes profound regret that Lecerf was not spared for the completion of a Reformed dogmatics on the scale of this introduction, he vindicated the Reformed position over against other approaches to the religious problem and to theology in general. While he makes some few concessions to biblical criticism, it is remarkable how clearly he stood as a champion for the inspiration of Scripture. After his death some of his studies were gathered together under the title *Calvinistic Studies,* published in 1949, and some of his heirs are now engaged in editing the notes he left on some of his courses in theology at the University of Paris.

It is proper here also to mention the name of Ruben Saillens (1855-1942). While this man was not a theological scholar in the technical sense of the term, he had a masterful grasp of the Christian faith and expressed his beliefs in a small volume entitled *The Mystery of Faith* (1931), which is marked by the literary qualities of this great evangelist and poet.

One should not underrate the influence of the conservative position of Emile Doumergue, (1844-1937), the great biographer and student of Calvin. While his view toward Scripture represented certain modifications of the doctrine of inerrancy, he must nonetheless be acknowledged as a stalwart champion of the evangelical faith. From more recent years additional names must be briefly mentioned. The editor of the *Revue Réformée,* G. Ch. Marcel, is one of the abler theologians of the present day. His monograph on baptism (1950) has been particularly significant. It has been translated into English under the title *The Biblical Doctrine of Infant Baptism.* Jean Cadier is professor of dogmatics at the Theological Seminary of Montpellier. He has written on the Lord's Supper and has made some contributions also on the subject of baptism. He is one of the editors of the new French edition of Calvin's *Institutes.* A. Lamorte, sometime dean of the Theological Seminary of Aix, wrote a doctoral thesis in which he makes certain concessions to biblical criticism, which he was led later to repudiate in an important statement published in *Études Évangeliques.* This may be the best place to mention also Dr. René Pache, who has published a number of clear expositions of biblical teaching. Pache does not commonly interact with the findings of theological scholarship, but he has a lucid style and his presentations have been helpful. His contributions include *The Person and Work of the Holy Spirit* (English translation, 1955), and *Eschatology.* Jacques Blocher has recently published a small work contrasting the evangelical view with the Roman Catholic position.

IV. GREAT BRITAIN AND THE DOMINIONS

At the turn of the 1890s in British lands the situation was very far from satisfactory from the evangelical point of view. Most theologians of note had been led to make important concessions to biblical criticism. Even in the Free Church of Scotland, which had earlier been such a bulwark of the evangelical faith, men who had made very damaging statements concerning the errancy of Scripture could not be convicted of heresy in Church courts: William Robertson Smith, A. B. Bruce, Marcus Dods and George Adam Smith were all maintained in good standing in the Church, and, except for Robertson Smith, all retained their professorial chairs. In 1889 in England the publication of *Lux Mundi* showed to what extent even among the Anglo-Catholics the effect of biblical criticism had been felt. Charles Gore, one of the leaders of the Anglo-Catholic movement, espoused a kenotic doctrine of the Person of Christ in order to account for the fact that the recorded statements of our Lord contained, as he thought, errors of fact with respect to the authorship of the Pentateuch and other matters related to the Old Testament criticism. Under those difficult conditions, one may perhaps understand that even stanch conservative men were sometimes moved to concede certain points to mediating theology. The name of James Orr (1844-1913) need be mentioned in this respect. Basically he was a very conservative scholar. He gave impressive defenses of the Christian faith in such books as *The Christian View of God and the World* (1893), *The*

Resurrection of Jesus (1908), *The Virgin Birth of Christ* (1907), *God's Image in Man* (1905), *Sin as a Problem of Today* (1910), and even took up the cudgels against biblical criticism in two volumes titled *The Bible on Trial* (1907) and *The Problem of the Old Testament* (1906). Nevertheless in his small volume *Revelation and Inspiration* (1910), otherwise committed to the defense of a conservative view of Scripture, he made the concession that the original Scripture may contain errors in matters of history and of science (James Orr, *Revelation and Inspiration,* 1910, pp. 163-169, 179-181, 213-215. Yet see also pp. 215-217 for an eloquent defense of the accuracy of the Bible). His *Sidelights on Christian Doctrine* (1909), *The Faith of a Modern Christian* (1910), and his volume on the history of dogma entitled *The Progress of Dogma* (1901), are also valuable contributions. His two volumes in criticism of Ritschlianism, *The Ritschlian Theology and the Evangelical Faith* (1898), and *Ritschlianism* (1903), certainly rendered great service to the evangelical cause. He was general editor of the best recent conservative Bible dictionary on a large scale, *The International Standard Bible Encyclopaedia* (1914), for which he wrote hundreds of articles, including "Bible" and "Jesus Christ." He was also one of the contributors of the well-known series of essays entitled *The Fundamentals* (1909-1915), from which the term "fundamentalist" has been coined. Thus, in spite of Orr's allowances to theistic evolution and to criticism, one is well justified in regarding him as one of the able champions of the conservative cause.

Beside Orr the names of James Denney (1856-1917) and of Robert Flint (1834-1910) may well be mentioned as those of men who defended in the main a conservative viewpoint, making, however, even more than Orr, concessions to the spirit of the age. Denney's best work from the conservative viewpoint was probably his volume on the *Death of Christ* (1902), which had very considerable success.

As representative of the old spirit of orthodoxy one may mention John Laidlaw (1832-1906) who published in 1895 the second edition of his great Cunningham Lectures on *The Bible Doctrine of Man* and prepared a fine summary on *Foundation Truths of Scripture as to Sin and Salvation* (1897), while his predecessor in the chair of systematic theology at New College, James Macgregor (1830-1894), published a conservative work about the Scripture entitled *The Revelation and the Record* (1893). Another evangelical work on this subject was Hugh M'Intosh's *Is Christ Infallible and the Bible True?* (1901). His answer was an unqualified "Yes" to both questions. John Urquhardt's *The Inspiration and Accuracy of the Holy Scriptures* appeared in 1895.

In the Free Church of Scotland, which continued separate after the union of the main body of the Free Church with the United Presbyterians, a very conservative mood prevailed. The name of John MacLeod (1872-1948), for many years principal of the Free Church College at

Edinburgh, may well be mentioned in this connection. His book on *Scottish Theology* (1943) is a valuable source of information from the pen of one who was deeply versed in the theological lore of Scotland.

In England at the turn of the 1890s some of the men who had represented most successfully the conservative view in earlier years were still alive but had reached an advanced age. Bishop J. C. Ryle (1816-1900), whose fertile pen had been so helpful to the conservative cause, was still writing, but not very extensively. From this period comes his volume entitled *Old Paths* (1897). Charles Haddon Spurgeon, the stalwart Baptist preacher, lived until 1892 but had come to the end of his prodigious activity in published material. Among the Plymouth Brethren William Kelly (1821-1906) also was aging and while his work was continuing, he did not produce extensively beyond 1890. The same may be said about Benjamin Wills Newton (1805-1898).

In the next generation we may notice the following men as conservative representatives of the evangelical faith: Henry Wace (1836-1924), whose ability was perhaps best displayed in his editorship of dictionaries and other important scholarly series, produced during this period a work on *The Sacrifice of Christ* (1898) and two volumes about biblical criticism (1902, 1903). Bishop H. C. J. Moule (1841-1920) was an indefatigable worker. His *Outlines of Christian Doctrine* appeared in 1889 but were republished in a large number of editions which came forth during the time under consideration. We may notice also his work on the Holy Spirit, *Veni Creator* (1890), some works about the sacraments (1890, 1896), and his short volume *Faith* (1909). W. H. Griffith Thomas (1861-1924) was another representative of the thoroughly conservative school. He is probably best known for his biblical expositions, but we should take notice of his large work entitled *Principles of Theology* (1930). This work, posthumously edited by Canon Dyson Hague, is an extensive commentary on the thirty-nine articles of the Church of England. It represents the mature judgment of this able theologian. He published also a work about the Lord's Supper in which a low church position is presented, *A Sacrament of Our Redemption*. His volume *The Spirit of God* (1913) is also recognized as helpful. Sir Robert Anderson (1841-1918) was not, strictly speaking, a professional theologian. Nevertheless he had some valuable insights in the field of theology and it may be proper here to mention his books on the deity of Christ, *The Lord from Heaven* (1910), on *Human Destiny,* and on the return of Christ entitled *The Coming Prince*. In many other areas he produced popular presentations always adhering closely to the most conservative faith. This was the attitude of the whole Plymouth Brethren movement, to which Sir Robert related himself, and they published frequently short popular summaries on various elements of the Christian faith. While these may hardly be viewed as belonging to the history of systematic theology proper, it would be unfortunate to fail utterly to mention them. One of the recent works of that nature is a small book by W. Hoste, *Studies in Bible Doctrine* (1948).

The great Cambridge trio of B. F. Westcott (1825-1901), J. B. Lightfoot (1828-1889), and F. J. A. Hort (1828-1892) falls almost entirely outside of the period under consideration. Furthermore, the main interest of each one of these men lay in New Testament studies, although Hort's *The Way, the Truth and the Life* (1893) and *The Christian Ecclesia* (1897), and Westcott's *The Gospel of Life* (1892) have an evident dogmatic import. Moreover, it must be owned that, while these scholars were conservative in their approach to particular issues of New Testament criticism, their position could not be viewed as fully evangelical in our sense. On the subject of the inerrancy of Scripture all three had reservations, and on the atonement Westcott held to the mystical theory (*The Victory of the Cross,* 1888). To the same general school of thought belongs Henry B. Swete (1835-1917), whose labors in the area of the Septuagint and of the New Testament are well known. Within our period he published important contributions on the doctrine of the Holy Spirit—*The Holy Spirit in the New Testament* (1909) and *The Holy Spirit in the Ancient Church* (1912), as well as works on the articles of the Apostle's Creed, *The Ascended Christ* (1910), *The Holy Catholic Church* (1915), *The Forgiveness of Sins* (1916), and *The Life of the World to Come* (1917).

The High Church party, as we have already remarked, often made very considerable concessions to the movement of Biblical criticism. Nevertheless it represented a conservative approach to many of the major doctrines of the faith. Among those who belonged to that group and whose labors in the field of dogmatic theology are especially noteworthy, one might mention Darwell Stone (1859-1941), T. B. Strong (1861-1944), and more recently L. S. Thornton (1884-) and E. L. Mascall (1905-). The presence of these names in this survey should not be construed as implying that these men consistently upheld the evangelical Protestant view, since the influence of Roman Catholic theology may be said to prevail in their thinking.

The Inter-Varsity Christian Fellowship developed a fine evangelical work among students. They engaged not only in practical work, but issued a number of books almost always written from a clearly evangelical viewpoint. Among the writers who contributed in the area of Christian doctrine, one should mention T. C. Hammond (1877-). His work on Christian theology is entitled *In Understanding Be Men* (1936). He wrote also a helpful manual, *Hundred Texts* (1939) which expounds the great elements of the Christian faith in a discussion of a hundred texts of Scripture. Archdeacon H. E. Guillebaud wrote a very fine work on the atoning work of Christ entitled *Why the Cross?* (1937). Other writers like D. F. C. Clark, Rendle Short and F. F. Bruce share the conservative position of the fellowship but did not particularly contribute in the area of systematic theology.

In Northern Ireland one may mention the Irish Evangelical Church, which publishes a monthly review *The Irish Evangelical*. The editor, W. J. Grier, has written a fine short work on the Second Coming of Christ from the amillenarian point of view, *The Momentous Event* (1945).

At the present time there is a wide movement both in Britain and in some of the Dominions for a more conservative theology. One of the more hopeful signs of this is the appearance in 1955 of a work penned by Leon Morris of Melbourne, Australia, *The Apostolic Preaching of the Cross*. In this volume a careful study is made of the various New Testament words connected with the doctrine of redemption, with a scholarly analysis of their background in Jewish Rabbinic writings, in the Septuagint, and also in the current Hellenistic language of New Testament times.

Since 1929 the *Evangelical Quarterly* has in general represented faithfully the conservative position. The contributors have not all supported the inerrancy of the Scriptures, but on the whole the journal was dedicated to a defense and exposition of the conservative faith and in this respect it has been a marked success.

In Canada the theological situation has, in general, closer ties with the United States than with England. In South Africa the prevailing influence, as indicated above, comes from the Netherlands. The theological seminaries of Potchefstrom, Stellenbosch, and Pretoria are important centers of evangelical learning. The English-speaking world is acquainted with Norval Geldenhuys, whose study on *The Supreme Authority* appeared in 1954. The name of Alexander Reese, who wrote a very careful treatment of *The Approaching Advent of Christ* (1937), will probably more readily be associated with the Dominions than with the mainland.

Although Arthur W. Pink (1886-1952) resided in Scotland, his influence was felt mainly in the United States, for it is there that his books, expository and doctrinal, were generally published. We may note the following titles: *The Sovereignty of God* (1918), *The Redeemer's Return* (1918), *The Doctrine of Sanctification* (1955), *The Satisfaction of Christ* (1955). Besides these books, he wrote a large number of shorter essays on various doctrines, and edited for years the monthly *Studies in the Scriptures*.

Before we leave the British Empire, we mention in passing a few names of men of great eminence who dealt with doctrinal issues in a popular or devotional style: Andrew Murray (1828-1907), F. B. Meyer (1847-1929), G. Campbell Morgan (1863-1945), W. G. Scroggie (1897-), T. T. Shields (1873-1953), H. Grattan Guinness (1835-1910). E. W. Bullinger (1837-1913) ought to be named here also, although his extreme dispensationalism has greatly undermined his influence among evangelicals.

V. OTHER EUROPEAN COUNTRIES

Scandinavia

The theological temper in Scandinavia has generally been more conservative than in the remainder of the Continent. To the best of our knowledge, however, there has been no significant scholarly movement of a clearly evangelical nature. Unfamiliarity with the original languages, however, discourages us from dogmatic assertion in this respect. The name of Ole Hallesby (1879-), of the Independent Theological Seminary of Oslo, should be noted here. Besides a two-volume dogmatics in Norwegian, *The Christian Faith* (1920, 1921), he wrote a number of works which have been translated into English: *Why I am a Christian* (1930), *Prayer* (1931; 34th ed., 1941), *Conscience* (1933), *The Christian Life* (1934), *Religious or Christian?* (1939). Some of these volumes have been reprinted repeatedly.

Hungary

Here again the ignorance of the language precludes this writer from expressing too emphatic an opinion. He is grateful, however, for the assistance of Professor Theodore Thienemann, of the Academy of Hungary. There are a number of conservative theologians in that country, the most noteworthy being Ladislau Ravasz, author of a greatly-esteemed volume, *Alpha and Omega*. The names of A. Csrkesz, A. Muraközi, and Bela Vassady may also be listed here. The last named, in some respects sympathetic to the Barthian theology, is at present in the United States, and has produced a small volume on *The Main Traits of Calvin's Theology* (1951).

VI. UNITED STATES

The situation in the United States developed along lines substantially different from that of Europe. For here, although widespread movements of departure had been in process long before 1890, the evangelical faith nonetheless still counted great numbers of adherents among the lay people, in the clergy, and in the theological seminaries. Not infrequently whole denominations could be listed among its stanch supporters. Many who wanted to escape the inroads of modernism and biblical criticism in Europe came to the United States as a haven of refuge. As late as 1893 the General Assembly of the Presbyterian Church U.S.A. suspended Charles Augustus Briggs, mainly because he favored a critical approach to Scripture and denied its inerrancy.

The period under study is one in which a theology indifferent to doctrinal issues, or actually opposed to the evangelical view, made increasing inroads into most of the major denominations. By the 1920s fundamentalists were frequently at bay, out-voted, commonly out-maneuvered in the major church assemblies of the north (Presbyterian U.S.A., Methodists, Disciples, Congregationalists, Baptists). In a number of cases their plight gave rise to new denominations and institutions, in some instances not wholly detached from personal motives. By 1924 in the Presbyterian Church U.S.A., the same which had condemned Briggs in 1893, some 1,274 ministers could be found to sign the Auburn Affirmation, a document stating that the inerrancy of Scriptures, the virgin birth, the vicarious atonement, the bodily resurrection, the miracles of Christ, are mere theories, and not essential doctrines of the Word of God nor of the Presbyterian standards. Even in the South, generally rated more conservative, considerable movement towards broader views could be observed.

After the late 1930s there was an almost steady decline of evangelical influence on theological scholarship. The vast numerical reinforcements due to their evangelistic zeal, their wide use of radio facilities, and the rapid growth of new sects, could bring but temporary relief to the prevailing impression that the evangelicals were fighting a losing battle. They were more and more viewed as an inconsequential group of pugnacious obscurantists in whom one should expect neither Christian graciousness nor adequate scholarship. In reverse, the evangelicals often regarded their opponents as unprincipled opportunists who subscribed to confessions of faith they did not believe in, who renounced the historic faith of the Church while appropriating its patrimony, and who deceived the masses by the use of pious phrases and attitudes.

By the late 1930s, and increasingly through the 1940s, the influence of a third protagonist in the field became operative: neo-orthodoxy. At many points it seemed to make common cause with evangelicals in their emphasis on the transcendence of God, the divine initiative, the need of special revelation, the importance of biblical theology, the innate sinfulness of man, the centrality of Christ, the reality of the supernatural, the importance of the eschatological hope. In some cases the similarity may well have been one of vocabulary rather than of basic concepts. In any case, profound differences remained even in the most favorable instances, especially in the matter of attitude toward the Bible. Nevertheless, the evangelicals were greatly encouraged in their struggle, first because a diversion was created, and secondly because the neo-orthodox seemed to attain a remarkable success, which they themselves had thus far failed to achieve, in displacing liberals in seminaries, learned societies, denominational positions, churches, and in the publishing field. This might well be an omen of better things to come.

For convenience's sake we shall subdivide our review according to the denominational ties of the men under consideration.

Lutheran

Among Lutherans, the Missouri Synod is noteworthy for its attachment to conservative theology. Its greatest leader, C. F. W. Walther (1811-1887), had died before the beginning of our period. His major theological work on *The Proper Distinction Between Law and Gospel* was published posthumously in German (1897) and translated into English in 1929. It is generally acknowledged to be one of the finest extant works on the subject, showing throughout a masterly grasp of Lutheran theology. The greatest dogmatician of the Missouri Synod was without a doubt Franz Pieper (1852-1931), noted especially for his monumental *Christian Dogmatics* in three volumes (in German 1917-1924, index 1928; in English 1950-1953). This work is probably the most widely acknowledged modern systematic presentation of conservative Lutheranism. It is marked by a deep grasp of the issues, a clear and pithy statement and vigorous defense of the Lutheran view, and a noteworthy mastery of the Scriptures, of Luther's writings and of the early Lutheran dogmaticians. Besides this major work Pieper produced also a small volume on *Conversion and Election* (1913), holding in this the straight Missouri doctrine on predestination against the views of F. W. Stellhorn (1841-1919), F. A. Schmidt and others. These men, also stanch evangelicals, wrote extensively in the interests of this controversy.

A. L. Graebner (1849-1904), another professor in Concordia Theological Seminary, wrote a short work, *Outlines of Doctrinal Theology* (1898). More recently J. T. Mueller, (1885-), author of numerous works of popularization, published a *Christian Dogmatics* (1934) in one volume in which an able summary of Pieper's work is presented. Other Missouri Synod men who made noteworthy contributions in dogmatics are Theodore Engelder (1865-1949), remembered especially for his large volume *Scripture Cannot be Broken* (1944); F. E. Mayer, author of a large work on the *Religious Bodies of America* (second edition, 1956); J. Pelikan; W. H. T. Dau.

In Wisconsin one of the main leaders was Adolf Hoenecke (1835-1908), whose large *Lutheran Dogmatics* in four volumes was published in German after his death by his sons (1909-1917).

To the Norwegian Evangelical Lutheran Church belongs Robert Preus, the author of a very fine analysis and defense of the seventeenth century Lutheran dogmaticians' views of the Bible, entitled *The Inspiration of Scripture* (1955). This work vindicates the so-called Lutheran Scholastics from many loose accusations commonly levelled at them, apparently because of insufficient acquaintance with them. In so doing the author also presents a vigorous and carefully drawn statement of the evangelical view of plenary inspiration. This is probably one of the best works of this century on the subject.

While the other branches of the Lutheran Church in America do not manifest the same unflinching allegiance to orthodox doctrine as the Synodical Conference, one acknowledges with pleasure that there have been very conservative theologians in the American Lutheran Conference (J. M. Reu, 1869-1943; F. W. Stellhorn, 1841-1919; F. A. Schmidt) and in the United Lutheran Church (Leander S. Keyser, 1856-1937; J. A. Seiss, 1823-1904; H. E. Jacobs, 1844-1932; Th. E. Schmauk, 1860-1920; J. B. Remensnyder, 1843-1927). For the history of Lutheran Theology in America great help can be derived from the quite conservative works of J. L. Neve (1865-1943): *Churches and Sects of Christendom* (third edition, 1944, pp. 182-233); *A History of Christian Thought* (1946, II, 297-311).

Presbyterian

The group of denominations indicated by this title has always been strong in doctrinal consciousness, and it is not surprising that in the present period a wide number of men deserve notice here.

We start with those associated with Princeton Theological Seminary, which was, especially until 1929, a bulwark of conservative faith. A worthy successor to Charles Hodge and A. A. Hodge in the chair of didactic and polemic theology was Benjamin Breckenridge Warfield (1851-1921). Like Charles Hodge an accomplished New Testament scholar, he made his mark particularly in the field of apologetics and systematic theology. During his lifetime he published comparatively few volumes of theology: *Two Studies in the History of Doctrine* (1897) on the Pelagian controversy and infant salvation; *The Lord of Glory* (1907, reprint 1950) on the deity of Christ; *The Plan of Salvation* (1915, reprint 1942) on the order of divine decrees; and *Counterfeit Miracles* (1918, reprint 1953) on the cessation of the apostolic *charismata*. Besides these there were a number of pamphlets, especially about the Westminster Standards, and four volumes of sermons or chapel talks, naturally oriented to dogmatic themes—*The Gospel of the Incarnation* (1893), *The Power of God Unto Salvation* (1903), *The Saviour of the World* (1915), and *Faith and Life* (1916).

In spite of the very great merits of these publications it is probably safe to say that Warfield's greatest contribution to theological science consisted in a vast number of learned articles published in encyclopedias and in various periodicals, especially the *Presbyterian and Reformed Review* (1890-1902) and its successor *The Princeton Theological Review* (1903-1921). Many of the most significant of these have been gathered by his literary executors and published in ten large volumes (1927-1932). Besides two volumes of theological essays ranging over the whole field of Christian doctrine—*Biblical Doctrines* (1929) and *Studies in Theology* (1932)—special tomes are devoted to inspiration—*Revelation and Inspiration* (1927) and *Christology and Criticism* (1929)—and sanctification, *Perfectionism* (2 vols. 1931).

In the field of history of dogma we note Warfield's special studies on Augustine, Calvin, and the Westminster Assembly. More recently the Presbyterian and Reformed Publication Company has regrouped and reissued a number of these articles. The series thus far numbers four volumes (*The Inspiration and Authority of the Bible,* 1948; *The Person and Work of Christ,* 1950; *Biblical and Theological Studies,* 1952; *Calvin and Augustine,* 1956). It is in these articles perhaps that Warfield's consummate ability comes best to light. There are some surveys in which the whole span of a doctrine is scanned in a few masterful pages, in which the essential is delineated and the secondary is bypassed with admirable skill (cf. "The Biblical Idea of Inspiration," "God," "Atonement," "Imputation," "Annihilationism"). In other articles, at the opposite extreme, a very limited subject is under scrutiny, and a most thorough investigation pursues, with painstaking care and a wealth of documentation, virtually every avenue of knowledge capable of shedding light on the issues at hand. (cf. "God-Inspired Scripture," "The Oracles of God," "The Printing of the Westminster Confession," "The New Testament Terminology of Redemption," and many others). In such articles Warfield's gigantic breadth of conception and scholarly care in the handling of details appear in their clearest light. There also his gifts for effective approach to controversy are exhibited: a firm grasp of the issues at hand, a deft handling of the opponent, an impressive marshalling of the evidence, often with crushing weight. These made him an opponent uncommonly difficult to gainsay. Warfield's critical reviews, veritable models of the kind, afford additional evidence of his scholarship. Friend and foe alike were ready to own to his masterful competency and to his consistent adherence to the tenets of the Reformed faith.

Although Warfield gave his attention to many areas of dogmatics, it may be proper to single out here those in which his contributions have been most significant. In the first place must undoubtedly be reckoned the doctrine of the plenary verbal inspiration of the Scriptures, which he vigorously defended from beginning to end. He also gave special attention to the deity of Christ, the atonement, sanctification, and historically to Augustine, Calvin, and the Westminster Assembly.

At the side of Warfield for over twenty-five years stood Geerhardus Vos (1862-1949), professor of biblical theology at Princeton from 1893 to 1932. In this chair he exercised a most decisive influence, first of all by giving biblical theology its due place in the orb of theological science as "that branch of exegetical theology which deals with the process of self revelation of God deposited in the Bible" (Vos, *Biblical Theology,* p. 13).

An unusually penetrating exegete, he always maintained a special interest in dogmatic theology which he had taught for five years in Calvin Seminary. His notes on this discipline were issued in mimeographed form in three volumes (*Dogmatic,* 1910). We are indebted to him for works on Christ (*The Self Disclosure of Jesus,* 1926, reprint 1954), and on eschatology (*The Teaching of Jesus Concerning the Kingdom of God and the Church,* 1903, reprint 1950; *Pauline Eschatology,* 1930, reprint 1952). In all his works Geerhardus Vos displayed extraordinary learning and exegetical acumen. His style as a result is at times quite ponderous. It may be something of a surprise for those who are acquainted merely with his scholarly works to find that he published several volumes of poetry both in Dutch and in English.

Francis L. Patton, (1843-1932), for some years president of Princeton Theological Seminary, lent the support of his incisive pen to the conservative faith. We have from him in this period *A Summary of Christian Doctrine* (1906) and *Fundamental Christianity* (1926).

Although Caspar W. Hodge, Jr., (1870-1937) never published a book, he deserves mention here on account of his articles and reviews in *The Princeton Theological Review.*

John Gresham Machen (1881-1937) was unquestionably one of the ablest champions of the evangelical faith in our period. Although his main interest lay in the field of New Testament studies, he was led to devote considerable attention to dogmatic issues and did so with a clarity of mind and style which characterized all the products of his pen. His great monograph on the *Virgin Birth of Christ* (1930, second edition, 1932), is the acknowledged classic defense of this dogma, exhibiting masterful control over the whole field and consummate skill in the handling of the argumentation and of the opponents. In *Christianity and Liberalism* (1923) we have the crystal clear statement of the conservative position as contrasted with Modernism. In *What is Faith?* (1925, reprint 1946) we have a searching analysis of this topic. In volumes of sermons and addresses (*The Christian Faith in the Modern World,* 1936, reprint 1947; *The Christian View of Man,* 1937, reprint 1947; *God Transcendent,* 1949; *What is Christianity?,* 1950) he gave a popular presentation of many great doctrines of the faith. An able biography of Machen was published by Ned B. Stonehouse in 1954. Machen's *The Origin of Paul's Religion* (1921, reprint 1947) is unmentioned above because it deals primarily with New Testament rather than with dogmatic issues.

Machen was one of the leading spirits in the foundation of Westminster Seminary in Philadelphia (1929), in which the conservative approach of the old Princeton was to be perpetuated when it appeared threatened in Princeton itself. Through the years this seminary has proven its attachment to the Reformed faith and is one of the present bulwarks of orthodoxy in America. *The Westminster Theological Journal,* published there since 1938, has been a vigorous and scholarly organ of the faculty. In 1946, under the title *The Infallible Word,* the whole faculty produced a symposium expounding the evangelical view of Scripture. A third edition of this work was already needed in 1953.

Faculty members of Westminster Seminary deserve mention here for their work in systematics. Cornelius Van Til (1895-) is best known for his labors in apologetics. We may rest satisfied here with mentioning his critique of neo-orthodoxy (*The New Modernism,* 1946), and his discussions on *Common Grace* (1947). In this latter area he has been under attack from some evangelical theologians, particularly James Daane in *A Theology of Grace* (1954) and William Masselink in *General Revelation and Common Grace* (1953). John Murray (1898-), professor of systematic theology, wrote on *Christian Baptism* (1950) and on *Redemption, Accomplished and Applied* (1955). He unites in a remarkable way exegetical insight with systematic grasp.

Also active in the Presbyterian Church of the North was W. G. T. Shedd (1820-1894), whose labors fell mainly before this period but who published after 1890 the third volume of his *Dogmatic Theology* (1894) and two other volumes, *Orthodoxy and Heterodoxy* (1893), and *Calvinism Pure and Mixed* (1893). He makes an interesting contrast to Charles Hodge, being a confirmed traducianist and holding the realistic view of original sin, yet agreeing with Hodge in the main tenets of the Presbyterian faith.

Floyd Hamilton (1890-) devoted special attention to creation (*The Basis of Evolutionary Faith,* 1931) and to eschatology (*The Basis of the Millennial Faith,* 1942). Loraine Boettner made his mark with the publication of his well-known volume *The Reformed Doctrine of Predestination* (1932). This work, intended above all to popularize the main tenets of Calvinism, enjoyed a great success, and a number of successive editions of it were quickly needed. The same author also wrote popular treatments of the doctrine of *Inspiration* (1937), *The Person of Christ* (1943), and *The Atonement* (1941), which he republished together with some of his theological articles in one volume entitled *Studies in Theology* (1947). Boettner excels in a presentation that may readily be understood even by the layman without antagonizing the scholar.

J. Oliver Buswell, Jr., (1895-), under the general title *The Lamb of God,* gave a succinct, popular presentation of the Christian faith in five small volumes (1937). David S. Clark (1859-) wrote a brief exposition of the Christian faith entitled *A Syllabus of Systematic Theology* which went through three editions. His son, Gordon H. Clark, recently published a volume on the Westminster Confession entitled *What Presbyterians Believe* (1956). Samuel G. Craig (1874-) is noted especially for his *Christianity Rightly So Called* (1946) and a recent volume, *Jesus of Yesterday and Today* (1956).

In the South, or Presbyterian Church in the U.S., we must take note of R. L. Dabney (1820-1898), whose *Syllabus . . . of Systematic and Polemic Theology* appeared in several revised editions in our period (sixth edition, 1927), and who wrote also a short work *Christ Our Penal Substitute* (1898). Some of his shorter works were published between 1890 and 1892 under the title of *Discussions.*

John L. Girardeau (1825-1898) was the author of *Calvinism and Evangelical Arminianism* (1890), *The Will in its Theological Relations* (1891) and *Discussion of Theological Questions* (1905). He was acknowledged as one of the ablest Calvinistic theologians of the South.

Francis R. Beattie (1848-1906) wrote a commentary on the *Presbyterian Standards* (1898). R. A. Webb (1856-1919) produced volumes on the *Theology of Infant Salvation* (1907), *The Christian Hope* (1914), *The Christian Salvation* (1921), *The Reformed Doctrines of Adoption* (1947). C. R. Vaughan published an esteemed work on *The Gifts of the Holy Spirit* (1894).

More recently we must name William Childs Robinson (1897-), author of a work on the deity of Christ, *Our Lord* (1937, second edition, 1949), and of *What is Christian Faith?* (1937), and *Christ—The Hope of Glory* (1945).

Connected with the Cumberland Presbyterian Church, a Presbyterian body with some Arminian leanings, were Robert Verrell Foster (1845-1914), author of a large *Systematic Theology* (1898), and James P. MacDonald (1861-), author of *Bible Studies in Christian Doctrines* (1939).

As a representative of the New School, we must mention E. D. Morris (1825-1915), of Lane Seminary, whose *Theology of the Westminster Symbols* (1900, second edition, 1911) is no doubt the crowning achievement of his life.

A special group among the Presbyterians is formed by those who espouse dispensationalism. The main figure in that group is unquestionably Lewis Sperry Chafer (1871-1952), author of an eight-volume *Systematic Theology* (1948) marked by unqualified adherence to the fundamentals of the faith and the consistent application of the principles of dispensationalism. The organization of the material leaves room for improvement, and there is little evidence of an awareness of present-day theological trends or of first-hand acquaintance with the great theologians of the past. Nevertheless these volumes contain many helpful discussions. They have received a wide hearing and exert a strong influence upon fundamentalist circles. Although a Presbyterian, Chafer advocates only a moderate Calvinism, denying, for instance, definite atonement. Other dogmatic works by Chafer include *Satan* (1909), *The Kingdom in*

History and Prophecy (1915), *Salvation* (1916), and *Grace* (1922). Chafer's successor at Dallas Seminary is John F. Walvoord, author of *The Doctrine of the Holy Spirit* (1943, second edition, 1954) and of *The Return of the Lord* (1955).

Compendious presentations of Christian doctrine from the same general viewpoint were published by William Evans (1870-), *The Great Doctrines of the Bible* (1912), and P. B. Fitzwater (1871-), *Christian Theology* (1948, second edition, 1953). Both of the above writers also wrote minor works on various Christian doctrines in a popular style.

During our period the interest of evangelicals in eschatology has been great. Among Presbyterians who published on this theme we would name F. C. Ottman (1859-1929), Nathaniel West (1824-1907), W. G. Moorehead (1836-1914), S. H. Kellogg (1839-1899), J. H. Brookes (1830-1897), W. E. Biederwolf (1867-1939), and more recently George Murray (1896-1956), Roderick Campbell, J. Marcellus Kik (1903-), Wilbur M. Smith (1894-), and Oswald T. Allis (1880-).

Reformed

The Reformed churches have always been very close to the Presbyterians in doctrine and government. The dogmatic interest of the latter has been shared by the former and we should not be surprised to find here again great productivity on the part of evangelicals.

We start with the Christian Reformed Church, a body well known for its attachment to conservative doctrine. Her seminary, Calvin Theological Seminary in Grand Rapids, Michigan, its teaching staff, its journal *The Calvin Forum* (1935-1956), and its alumni have been throughout the years stanch upholders of Reformed orthodoxy. As late as 1922, a professor, Dr. Ralph Janssen, was deposed from office mainly on the charge that he had made important concessions to Old Testament criticism. There is some question as to whether the charges were sufficiently founded, but the impressive feature is that this trial proved that, in this denomination at least, yielding to biblical criticism was deemed as a sufficient reason for deposition.

The list of Christian Reformed men who made contributions in the area of dogmatics would be a long one. We can do no more than name Henry Beets (1869-1947), H. Beuker (1834-1900), M. J. Bosma (1874-1912), Y. P. de Jong, G. K. Hemkes (1838-1920), J. van der Werp, S. Volbeda (1881-1953), and more recently R. J. Danhof, J. K. Van Baalen, Fred Klooster, E. H. Palmer, Lewis Smedes. All of these men published materials dealing with Christian doctrine, either as a whole, or in some particular aspect.

Two areas received special attention during this period in the Christian Reformed Church: common grace and eschatology.

In the matter of common grace, the radical views of Henry Danhof and Herman Hoeksema, expressed in their joint volume *About Sin and Grace* (1923), were condemned by Synod in 1924. Alexander C. de Jong has well summarized the controversy which ensued in his thesis entitled *The Well-Meant Gospel Offer* (1954). Among those who dealt with this subject then or later we may note Herman Kuiper, L. Berkhof, James Daane, and William Masselink. Herman Hoeksema founded the Protestant Reformed Church and is perhaps best known for his ten-volume exposition of the Heidelberg Catechism under the general title of *The Triple Knowledge* (1943-1956).

Among those who dealt with eschatological themes one may list H. Bultema, D. H. Kromminga (1879-1946), Louis Berkhof (1873-), Y. P. de Jong, W. Masselink, W. Hendriksen, W. H. Rutgers, M. Wyngaarden.

William Heyns (1856-1933), for many years professor at Calvin Seminary, wrote a *Manual of Reformed Doctrine* (1916, in English, 1926) and many works on ecclesiology. Foppe Ten Hor (1845-1934) wrote a *Reformed Dogmatics* in Dutch. H. H. Meeter published an important thesis on *The Heavenly High Priesthood of Christ* (1916) and two volumes on Calvinism (1930, 1939).

Berkhof started as professor of New Testament (1906-1926), then turned his attention to dogmatics. He is particularly noted for his large *Reformed Dogmatics* in four volumes (1932-1937). A second edition of Volume I appeared in 1946. Volumes II and III were rewritten and published in one volume under the title *Systematic Theology* (1938). In this work, which underwent several editions (1941, 1946, 1949), Berkhof exhibits a remarkable ability in stating the issues in clear, concise language. The view which he advocates is contrasted with one-sided or faulty views. Abundant reference is made to Scripture and a far-reaching knowledge of the relevant theological literature is manifested. Full advantage is taken of the labors of his predecessors, and historical perspective is given through carefully drawn summaries of the history of dogma. Bibliographical helps are subjoined to each chapter and at the end of the volume. The material is carefully organized and the whole subject matter of dogmatics is expounded in proper balance. It may be observed that this book does not often suggest new and original solutions to the perennial problems of theology, but it is up-to-date (1938), orthodox, and admirably suitable as a textbook. It has been hailed "as the most important work on systematic theology from an American source that has appeared in recent years" (S. G. Craig). In addition to this *magnum opus* Berkhof produced some shorter expositions of the Reformed faith (1923, 1938), and volumes on *The Assurance of Faith* (1928; second edition, 1939), *Vicarious Atonement through Christ* (1936), *The Kingdom of God* (1951), *Aspects of Liberalism* (1951), *The Second Coming of Christ* (1953) and *Recent Trends in Theology* (1944). Berkhof's characteristic qualities appear in these works also.

Among members of other Reformed groups some names must be mentioned here. D. J. Burrell (1844-1926) wrote on the doctrine of inspiration (1904-1917); G. H. Hospers (1864-) on *The Reformed Principle of Authority* (1924); G. S. Bishop (1836-1914) on *The Person and Work of the Holy Spirit* (1897); and on *The Doctrines of Grace* (1919); E. J. Blekkink on *The Fatherhood of God* (1942); Winfield Burggraaff on *The Rise and Development of Liberal Theology in America* (1928). Each of two returned missionaries, Samuel M. Zwemer (1867-1952) and Albertus Pieters (1869-), wrote a number of volumes dealing with doctrinal themes. The brothers, J. H. and Henry De Vries are perhaps best known as the translators of several of Abraham Kuyper's works. Henry De Vries wrote also a volume on the person of Christ, *The Incarnate Son of God* and another on the work of Christ, *The Lord's Anointed* (1926).

Episcopalian

We may perhaps start with the Reformed Episcopal Church, a thoroughly evangelical body founded in 1873. To it belong such men as James M. Gray (1851-1935), Frank E. Gaebelein (1899-), William Culbertson (1905-), who without being professionals in dogmatics, yet produced helpful volumes with popular appeal.

In the Protestant Episcopal Church, Cornelius Walker (1819-1907), will be remembered for his *Outlines of Christian Theology* (1894). The greatest theologian which this church produced undoubtedly was the quite conservative Francis J. Hall (1857-1932), author of a monumental *Dogmatic Theology* in ten volumes (1907-1922), of an incisive work on *The Kenotic Theory* (1898), and of a vigorous defense of conservative theology, *Christianity and Modernism* (1924). Because of his very "High Church" position and because of some concessions to biblical criticism and to evolutionary hypothesis, he does not fit perfectly in the framework of the present history. Nevertheless it is desirable at least to make mention of this very able theologian.

Methodist and Holiness

There are not in the Methodist churches many acknowledged scholarly dogmaticians who unqualifiedly espoused the evangelical theology during our period. John Miley (1813-1895) was reaching the end of his fruitful career and published his two-volume *Systematic Theology* (1892-1894), substantially conservative yet with some mediating tendencies. J. A. Faulkner (1857-1931) in his *Modernism and the Christian Faith* (1921) and *The Miraculous Birth of Our Lord* (1924) upheld substantially the same position. Bishop R. J. Cooke (1853-1931) wrote a conservative volume, *The Incarnation and Recent Criticism* (1907). At Nast Theological Seminary, F. W. Schneider wrote his *System of Christian Doctrine* in German (1908), in which the idea of divine love is the controlling principle of division. At the present time Asbury Theological Seminary in Wilmore, Kentucky, espouses wholeheartedly the evangelical position and publishes *The Asbury Seminarian* (1947-).

On a popular level we must note the almost phenomenal success of W. E. Blackstone's little book *Jesus is Coming* (1908). A. C. Gaebelein (1861-1945) was the author of at least forty volumes dealing with doctrinal issues, particularly eschatology. As editor of *Our Hope* from 1894 he wielded a very great influence. George P. Eckman (1860-1920) deserves mention here also for his *When Christ Comes Again* (1917).

J. J. Escher (1823-1901) was a Bishop of the Evangelical Association. His *Christian Theology* in two volumes in German (1899-1901) is the first systematic theology produced by his church. A third volume might presumably have been added to deal with ecclesiology and eschatology if the life of the author had been spared longer.

Among United Brethren a mere mention of Bishop Weaver's (1824-1901) *Christian Theology* (1900), and of J. A. Miller's (1866-1936) *Christian Doctrine* (1946) will suffice. The Brethren have a very conservative school at Winona Lake, Indiana, Grace Theological Seminary.

The Church of the Nazarene, an evangelical and evangelistic body, is represented by E. P. Ellyson's *Theological Compend* (1905), A. M. Hills's (1848-) *Fundamental Christian Theology* (2 vols., 1931), and especially H. Orton Wiley's (1877-) *Christian Theology* (3 vols., 1940-1946). This last work is well documented and provided with an extensive bibliography. A one-volume abridgement of it has appeared under the title *Introduction to Christian Theology* (1947).

In the Church of God (Anderson, Indiana), we may note F. G. Smith (1880-), whose book *What the Bible Teaches* (1913) has had at least fifteen editions (1945); Russell Byrum (1888-), who wrote *Christian Theology* (1925); and A. F. Gray (1886-), who published a *Christian Theology* in two volumes (1944-1946).

In the Assemblies of God, Carl Brumback has written a lengthy discussion of the gift of tongues, *What Meaneth This?* (1947). Myer Pearlman wrote a volume entitled *Knowing the Doctrines of the Bible* (1937), and very recently Ernest S. Williams published a three-volume *Systematic Theology,* unfortunately somewhat disappointing in scholarship.

The Christian and Missionary Alliance claims A. B. Simpson (1844-1919), author of a number of doctrinal books written in a popular or devotional vein. Frederick Farr and George Pardington (1866-1915) wrote summaries of Christian doctrine from this viewpoint.

Congregationalists

R. A. Torrey (1856-1928) may be remembered for his *What the Bible Teaches* (1898) and his *Fundamental Doctrines of the Christian Faith* (1918), as well as for a good number of volumes on particular aspects of doctrine in a popular vein. Also predominantly popular or homiletical are the doctrinal works of C. I. Scofield (1843-1921), A. Z. Conrad (1855-1937) and Harold J. Ockenga (1905-), author of such penetrating works as *The Church In God and The Comfort of God.*

Baptist in the North

At the turn of the 1890's there were a number of evangelical theologians among the Baptists. John J. Butler (1814-1891) and Ransom Dunn (1818-1900) represented the Free Will Baptists and published their *Lectures on Systematic Theology* (1892). Alvah Hovey's (1820-1903) pen was still active: *Studies in Ethics and Religion* (1892), *Christian Teaching and Life* (1895), *Manual of Theology* (1900). F. L. Chappell's (1836-1900) *Biblical and Practical Theology* was published shortly after his death in 1901. In 1895 Carl G. Lagergren (1847-1941) published in Swedish his *Fundamental Bible Doctrines* in seven volumes (second edition, 1922-1924). His influence over Swedish Baptists has been very great. A. J. Gordon (1836-1895), not a professional theologian, yet a keen thinker, issued in our period two volumes on the Holy Spirit: *The Holy Spirit in Missions* (1893) and *The Ministry of the Spirit* (1894). Ezekiel G. Robinson's (1815-1894) *Christian Theology* (1895) appeared shortly after his death. Although in the main a conservative work, it represents a surprising number of departures from traditional theology (for a careful study of Robinson's views see C. F. H. Henry, *Personal Idealism and Strong's Theology* [1951], pp. 20-47). Robinson was the teacher of E. H. Johnson and A. H. Strong and exercised a great influence upon both of them. Elias H. Johnson (1841-1906), of Crozer Seminary, published *An Outline of Systematic Theology* (1891, second edition, 1895), for which H. G. Weston (1820-1909) supplied the treatment of ecclesiology.

Augustus Hopkins Strong (1836-1921) is no doubt the outstanding Baptist theologian of his generation. Besides his imposing *Systematic Theology* (first edition, 1886, eighth edition and last revision in three volumes, 1907-1909), he produced two important volumes of theological essays, *Philosophy and Religion* (1888) and *Christ in Creation and Ethical Monism* (1899), studies on the theology of various poets (1897, 1917), a volume on *Union with Christ* (1913), and at the very end of his life a summary of Christian doctrine, *What Shall I Believe?* (1922). Strong's work is noteworthy for his talent of organization, for his extensive acquaintance with both philosophical and theological literature, abundantly referred to and quoted in the small print of his major work, for his firm support of most evangelical doctrines. One major weakness is the increasing influence of idealistic monism which led him to dangerous modifications of the orthodox faith, particularly with respect to creation and atonement (for a careful study of the chronology of Strong's development along this line see C. F. H. Henry, *op. cit.*).

Unfortunately for the evangelical cause many of Strong's students (e.g., Walter Rauschenbusch) carried out the logical implications of monism much further than their teacher.

Nathan E. Wood (1849-1937), another conservative with occasional mediating tendencies, is known mainly for his book on *The Person and Work of Jesus Christ* (1908), which deals with Christology and soteriology. His son, Nathan R. Wood (1874-), published in 1905 a brief work on *The Witness of Sin,* then in 1932 a very stimulating study of the reflections of the Trinitarian Being of God in nature and man, *The Secret of the Universe* (tenth edition, 1955). His *Seven Lamps of Fire* (1943, second edition, 1950, entitled *The Open Secret of Christianity)* is a series of studies in various Christian doctrines.

John B. Champion (1868-1943), of Eastern Baptist Theological Seminary sought to expound what he called genetic theology in a series of volumes: *The Living Atonement* (1910), *The Virgin's Son* (1924), *More Than Atonement* (1927), *Sovereignty and Grace* (1933), *Personality and the Trinity* (1935), *Inspiration Explains Itself* (1938). While we gladly acknowledge that this author was earnestly contending for the evangelical faith, it must be owned that his view of the atonement is uncommonly obscure and seems to fail to do justice to the forensic element of that doctrine.

A. K. de Blois (1866-1945), for many years president of the same seminary, edited a volume of papers by the faculty entitled *The Evangelical Faith* (1931).

A brief notice may be given to Colin M. Cline (1873-), who wrote *A Manual of Theology* (1936); to Emery H. Bancroft (-1944), whose *Elemental Theology* (1932) and *Christian Theology* (1925) are written from a dispensational viewpoint; to H. C. Thiessen (1885-1947), mainly a New Testament scholar, whose *Introductory Lectures in Systematic Theology* were published after his death (1949).

Among Baptist writers who dealt with doctrinal themes mainly in a popular or homiletical fashion, we may mention I. M. Haldeman (1845-1933), W. B. Riley (1861-1947), W. L. Pettingill (1866-1948), J. C. Massee (1871-). Chester Tulga has issued a series of small booklets entitled "The Case for . . ." or "The Case Against . . ." The former are probably the best evidence of his ability, while the latter are often good representations of the worst features occasionally encountered in Fundamentalism: vitriolic attacks, hasty generalizations, frequent use of the charge of guilt by association, a general bitterness of spirit, all this deeply disappointing in anyone who claims to uphold the cause of Christ.

In the present generation there are a number of promising young Baptist theologians who have already given samples of their ability. Carl F. H. Henry (1913-) made a keen analysis of the present doctrinal situation in his *Protestant Dilemma* (1949). His work on A. H. Strong (1951) and his history of twentieth century theology (1950) have been noted earlier. His *Notes on the Doctrine of God* (1948) is a valuable contribution on this subject. Edward J. Carnell (1919-), mostly interested in the philosophy of religion, wrote a critique of *The Theology of Reinhold Niebuhr* (1951). Paul K. Jewett published a searching study of *Emil Brunner's Concept of Revelation* (1954). George E. Ladd (1911-), mainly interested in New Testament studies, issued two books on eschatology, *Crucial Questions About the Kingdom of God* (1952) and *The Blessed Hope* (1956). These, it may be hoped, are but the first fruits of a much more abundant harvest to come.

Baptist in the South

The South has traditionally been conservative, and the Baptist movement has had great success in that region.

E. Y. Mullins (1860-1928), for many years Professor of Theology and President of Southern Baptist Theological Seminary (1899-1928), was one of the stalwart representatives of the evangelical faith. His main work, *The Christian Religion in Its Doctrinal Expression* (1917), is a helpful contribution, although it does lay undue stress upon religious experience as a source of truth. This led Mullins to questionable positions on the doctrine of the person of Christ and of the atonement. Other dogmatic works by Mullins include *Axioms of Religion* (1908), *Baptist Beliefs* (1912), *Freedom and Authority in Religion* (1913,) *The Life in Christ* (1917) and a defense of evangelical theology against Modernism, *Christianity at the Crossroads* (1924).

E. C. Dargan (1852-1930) was primarily concerned with practical theology, but he wrote a bulky *Ecclesiology* (1897, second edition, 1905), and a smaller volume on *The Doctrines of the Faith* (1905).

T. P. Stafford (1866-1942) wrote a substantial volume, *A Study of Christian Doctrines* (1936) as well as *A Study of the Holy Spirit* (1920) and *A Study of the Kingdom* (1925). T. P. Simmons is the author of *A Systematic Study of Bible Doctrines* (1936, second edition, 1938). J. B. Tidwell (1870-1946) wrote a popular work on *Christian Teachings* (1929).

Walter T. Conner (1877-1952) of Southwestern Baptist Theological Seminary published in 1924 *A System of Christian Doctrine,* which he later developed into two volumes, *Revelation and God* (1936) and *The Gospel of Redemption* (1945), and abridged into a smaller compendium, *Christian Doctrine* (1937). He wrote further *The Gospel Doctrines* (1925), *The Resurrection of Jesus* (1926), *The Faith of the New Testament* (1940), *The Work of the Holy Spirit* (1949), *The Cross in the New Testament* (1954). While this author's influence has been beneficial to the conservative cause, it must be owned that in his treatment of the atonement he opposed penal substitution, and that his definition of justification fails to set forth the purely declarative nature of this blessing.

Mennonites

The Mennonite General Conference ordered two doctrinal symposiums to be prepared under the editorship of Daniel Kauffman (1865-1944). The former, *Bible Doctrine,* appeared in 1914, the latter, *Doctrines of the Bible,* in 1929. Both are large volumes written in popular style. More recently J. C. Wenger (1910-) wrote *The Doctrines of the Mennonites* (1950) and a very competent *Introduction to Theology* (1954). This latter work is well documented and abreast of recent trends. Among those who took the cudgels against the inroads of liberalism in the 1920s one should name John Horsch and his *Modern Religious Liberalism* (1921). J. A. Huffman (1880-), of the Mennonite Brethren in Christ, wrote a number of doctrinal volumes in a popular vein.

Miscellaneous

Under this title we shall give a brief notice to some evangelical efforts in denominations which do not fit into any of the groupings thus far reviewed, and also to some men whose denominational connection the present writer has been unable to ascertain.

Among the Advent Christian we must mention G. L. Young, who wrote a number of volumes on eschatology and a work entitled *Fundamental Christology* (1906). Clarence H. Hewitt (1890-1954) also wrote extensively on eschatology, culminating in his *Classbook in Eschatology* (1942). He also published *Faith for Today* (1941) and *Vital Atonement* (1946). The last-named volume advocates a form of the mystical view of the atonement and has been the object of the incisive criticism of James A. Nichols, Jr., in *A Critique of the Theory of Vital Atonement* (1955).

The Seventh-Day Adventists are not usually classified among the evangelicals. Nevertheless it may be proper at this time to acknowledge that some of the more learned among them are being gradually weaned from the teachings of Mrs. White. L. E. Froom (1890-) has recently completed a monumental study of prophetic interpretation in four large volumes, *The Prophetic Faith of Our Fathers* (1946-1954).

Among the Plymouth Brethren we often find men with a considerable knowledge of the Bible, but seldom men versed in dogmatics. A marked exception is F. W. Grant, who died in 1903. Philip Mauro (1859-1952) was the author of a large number of volumes dealing principally with eschatological and prophetic interpretation. A radical shift in his views away from dispensationalism took place in about 1929. His small volume

Life in the Word (1909) is a very stimulating work on inspiration. H. A. Ironside (1876-1951) is well known for his numerous books, several of them on doctrinal themes, in a popular style.

A few lines should be devoted to the Irvingite, S. J. Andrews (1817-1906), a man of great learning, author in this period of *Christianity and Anti-Christianity in Their Final Conflict* (1898).

Harry Rimmer (1890-1953) was first a Quaker, then a Presbyterian, and wrote a large number of volumes attempting to relate science to the Scripture in defense of inspiration. According to the best information available to this writer, his presentation was commonly marked by superficiality and was not of a nature to satisfy either real scientists or competent theologians.

The present writer has been unable to determine with accuracy the denominational connection of the following men: Mark G. Cambron, *Bible Doctrines* (1954); David L. Cooper (1886-), *What Men Must Believe* (1943), and a whole series of books about the Messiahship of Christ; E. Schuyler English (1889-), *Things Surely to Be Believed* (1946). To these might be added the names of C. L. Feinberg (1909-), C. C. Ryrie and H. W. Frost (1858-), who dealt with eschatology. All six of these men are inclined to dispensationalism.

VII. CONCLUSION

It appears quite clearly from the foregoing pages that the evangelical output in systematic theology has been quite considerable in the course of the period under review. So large has this contribution been, in fact, that it has been impossible within the limits of this chapter to do much more than to list major authors and their principal works with a brief critical appraisal. Full use could not be made here, therefore, of the potential represented by the contribution in this discipline, which has engaged evangelical attention in a paramount fashion. A full volume, rather than a mere chapter, would certainly be needed to that end. It may be fitting, however, in a few pages of conclusion, to assess the main evangelical contributions by areas, and to cast a glance at the tasks still most urgently requiring their attention.

In bibliology, obviously, the evangelicals have a crucial stake, for the attitude to the Bible is determinative for the whole position. As noted above, important contributions have been made in this area by various authors (Rohnert, Koelling, Kuyper, Dijk, Berkouwer, Lecerf, M'Intosh, Orr, Engelder, the Westminster Faculty, Preus), and in the most impressive way perhaps by Warfield.

These and other able presentations should have removed all excuse for confusing the evangelical view with the mechanical theory of inspiration, at least by those who would lay claim to competent scholarship. We regret to say, however, that such confusion is still very widespread, and seems to lie at the basis of many attacks leveled at the evangelical view. Somehow, therefore, this distinction must be reasserted and emphasized, until the strawman of "dictation" is definitely laid to rest in the theological grave. Meanwhile, no one should be surprised if evangelicals are scarcely impressed by arguments intended to refute or discredit their view, but which, in fact, fundamentally misconstrue their position.

There are a number of areas in which a modern, competent evangelical treatment is greatly to be desired: we need a study of the historical course of the doctrine of inspiration from the beginning to our day, which will compare with the work of the Roman Catholics Dausch or Pesch; we need a rather extensive discussion of the Canon of Scripture, especially in its dogmatic implications; we need a full-orbed balanced discussion of the whole doctrine, giving adequate attention to modern trends and problems and dispelling current misgivings. Truly in this crucial area the task ahead is very great.

In theology proper we do not note a particularly large output by evangelicals, although various divine attributes and the doctrine of the Trinity are indirectly the object of careful attention in various dogmatic investigations related to other *loci*. Particularly the study of the atonement is apt to set forward divine attributes, and discussions on the person of Christ and on the Holy Spirit naturally are closely related to the Trinity. Even so, it must be owned that few full-size volumes on this *locus* have been produced, albeit the indigence of evangelical thought on the Trinity, for instance, is hardly as great as Claude Welch suggests. *(In This Name,* p. 100, 1952. Note the absence of any reference to Bavinck, Kuyper, Pieper, Berkhof, Wood, etc., in this otherwise well-documented work.) The doctrines of the decrees of God and of Providence, on the other hand, have been the object of a number of rather extensive studies: the names of Berkouwer, Boettner, Dijk, Girardeau, Polman and Warfield readily come to mind in this connection. The doctrine of creation has been the object of very considerable attention, particularly in connection with evolutionary thought. This phase of doctrine properly belongs to another chapter of this volume, touching science and the Bible.

In anthropology and hamartiology we do not have in this period many great evangelical monographic studies, although we should not forget Orr's *God's Image in Man* and *Sin as a Problem of Today,* nor the second edition of Laidlaw's great classic, *The Bible Doctrine of Man.* The handling of these *loci* in most full-size systematic theologies is competent. The subject of the covenants has been the object of several extensive and able treatments, especially among the Reformed Churches of the Netherlands. During our period there was a drastic change of the general theological atmosphere from a widely prevailing mood of optimism to a much more realistic appraisal of man's predicament, sometimes verging to an extreme form of pessimism with slight biblical warrant. This change of current, however, appears to have been due more to the course of events and to the internal difficulties of the old-fashioned optimistic liberalism than to overpowering contributions by evangelicals. We need evangelical works which might come closer to match the offerings of Barth, Brunner, Niebuhr and others, and to manifest correlation with the latest insights of depth psychology and psychiatry, even though these may often be vitiated by faulty presuppositions and an almost morbid character may at times attach to the present day interest in these fields.

Christology has been in the forefront of evangelical attention. Many of the key issues of the fundamentalist controversies have been Christological. Under these conditions we are not surprised to find a substantial body of evangelical literature on the person and work of Christ. It will be sufficient here merely to name Kuyper, Berkouwer, Warfield, Vos, W. C. Robinson, H. de Vries, F. J. Hall, Cooke and N. E. Wood in connection with the incarnation and deity of Christ (a composite volume written by ministers of the Reformed Churches of the Netherlands, *Christ the Savior* [1948] may also be mentioned); Orr and Machen on the virgin birth; Orr on the resurrection; Koelling, Berkouwer, Denney, Guillebaud, L. Morris, Pink, Murray and Dabney on the atonement. During this period the kenotic view, so enthusiastically espoused up to 1920, gradually waned and lost almost all support since that time. The two-nature doctrine, which had been the target of heavy criticism, received new attention, although not always wholehearted support. In the doctrine of the atonement the trend has been away from purely subjective views toward more objective approaches, yet short of a doctrine of penal substitutionary satisfaction. The evangelicals have reason to rejoice over these changes, although they have to grant that not all of them have come to pass as a result of their efforts. There is still room for cogent evangelical presentations of the person and work of Christ.

Pneumatology has been the object of particularly ample attention from evangelicals. Beside the major works of Kuyper and Swete, it is fitting to remember the offerings of Koelling, Hepp, Pache, Moule, G. C. Morgan, Griffith-Thomas, Vaughan, Walvoord, Bishop, A. B. Simpson, A. J. Gordon, Stafford, Conner, and a galaxy of popular or devotional works on this theme. Here fits also a composite work by ministers of the Reformed Churches of the Netherlands, *The Holy Ghost* (1949). This is one of the areas in which the most satisfactory coverage has been given by evangelicals in this period.

Soteriology has been treated with only moderate extensiveness. The names of Webb and Berkouwer, each of whom wrote three volumes in this area, perhaps stand foremost, although we should not forget the contributions of Kuyper, Walther, Murray, Chafer and Bishop on grace and salvation in general; of Boehl on justification; of Machen, Moule and Berkhof on faith; of Bavinck and de Groot on regeneration; and of Pink and Warfield on sanctification. There is still a need for scholarly productions on justification and on the new life, especially in relation to current advances in psychology.

Ecclesiology has been very much in the forefront of theological thought in recent years, particularly in connection with ecumenical thinking. The evangelicals have not written extensively in this area: J. J. Bannerman's masterly treatise on *The Church of Christ,* soon to be reprinted, dates back to 1868, Dargan's *Ecclesiology* to 1897, Dana's *Manual of Ecclesiology* in its second edition to 1944. Without wanting to underrate the significant contributions of Schlatter and of the Dutch writers (Kuyper, H. Steen, H. Bouwman, J. Janssen, Sillevis Smitt, the Kampen Theology Faculty), we may well assert that a cogent, scholarly treatment of the evangelical application of biblical principles to the subjects of Christian fellowship and the Church is very much to be desired. In this connection it may be observed that evangelicals frequently differ widely among themselves in this area, and that an attitude of wary suspicion or outspoken opposition toward the ecumenical movement, while not infrequent among fundamentalists, is not invariably present in evangelical circles. On the subject of the means of grace, also very much in the limelight in our day, the evangelicals have produced more amply: Berkouwer's work may be noted here, as well as G. Kramer, E. Smilde, Diermanse, Marcel and Murray on baptism; Moule and Griffith-Thomas on the Lord's Supper. Even so, the evangelical voice could well be heard to advantage in additional scientific treatments of this area.

Eschatology has been in a remarkable way a focus of interest for the evangelicals throughout our period, long before the general attention of the Protestant world had converged on this topic in connection with the Evanston Assembly (1954). The evangelical productivity in this area has been almost phenomenal, particularly with respect to the Second Coming of Our Lord and the accompanying events. It is true that all this literature is not always notable for its scholarship, but there is no dearth of very competent handling of these difficult themes. A. list of the names of those whose contribution is noteworthy would be too long here, but it is imperative to single out for attention the extensive treatises of Kuyper, Dijk and Froom, embracing eschatology as a whole, and to acknowledge the valuable discussions of Sauer, Pache, Reese, Vos, Allis, W. C. Robinson, Berkhof, West, Kellogg, Ladd, Mauro, Kromminga, Eric Lewis and Schilder in connection with particular topics. In spite of this abundance of material, we are still eager to see the appearance of additional works dealing with the various aspects of eschatology in a sane, temperate and scholarly way, without seeking to outline an absurdly detailed program for the future or engaging in other precarious speculations utterly lacking in substantial scriptural support. Inasmuch as the evangelical view of inspiration affords a peculiarly adequate ground for the recognition of the true validity of prophetic parts of Scripture, it appears without further discussion how suitably eschatology may be developed from this vantage point. In fact, the assumption that we have an authoritative disclosure from God is the only ground on which, it would seem, any eschatology may be built which can lay claim to be more than wishful thinking or debatable speculation.

In conclusion it may well be urged that the evangelicals have not been wholly lacking in able scholars who have upheld this position not because of ignorance or naiveté, but in clear recognition of the issues at hand, in competent mastery of the field, and in conscious commitment to the basic principle of supernaturalism. In addition to the particular contributions of many such scholars to special areas of dogmatics, we must here note that the present period has seen the production of bulky and able evangelical systematic theologies, equalling and sometimes exceeding in ability and insight most of similar productions of the past and of competing contemporary theological trends. To name only the most eminent, we list Bavinck, Kuyper, Polman, Berkouwer, Pieper, Hoenecke, Vos, Shedd, Dabney, R. V. Foster, Berkhof, F. J. Hall, Chafer, Miley, Wiley, Lagergren, A. H. Strong, and Conner: this is a list which must indeed appear impressive to any unbiased informed observer. The list could be increased to include at least seventy-three names, if all systematic theologies mentioned in the present article were taken in consideration. The present writer is inclined to doubt whether there be any school of theological thought which could, for that same period, set forth a comparable roster in this area, matching this one in mastery of the subject, in variety of approach, in denominational and geographical diversity, in exegetical skill, in consistency of presentation, in coverage of the relevant literature.

In view of the achievements noted above, one may express some surprise and chagrin at the cavalier manner in which too often the evangelical contributions are dismissed or disregarded by those who do not share the position. Those who feel, by the use of such weighted words as "obscurantists," "repristination," "snake handlers," "bibliolatry," "mechanical inspiration," and so forth, that they have adequately and finally disposed of the whole movement, are themselves hardly giving thereby evidence of real learning or competent scholarship.

The labors of worthy champions of the evangelical cause in the past, far from causing their successors to rest on their laurels, should on the contrary supply a wholesome incentive to press on with earnest zeal and to carry on where they have left off, in a spirit of wholehearted allegiance to God's Word written, in an attitude of fearless honesty, and with the equipment of the best tools and methods which modern scholarship can supply.

ETHICS

Dirk Jellema

Dirk Jellema graduated from Calvin College in 1947, and received his Ph. D. degree from the University of Wisconsin in 1951. He has written numerous articles and book reviews for various journals, and has also translated from the Dutch Abraham Kuyper's Christianity and the Class Struggle *(1950). His research fields include medieval and early modern social and intellectual history, nineteenth century Dutch Calvinism, Protestantism and Capitalism. He is at present professor in the department of social studies at Case Institute of Technology in Cleveland.*

4. *Dirk Jellema:*

ETHICS

WHAT WE ARE to do in the essay which follows is to discuss the current position of evangelical thought in the field of ethics. In order to do this meaningfully, we will consider the rise, dominance, and decline of liberal Protestant ethics; then the more recent emergence of a revival of a Christian ethics; and finally, what contemporary evangelical thought has produced, and the situation it faces.

The term "ethics" can be used in various senses. It can be used loosely, to mean codes of conduct, social customs, and the like; or narrowly, to mean a subdivision of philosophy which deals with values; or broadly, to mean an organized statement of what man should do. We will use the term in this last sense.

"Evangelical" is perhaps also a somewhat ambiguous term. We will use it to mean especially two groups: that group which can be called "fundamentalist," which has its historical background in Reformation Anabaptism, English Non-Conformism, and Wesleyan Methodism; and that group which has held to Reformation Calvinism or Lutheranism. "Neo-evangelical" will then mean the contemporary thought emerging from these two groups which calls for a revitalized evangelical presentation.

We will also consider two other groups which lay some claim to be called orthodox, and which offer a form of Christian ethics as an alternative to liberal ethics: the neo-medieval thinkers of Catholicism and (High) Anglicanism; and the neo-orthodox thinkers who have revolted against liberalism in the name of some major aspects of Reformation thought.

I. ETHICS AND WORLD-OUTLOOK

We have said that "ethics" as used here would mean an organized statement of what man should do. This can be expanded into the following: *ethics is an organized statement, based on a comprehensive world-outlook, of what man should do in his contemporary situation.*

This implies that ethics must be based on a world-outlook, a *Weltanschauung,* and that it takes its basic presuppositions from its parent world-outlook. It means that we can determine what man should do only after we know what man is. Any developed ethics implies the development of a parent world-outlook.

The development of an ethics is part of the development of the parent world-outlook. A *Weltanschauung,* a developed world-outlook, means an ethics. An undeveloped world-outlook will not necessarily have an ethics in our sense. The Greeks of Homer's day had a world-outlook, in a sense; they had made their basic assumptions about the cosmos. But a developed world-outlook came only at a later time. The implications were not worked out until later.

Likewise, the early Church had a world-outlook in a sense. But the development of Christianity into a systematized world-outlook did not come until later. Nor did the development of an ethics in our sense. The Nicene theology was not formulated until three centuries after Christ; and Augustine's *City of God* until four centuries after Christ.

The Bible contains the seeds for a systematized ethics, an ethics which takes up systematically the contemporary problems of man and society. But it took time for these seeds to grow. It was the achievement of the Church Fathers, and again of the Middle Ages, and again of the Reformation, to nurture these seeds, to make them grow into a Christian ethics in our sense. Or, to vary the metaphor, the Bible contains a Christian ethics in the sense that the earth contains treasure: it must be searched for.

The point we are getting at is this—a Christian ethics is an *achievement.* It has to be *worked for.* It is implied in God's Word, it is there in God's Word; but the full implications of God's Word have to be worked out, and worked for.

Hence, those centuries which did this did something which was an achievement. They produced a systematized answer to contemporary ethical problems in terms of Christianity. And this was not an easy thing to do. It has been done perhaps three times in the history of the Church: by the Church Fathers (300-400); by the Scholastics (1200-1300); and by the Reformation (1500-1600). And, perhaps, by Neo-Evangelicalism (1950-).

A Christian ethics, in our sense, is not necessary for salvation. It *is* necessary for a "full-orbed faith." *It is necessary if the full imperative of the Gospel is to be carried out.* And, indeed, the tendency of Christians has always been to try to sidestep the problem of building a Christian ethics. The easy way, the path of least resistance, is to accept whatever non-Christian or semi-Christian ethics happens to dominate the contemporary society.

There are two, or perhaps three, ways in which the church can rationalize its avoidance of a Christian ethics. The first is the way of *separation from society,* and a concentration on building an ethics for a small separate group. This might still perhaps be regarded as taking up the problem of a Christian ethics, in a rather special sense. This was the way followed by medieval monasticism, by some elements in Reformation Anabaptism, and by some elements in fundamentalism. And, for that matter, this might be regarded as a partially valid answer. A Christian ethics for a Christian group is surely better than no Christian ethics for society at large.

Another way is *over-simplification of the Gospel.* The message of Christianity is over-simplified, taken to mean only personal salvation. "We have Christ; what more is needed?" This means, in practice, that the Church concentrates on salvation to the exclusion of Christian ethics; and that the ethics of the contemporary society is simply adopted or avoided. This was the way followed by Christianity during the Dark Ages, and in some respects by what might be called revivalistic Christianity during the hey-day of liberalism. The moral "difference" in the Dark Ages lay in pious attention to relics, ostentatious external piety; in the twentieth century, on abstinence from smoking, card-playing, motion pictures, and other so-called worldly amusements.

A third way is *formal repetition* of previous formulations of Christian ethics. This has the effect of evading the problems of a contemporary society by giving a series of irrelevant answers. Thus late medieval Catholicism evaded the application of Christian ethical principles to the rising bourgeois society by formalistic repetition of the answers developed for an earlier set of problems. And thus Protestant orthodoxy evaded the application of Christian ethical principles to the problems raised by the Industrial Revolution.

"What is the most effective type of economic system?," asked the young man. "That is a worldly question," answered his father. This illustrates *separation.* "What is the most effective type of economic system?," asked the young man. "God is Love," answered his father. This illustrates *over-simplification.* "What is the most effective type of economic system?," asked the young man. "Arabian steeds are the best kind of horses," answered his father. This illustrates *formalism,* giving valid answers to a set of questions different from those being asked.

A society where men are saved but where the society is barbarian is possible, and has existed. A society where men are saved but where the ethics of the society is non-Christian is possible, and has existed. A Christianity which is orthodox but which simply accepts in practice the ethics of the contemporary society, rather than working out a Christian ethics, is possible and even likely. It can hardly be called, however, the best kind of orthodox Christianity.

II. THE ETHICS OF THE LIBERAL WORLD-OUTLOOK.

Man, in his contemporary mid-twentieth-century society, is looking for an ethics. This fact gives orthodox Christianity an opportunity it has not had for some centuries: the opportunity to develop a Christian ethics which has a good chance of being accepted by a contemporary society.

How and why has this situation arisen? In order to understand the current opportunity which orthodox Christianity has, and the challenge which it faces in the field of ethics, we must next consider the rise, domination, and failure of liberalism.

The dominant world-view, and the dominant ethics, during the past three centuries has been what we call liberalism. This was a world-outlook and an ethics which was humanist, secular, and bourgeois. It stressed man, reason, and property. Around 1650, it began to replace the older Medieval-Reformation ethics and world-outlook. And by 1950, it was almost everywhere in the process of being replaced.

The basic assumptions of liberalism took this course: (1) Man is essentially good, and evil is due to lack of freedom to develop man's natural goodness. (2) The universe is governed by rational laws, which can be discovered by man's reason, his most important characteristic. (3) The moral life of society, and of the individual, is governed by rational laws, which can be discovered by reason.

These basic beliefs have implications. They can be used as the basis for developed ethics. The intellectual history of the past three centuries is in large part the story of the working out of these implications (i.e., the development of a liberal ethics) in various fields. Though, from the Christian point of view, the basic beliefs of liberalism are incorrect, the application of these beliefs to various fields did produce much that was valuable, notably in science and technology.

During the first five generations of liberalism (1650-1750), inspired by the scientific synthesis of Newton, these ideas were outlined and expressed, and became the property of the educated classes. During the next five generations (1750-1850), the implications were worked out in detail, and the liberal ethics became important enough to inspire a series of revolutions (American Revolution, French Revolution, Revolution of 1830, Revolution of 1848). The next five generations (1850-1950) saw, first, the apparent triumph of liberal ethics as the determining force in society's behavior; and, after World War I, the increasing breakdown of liberal ethics as a vital and dynamic force.

Liberalism, by and large, was not anti-religious, although there was always a "left wing" which held to agnosticism or atheism. It was opposed, however, to a Christian ethics in our sense. The real ethics of society and individual, the basis for decisions of importance, the real molder of moral codes, was not to be Christianity but liberalism. Apart from that requirement, orthodox Christianity was tolerated, and in many cases, cheerfully mixed with a liberal ethics.

More typical, however, was the effort to apply reason to religion; to emerge with a "reasonable Christianity." This produced the deism of men like Jefferson, Franklin, Voltaire and others. Said Voltaire, in support of this type of liberal religion: "Every man of sense, every good man, ought to hold the [old-fashioned] Christian sect in horror. The great name of Deist, which is not sufficiently revered, is the only name one ought to take. The only gospel one ought to read is the great book of Nature, written by the hand of God and sealed with his seal. The only religion that ought to be professed is the religion of worshipping God and being a good man" (Cited from J. H. Randall, *The Making of the Modern Mind,* 2nd ed., Boston, 1940, p. 202).

Christ was regarded, by deists such as Voltaire and Jefferson, as a great man, a great teacher. The basic outlook of nineteenth-century religious liberalism was already there. It only remained to apply reason systematically and carefully to religion. This was done by Hume, by the German higher critics, and by many others. The romantic movement, with its stress on emotion as good, changed the picture somewhat: Christ became associated with tenderness, mildness, sentimentality.

Liberalism felt, in brief, that religion is fine, but not a Christian ethics. God, in liberalism, occupied a position somewhat similar to that of the Negro in Mississippi: his co-existence was tolerated so long as he stayed in his place.

There was little room for Christian ethics in liberalism, and not much room for the Christian God. He could, if one wished, be tacked on as an afterthought to a list of affirmations; but he was of little *real* importance. If there was a real God, he was not the Christian God, but something like the rational mathematician of deism, or the pantheistic World Spirit of Hegel. And, to many liberals, there seemed no need for a God at all. The declension from orthodoxy can be charted: in Europe, Pascal's Christian God, Hegel's World Spirit, Haeckel's Materialism; in the United States, Jonathan Edwards' Christian God, Ralph Waldo Emerson's Transcendental Spirit, John Dewey's Naturalism.

The effect of liberalism, then, was not so much atheism or agnosticism as this: *Christianity's sphere of relevance constantly shrunk.* It lost more and more areas of social and individual life to a non-Christian ethics.

Even those groups which retained some dogmas confined them more and more in a vacuum. Christian ethics, in our sense, became a thing of the past.

The development of a liberal ethics took time. The implications of the basic liberal beliefs were worked out gradually. And these implications were slowly applied to actual practice and institutions. The idea that liberal ethical principles demanded that the individual business man should be free to buy and sell as he pleased, for example, had been stated by 1650, and worked out in detail by 1750; yet it was not for another century that legislative reforms carrying out this idea became general. We might examine briefly the ethical implications of the liberal outlook, remembering that each of the ideas given below developed gradually, and in a much more complex way than can be given here.

What is man? A rational being, we have said. What should govern his actions? Obviously, reason. What general truths about ethical actions can reason give us? Here various answers are possible. Early liberalism retained the idea that there was a realm of natural moral law which could be discovered by reason, and which was outside of man (i.e., that an objective non-theistic realm of values exist). Reason could prove these laws, and give us data about them, just as the Greek philosophers had been able to do in the days of Plato. But this idea of natural moral law proved increasingly difficult to maintain in the face of sceptical criticism. There was, in liberalism's second stage, a tendency to retreat to values which exist only in humanity, in man-as-a-whole, but which are binding on the individual. After 1850, philosophical analysis showed that this position was also difficult to maintain. There was an increasingly desperate search for something else to ground values in—the evolutionary process, the pragmatic results of actions, the welfare of the race, and so forth.

One of the most popular general systems of ethics (popular perhaps because of its superficiality) was the Utilitarianism of Bentham and Mill. This attempted to base ethical actions not on an objective moral law, but rather on the desire of every individual to gain his own happiness. Each individual should be left free to do this (unless he interferes with the similar freedom of others), and if each man looks out for his own individual welfare, the general welfare would automatically benefit also.

How should liberal ethics apply to economic systems? Here again, reason gives the answers, said early liberalism. Economics is governed by rational laws (supply and demand, and so forth), which reason can discover. The best economic system is that which protects the right of every man to be free to act according to his reason. This means that every man must be free to make contracts. The rational laws which govern economics should be allowed to operate unhampered by interference by government or church or feudal institutions or artificial barriers of any kind. The less desirable implications were not yet apparent, namely, that every worker is free to contract to work fifteen hours a day, that the people are free to contract to live under a dictator, and so on. A whole series of legislative and social reforms was projected from this standpoint of reason and liberty. The ethical duty of the individual business man is primarily to operate according to the rational law governing economic life.

Man according to the liberal view, which implied a denial of original sin, is basically good. He needs only freedom to be able to express this goodness. Past environment has held back his use of reason. Once these restrictions have been removed, utopia will be in sight. Man can progress, and progress rapidly. (The liberal idea of progress, shared by many evangelical churchgoers today, actually implies a denial of original sin.) Reason, through science, has made possible more progress in a few centuries than man has achieved in all his previous history. Progress can be defined in terms of increased use of reason, or, as an approximation, a higher standard of material welfare.

What are the ethical goals of the state? It must promote reason, freedom, and property. Education in reason is basic to these goals. Education is therefore the function of the state, and education should be education in reason. In England and America, where liberalism usually appeared as a watered-down Christianity, this objective did not cause the trouble it did on the Continent, where it became a major issue between church and state. And protection of property, which reason shows us is necessary for freedom, is the function of the state. Apart from this, the state, said classical liberal ethics, should keep hands off (laissez-faire): the best state was that which governs least. Later liberalism shifted this emphasis somewhat; by 1900, the best state was that which preserved freedom by extending property to the masses, i.e., raising the material standard of living.

What group has the ethical right to govern the state? The group most concerned with the ethical goals of the state. The first liberal century (1650-1750) thought this was a rational elite ("enlightened despotism"); the second liberal century (1750-1850) answered that it was the men of property, by means of a parliament and a restricted franchise; the third liberal century (1850-1950) felt that it should be the educated masses ("mass democracy"), through universal suffrage.

What is the ethical basis for the state's power? A rational contract between ruler and ruled. Is revolution ethically permissible? Whenever this rational contract has been broken by the ruler. What was marriage? A rational contract between free individuals. What was the ethical principle underlying law? The protection of rational contracts. What did management owe labor? Rational contracts (cf. R. Tawney's *Religion and the Rise of Capitalism* for a sketch of the liberal displacement of the

Medieval-Reformation outlook). What was the ideal figure, the hero, in a society dominated by liberal ethics? Not the saint, but the business man; not the missionary, but the engineer.

What is society? A collection of individuals. What are individuals? Men who have reason. What is the ethical basis for any social institution? Reason. What is an individual's main right? Freedom. What is a nation's right? Freedom, self-determination. So tangential to this outlook was the Creator-Redeemer God that already in the nationalistic spirit of the 1800s the substitution of state-worship for God-worship could be detected.

Hobach summed it all up: " 'Oh thou,' cries Nature to man, 'who, following the impulse I have given you, during your whole existence incessantly tend towards happiness, do not resist my sovereign law. . . . Dare, then, to affranchise yourself from the trammels of superstition, my self-conceited, pragmatic rival, who mistakes my rights. . . . It is in my empire alone that true liberty reigns' " (cited from Randall, *op. cit.,* 278). Or, as Condorcet put it a little later, in George Washington's time: "What a picture of the human race, freed from its chains, removed from the empire of chance as from that of the enemies of its progress, advancing with a firm and sure step in the pathway of truth, of virtue and of happiness, is presented to the liberal philosopher. . . . It is in contemplating this vision that he receives the reward of his efforts for the progress of reason, for the defence of liberty" *(ibid.,* p. 384).

By 1850, liberal ethics had apparently won out; it had reached the position where it molded the ethics of society, state, and individual. Its success was due to two things: first, the previous decline of Christian ethics, in the years before 1650; second, the fact that liberalism seemed to *work.* Had not the marvelous advances of science, based on a belief in rational law, shown what reason could do? Had not humanity made progress since the days when Calvin burned Servetus, or when Wesley believed in witchcraft? Had not liberalism given parliamentary government to millions through the application of liberal ethical standards to government? Had not liberal ethics applied to economics produced a dynamic capitalism? Had not Christianity, therefore, been shown to be irrelevant to man's important decisions—those touching the social concerns? Men still believe in God, in 1850. Some, indeed many, are still Bible-believing Christians. But not in the old sense. Men no longer think of basing society on Christianity, of making political decisions on the basis of Christian presuppositions, or indeed of making important personal decisions on the basis of Christian ethics. God on Sunday, liberalism the rest of the week—except for small taboos.

But at the very time when liberalism was settling down to enjoy the triumph of liberal ethics, the basic beliefs of liberalism, the bases for liberal ethics, were coming under attack.

These difficulties became apparent first to liberal intellectuals. It became increasingly clear, after 1850, that reason could be used to dethrone reason. Rational moral law had already come under attack, and the development of Marxian Socialism cast doubt on the validity of Utilitarianism by following its premises to disturbing conclusions. Darwinian evolution, which was at first hailed as a scientific vindication of laissez-faire economic capitalism, seemed on second thought to justify a Nietzschean Superman. (Cf. R. Hofstadter, *Social Darwinism in American Thought,* 1944, available in Beacon paperbacks. William Jennings Bryan's *In His Image* shows an intuitive grasp of the potentially anti-democratic implications of Darwinism—an intuitive grasp unsupported by knowledge and understanding, unfortunately.) Freud and his theories of psychoanalysis seemed to show that rational man was a figment of the imagination, and that man was governed by a set of irrational drives. Pavlov, Watson and others produced evidence which seemed to show that, even worse, man is merely a set of automatic conditioned reflexes. And, finally, developments in the field of subatomic physics seemed to shatter the very citadel of the liberal outlook, objective natural law.

It also became increasingly clear, after 1850, that liberal ethics did *not* seem to work in many fields. Freedom of contract seemed to have produced a society where a new aristocracy ruled—the rich. Education in reason produced a generation which read tabloid journals rather than liberal economists. Freedom of self-determination among nations produced a nationalism which often took anti-liberal forms. The rational contract between management and labor produced working men who turned to Marxism. The machine produced unemployment.

By 1900, a modified liberalism had emerged, a "welfare liberalism." The ethical purpose of the state was regarded not as freedom but as security in a material sense. A related movement was the liberal "social gospel," where (for the last time) something of the former dynamic of the liberal outlook was captured.

The generation after 1900 was the last generation which lived in a calm belief in liberal ethics. That generation marked the twilight of liberalism though few realized it at the time. The basic assumptions of the liberal outlook were under attack by the ablest thinkers of the day. And, despite the social gospel, a slightly modified liberalism had been unable to cope with the underlying problems of the Age of the Machine.

Liberal complacency was shattered, in Europe, by the first World War; and in America, by the great depression. Liberal ethics were regarded more and more as old-fashioned. In Italy, Germany, and Russia, liberalism was denounced as reactionary superstition as new faiths struggled for supremacy. By 1950, in Western Europe, the once-great liberal political parties were reduced to impotence, and liberal ethics regarded as Victorian nonsense. By 1950, in the American religious scene, the voice of an unreconstructed liberal Henry Nelson Wieman sounded like a voice from the past. Liberalism had an air of unreality about it in Europe, and an air of old-fashioned respectability in America.

The dream of Condorcet seemed, to many, to have evaporated on the bloody fields of Flanders, or to have vanished in the dreary bread-lines a decade later.

III. CHRISTIAN ORTHODOXY IN THE LIBERAL SOCIETY

What was Christian orthodoxy doing during the three centuries of liberal ethics and liberal society? It did not vanish. It accomplished much in certain fields: the cultivation of personal piety, the development of missions, the promotion of revivals. In some of these areas, it did much more than Medieval-Reformation Christian orthodoxy had done. But, at the same time, it gradually gave up its earlier claim that Christian ethics was the basis for the real decisions of society and the individual.

The century from 1650 to 1750, when liberal ethics was being formulated in broad outline, was marked in orthodox circles by an increasing sterility. The controversies of the 1500s were debated over again and again, and the ethical questions involved in the rapid development of a modern European society ignored. When liberalism was attacked (as when Voetius attacked Descartes), the attack was blind and ineffective.

The century from 1750 to 1850, in which liberalism fought its way to apparent trimph in European Protestant churches, produced various ways of rationalizing the failure of orthodoxy to build a contemporary Christian ethics. One reaction was separation from society; this was in general the Catholic answer during this period. The Popes contented themselves with hurling anathemas at liberalism, and warning the faithful to refuse to participate in the liberal society which had emerged. Another reaction was evasion through formalism and sterile repetition of a Christian ethic designed to meet the problems of three centuries before. This reaction can be seen, for example, in New England Puritanism during this period. A third reaction was over-simplification of the Gospel message, a limiting of Christianity to a message of personal salvation. This can be seen in German pietism and American frontier revivalism. Some exceptions can be found—Alexander Campbell's interest in political thought; the inspiration of Abolitionism in part by revivalism—but the generalization will stand.

There was a tendency in this third type, the orthodox reaction to the increasing dominance of liberal ethics, to make Christianity a matter of the emotions and feelings rather than of the whole man. And it is curious that, at roughly the same time, the early 1800s, some liberal Christians were resorting to the same approach, as a defense against attacks by liberal agnostics. Schleiermacher, with his liberal Christianity based on feeling and emotion, is in some ways close to a backwoods American revivalist of the same period. The differences are due to the different faiths which they use emotion to defend. The similarities are due to this, that both have given up a Christian ethics.

The century from 1850 to 1950 was characterized by the apparent triumph of liberal Christianity in America as well as in Europe; and, after 1914 and 1929, its decline. In America, with men like Henry Ward Beecher, liberal Christianity was at first tied in with an ardent defense of laissez-faire liberal capitalism. Later, as the need for a revised liberal ethics in the field of economic life became clear, liberal Christianity was tied in closely with that last flowering of liberal idealism, the social gospel.

In Europe, by the last half of the nineteenth century, the first faint signs of a revival of a Christian ethics were beginning to appear. Isolated attempts to revive a Christian ethics were made from divergent standpoints by Kierkegaard, Grundtvig, Kuyper, Maurice and others. Their main importance, however, was that of precursors to the events of the twentieth century. In America, orthodoxy continued to evade the problem. Frontier revivalism merged into fundamentalism around 1900. Men like Dwight L. Moody and Billy Sunday gave their talents to revival campaigns which did much to keep the Gospel alive; but they did not take up Christian ethics in our sense.

Another type of orthodox reaction, that of "handing down the faith of the fathers," found notable champions also. Men like Charles Hodge, B. B. Warfield, W. G. T. Shedd, and others produced notable defenses of the Reformation outlook. So far as sheer erudition went, they were a match for any liberal of the day. But they had little success in overcoming the dominance of liberal ethics. This was due in large part to their failure to develop a Christian ethics which would mold the contemporary society. They concentrated their efforts on "holding fast," which in practice often meant taking a firm stand on issues which were vital no longer. One can search the turn-of-the-century "giants" in vain for any examination of the ethical problems raised by the emergence of mass industry—surely the main social force of their age. One can hardly avoid the impression that the giants of orthodoxy around 1900 had done a magnificent job of keeping intact a system which was oriented to the ethical problems of the sixteenth century. (Hodge and Warfield, at least, though, held fast their inheritance, an achievement unduplicated after their era.)

In the thought of many of the age's leading figures, a marriage of Christian dogma and liberal ethics can be seen. And though the marriage partners might seem to many to be at least superficially compatible, the marriage was hardly one made in heaven. Charlemagne had held to Christian dogma, but acted as a barbarian; in much the same way, the nineteenth-century millionaires held to orthodox dogma, but acted as liberal business men. Society, from one point of view, was becoming dangerously schizoid. The writers of the day (cf. Mark Twain's later writings or a novel such as Melville's *The Confidence Man*) discerned this more quickly than the theologians.

The last attempt, a desperate attempt, to stop liberal Christianity in the United States occurred in the 1920s in the fundamentalist-modernist controversy. The attempt was too little and too late. With no system of Christian ethics available, the fundamentalist protest was regarded by society at large as irrelevant to the trends of the day. The attempt is worth sketching (cf. N. F. Furniss, *The Fundamentalist Controversy 1918-1931,* and E. A. White's more sympathetic evaluation in *The Pacific Spectator,* 1951).

In 1910, a group of evangelicals attempted an intellectually respectable attack on liberal Protestantism. R. A. Torrey, E. Y. Mullins, Philip Mauro and others collaborated in writing *The Fundamentals,* which called for adherence to the basic Christian doctrines in the face of liberal aggression. "Fundamentalist" groups soon began rallying around this banner.

After the first World War, fundamentalist leaders began to stir up sentiment and call for action, centering their attacks on the teaching of evolution in the public schools. The more scholarly and moderate voices (Mullins, J. Gresham Machen) were soon drowned out, and crusaders like W. B. Riley, John Roach Stratton, A. C. Dixon and others began beating the drums of emotion. The aged Bryan was chosen leader of the crusade. In the South, the crusade gained much popular support, and politicians were forced to reckon with it. Moderation vanished in the crusade; in Kentucky, fundamentalists forced the dismissal of a teacher who taught that the world was round, thus "contradicting Scripture" (see *New York Times,* January 27, 1922); in South Carolina, the Governor trumpeted that no school book should even "print pictures of a monkey and a man on the same page"!

The high point of the attack on liberal religion came in the Scopes trial of 1925. But it was a defeat, not a triumph. Bryan, humiliated, died soon afterwards, and there was no one else of sufficient stature to lead a united fundamentalism. Fundamentalist leaders fell to squabbling among themselves, and the country lost interest in the whole controversy. By 1929, fundamentalism had dropped into an attitude of separation from the main trends in society.

The dream of some of the abler leaders in the movement had been to start a chain of Christian colleges, to produce men who could fight liberalism on equal terms. This dream, by 1929, had also failed. The ill-fated attempt to build a Christian university out of Des Moines College was all too typical. Indeed, moderate fundamentalism all during the Twenties was a rather lonely position. And inside the fundamentalist colleges, the conception of a Christian ethics in our sense was lacking: divinity students at Northern Baptist Theological Seminary, for example, could for many years enroll in either economics or ethics.

In the late Twenties, J. Gresham Machen, on whom the mantle of Hodge and Warfield had fallen, made a last effort to preserve orthodoxy in the Presbyterian Church U. S. A., where Princeton Seminary was falling into the hands of liberal Protestants. Machen avoided the term fundamentalism, although in doctrinal matters he shared its leading tenets. Machen was able to show that liberal Protestantism was not orthodoxy. But, since no orthodox ethics was available, Machen's attempt to reverse the course of events was doomed to failure. (The fact that Machen's writings received respectful notice from Walter Lippman and H. L. Mencken perhaps indicates what evangelicalism might have been able to do if a real Christian ethics had been available.)

The founding of Westminster Seminary in 1929 by Machen and like-minded associates can be thought of as a retreat to the last bulwarks of defense: orthodoxy had now lost most of its former territory. Indeed, to an observer in 1929, it would have seemed that orthodoxy in the United States, even using the term in its widest sense, was not only sterile, but dying.

This proved to be a false impression. A generation after 1929, the liberalism which had seemingly won out in every field was itself sterile, and threatened by a revival of Christian ethics.

IV. THE NEW ORTHODOXIES

The revival of a Christian ethics, an "organized statement of what man should do in his contemporary situation, based on Christianity as a world-outlook," was carried on in terms of two approaches in the period between the wars. The first might be termed "neo-medieval," and the second is usually called "neo-orthodox." Since World War II, another approach is beginning to be worked out: the neo-evangelical, based on the evangelical foundations which seemed so nearly demolished in 1929. One main difference between neo-evangelicalism and the older evangelicalism is precisely this, that neo-evangelicalism recognizes the need for a Christian ethics in our sense.

The impact of the revival of Christian ethics by the neo-medieval and neo-orthodox thinkers between the wars has been fairly great. It is far too soon to say that Christian ethics will replace liberal ethics; other aggressive contenders are in the ring also. But Christian ethics (of one variety or another) now is generally recognized as a contender. And that is something which has not been true for centuries.

The task of working out a Christian ethics is a complex one, and the summaries which follow should be recognized as no more than summaries. It may sound simple to say that "man is a person, not an individual," as Christian ethics does say, in contrast to liberal ethics in its heyday. But to give this statement *meaning* in terms of contemporary thought is a difficult thing, involving some analysis of, say, Freudian psycholanalytic thought, sociological discoveries of the past century, Marxian dialectic, post-Kantian philosophy, and the like. Until this is done (and it has been done by neo-medievalism and neo-orthodoxy both), such a statement will be true but trite; it will have no contemporary meaning; it can not be called a meaningful contribution to Christian ethics.

And once this has been done, and meaning given to the statement, there still remain further problems. How can this meaning be *communicated* to contemporary society? And, how can this thought be expressed in terms of legislation, social institutions, and personal codes? What does this now meaningful statement *imply* with regard to current problems?

"Man is a person, not an individual," we have said. Fine; and suppose we know what this *means;* what then should be *done*? Suppose man's person-ality implies love for one's neighbor as a basic component of man's life. Fine; but what does this mean in terms of contemporary mass society? How can I show love for my neighbor when I have no contact with him? And so on and so forth. Does man's person-ality imply that urban concentrations are harmful to spiritual life? That the assembly line deadens the soul? That the goals of labor unions should be more than material benefits? That a Christian business will be run along very different lines than an ordinary business? That a Christian choice of vocation should depend on the opportunities it gives for love of one's neighbor? That small farms are better than big farms because they help develop personality more? That our farm program should be based on this? That a man should be willing to give up a high-paying job in Chicago because urban life stultifies man's soul? And so on and so forth. We do not at this point imply a necessary answer one way or the other, but specify questions of the kind a relevant Christian ethics must answer. This particular line of questioning has produced some significant works on Christian ethics as it relates simply to one problem: the person in a technological society.

Every statement in the summary which follows can lead to similar lines of questioning. This is how liberal ethics was developed; this is how neo-medieval and neo-orthodox ethics were developed (and are developing); and this is the way neo-evangelical ethics will have to develop.

The *basic* assumptions or beliefs (or truths) which underlie a Christian ethics are already given, in the orthodox creeds, or in the Bible as the inspired rule of faith and practice. These are accepted by the neo-medieval approach and also (with considerable qualification) by the neo-orthodox approach. The basic outlook, however, is on a universe very different from the liberal universe. Man is not essentially good, but essentially evil, in need of a radical conversion. Not rational laws, but a personal God, determines how the universe runs. Man is man not because he can think but because he is in touch with the trans-natural, the eternal realm of God. The task of the state is to carry out God's revealed will. The task of the individual is to glorify God by obeying His will. And so on: the basic outlook is familiar enough to the readers of this essay.

The Neo-Medieval Approach

One approach to the problem of developing a Christian ethics is taken by two groups, the Roman Catholic and the Anglican. It may be called "neo-medieval" because the Christian Middle Ages is taken as the most promising model for a contemporary approach. Both groups stress the medieval synthesis of faith and reason, the medieval trust in reason as a handmaiden of faith, and the medieval reliance on hierarchy and tradition. And both groups took up the problem of building a Christian ethics which would have meaning in modern society.

The revival of a Catholic Christian ethics as an important intellectual force in the modern world goes back to Vincent Pecci, better known as Pope Leo XIII, in the 1880's. Leo did three things of great importance in this respect. First, he called for a revival of the thought of Thomas Aquinas in modern terms, as the philosophical basis for a Catholic ethics in our sense. Second, he attacked the basic presuppositions of liberalism and pointed out the dependence of liberal ethics on these presuppositions. Third, he asked Catholics to participate in the political life of liberal countries, by means of Catholic political parties, rather than separating themselves from the liberal state. Fourth, he denounced both laissez-faire capitalism and Marxian socialism as false and un-Christian, because of their acceptance of liberal ethics.

The papal encyclical *Rerum Novarum* (On Capital and Labor), released in 1893, is perhaps the manifesto of the Catholic attempt to build a contemporary Christian ethics.

Leo's encyclicals were greeted with enthusiasm by Catholic intellectuals. The Church at large responded slowly and with only gradually thawing indifference.

Despite general Catholic apathy, action was begun. Catholic universities began the task of working out Thomas's philosophy in contemporary terms. Catholic political parties, with Catholic political programs, were started, Catholic primary and secondary education was extended. Catholic trade unions were started. Canada today has a separate Catholic trade union in Quebec, while in the United States, where the unions are regarded as "neutral," Catholic cell groups, united in the ACTU (Association of Catholic Trade Unionists) have been formed within the unions.

By 1914, a Catholic "renaissance" was beginning to gather momentum. Writers like Peguy and Bloy and Claudel were expressing dogma in terms of contemporary literature. Etienne Gilson and Jacques Maritain and many others were emerging as the leaders of neo-Thomism, couched in modern terms, and providing an intellectually respectable rival of liberal philosophies, and a philosophical basis for a Christian ethics.

In the era of armed peace (1919-1939), despite the triumph of another anti-liberalism (i.e., totalitarianism) in Germany and Italy, the movement went forward. Neo-Thomism became a force to reckon with in philosophical circles. By the second World War, a "second generation" had come forward; philosophers trained under Gilson and Maritain continued the development of neo-Thomism; Catholic writers like Graham Greene, Evelyn Waugh, Georges Bernanos, François Mauriac, and others, pictured a vital Christian ethics as the only answer to the problems of the twentieth century.

After the second World War, the United States began to feel the impact of the revived Catholic ethics. Philosophers like Von Hildebrand, popularizers like Fulton J. Sheen, writers like Thomas Merton, all in their own way expressed the Christian ethics which had been developed since Leo XIII called for a vital and relevant restatement.

The related revival of the medieval outlook within the Anglican church also has a historical background in the nineteenth century. The attempts of John Henry Newman and Frederick Maurice to work out a meaningful alternative to liberalism perhaps mark its beginning. Newman attacked many of the basic liberal assumptions, while Maurice was interested in attempting a Christian social ethics. Maurice's "Christian socialism," with its emphasis on cooperation rather than competition, has greatly influenced later developments in Anglican social ethics. Around 1900, T. E. Hulme was attacking liberalism as a "false theology," and pointed out the basic error of liberalism—the belief in man's natural goodness, which implied a denial of the need for salvation.

During the armed peace (1919-1939), an important body of Anglican thought was developed, much of it closely connected with Christian ethics. The expatriate American, T. S. Eliot, emerged in the Twenties as a major poet, and one whose poems (after his conversion) are attempts to communicate the meaning of Christian dogma, and Christian ethics to an extent, in the forms of contemporary poetry. Eliot's *The Hollow Men* (1925) would perhaps do as well as anything for a manifesto of Anglican neo-medievalism.

Eliot soon was joined by other figures: Dorothy Sayers, Wyston Hugh Auden, C. S. Lewis, and many others. All were interested in the problem of *communication* of dogma and ethics through literature. Lewis's *Screwtape Letters* is perhaps the best known result of this concern.

Meanwhile, men like M. B. Reckitt, William Temple, and others were following in the footsteps of Maurice and producing a significant body of work dealing with Christian ethics in society. The Malvern Conference (1941) showed that a closely argued alternative to liberal social ethics had emerged.

Since the second World War, the influence of Anglican neo-medievalism has increased. In America, philosophers like John Wild, and popularizers such as Chad Walsh, are not only transmitting but also adding to the work done in England.

Neo-Medieval Ethics

Neo-Thomism, and the Catholic approach generally, and the Anglican approach generally, are orthodox in the sense of accepting the orthodox *creeds* as statements of truth. The basic beliefs of any orthodox Christian —as summed up in the Apostles' Creed, say—are accepted. Beyond that, too, the general approach is the same, though there are differences between Gilson and Eliot, or Maritain and Temple, and so on. The point of departure is the Christian Middle Ages, rather than the related but different Protestant Reformation.

This means that there is a greater trust in reason (understood in the Christian rather than the liberal sense) than there is in most thinkers of the Reformation. Reason for the neo-medievalist is not autonomous reason; it is a gift of God, dependent upon God, and tied in with the Logos. Yet reason, even detached from faith, can give us truth in morality—up to a point. Reason can take us so far, and then faith is needed. The tendency is to view Christianity as a fulfillment and completion of what reason can tell us, rather than as a transvaluator of values. Revelation adds to reason; reason can approach the truth; reason can get us on the road to Christianity.

Thus a distinction is made between reason and faith, natural and supernatural, secular and sacred. But in each case the latter is viewed as the fulfillment of the former rather than, say, the sole normative realm, or an opposed realm, or an unrelated realm. Reason, natural and secular things: these are not evil but relative goods, which point to faith, to supernatural and sacred things.

Likewise, salvation tends to be thought of in terms of coming closer to God. The Logos made flesh is the fulfillment and completion of the Logos which has always lighted man's ways. Christ as the God-Man, rather than Christ as the Sacrificial Lamb, attracts the major share of attention.

Man, though reason is an important part of him, is not the rational individual that classic liberalism pictured. He is a rational *person;* he has a soul. He is not naturally good, but in need of salvation. Evil is distance from God, alienation from God. A reconciliation is possible only through faith. Thus the real goal, the ultimate goal of man, is to know God. Many proximate goals are, however, part of the natural order and can be discovered by reason. Plato discoursed on justice, after all. This natural moral law rests on and depends on the will of God. It cannot exist alone.

Society is not a rational contract, but an organic whole. The state's ethical duties are moral, to carry out the will of God as revealed in natural law. The church deals with the supernatural sphere especially, and is independent of the state. When society is made up solely of Christians, as in the Middle Ages, the lines which separate church and state are drawn with more difficulty, but in a "mixed society," as is the case today, this formula stands. Society is made up not so much of individuals as of *groups,* the most basic of which (in the natural realm) is the family. Other groups are ranged in hierarchial order, up to the state.

Society, if it is to follow a Christian ethics, must reject both the main varieties of liberal social ethics, laissez-faire capitalism and Marxian socialism. Christianity teaches cooperation rather than competition.[1] Labor and capital are both organic groups within society. They should cooperate, and cooperate meaningfully. Hence the *Mittbestimmungsrecht* laws of post-war Germany, put through by the Catholic party and the Catholic trade unions, providing for union representatives to cooperate on management decisions, i.e., have a voice in making them. The Dutch Calvinist trade unions, incidentally, have backed similar legislation, so that the social thought behind the laws is perhaps not specifically Catholic. The common aim of all such groups should be the general welfare of the society, this general welfare being understood in moral as well as material terms.

Christianity and culture are closely related, as are faith and reason. Just as faith implies reason, so Christianity implies culture. The natural must be used in the service of the supernatural, and hence culture must be used in the service of Christianity.

That, then, is a brief and over-simplified summary of some of the main attitudes of neo-medieval ethics. We have next to consider the neo-orthodox movement. This can also be divided into two groups: neo-orthodoxy properly so-called (Karl Barth, Emil Brunner, Reinhold Niebuhr); and the related "neo-Lutheran" approach of Anders Nygren, Nels Ferré, Gustaf Aulén, and others.

---

[1] This does not imply that capitalism is necessarily unethical and unchristian, but simply that it must be "under God" to be neither. Nor does the fact that modern socialism makes a cliché of "cooperation" certify that it supplies the ideal or preferential framework for economic life.—ED.

The Neo-Orthodox Approach

The neo-orthodox approach includes a number of thinkers who have taken up the task of building a meaningful Christian ethics based on this approach. They have these characteristics in common. First, they are in revolt against liberalism. Second, they find their "orthodoxy" not in the Middle Ages but in the Reformation. Third, they stress those elements (or, indeed, accept only those elements) of the Reformation which accord with the approach and insights of contemporary dialectical or existential philosophies.

Neo-orthodoxy emerged first in Europe, where the crucial date which marked the end of liberalism's dominance was 1914. It came somewhat later to the United States, where the crucial date was 1929. If a "manifesto" for each of these would have to be chosen, Karl Barth's *Römerbrief* (1919) and Reinhold Niebuhr's *Moral Man and Immoral Society* (1932) would do as well as any.

Barth, with a prophetic vigor, called for a return to the realistic insights of the Reformation regarding sin and the terrible condition of godless man, and scathingly denounced the shallow naïveté of liberalism. He was followed by others, notably Emil Brunner. And, especially in Scandinavia, a return to Luther was under way; theologians influenced by the rediscovery of the "first existentialist," Kierkegaard, began to wonder whether Luther was not more contemporary than liberalism.

Niebuhr's manifesto in 1932 was followed by a series of attacks on liberalism, and a fruitful study of the problems of a Christian ethics. The American neo-orthodoxy, also, stressed the sinful condition of man, and the need for a confrontation of God, Reality. As it gained strength, it gained converts; and after World War II, a "second generation" appeared, men trained under or influenced by Niebuhr and other neo-orthodox leaders.

Neo-orthodoxy (using the term in the narrow sense, now) looked back to certain aspects of Calvin's thought. The neo-Lutheran movement looked back to Luther, whom it pictured as a Kierkegaardian rebel against medieval formalism. Luther's dualistic contrast between nature and grace, sacred and secular, faith and reason, was accepted. Nygren developed Luther's notion of God's love into a treatment of *agape* (disinterested love) and *eros* (self-interested love) which he took as a distinction of basic importance in Christian ethics. Ferré brought many of the neo-Lutheran emphases to this country.

Neo-Orthodox Ethics

Just as Thomism (and neo-Thomism) adopted much of the philosophical framework of Aristotle as the best framework for justifying Christian ethics, so neo-orthodoxy went in debt to the existentialist philosophy (or philosophies) of the years of the armed peace. There is much of Heidegger and Jaspers in Niebuhr, just as there is much of Aristotle in Gilson. Mention might be made also of Gabriel Marcel, the Catholic existentialist, an exception to the general trend of Catholic philosophers, since his exposition is much more along neo-orthodox than neo-Thomist lines. By both traditions, of course, philosophy is used critically, and invoked in the service of Christianity.

Neo-orthodox ethics begins with man as sinner, and concentrates on man as sinner. Man is, by himself, lost: just as Calvin and Luther proclaimed (and also existentialism). He is always in a state of *anxiety*, which he tries in vain to hide. His reason cannot help him. Reason is corrupted and ineffective. He cannot reach God; God must reach him. God speaks to man through revelation, which cannot become effective until man *encounters* it, grapples with it. The Bible is not the Word, but God speaking in the Bible is the Word; or, the Word does not influence man until he realizes it is the Word; until there is an encounter between man and God, the Bible is just a book. God is not the fulfillment of reason, nor the supernatural in close relationship with the natural, nor a Being who can be partially apprehended by reason: he is, rather, a *Deus absconditus*, Wholly Other, an alien Being who speaks in awful tones from the Beyond Reason, who gives Himself to us because of an *agape* we cannot understand.

This emphasis on man's inability to contact God, this suspicion of reason, sometimes goes so far that the very possibility of a systematized Christian ethics is virtually denied (e.g. in Brunner's *The Divine Imperative*). To systematize *agape*, to bind the Wholly Other in an ethical code, is presumptuous pride. In any given situation, we must act according to the spirit, according to faith; not according to reason. We cannot give general rules for existential situations.

Man is a slave to sin, his reason is a slave to sin, his values are infected by sin, his political programs (even if "Christian") are infected by sin, his societies are infected by sin. Hence Barth's distrust of "Christian politics" and his tendencies toward "neutralism" in the Cold War. Man is in an existential situation where he can do nothing except await the unmerited *agape* of the Wholly Other. On the other hand, the Christian *must* act; he must have concern, he must help his fellow men, he must love his fellow sinners. Thus there is, in neo-orthodox thought, a constant tension between the need to act (and the necessity for a Christian ethics of a systematized nature), and the inability to act well (and thus the inability to produce a valid Christian ethics of a systematized nature).

Man is a person; he has a soul. Society is a collection of persons. Any society is only relatively good; all are infected by sin. (Indeed, there is always a tendency to excuse the Worse because all are Bad.) Democracy, Capitalism, Marxism—all are infected by sin. The Christian is thus committed, in a sense, to action which he knows will fail; that is, any Christian ethics will itself be infected by sin.

Neo-Lutheran thought has many of the same emphases. God is thought of as the Other, who intrudes mysteriously into a world of men enslaved by sin. Reason is of little value. The realm of nature and the realm of grace have little contact. Nygren stresses *agape* so much that justice is forgotten. Man's existential dilemma, his powerlessness, is emphasized, and the imperfection of what he can accomplish.

This type of thinking can be supported by some emphases in Luther and Calvin, surely. On the other hand, there is a tendency to pick and choose from the Reformation only that which accords with neo-orthodoxy. *Agape,* fine; justice, no—it doesn't fit in. Total depravity, fine; common grace, no—it doesn't fit in. And the same is true of the Bible. The "existentialist" elements of biblical thought—as that truth is for the sake of obedience, and that man is confronted always by the inescapability of ultimate decision—are accepted; other elements played down.

Neo-orthodoxy, theologically, includes a fairly broad spectrum of thinkers. None maintains the old liberal view of revelation; few if any are strictly orthodox. There is a tendency to rely on the concept of *myth* (i.e., truth expressed in symbolic form) rather than on the concept of historicity. That sense of incarnation, God entering history, which is so prominent among the neo-medievalists, is largely lacking among the neo-orthodox. The world of the existentialist, after all, whether he is Christian or not, has little place for history but a great deal for encounter.

Neo-orthodoxy, in short, has a semi-orthodox view of sin, but a fuzzy approach to God. Neo-medievalism has an orthodox (even if incomplete) view of God, but a fuzzy view of sin.

The neo-evangelical, in his approach to the problem of building a Christian ethics, can and should *learn* from what these other groups have done. Carping criticism of secondary features is the easy way out.

Two old men were talking about a third one day in the village square. "He's no good," said the first. "I plan to hit him over the head and tar and feather him." But he did nothing. The second got up, walked over, and felled the third old man with a hard right hook, and then returned. The first old man said merely, "Huh! You didn't tar and feather him, like I would!" and sat complacently back. Our attitude towards neo-medievalism's attack on liberalism should not be of this nature.

And, once the neo-evangelical has learned from these two attempts, he should avoid their shortcomings in building a Christian ethics, and contribute a vital contemporary alternative to liberal ethics—and to the other anti-liberal ethical systems which have appeared since the first World War.

There is, in the evangelical tradition, much material of value. Luther and Calvin, and indeed the Anabaptists, do have a social ethics and a personal ethics which are well worked out in terms of *their* contemporary problems, and which would be a basis for a neo-evangelical Christian ethics. (E. Troeltsch, *The Social Teaching of the Christian Churches* [2 vol., New York, 1949, a translation of the 1911 German classic] includes a most provocative section on the Reformation, of interest especially in showing how theology and Christian ethics are related in Calvinism, Anabaptism, and Lutheranism.) Much of it has been forgotten. But there is in the Reformation a synthesis of reason and faith, love and justice, individual and society, secular and sacred, which (we personally think) gives promise of a more adequate formulation of a contemporary Christian ethics than neo-medieval or neo-orthodox thinkers have been able to produce.

But, so far, we are a long way from such a formulation. Neo-evangelicalism is a young movement; and it has, essentially, advanced only to the position of *seeing the need* for a Christian ethics, rather than having worked out a Christian ethics.

V. THE BEGINNINGS OF A NEO-EVANGELICAL ETHICS

A third approach to the problem of building a Christian ethics as an alternative to liberal ethics has emerged since the second World War. It can be called, for convenience, "neo-evangelical."

As used here, this approach includes three groups. First, what might be called a neo-fundamentalist group. This has its historical background in the more scholarly aspects of the fundamentalist movement of the Twenties, and includes a number of figures—Carl F. H. Henry, Harold John Ockenga, Bernard Ramm, and others. Second, a group (closely related) stemming from J. Gresham Machen and Westminster Seminary, and looking back, beyond that, to the Princeton Seminary of Charles Hodge. Third, a group (closely related) with its historical roots in the "neo-Calvinism" of the Netherlands, around the turn of the century. (Cf. J. VanderKroef in *Church History,* 1948. Kuyper, the leader of the movement, was a theologian, political leader, and social theorist [cf. his *Calvinism,* 1898, Grand Rapids, 1943; *Christianity and the Class Struggle,* 1891, Grand Rapids, 1950]).

The "manifesto" of neo-evangelicalism, if one single thrust had to be picked, would probably be Henry's *The Uneasy Conscience of Modern Fundamentalism* (1947), which really amounts to an ardent plea for a neo-evangelical ethics.

In the decade since then, some progress has been made. Various neo-evangelical authors have written. So far, the works have been primarily in one of two categories: attacks on liberalism and neo-orthodoxy, or general attempts at formulation of an orthodox Christian position.

In the first category, that of criticism, might be mentioned such books as the following: Cornelius Van Til, *The New Modernism* (1946), a harsh critique of neo-orthodoxy as being essentially liberal; G. C. Berkouwer, *The Triumph of Grace in the Theology of Karl Barth* (1956), a more sympathetic view stressing the orthodox elements in Barth; Carl F. H. Henry, *The Protestant Dilemma* (1948); Edward John Carnell, *The Theology of Reinhold Niebuhr* (1951), both containing valuable critiques of neo-orthodoxy. Though mainly concerned with criticism of neo-orthodox theology, they contain by implication some criticism of neo-orthodox ethics. The same can be said of L. Smedes, *The Incarnation: Trends in Modern Anglican Thought* (1953), a criticism of the theological basis of much Anglican ethics.

In the second category, general statements of orthodoxy as a world-outlook, there have been such books as: Henry, *The Drift of Western Thought* (1951); Carnell, *An Introduction to Christian Apologetics* (1948); Gordon H. Clark, *A Christian View of Men and Things* (1952). Clark's earlier *A Christian Philosophy of Education* (1946) contrasts biblical values with the moral values assumed and supported in contemporary public education. Berkouwer, *Modern Uncertainty and the Christian Faith* (1953), reflects a European orthodox Calvinist outlook. This second category, too, has some relevance to ethics, though indirectly.

Philosophy is closely connected, in a sense, with Christian ethics. There has been increasing neo-evangelical interest in the problem of a Christian philosophy. Carnell has used the personalism of Edgar S. Brightman in a profitable manner in his works. There have been two attempts to develop a full-fledged orthodox philosophy, both stemming from the Dutch neo-Calvinist tradition: W. Young, *Towards a Reformed Philosophy* (1951), discusses the background. H. Dooyeweerd's *A New Critique of Theological Thought* (3 vols.; vol. 1, 1953) is a Dutch synthesis of Calvinism and phenomenology, notable for its critique of post-Kantian philosophies (cf. also the critique of Dooyeweerd in the *Calvin Forum,* 1954). The neo-Augustianian philosophy of W. Harry Jellema is unfortunately still in manuscript. An appreciative reflection of it can be found in Henry, *Remaking the Modern Mind* (1946) (cf. also Jellema, "Calvinism and Higher Education," in *God-Centered Living,* 1951; and "The Curriculum in a Liberal Arts College," available from Calvin College).

There have been some works dealing with Christian ethics taken in a narrower sense than we here use it. J. A. Springer, *Practical Christian Living* (1951), is a popular survey dealing especially with borderline personal problems. The symposium *The Fulness of Christ* (1950) has some material on ethics, but is of interest mainly as reflecting a neo-evangelical trend among some Low Church Anglicans.

C. Van Til, "Christian Theistic Ethics" (syllabus, Westminster Seminary, Philadelphia) deals with some philosophical emphases which influence ethics. John Murray's *Aspects of Biblical Ethics,* scheduled for publication by Eerdmans, supplies fundamental outlook and does begin to grapple with central problems. Henry's *Christian Personal Ethics* is a new work which gives an intelligent statement of Christianity's outlook on personal actions.

The problems which must be faced if a neo-evangelical social ethics is to be built up are touched on in several symposiums of Calvinist background: *God-Centered Living* (1951), *Calvinism in Times of Crisis* (1943), *The Reformed Faith and Its Ethical Consequences* (1938). These again, unfortunately, are general in nature, containing much more exhortation than real accomplishment. Some of the individual essays, however, are valuable. *The Secularization of Modern Life* (1953), the latest of these symposia, is more specific than most, and contains essays by S. Stob, Dooyeweerd, S. Reid, and others. (This symposium is rather difficult to obtain, but may be secured from Baker Book House, Grand Rapids.)

Neo-evangelical institutions or even groups dealing with the application of Christian ethics as yet would seem to be in the future. The Social Action Committee of the National Association of Evangelicals (NAE) is a useful clearing house, but so far, little more. The Dutch Calvinist Christian trade union movement has produced an as-yet feeble reflection in this country in the Christian Labor Association (CLA), a small trade union based on Christian principles. The CLA, now twenty-five years old, is centered in Western Michigan. It has been hampered by an emphasis on withdrawal from "godless unions" rather than on a positive program, although such an effort has recently been outlined in "Pioneering Towards a Christian Society" (available free of charge from the CLA, 1600 Buchanan Street S.W., Grand Rapids).

So far, then, a neo-evangelical approach to the problem of building a Christian ethics is in its infancy. It has, however, seen the problem, and it has begun to get at it.

While it may be justly complained that neo-evangelicalism has so far displayed a penchant for criticism of other ethics and calls for a neo-evangelical ethics more energetically than it actually progresses in building such an ethics, it should also be pointed out that the building of an ethics proceeds slowly, and of necessity proceeds slowly. Exhortation is still needed. Neo-evangelicalism so far has influenced primarily a small group of thinkers within the evangelical churches. The average evangelical is still not aware of the *problem* of building a Christian ethics.

It was roughly a decade ago that the neo-evangelical approach began to appear in print. Some of the remarks made then are, alas, still all too relevent a decade later.

"Fundamentalists have in the past paid no attention to philosophy

. . . they have neglected the philosophical, scientific, social and political problems that agitate our century," said Gordon Clark a decade ago. "Fundamentalism is prodigally dissipating the Christian culture accretion of centuries, a serious sin," cried Harold Ockenga a decade ago. "Whereas once the redemptive gospel was a world-changing message, now it has narrowed to a world-resisting message," said Carl Henry a decade ago!

These remarks still apply all too much to contemporary evangelical groups. But, in the past ten years, a good deal of progress *has* been made. A neo-evangelical approach to Christian ethics has begun to take shape.

It should not be assumed that neo-evangelical ethics, once it is formulated, will automatically be influential; nor, indeed, that neo-medieval or neo-orthodox ethics will succeed in replacing liberalism. A Christian ethics is only one of the alternatives to the liberal ethics which is no longer dominant. There are other options for Western man today. Fascism or Communism may win out in Europe. And in America, a post-liberal ethics is emerging also, which is not a Christian ethics. The literature on this is assuming sizable proportions (cf. D. Riesman, *The Lonely Crowd,* available in Anchor paperbacks; cf. W. Herberg, *Protestant, Catholic, Jew* [New York, 1956], for the emergence of "believe in God, any respectable God"). An outlook is emerging somewhat as follows: (1) morals are subjective; (2) if "good" has any meaning, it means whatever raises my standard of living or increases my emotional security; (3) this will be, in most cases, whatever my group believes in. Hence, for such a person, "religion is true if you believe in it," "God exists if you believe he does, but not otherwise," "Church going is good because the group approves." This attitude (which has some interesting parallels with Jean Paul Sartre's atheistic existentialism) may prove to be a more deadly foe than liberalism ever was.

Liberal ethics has been discredited. The throne is vacant. Christian ethics is one of the leading contenders for the throne. It has been developed in terms of two approaches, neo-medieval and neo-orthodox, in ways that can be studied and used by evangelical Christians with a great deal of profit. It is beginning to be developed by a third approach, neo-evangelical. In the past decade, this approach has made a significant beginning.

APOLOGETICS

Gordon H. Clark

Gordon H. Clark is in the front rank of competent Christian philosophers in our generation. He holds the Ph.D. degree from the University of Pennsylvania (1929), and is professor of philosophy at Butler University. He is author of Readings in Ethics *(1931),* Selections from Hellenistic Philosophy *(1940),* A Christian Philosophy of Education *(1946),* A Christian View of Men and Things *(1952),* What Presbyterians Believe *(1956), and* Thales to Dewey *(1957).*

5. Gordon H. Clark:

APOLOGETICS

SHORTLY after the inauguration of a certain college president, the faculty discussed dropping the course in theism which the previous president had required. The head of the history department (and the new president had been a member of the history department) argued in favor of dropping theism on the ground that a course in theism had never converted anybody. A course in history should be required in its stead.

Aside from college politics, this incident raises the question, What is theism or apologetics? What is its aim? What is it intended to do? Is the course supposed to convert the students? Or is it supposed to equip the students so that they may more effectively preach the Gospel after they have left the classroom? In the latter case, couldn't they put on a better evangelistic campaign if they had learned to play cow bells and a xylophone instead of having studied apologetics? What then is the purpose of apologetics?

I. THE PURPOSE OF APOLOGETICS

Among the writers who are most thoroughly biblical there is considerable unanimity. Farthest removed from hill-billy evangelism both by academic temperament and professional background, Cornelius Van Til of Westminster Seminary is one of the most outspoken on the evangelistic aim of apologetics. In *The Defense of the Faith* (p. 303) he asks, "How shall Christians win unbelievers to an acceptance of Christian truth?" A long section which follows shortly after is an applied lesson in contrasting methods of personal evangelism. And at an indefinite number of points in the volume Dr. Van Til's concern for evangelism is clearly seen among the technical arguments on Aristotle, Kant, and Hegel. With one or at most two exceptions the other writers considered here are equally explicit.

Yet with this unanimity there is some diversity or at least hesitation as to how closely an apologetic argument should resemble an evangelistic service. Should the contents of a course on theism or of a book on apologetics be within the grasp of a high-school sophomore? Not in the case of Van Til, at any rate. But another book gives a mixed impression.

Kenneth S. Kantzer in his foreword to *A Christian Approach to Philosophy* by Warren C. Young, professor of philosophy of religion at Northern Baptist Seminary, hails the volume as an evidence of the revival of letters. He speaks of Young's vigor of thought and breadth of understanding. He sees in Young's book the Augustinian tradition in its purest form. Thus apologetics and philosophy are made to appear intellectual disciplines which, though they may eventually aid evangelism, are in the first place above the level of secondary education. But then, in the same few pages, Kantzer strangely commends Dr. Young for refuting other Christian apologetes on the ground that their arguments did not convert Sophie the Scrubwoman.

Perhaps Professor Young himself would not want the value of his book to be judged by its appeal in an evangelistic campaign. He discusses epistemology, the origin of life, and the nature of consciousness. These are hardly evangelistic themes. Yet it is not clear precisely how Young views the nature of apologetics. On page 200 he says that if "philosophy" be understood to mean a world-view, then Christianity is a "philosophy." If philosophy is an attempt to see life steadily and to see it whole, if philosophy attempts to give a coherent account of all of one's experience, then Christianity has a philosophy. On the other hand, only a dozen lines below these sentiments, Young asserts that "our present task is not one of attempting to demonstrate to all comers that Christian realism is a more coherent world-view than those systems which other thinkers have to offer . . . Converts from one world-view to another are seldom made by demonstrating that one's own particular philosophy is more coherent than all others." These words (although a conscientious effort should be made to avoid misinterpreting any of these authors) have the appearance of disparaging whatever is recondite or too profound.

Edward John Carnell and Carl F. H. Henry of Fuller Theological Seminary define apologetics much as Van Til does. President Carnell once put the matter very simply in an article in the *Moody Monthly* (January, 1950). "Every personal worker faces many stock objections to his faith. Who married Cain? How did Noah manage to put all the animals into the ark?" These are the sophomoric questions. Then Carnell continues, "There are others far more basic, affecting the very foundations of the Christian faith." These others lead Carnell to consider atheism, agnosticism, and naturalism. And the intricacies will be lost on Sophie the Scrubwoman. Henry, whose many books have more of the content than the form, believes that apologetics includes internal criticism of competitive views to lay bare their inner contradictions; external criticism of competitive views to show that biblical theism avoids compromising elements and safeguards whatever truth other views may have, transforming these positive elements within the perspective of special revelation; and personal testimony because the believer alone has weighed both views as live options.

Such general remarks may be amplified and a clearer notion of the contents of apologetics may be had by observing the topics that apologetes discuss. In this respect also, recent evangelical apologists show considerable uniformity, although the diversity makes a stronger impression in some cases. Men who ask us a reason for our faith ask many different questions; and because a list of them would be an unsystematic aggregate of topics, apologetics can be considered an illegitimate subject of study. Such is the view of Dr. Samuel M. Thompson, professor of philosophy in Monmouth College. In *A Modern Philosophy of Religion* (p. 30) he speaks of apologetics as having been born in confusion, as an illegitimate discipline caught in a dilemma that can be disguised only by sleight of hand. Such a summary dismissal of apologetics is reminiscent of the contention made by the Roman Catholic writer, Etienne Gilson, to the effect that Calvinism cannot have a philosophy. Gilson's reason is that the Thomist conception of philosophy is incompatible with Calvinism; and since the Thomists are unwilling to call anything philosophy that is not built on their first principles, they naturally conclude that Calvinism provides no room for any (Thomist) philosophy. Transparent as such a device is, Thompson's view of apologetics is at least based on the undeniable fact that answering desultory questions cannot constitute a neat systematic science. Even when the trivial questions are set aside in favor of really important matters, the list still exceeds the scope of any single science. Bernard Ramm of Baylor University, for example, writes on *The Christian View of Science and Scripture*. He discusses evolution, cosmology, the antiquity of the human race, and certain miracles. Although Professor Ramm in these discussions is defending Christianity, none of these subjects is found in Van Til's book. In fact, Van Til might possibly assert that these subjects are rather to be called evidences than apologetics. For him apologetics is concerned with reality, unity and plurality, God's knowledge and man's knowledge, as well as with idealism and rationalism. Consider also the excellent volume, *The Basis of Christian Faith* (third edition) by Floyd E. Hamilton, onetime missionary and professor in Pyengyang, Korea. The book gives many reasons for the faith; it aims "to prove the truth of Christianity" (p. 15). In doing so, Hamilton discusses Old Testament criticism, the recent discoveries of archaeology, the fulfillments of prophecy, and the resurrection of Christ; besides which he examines Gibbons' theory of the early spread of Christianity, the evolutionary hypothesis, and something of the biblical texts and versions. The book is an admirable handbook of information useful to the college student; but although Hamilton shows himself quite ready to give an answer to those who ask a reason, only the first fifty-five pages are apologetics in the stricter academic sense of the word.

A stricter sense is a necessity. Without some more or less arbitrary limitation of subject matter, apologetics could not be distinguished from evidences or from an evangelistic sermon. Certainly there is a place for evidences in the propagation of the faith. Certainly the resurrection of Jesus Christ should be preached and the testimony of the eye witnesses recounted. But after we have published abroad His wonderful name, and after we have declared our faith, the auditors may ask us a reason. Apologetics therefore has its place too, but in the temporal order it is a later place. And over the years the questions and reasons to which the term apologetics has been attached have been restricted to certain basic problems. However interesting archaeology may be, and however important biblical criticism is, there are still more fundamental matters. The details of biblical criticism change, sometimes with great rapidity. But the foundations on which all the rest is supported remain the same, and questions concerning these foundations recur in every age. Does it matter where Cain got his wife or how many years ago man appeared on earth, if there is no God? And would it be possible to answer these or any other questions, if the human mind were incapable of grasping truth? Other issues are frequently included, but these are the absolutely inescapable topics that form the core of apologetics.

To conclude this short introduction, the relationship between the evangelistic motive and the academic content can perhaps be exemplified by the relationship between engineering and mathematics. The former is immediately concerned with an individual practical situation; its procedure is rough rather than rigorous; and everyone is satisfied if the bridge or building is serviceable despite some minor inconveniences. But the mathematics which the engineer used, the theory which he applied, was developed with the utmost exactitude; and if Leibniz and Newton had been preoccupied with bridges and buildings, they would never have invented calculus.

II. HISTORY AND MORALS

After the preceding introduction it might seem that a discussion of history and morals would be out of place. On the contrary, a brief consideration of ethics will serve as well or even better than anything else to emphasize and to amplify what has already been said.

Traditional apologetics has never neglected questions of morality. Bishop Butler, Thomas Aquinas, St. Augustine, and lesser authors as well have all given their arguments. In too many cases, however, without giving reasons, it has been assumed that Christian morality is superior to other ideals of life, and that therefore this superiority in morals is itself a reason for recommending the Christian system as a whole. In addition, it has also been frequently maintained that a none-too-prejudiced pagan, by his own reflection, would arrive at something pretty close to the Christian standards. Does not everyone condemn theft and murder? Even Carnell in *An Introduction to Christian Apologetics* (p. 329) says, "All ethicists agree that murder is wrong." But this does not happen to be the case. The ancient Greeks condoned the murder of defective infants. Communists today openly espouse violence, torture, and murder. It is irrelevant to reply that the Marxist does not approve of someone's murdering him. A personal disinclination to being killed is not the equivalent of the moral principle that every case of murder is wrong. Naturalism and Humanism have attacked the superiority of the Christian ideal on other points also. Edwin A. Burtt criticizes what he believes are moral deficiencies in the character of Jesus; and he notes that many humanists approve of promiscuity. Before him, Hastings Rashdall and others repudiated orthodox Christianity as a nauseous, selfish, soul-saving religion. Therefore an evangelical apologist of today misses the mark if  he argues from the supposed superiority of Christian morality to the truth of the system as a whole; he is required to give reasons in favor of his position on morals.

Professor Young's discussion of ethics is mainly a description of the naturalistic, the idealistic, and the Christian viewpoints without detailed arguments in favor of the latter or in opposition to the former. His motive in this omission is problematical, but a point of agreement among several of these authors suggests a reason. Young asserts that "Value . . . is simply the will of God for the Christian life" (p. 136), and he further implies that we ought to value certain objects "because it is commanded by God." Carnell (pp. 322-329) also argues for the primacy of the Lawgiver, as opposed to Plato's and Leibniz' primacy of law. Van Til writes, "the good is good for man because it has been set as good for many by God. This is usually expressed by saying that the good is good because God says it is good. . . . We do not artificially separate the will of God from the nature of God" (p. 69). If now this point of agreement is the truth, it follows that a reply to the naturalistic objections to Christian morality cannot be framed on a narrowly ethical basis. Rather it must await the establishment of strictly theological propositions. That is to say, if morality is the command of God, the Christian apologete must first discuss the existence and nature of God before he can support Christian standards of ethics.

Now, if God comes first, and ethical standards are established by His command, there is another factor to be considered in the discussion of morality. Professor Van Til, more than the others, stresses the defilement of man's conscience caused by sin. Since man is at enmity with God, he tries to suppress his knowledge of God. Therefore the dictates of his conscience are sure to be mistaken. Hamilton, who also insists on the effects of sin, believes that on some occasions, perhaps rare occasions, and by accident, a man's conscience might coincide with the command of God; but Van Til seems to imply that the unregenerate mind never makes a moral judgment that conforms to divine standards. "He cannot even know what the good is" (p. 71). Therefore he concludes, "It is *Scripture and Scripture alone* [italics his], in the light of which all moral questions must be answered" (p. 71). Insistence on the necessity of Scripture, however, does not depend on the unusual claim that an unregenerate mind can have no moral knowledge. Even if mankind occasionally agrees with divine standards, the prevalence of error and the methods of arriving at a decision prevent a sure judgment between what is true and what is false. Once more therefore Christian morality cannot be defended without the prior principle of revelation. The most that can be done within the sphere of ethics alone, i.e., apart from and prior to the establishment of propositions on theism and revelation, is to show that naturalism and other non-revelational theories fail to justify any moral principles whatever. Carnell, in discussing scientific law as well as moral law, argues that non-theistic principles remove all confidence for the future. Without God there is no reason to believe that the laws of science or the standards of morality will be the same tomorrow as they are today (cf. pp. 94, 153, 326). Gravitation and honesty in the past; relativity and theft in the future. This is a point that deserves to be made, but it is not a devastating point unless in the past there have been instances of radical and sudden changes. The naturalists can easily reply: true, we have no absolute confidence that tomorrow will be like today; in fact, the world is constantly changing; we have adapted ourselves to these changes in the past, and we shall have to take our chances with the future; therefore we admit your contention but deny that it damages our position. In *A Christian View of Men and Things* the present writer by-passes this reply in a detailed examination of the chief types of ethical systems. His conclusion is that, without worrying about tomorrow, non-revelational ethics cannot justify rational choices for today. Neither utilitarianism nor Kantianism can conclude in favor of any one action as against some other. Naturalistic philosophies fail to establish any normative propositions whatever. The only basis for moral distinctions must therefore be the preceptive will of God, and these precepts are found only in the Scripture.

In fairness and for a greater degree of completeness it should be noted that one contemporary evangelical apologete, Dr. J. Oliver Buswell, Jr., in *The Bible Today* (November, 1948, p. 53), takes issue with the position that moral distinctions are based on the will of God. As the passage is short, perhaps nothing more should be said, for fear of reading extraneous ideas into the text.

If the problem of morality has taken on a new form in contemporary apologetics, the idea of history is almost completely an innovation of this century. Naturally, the older writers, such as James Orr in *The Christian View of God and the World,* were interested in the Incarnation as an historical event and in a certain amount of eschatology. But during the nineteenth century, growing out of the work of Hegel and of Darwin, philosophies of history were attempted by Karl Marx, Auguste Comte, Herbert Spencer, and recently in more elaborate form by Oswald Spengler, Arnold Toynbee, R. G. Collingwood, and others. Now the idea of a philosophy of history is originally a peculiarly biblical concept, and St. Augustine exploited the material in his great *City of God.* But it has taken the studies of the recent secular scholars to stimulate a renewed interest in history among the evangelicals.

In point of publication Carl Henry seems to have been the first to pick up this theme. The second chapter of his *Remaking the Modern Mind* discusses the inevitability of progress; and the third chapter discusses the inherent goodness of man, so closely connected with it. Far from limiting himself to the nineteenth century theories, Henry says relatively little about Marx and Spencer, while he surveys the twentieth century of Russell, Flewelling, Berdyaev, and particularly Niebuhr. In part, his argument shows that even the non-evangelicals of today are not so optimistic about history as were the modernists and secularists of fifty years or more ago. In *A Christian View of Men and Things* the chapter on history analyzes the concept of progress and attempts to show the ineffectiveness of its alleged causes; then after a review of Spengler and Toynbee there is a statement of the Christian principles of history, with emphasis on the need of revelation if the laws of history are to be understood. This again shows that the study of these subjects cannot be carried on without a prior appeal to the more fundamental problems of the nature of God and the reality of revelation. Thus the argument has brought us to the central theme of apologetics—the existence of God.

III. THE COSMOLOGICAL ARGUMENT

When we come to examine the arguments for the existence of God, there arises at once the question of distinguishing between evangelical and non-evangelical apologetics. St. Thomas Aquinas and contemporary Roman Catholic philosophers believe that a formally valid argument can start with sensory perception of the physical world and conclude with God's existence. This argument, as it is worked out in detail, is extremely complex and involves a great mass of scholastic philosophy which the Reformers considered inimical to evangelical Christianity. When, now, Dr. Thompson, although he is a professor in a United Presbyterian college, so wholeheartedly adopts the Thomistic position, one wonders whether the argument should be discussed under the title of evangelical apologetics. At the same time, there are other writers, conspicuously Reformed in their theology, such as Floyd E. Hamilton, who hold, not precisely to Thomism, but to some form of the cosmological argument for God's existence. In any case there may not be a necessary connection between the Thomistic proof of God's existence and the unacceptable parts of Romish theology. Hence Thompson's argument will not only be included here, but, because of his extended and proficient exposition, he will be taken as the chief representative of the empirical and cosmological viewpoint.

Of great importance, as will be heavily underscored in the final section of this chapter, is the starting point. From what does the argument for God's existence begin? Thompson very clearly states in his preface (p. vii), that God's existence "is not the unacknowledged premise of the argument," for this, he believes, would make the argument circular and valueless, but rather it is "the conclusion required by the facts." Facts therefore are the starting point. Or, better, sense perception, which gives us the facts, is the starting point. "The first foundation of knowledge," he says (p. 50), "is sense perception." However plausible this may seem as a starting point, it takes but a smattering of philosophy to recognize that many difficulties are hidden in such a statement. Sense perception is not to be equated with sensation. Thompson admits that sensation alone does not provide knowledge. In looking at a rose I may have the sensation of red, but my perception takes in far more than the quality red. Perception grasps the rose. "In perception there is recognition and interpretation as well as sensation" (p. 51). This, he says (p. 59), is our one means of contact with external existence.

At this point an interruption may be permitted. Dr. Carnell, although his general viewpoint is far removed from Thompson's, also stresses facts and perception. Sense perception, he says (p. 49), is a source of truth; a judgment is true when it sticks together with all the facts of experience (p. 56); formal validity without real facts is empty (p. 59); in science, sense perception is a check; and knowledge is inference drawn from facts (p. 92). Hamilton too, though notably rejecting the Aristotelian theory of abstraction and denying that all our ideas are originally contained in sense perception or memory (p. 19), nonetheless has sensation as at least one starting point, in the sense that "sensations are the raw materials of knowledge" (p. 27).

Something ought to be said (but in this chapter not very much can be said) about the difficulties inherent in appeals to sense perception and facts. First, as to facts. The English word *fact* has too many connotations to be useful in a carefully formulated theory. An historical event like the crucifixion of Christ or the San Francisco earthquake is called a fact. In science the exact length of an individual pendulum is called a fact to distinguish it from an equation called a law; but sometimes the law itself is called a fact. Another person may say that it is a fact that God exists. These several usages of the word are so different that confusion results when fact is made the basis of knowledge. For example, in determining the length of a pendulum a scientist will make a large number of measurements, compute their average, and call the average the true length. Is this length a "fact" or is it an inference drawn from many facts? Thus, when the law of the pendulum, an historical event, and the existence of God are also called facts, it is clear that the word has no fixed meaning. Now, second, to avoid such confusion more careful thinkers have selected sensation as the basis for knowledge. What is immediately given in sensation is supposed to have undergone no intellectual elaboration and therefore to be free from error. In modern times Kant and the post-Kantians sought, unsuccessfully, to isolate the immediately given from the combination of subjective form and external content. Many years previously, St. Augustine had taught that there is no perception apart from intellectual interpretation; that is to say, pure sensation never occurs. But if there is always interpretation, one cannot find in perception the freedom from error that would be so desirable as a foundation for knowledge. Of course, both Carnell and Thompson recognize that perception may be mistaken. The color red may be interpreted as a rose when in the particular case it should have been interpreted as a tulip or even as a bottle of perfume. Carnell (Chapter III) well enough points out the possibilities of error and the imperfections of several criteria of truth; but then he seems to proceed as if none the less we had the "facts." Thompson apparently uses two devices to surmount this hurdle. First, taking the admitted proposition that an error in perception does not imply that perception is always erroneous, he seems to transform it into the very different proposition that perception is trustworthy. To this he adds the explanation that errors in perception occur when conditions are not right. But what these conditions of the correct interpretation of sensations are, and how we may recognize their presence, are questions which Thompson is not alone in dodging.

After this short account of the difficulties in Thompson's starting point, it is best to jump nearer to the end of his argument. Let us assume that he has satisfactorily demonstrated the existence of an external world. He then wishes to prove that this perceived external world neither exists by itself nor contains any self-existent part. When further it is shown that such a world depends on something that does exist in and of itself, the final conclusion that God exists is but a step further on.

To prove that neither the world as a whole nor any of its parts is self existent, Thompson asserts that to endure for a time means to change and to be contingent. To be a natural thing is to be a process. What a thing was five minutes ago cannot be what it is now, for if the two *whats* were identical, the two times would be identical, and now would be five minutes ago (pp. 307-309). These assertions, which may surprise the unwary, depend on the Aristotelian analysis of time as the measure of motion. If there is no motion or change, there is no time. Nor can one thing remain unchanged through the time or change of another thing, for "there is no single all inclusive time which exists somehow in independence of all individual durations, against which they can be measured" (p. 311). And to suppose that there are unchanging *atoms,* as contrasted with *things,* is to suppose that sensory objects are not real. But this is to reject sensation as the test of existence, which in turn would make all knowledge impossible.

Further, if one denies the principle of potentiality (a concept Aristotle himself could not define), and still asserts motion and duration, one would have to say that motion is from point to point. Such a denial of continuity, Thompson asserts, opens the way to Zeno's paradoxes, or at best reduces the world to the separate flashes on a cinema screen.

To those who are not skilled in scholastic philosophy, this argument may seem heavy and uninteresting. But if it proves, really proves, the existence of God, it cannot be unimportant. Nor could we expect so profound a matter to be as easy as tick-tack-toe. One cannot on principle object to a difficult argument. Euclid has taken us step by step through great complexities until the regular solids are inscribed in the sphere. Perhaps the argument for God's existence is as intricate as Euclid: the intricacy is not per se an evidence of invalidity. But, if we must avoid an interminable examination of potentiality, time, and motion, it may be noted that Euclid has proceeded step by step with such clear cogency that no one but a high school student questions the formal validity of his arguments; whereas great numbers of highly trained philosophers have not been convinced of the necessity of many steps in Aristotle's reasoning. However, since theological treatises and even ordinary sermons often mention the cosmological argument, it is worth the effort, at least once in a life time, to read through a summary of it. And the summary must be taken from the scholastics, for they are the only writers who make a serious effort to state the proof in full. Therefore let us follow Thompson for a few more paragraphs.

Thompson defends Aristotle against the common charge that he committed the "school-boy fallacy" of composition in arguing from the contingency of the parts of the world to the contingency of the world as a whole. Aristotle was aware of this fallacy; he well knew that the properties of a part are not necessarily the properties of the whole. Aristotle did not argue that the property of contingency in a part implies the property of contingency in the whole. For, says Thompson, to be contingent is not to have contingency as a property. Further, and more convincing than this little bit of scholastic brittleness, nature does not exist as a whole; the existence of the parts is the only existence nature has: nature exists bit by bit in time.

Then comes the crux of the argument—a point that apparently seems so obvious to modern Aristotelians and so unnecessary to all others. The series of existing things and events cannot be infinite. History goes back from A.D. 1956 to A.D. 56 to 56 B.C. to 1956 B.C., but the series of historical events, biological events, geological and cosmological events cannot be an infinite series. "To designate a series . . . as infinite is to deny that it is a series . . . of real existence" (p. 320). Infinite series can be constructed in mathematics, Thompson argues, because there is a real continuum from which we abstract parts. The continuum is not something put together out of the items of the series; on the contrary the items of the series are cut off out of the continuum. But when the parts of a whole are themselves really existing things, and the whole is constructed from them, as is the case with nature, then the sum of the parts is finite.

Concerning these remarks one may ask whether they form an argument or whether they are sheer assertions begging the question. Has the author given reasons for suggesting in the last sentence of the exposition that nature is a whole and a sum of parts? Earlier he had repudiated the idea that nature as a whole exists. And if nature is not a whole or sum, but a series, why may not the series of events be infinite? It would seem that at this crucial point in the argument for God's existence, there is no argument, and that the gap is bridged by an unsupported assertion.

Thompson carries on. To cross from contingency to self-existence, he needs the principle of causality. Not only must there be causes of things in nature, but above all there must be a cause of nature. Either there is real causality or we cannot maintain the distinction between actuality and potentiality. These themes Thompson works out with his usual attention to detail; but perhaps enough has been given here to serve as a fair sample of the argument for God's existence.

Thompson is not the only one who holds to the validity of the theistic proofs. As was indicated above, Hamilton takes a somewhat similar position. Though he does not follow all the Aristotelian apparatus found in Thompson, and though he holds that God may be the immediate cause of sensations without the intermediary of an external world (pp. 40-42), he still argues from sensory experience, through the innate principle of causality (pp. 21, 44), to the existence of God; and of the conclusion that man has a moral creator he says, "The preceding arguments are so plain that the conclusion is inescapable" (p. 54). Hamilton therefore apparently holds to the formal validity of the theistic proofs. But herein lies a difficulty. Hamilton's argument is a couple of hundred pages shorter than Thompson's. If now he does not accept all the Aristotelian details, what precisely are the steps by which he would advance from the self and its ideas to God? Hamilton's statement is longer than the summary references often found in other evangelical writers. Of them all the more must it be asked by what steps do they proceed from premises to conclusion? An argument cannot be appraised unless it is stated. How could anyone judge of the inscription of the regular solids in the sphere, if a third or two-thirds of the previous theorems were omitted?

Strange as it may seem, and it will seem still stranger as we proceed, Van Til also asserts "the Reformed apologist maintains that there is an absolutely valid argument for the existence of God" (p. 121). Van Til, of course, is less Aristotelian than Hamilton. If then Van Til does not start from sensory experience, he ought to state his basic premises and give the argument step by step. He seems to suggest that the premises have something to do with the doctrines of creation and providence, and "when the proofs are thus formulated they have absolute probative force" (p. 196). Here one must ask whether it is valid to argue from creation to the existence of God, or whether the notion of creation does not already presuppose the existence of God? Has not Van Til interchanged premises and conclusion? However, though the phrase "probative force" suggests valid demonstration, Van Til immediately disclaims the pure deduction of one conclusion after another from an original premise. Instead of syllogisms he prefers a method of analogy, to which reference will be made later. Finally he repeats "The argument for the existence of God . . . is objectively valid. We should not tone down the validity of this argument to the probability level. The argument may be poorly stated, and may never be absolutely stated. But in itself the argument is absolutely sound" (p. 256).

One pauses to ask only how an argument can be known to be objectively valid and absolutely sound, when the argument has never been formulated. Could we judge the Pythagorean theorem, if it were defectively stated? The Roman Catholics appeal to Romans 1:20 as guaranteeing the validity of the cosmological argument. Similarly, Dr. Buswell in *The Bible Today* (Oct., 1947, p. 6) writes, "The so-called cosmological argument is precisely the teaching of Paul in Romans 1:20." But surely Paul did not mean precisely to confer infallibility on Thomas Aquinas. Still less did he confer formal validity on the sketchy summaries of other writers. And to avoid all confusion, it should be noted that any assertion to the effect that Romans 1:20 *is* the cosmological argument is false. The verse has neither premises nor conclusion; it contains no hint of an implication; it is a simple statement, and simple statements are not arguments and can be neither valid nor invalid. Beyond this, there is no point in talking about a perfect argument that no one has ever correctly formulated. The actual implications that have been printed in books are simply not valid, and evangelicals do themselves a disfavor if they imitate the scholastic legerdemain of Aristotle and Aquinas.

IV. THE PROBLEM OF KNOWLEDGE

The formal defense of the cosmological argument is hardly ever undertaken by contemporary evangelical theologians, and the reasons therefore bring us to the last and most profound problem of apologetics. This problem of knowledge divides into three sub-sections: (1) demonstration and consistency; (2) the starting point; and (3) analogy.

Demonstration and Consistency

Presumably the cosmological argument begins at some starting point, progresses through a series of steps, and allegedly reaches a conclusion. In the previous section it has been argued that this series of steps does not constitute a formally valid demonstration. An example of a formally valid argument is: All the heroes of the Iliad died young; Alexander was a hero of the Iliad; therefore Alexander died young. An example of an invalid syllogism is: Some Greeks are Athenians; some Athenians are traitors; therefore some Greeks are traitors. This latter syllogism may sound good to a careless thinker, but it would flunk a student in a logic class. Somewhat similarly in the cosmological argument the conclusion is acceptable, while it remains unnoticed that the premises do not necessitate it. Rather than change the premises (which is a matter of the starting point) some earlier writers hesitantly admit that the cosmological argument is not "mathematically" conclusive, though they avoid calling it fallacious. Floyd Hamilton, for example, in spite of the wording quoted above grants that it does not follow strictly the rules of the syllogism; but he wishes to call it a proof in some looser sense of the word proof. Whether or not Dr. Buswell denies the formal validity of the argument is hard to discern. In *The Bible Today* (May, 1948, pp. 239-242), where he is attacking Carnell, he tries to maintain that Aquinas did not present his arguments as a necessary deduction. This is an historical blunder, and one might guess that it was motivated unintentionally by a desire to retain as evidence convincing for practical purposes an argument that is a formal fallacy. Then too, in stating one part of the argument, Buswell labels it "most probable." But the matter is not clear, for in rephrasing other parts, he gives implications that seem to be intended as necessary.

If one wishes to use the cosmological argument without asserting its formal validity, there is a difficulty that requires explanation. The expression that the natural evidence for God's existence is convincing for all practical purposes must be understood as simply a form of enthusiastic speech, for obviously it cannot be taken literally. There are many people, both Christians and unbelievers, to whom this argument is by no means convincing; nevertheless the conversion of the unbelievers and even the enlightenment of the Christians would have to fall within the class of all practical purposes. If then it is not satisfactory for all practical purposes, can it be defended as satisfactory for some practical purposes? After all, it is convincing to those who use it. But this explanation is no better. People are frequently convinced by the flimsiest of evidence and the most glaring of fallacies. If it is justifiable to use an argument merely because it serves some practical purpose, would not evangelism be reduced to utter sophistry? Any evidence or any fallacy could be used, if only it were convincing to the person addressed. And this would remain the case even when the evangelist himself knew that his arguments were inherently unsound. The confusion arises from the unwillingness to see that an argument is either valid or fallacious. There is no third possibility. And in choosing arguments there is no substitute for valid logic.

The importance of necessary inference or valid argumentation goes beyond the cosmological argument. The wider question involved is whether or not reasons, rational arguments, or necessary inference can be used to support the Christian system as a whole. Or, one might even ask, Is Christianity a rational system of thought? Before other writers are quoted, another reference to Buswell is in order. In *The Bible Today* (Oct.,1947) Dr. Buswell incorrectly attributed to the present writer one of Van Til's views (p. 4); he also asserted (p. 6) that I had ignored the Cartesian form of the ontological argument, although the very page from which Dr. Buswell quotes contains a summary of it. Because of these misunderstandings there was an exchange of views in the December, 1947, the January, 1948, and the March, 1948, issues of the periodical. At first Dr. Buswell shied away from the notion of a system, a perfectly self-consistent, rational system, and tried to define system as "a more or less consistent or inconsistent complex of thought" (December, p. 72, and January, p. 115). Finally, however, in spite of this initial hesitation, he accepted the proposition that "the truth is a perfectly consistent system." For an author who uses the cosmological argument, this acceptance of consistency should, one would think, imply that the cosmological argument is formally valid.

But not all writers accept the notion of perfect consistency. In the past mystics and anti-intellectuals have been a definitely small minority; but inasmuch as neo-orthodoxy today proposes to do great things with illogical paradoxes, the relation of Christian truth to logic is pertinent and timely. Although many popular preachers use the unscriptural antithesis of head versus heart, anti-intellectualism is still a minority view among evangelicals. Carl Henry writes on "The Reasonableness of Christianity" in *Remaking the Modern Mind:* "Revelational theism has never offered itself as an escape from rationality . . . it offered a rationally consistent view of existence" (pp. 213, 215), and he clearly expresses his displeasure with anti-intellectualism. Carnell commences his "Preface" by accepting the task of constructing a rational explanation for the whole course of reality; he emphasizes systematic consistency (though he believes that consistency is insufficient and must be supported by coherence—a different concept, though many other writers use the two terms as synonymous), and he even dares to accept the term rationalism (pp. 7, 56, 152, 153). My own writings also emphasize logic.

But Warren Young disagrees. He does not accept the task of attempting to demonstrate that Christian philosophy is more coherent (consistent?) than other systems (p. 200); coherence itself is always relative, depending on assumptions of faith rather than on rational demonstration (p. 201). And in particular, "We object to the coherence approach advocated by . . . E. J. Carnell . . . his apparent basic assumption that Christianity can be shown to be the most rational or coherent world view must be questioned . . . The same general view is to be found in . . . G. H. Clark . . . he too seems to become a victim of the coherence [consistency] fallacy when he says, . . . 'if one world-view is consistent while others are self-contradictory, who can deny us . . . the right to choose the most promising first principle?' But who is to determine which view is consistent and which is self-contradictory? Sidney Hook? Edgar Sheffield Brightman? Or Gordon H. Clark?" (p. 221).

The literal answer to these last questions is of course that each man must decide for himself, even Sophie the Scrubwoman, and not surrender his responsibility to some philosophic Pope. But Young has asked the wrong question. Instead of asking, Who decides? he should have asked, On what grounds can a decision legitimately be made? One must seriously consider whether even the totality of Christian evidences —which, since it is evidence, falls short of logical necessity—can furnish a reason, if the law of contradiction be abandoned. Unless self-contradiction is a perfect reason for rejecting a complex of propositions, conversation becomes meaningless. Suppose some unbeliever who wishes to attack Christianity should assert that one passage of Scripture contradicts another: how shall we answer him? Shall we say, "We do not claim that the Bible is rational or self-consistent; on the contrary, it is you who are a victim of the coherence fallacy; though the passages contradict each other, they are both infallibly inspired"? Such an answer would qualify as paradoxical.

The Starting Point

On several occasions in the preceding discussion the question of the starting point has come to the surface. Once it was asked whether Van Til began with the doctrine of creation and argued to God's existence from this doctrine. Carnell seems to have based some of his argument on an appeal to common facts and accepted principles of morality. Thompson began with sensory experience. Now, if in some cases these starting points beg the question and in others the inferences are invalid, a search for a suitable starting point seems called for. With what can the apologetic endeavor begin?

In opposition to the Aristotelian procedure of learning about God from the world, there is the Calvinistic position that the knowledge of God comes first. Two volumes, both published in 1946, take this position. In *A Christian Philosophy of Education* (p. 38) I said, "instead of beginning with the facts and later discovering God, unless a thinker begins with God, he can never end with God, or get the facts either." Carl Henry's *Remaking the Modern Mind* (p. 225) argues that the Thomistic proofs contain within themselves the seeds of their own destruction; their presuppositions rule out a Christian philosophy; one "must begin with God, not only to get to God, but to get to anything" (p. 232). At the same time Floyd Hamilton, cognizant of the trend of thought, had been revising his *Basis of Christian Faith* (1927), and the same year (1946) issued a third edition, in which, though modifying his earlier expressions, he attempts to defend the theistic proofs. Later (1947-1948) Dr. Buswell not only disagreed with me, but criticized Carnell also, who by this time had published similar views; and most recently (1955) Van Til, who also insists on putting God first, has criticized Hamilton, though unfortunately in using the 1927 edition he quotes sections which Hamilton had retracted and replaced nine years previously. The very fact that Hamilton thought it wise to make these alterations is itself evidence that the old Augustinian position rather than the natural theology of Thomism is a prominent and perhaps the growing opinion of contemporary evangelical apologetes. This necessitates a consideration of the starting point in apologetics.

Note well, the question does not refer to the starting point of an evangelistic campaign, nor to the start of a conversation designed to lead a particular person to Christ. Such a conversation might begin with references to football, fishing, or burdensome taxation. Evangelism was compared with practical engineering that must adapt itself to the local conditions; while apologetics is similar to the mathematical theory which engineering applies. Therefore the starting point here discussed is not a temporal but the logical starting point. This is elementary, but in studying the thought of the several apologetes, one must consider whether they keep this distinction constantly in mind or whether they unconsciously confuse the two.

First, let us consider Carnell. Notwithstanding his occasional appeal to facts and perception, including the puzzling statement, (All?) "Knowledge is inference drawn from facts,"—a statement implying that neither ultimate premises nor the facts themselves can be known—there is another and apparently more pervasive strand in his thought. Rather than proving the authority of God's word by an inference from facts, he says (p. 66), "The word of God is thus self-authenticating . . . If the word required something more certain than itself to give it validity, it would no longer be God's word. . . . It would be a derogation to the efficiency of revelation to suppose that any more than God's Spirit is needed to seal the word to the hearts of believers," and he quotes a remarkable sentence from Charles Hodge. Later (p. 89) Carnell refers to the existence of God as the "ultimate postulate" of the Christian world-view. Again (p. 124) he says the Trinity is the starting point; he rejects the theistic proofs (pp. 126-139); instead of the existence of God being demonstrable "his existence is the *sine qua non* for all demonstration" (p. 159). In addition to these sometimes scattered remarks, Chapter VII explicitly discusses the starting point of apologetics. Opposing Brightman, Carnell says, "The Christian believes that the starting point controls both method and conclusion" (p. 120). Certainly it is obvious, we may remark, that the axioms of geometry control the theorems. Then Carnell continues, "philosophy is like a railway without switches—once a man is committed to a given direction, he is determined in his outcome. Should he change his mind about the wisdom of the course, his only recourse is to go back and start on another track. A change from idealism to pragmatism involves a change in starting point, method, and conclusion" (p. 123).

Buswell, in *The Bible Today* (May, 1948), vigorously criticizes this railroad illustration. He pictures a bewildered traveler in New York who is about to get on a train for Boston, thinking it will take him to Philadelphia. Buswell would correct the man by pointing to the sign over the gate and asking the gateman. Carnell, on the other hand, as Buswell understands him, is accusing Buswell of letting the man get on the wrong train, of even getting on with him, on the assumption that the train is going to Philadelphia. This reproduction of Carnell's illustration, however, is an instance of the dangers of illustrations. Even Christ's parables were and are occasionally misunderstood. To be sure, there are signs and gatemen in the railroad station; but in philosophy there are no gatemen; there is the starting point only at the start. When we are writing down the axioms, we do not yet have any of the theorems; and the only way to see where the axioms go is to board the train of thought and deduce the theorems. Deduction is "going to Boston." Now, Carnell is saying, if you do not care for the theorems you are getting, you must discard all your deductions, go back to the start, and take another train, i.e. another set of axioms: you cannot switch from theorem fifteen of Euclid to theorem sixteen of Riemann. Buswell nevertheless asserts that the metaphor is meaningless: "What could the words 'go back and start on another track' mean in this time-world of intellectual experience?" (p. 245). Saul met Christ on the road to Damascus; before this meeting Saul had been on the wrong track; now, says Dr. Buswell, Saul did not go back at all; his past was still past; he simply switched over onto an entirely different track. Unfortunately, this is a total misunderstanding of Carnell's meaning. Carnell is not requiring Saul to go back to Jerusalem; he is surely not requiring Saul to reverse the direction of time, but he is insisting that Saul drop his starting point, the axiom that Jesus is an impostor, a blasphemer, an enemy of the true religion, and start anew on the different axiom that Christ is the Lord. Carnell is perfectly clear—he even puts it in an italicized subhead—that the temporal starting point is of no importance, and that he is writing of the logical starting point. "The logical starting point is the coordinating ultimate which gives being and meaning to the many of the time-space universe. For Thales it was water; for Anaximines it was air. For Plato it was the Good; and for the Christian it is the Trinity. The logical starting point is the highest principle which one introduces to give unity and order to his interpretation of reality. This is why it is the *logical* starting point—it is what one logically conceives as the over-all synthesizing element which unites the particulars." It would seem therefore that preoccupation with evangelistic engineering has blunted Dr. Buswell's appreciation of pure mathematics.

Carnell, however, has several passages—his appeals to facts, his remark about murder cited in the section above on morality, as well as others not yet referred to—which might cause the careful reader to wonder whether or not he has consistently followed out his understanding of the starting point. Another (and one might say a more vigorous) attempt to make God the starting point is that of Professor Van Til. Let us summarize his construction for purposes of comparison.

Van Til emphatically asserts that no "area or aspect of reality, any fact or any law of nature or of history can be correctly interpreted except it be seen in the light of the main doctrines of Christianity" (p. 113). Therefore an apologist cannot "agree with the non-Christian in his principles of methodology to see whether or not Christian theism be true." Romish and Arminian apologists, e.g. Thomas, Butler, A. E. Taylor, to the extent that they believe in human autonomy, try to use the unbeliever's methodology; but a truly Reformed Christian must disagree "with the natural man on the nature of the object of knowledge

[and] . . . on the method to be employed in acquiring knowledge" (p. 116). In total opposition to Thompson's point of view, the Reformed apologist frankly admits that his methodology presupposes the truth of Christianity. The basic doctrine of the Trinity controls a truly Christian methodology. Therefore "the issue between believers and unbelievers in Christian theism cannot be settled by a direct appeal to 'facts' or 'laws' whose nature is already agreed upon by both parties to the debate" (p. 117). Since "there is one system of reality of which all that exists forms a part," and since "any individual fact of this system is what it is in this system," it follows that apart from Christion presuppositions "no facts mean anything at all" (p. 164). "All reasoning is, in the nature of the case, *circular reasoning*. The starting point, the method, and the conclusions are always involved in one another" (p. 118). These quotations, of course, seriously abbreviate Van Til's exposition, but if one keeps in mind the acknowledged control of axioms over theorems, and the theorem's presupposing the axioms, in which sense geometry itself may loosely be called circular reasoning, it will not be too difficult to grasp Van Til's thought.

But apologetics is more complicated than plane geometry, and the matter of the starting point becomes involved with the notion of a common ground, the noetic effects of sin, and a theory of analogy.

In this discussion of the starting point with the example of the axioms and theorems of geometry, it is immediately obvious that there can be no theorem common to two systems of geometry. Euclid and Lobachevsky may both use the phrase "parallel lines," but they mean different things; and when a perpendicular crosses them, Lobachevsky's results differ from those of Euclid. Similarly, in Christianity and in a naturalistic philosophy the words fact, reason, and God may occur, but the meanings, determined by the axioms, are not the same. Hence even if two sentences are composed of identical words, if one is in a naturalistic system and the other in a Christian system, it does not indicate that the two systems have a proposition in common.

Does it follow, however, that two persons, a Christian and a naturalist, can have no knowledge in common? A person is not a system, and hence we cannot say of a person what we say of a system, unless some further reasons be adduced.

Van Til's answer to this question is somewhat confused. His first answer is as follows: "It will be quite impossible then to find a common area of knowledge between believers and unbelievers unless there is agreement between them as to the nature of man himself. But there is no such agreement" (p. 84). Particular examples are found here and there through the book; for example, the natural man, blinded by sin, does not have the right (the power?) to judge by means of his reason between what is possible and what is impossible, nor to judge by his moral nature what is good or evil (p. 99). "The 'reason' of sinful men will invariably act wrongly" (p. 100). And on the bottom half of page 110 he says, in a complicated form of expression, that we cannot admit the unbeliever's ability to interpret any area of experience whatever. Later (p. 262) he writes:

> Aquinas and Butler hold that the natural man . . . has some correct notions about God. I mean correct notions as to content, not merely as to form. Anyone who says, 'I believe in God,' is formally correct in his statement, but the question is, What does he mean by the word *God?* The traditional view assumes that the natural man has a certain measure of correct thought content when he uses the word God. In reality the natural man's 'God' is always a finite God . . . The natural man's god is *always* [Italics his] enveloped within a Reality that is greater than his god . . . he makes Reality to be inclusive of God and himself. And there is not much that the traditional apologist can do about this. He has bound himself to confusion in apologetics as he has bound himself to error in theology. He must tie on to some small area of thought content that the believer and the unbeliever have in common without qualification when both are self-conscious with respect to their principle. This is tantamount to saying that those who interpret a fact as dependent upon God and those who interpret that same fact as not dependent upon God have yet said something identical about that fact. All this is bound to lead to self-frustration on the part of the traditional apologist.

Do not these assertions imply that the natural or unregenerate man is totally devoid of knowledge? The first quotation in the preceding paragraph denied that there was a common area of knowledge; a later one says that reason of sinful man *invariably* acts wrongly; then, the unbeliever cannot interpret any area of experience; and finally, the traditional view that the natural man has a certain measure of correct thought content leads to self-frustration. Certainly these passages imply that an unregenerate man is totally ignorant.

Carnell, however, gives a different answer. Quoting from *A Christian Philosophy of Education* (p. 164), Carnell distinguishes between a philosophic system as such and a person who understands and accepts more or less of the system. It should be obvious that there cannot be any common ground, any common proposition, shared by two systems. But since living persons are not so ideally consistent, they may, as limited in intelligence and subjected to diverse educational influences, sincerely think and believe actually contradictory propositions. Buswell's vigorous statements in *The Bible Today* seem to have been caused by this failure to distinguish between a confused person and a logical system. Apparently even Carnell himself does not follow through to the end. Instead of remaining with the distinction between person and system, Chapter XII of his *Introduction to Christian Apologetics* diverges into a distinction between science and metaphysics. At first he seems to say that the problem of a common ground has no relevance in science: "Scientific conclusions as such do not depend for their meaning upon one's logical starting point. Water is H_2O for the Christian no less than for the non-Christian" (p. 214). In these two sentences there appears to be a shifting and confusion. The first refers to scientific conclusions as such; the second speaks of persons. Did Carnell mean to say, Water is H_2O both on naturalistic principles and on theistic principles as well? And if so would he also add that the words bear the same meanings in both systems? At any rate, so far as the first sentence is concerned, in the chapter on Science in *A Christian View of Men and Things,* I have taken pains to show how definitely scientific conclusions depend, though sometimes unrecognized by the scientist, on one's logical starting point. But perhaps Carnell and I are closer in our views than this much indicates, for he goes on to say that (although there is a common ground in science [?]) there is no common ground in metaphysics. In one place he says there is a line that divides science from metaphysics; but then, this line is almost invisible, and down the page (215) he admits that the reach of metaphysics is absolute and overshadows every level of meaning. The metaphysical level is so penetrating that it succeeds in reflecting back upon the scientific level also. This would imply that science also furnishes no common ground. But then Carnell introduces another modification to the effect that while metaphysics is implicit in every formula, common ground concerns only explicit metaphysical meaning (p. 216). This distinction between explicit and implicit meaning seems to be ambiguous. Logically the theorems are implicit in the axioms; and if this is the sense of Carnell's distinction, he would in effect be saying that naturalistic axioms cannot be found in Christianity, but that a given theorem may occur in both systems. This conclusion both conflicts with other things Carnell has said and also seems to be untenable in itself. On the other hand, Carnell's distinction between implicit and explicit may be taken in a personal sense; that is to say, an unregenerate and unphilosophic business man may believe that water is H_2O without the least reflection on naturalistic presuppositions. Or, he might believe a given historical statement in the Bible, though he disbelieves all of the doctrine. If thus Carnell's meaning refers to the confusion and inconsistency of superficial minds, it must be judged to be inadequately expressed, with the result that the material on the pages now under discussion is not an improvement upon his introductory statement.

Then again, two years before Carnell's book appeared, Hamilton was putting out the third edition of his *Basis of Christian Faith.* Perhaps he has not expressed the distinction between person and system with the clarity one might like. Yet how otherwise can pages 16, 25, 28, 55, and

323 be understood? This last page in particular has Van Til directly in view. Since at that time these points were subjects of controversy between Van Til on the one side and Hamilton and myself on the other, it is all the more regrettable that Van Til ignored this material in his recent criticism of Hamilton.

One important reason for maintaining the distinction between consistent systems and inconsistent persons is that unregenerate persons are thereby permitted to have at least some knowledge. Since the Scriptures base responsibility on knowledge, and since Romans 1:32 assigns to the wicked an amount of moral knowledge sufficient to make them guilty of sin, the evangelical must frame a theory by which this knowledge is shown to be possible. Were a man totally ignorant, he could not be guilty of sin.

Now, strange as it may seem, although Van Til's statements, quoted above, inexorably imply that the unregenerate are totally ignorant, Van Til makes some contradictory remarks. Contrary to all he has said, Van Til quotes Warfield, apparently with approval, to the effect that "the conviction of the existence of God bears the marks of an intuitive truth . . ." (p. 102). Then later, "The apostle Paul speaks of the natural man as actually possessing the knowledge of God" (p. 110). And above all, "The point of contact [common ground?] for the gospel, then, must be sought within the natural man" (p. 111). Again, "All men have not only the ability to know but actually know the truth" (p. 194). In answer to his critics Van Til asserts "I have never denied that he [the natural man] has true knowledge" (p. 285).

These quotations when compared with those cited previously impose a burden upon anyone who wishes to understand Van Til. How is it possible to reconcile the assertion that "all men . . . actually know the truth" with the earlier assertion "It will be quite impossible then to find a common area of knowledge between believers and unbelievers . . ."? Or again, "It is natural and consistent for Roman Catholic apologetics to seek its point of contact with the unbeliever in a 'common area' of knowledge . . . But herein precisely lies the fundamental point of difference between Romanism and Protestantism" (pp. 93, 94). Does this sound like "The point of contact . . . must be sought within the natural man"? How can Van Til quote Hodge with approval to the effect that the natural man has "no true knowledge of God" (p. 91) and then assert "I have never denied that he has true knowledge"?

Indubitably Van Til has said that the natural man actually has true knowledge. It is also indubitable that Van Til has denied a common area of knowledge. Is not one forced to conclude that Van Til has, first, contradicted himself, and then, second, has forgotten his previous remarks to say, "I have never denied that he has true knowledge"? *The Defense of the Faith* is not the only product of Dr. Van Til's pen. In another document also he denies true knowledge to the unregenerate. As a matter of fact he goes still further and implies that no human being can have knowledge.

The Text of a Complaint (p. 5, col. 1), a product of a collaboration by Van Til and some of his colleagues, asserts that "there is a qualitative difference between the contents of the knowledge of God and the contents of the knowledge possible to man." This qualitative difference does not lie in the psychological procedure of knowing; it is not that God knows intuitively and man knows discursively; the assertion is that the *contents* of knowledge are different. To make it clearer, the document continues (p. 5, col. 3), "We dare not maintain that his knowledge and our knowledge coincide *at any single point,*" and the authors, including Van Til, proceed to repudiate the idea "a proposition would have to have the same meaning for God as for man." They also deny (p. 7, col. 3) that "propositions *have the same content, mean the same,* to God and man." Now, if God knows all truths and knows the correct meaning of every proposition, and if no proposition means to man what it means to God, so that God's knowledge and man's knowledge do not coincide at any single point, it follows by rigorous necessity that man can have no truth at all. This conclusion is quite opposite to the views of Calvin *(Institutes* II, ii, 12-15), and undermines all Christianity.

Analogy

There is an expedient which extends hope that Christianity may yet survive these fatal implications. After stressing the fact that God's knowledge of the universe, unlike man's, depends on God's knowledge of Himself, Van Til asserts that "human knowledge is *analogical* of divine knowledge" (*Defense,* p. 56). Roman Catholic apologetics also hold that human knowledge is analogical.

Professor Thompson, though not a Romanist, is rather thoroughly Thomistic. In his *Modern Philosophy of Religion,* Chapter XXIII discusses "Knowledge by Analogy." It is impossible to trace the argument through its many scholastic subtleties; it is still less possible to evaluate what appears to be Thompson's slight modification of Thomism in the interest of making analogical knowledge more positive, for the result does not seem to differ greatly from the original theory. Thompson says:

> We, as contingent beings, do not know self-existence in ourselves. So we do not and cannot know self-existence as it is. . . . To know the goodness of God by analogy is not to know goodness as it is in God . . . We can know nothing, except what is negative, of what it is like *to be goodness,* as God is goodness. . . . The goodness of God is beyond anything we can conceive or imagine . . . Analogy does not enable us to conceive God's goodness as identical with his essence but to affirm it as identical with his

> existence. . . . Our idea of good is not the concept of God's essence, but of our own nature; yet we can use it to refer to God . . . Analogy does not capture for our minds the goodness of God in terms of what that goodness is; so far as its actual content is concerned, it finds the goodness of God only in terms of what it is not. But it really finds the goodness of God in these terms. . . . Once we forget that our assertions about the nature of God are true only by analogy, once we take them to be true univocally (i.e., literally), they collapse into mere negations (pp. 389-391).

Is not this an elaborate and somewhat misleading way of saying that we have no knowledge of God? Apparently Carnell (pp. 143-151) thinks so, and I also *(op. cit.,* pp. 309-312) argue against the analogical method of knowledge.

Now Van Til's comment on Thomism is not that analogy is a fruitless expedient, but, quite the reverse, that Romanism does not take analogy seriously enough (p. 56). Romanism still retains too much, shall we say, univocity. Not Christian thought, but, says Van Til, "Nonchristian philosophies hold that human thought is univocal instead of analogical" (p. 65). In view of the fact that Romanism allows univocal predication in the sphere of science and of ordinary experience, Van Til's assertion is most easily understood to mean that univocal predication is impossible for man in any subject. In this Van Til shows a close affinity to neo-orthodoxy. The adherents of the dialectical theology teach that all language, or all religious language, is analogical, metaphorical, or symbolic. Not language only, but conceptual knowledge also. Intellectual knowledge, *Es-Wahrheit,* is only a pointer, a pointer to something that cannot be thought. Therefore creeds are not to be taken univocally or literally, but in some analogical and therefore undefined meaning.

To be sure, this is paradoxical. Van Til says, "Our knowledge is analogical and therefore must be paradoxical" (p. 61). On this point, we are glad to say, Van Til diverges from neo-orthodoxy. The dialectical theologians weave actual, irresolvable contradictions into the warp and woof of reality. They picture God as irrational. But Van Til uses the term paradox in the earlier and usual sense of seeming contradiction. Hence he is saying that for men "there must seem to be contradiction" (p. 62). But one wonders whether this is worth saying. Of course the disability of the human mind darkened by sin leads us all into confusions; and perhaps Adam before the fall was not immune to the enigmatic. But the philosophic or systematic value of paradoxes is diminished by the fact that what is a paradox for one person is not paradoxical for another. Theorem fifteen may be a paradox to the high school student, but not to the teacher. As an example of a seeming contradiction, in fact, as "one of the outstanding paradoxes of the Christian interpretation of things" (p. 61), Van Til gives these two propositions:

"Prayer changes things and . . . everything happens in accordance with God's plan and God's plan is immutable." Undeniably this is a paradox, for the two statements seem contradictory to Van Til. Undeniably also this is not a paradox because they do not seem contradictory to some other people. A paradox is not a quality inherent in pairs of propositions, as the relationship of contradiction is. Since a paradox is only a seeming contradiction, it exists only in so far as these statements seem so to some individual. But such irregular, personal reactions cannot be lifted to the level of principal importance. Let us then have done with paradoxes; let us restrict analogy to a literary embellishment; let us eschew fallacy, pursue valid reasoning, and acknowledge God as the source of all truth.

V. CONCLUSION

The Protestant Reformation swept away the superstitious idolatry of Romanism and the scholastic philosophy as well. But whereas it replaced the false worship with the pure Gospel, it failed to replace scholasticism with anything. Protestantism has never had an official philosophy—a fact of which we may be glad; but it is not so fortunate that we have not had a semi-official philosophy or at least a wide area of agreement. Not that there has been too much disagreement: rather the difficulties of philosophy have been neglected, even by those who are most doctrinally conscious and who therefore ought to assign a proper value to truth. In pragmatic America especially where the educational standards are so far below those of Europe, the evangelical movement has been nothing less than deplorable in this regard. Attention has been paid to evidences; archaeology evokes a degree of interest; but a thorough and patient study of the more profound issues is often avoided. Even the preaching of the Gospel itself is frequently reduced to half a dozen fundamental doctrines. Such impoverishment betrays the cause of Christ. If Christianity instead of its modern imitations is to make an impact on our society, preaching must become richer, fuller, and more profound. And in addition, the faith that is preached should be defended against the attacks of its enemies by the formulation and exposition of a thoroughly biblical world-view. This requires more scholars, more discussion, more publication, and a wider appreciation of the importance of the task.

EDUCATION

Frank E. Gaebelein

Frank E. Gaebelein has been for many years Headmaster of the Stony Brook School. A Phi Beta Kappa graduate of New York University with an A.M. from Harvard, he holds honorary degrees from Wheaton and the Reformed Episcopal Theological Seminary. Dr. Gaebelein is known here and abroad as a preacher and as a lecturer in biblical and educational subjects. Among his eleven books are Christian Education in a Democracy *(the Report of the National Association of Evangelicals) and* The Pattern of God's Truth; Problems of Integration in Christian Education, *both published by Oxford University Press.*

6. *Frank E. Gaebelein:*

EDUCATION

CONTEMPORARY evangelical thought in the field of education may be likened to a fabric in process of weaving—not a mere patchwork but a tapestry, unfinished, to be sure, yet with design so unmistakably woven into warp and weft that there can be no doubt of its nature. The purpose of this chapter is to examine this fabric in order to see the nature of the design which, as the tapestry grows, is being unfolded.

I. THE EVANGELICAL PRESUPPOSITION IN EDUCATION

Without laboring the analogy, we may begin by pointing out that evangelical education, or, for that matter, any other type of education, exists within a frame. As a tapestry is woven upon a loom so education has for its context a frame of reference. In the case of evangelical education that frame of reference is historic Christianity, set forth in Scripture and expressed in the great doctrines of Protestantism, such as the existence of God the Father, the Maker of heaven and earth; man's creation in God's image, an image ruined through sin but not beyond God's power to regenerate; the incarnation of God the Son for the redemption of lost humanity; the work of God the Holy Spirit in calling out of the world a community of believers, the Church; and, finally, the end of earthly history through the "glorious appearing of the great God and our Saviour Jesus Christ." To these there is always basic the divine inspiration of the Bible, the infallible Word of God.

As the loom does not change while the tapestry is being woven, so these truths remain the unalterable context of evangelical education. But the weaver of a tapestry is free, within the framework of the loom and the limits of the warp strung upon it, to develop his design. So Christian education works out its own particular practices and patterns within a spiritual framework which, while usually expressed in doctrinal terms, may also be summed up in the single word—"truth." And by "truth" is meant not just religious truth, but truth in all its myriad manifestations—in science, in art, in literature, in human endeavor and human relations of every sort—for it is axiomatic that there can be nothing true that is not of God.

It is not the purpose of this chapter to debate the theological context of evangelical education; it is assumed that it consists of those central doctrines, summarized above, that are the common heritage of Protestantism and that are set forth in the inspired Word of God. Evangelical education has a long and honorable history in the United States, a history during which the theological frame of reference has in its essentials not changed. Emphasis may indeed vary from generation to generation, but revealed truth is not relative but absolute. This does not mean, however, that it is ever fully comprehended at any particular time; the great doctrines of sin and redemption, of God and what He requires of man in worship and service and of how He governs the world —these contain depths yet to be sounded. Composed of truth of infinite dimensions, this frame of reference is spacious enough to enclose all that man can know and plan and do in the field of education as well as in any other field.

II. THE BACKGROUND OF EVANGELICAL EDUCATION

Within this frame, or, to go back to our original figure, upon this loom, how is the tapestry of evangelical education being woven in America today? To answer the question, we must first of all see contemporary evangelical education against its background. That background consists broadly of several periods. First, there was the time of beginnings when all of American education was evangelical, because biblical truth was the spiritual matrix of our first schools and colleges. This was succeeded by a period during which many institutions which were once evangelical shifted in response to pressures of current thought from the biblical to a secular frame of reference and thus drifted from their historic orientation. This in turn was followed by a time when, spurred by the controversy between modernism and conservatism, evangelicals either founded new institutions committed to the biblical frame of reference or strengthened old ones in their allegiance to such truth. That evangelical education is still in this period is evident from its progressive "coming of age" in relation to awareness of its educational philosophy and a concern for intellectual standards.

Now to confine these periods to precise spans of years is impossible. Schools and colleges are living organisms; like individual human beings they develop at different rates. Similarly their response to the climate of opinion and the thousand and one other influences that lead to educational change varies according to such things as the traditions, control, student body, and locale of the particular institution. The most we can say is that the first period began with the founding of Harvard in 1636 and extends until the impact of evolution and the higher criticism upon American theology—i.e., the post-Civil War period. For it is a fact that historic, evangelical Christianity is the true alma mater of the American school and college. In some cases, as with Harvard, the shift from biblical doctrine began comparatively early with the influence of New England Unitarianism and transcendentalism. In other instances, it was delayed until well after the post-Civil War years. Also within this first period there were ebbs and flows of spiritual vitality inside the various institutions, as at the end of the 18th century when Deism and French rationalism all but stifled the Christian life of the colleges, so that at Princeton there were reported to be only two professed Christians among the students, and not more than five or six who did not use profane language in common conversation. (J. Edwin Orr, *The Second Evangelical Awakening in America,* p. 18). Such fluctuations of belief, however, left the religious frame of reference unaltered with the result that when, as at Yale and Princeton, revival came, there was a general return to the original Christian commitment of the institution.

The second period was a shorter one, stretching from after the Civil War to World War I, although here again changes came to different institutions at different times, so that in some instances the retreat from evangelicalism was still in process after 1918.

As for the third period, this, at least in part, overlaps the second. Generalizing again, we may say that it began with the early years of the present century and is continuing today. Particularly since the Twenties there has been an upsurge in evangelical education; new schools and colleges have been founded and old ones have witnessed new access of life and strength.

In these mid-century years, evangelical education is coming of age. Materially it is receiving growing support. Intellectually and culturally its position is being consolidated. Philosophically it is showing an awareness of educational ends and a self-consciousness in relation to method that is leading to higher standards. At the same time it shows signs of moving out of the spiritual and intellectual parochialism that has in the past limited its witness.

III. THE TRENDS IN EVANGELICAL EDUCATION

Such, sketched in a few broad strokes, is the background of evangelical education today. From this background we turn to a closer view of our Christian schools and colleges, of the thinking and planning that underlie their work, and of the direction in which they are going. There are two ways to take such a conspectus of the present educational scene. One is the way of precise documentation, whereby quotations build up the picture. The other is through passing in review the significant trends and movements in evangelical education, not forgetting also its inter-communication with thought beyond its own immediate territory. To be sure, this too requires documentation, but in a chapter of these dimensions not to the extent of the first method. As we continue, ours will be the second way of approach.

The trends in contemporary evangelical education that we shall pass in review are seven in number: first, the growing awareness of the need for the study and formulation of the Christian philosophy of education; second, an increased consciousness of the value of higher intellectual standards not only as a requirement for accreditation but also as an obligatory accompaniment of Christian education; third, a new consciousness of the relation of Christianity to culture; fourth, a penetration of isolationism in evangelical education through the recognition of values in the educational philosophy and practice of other Christian groups not commonly associated with evangelicalism; fifth, a mounting realization of the need for the Christian education of youth on the elementary and secondary levels; sixth, a concern regarding the secularism dominant in public education; seventh, a growing drive toward a more articulate and competent scholarship, especially on the graduate and seminary levels.

Doubtless other observers would identify somewhat differently the chief tendencies in evangelical education. Yet a consideration of these seven trends will go far toward giving us a conspectus of the present state of evangelical Christian education.

IV. THE TASK OF EVANGELICAL EDUCATION

(1) *The growing awareness of the need for the study and formulation of the Christian philosophy of education.* At once honesty compels an admission. Until very recent years, evangelical education, at least in the last of the periods we have identified, has been backward in formulating its philosophy. It was not always so. One may find among the older evangelicals, such as A. A. Hodge of Princeton (*Popular Lectures on Theological Themes,* 1887, pp. 283 ff.), some acute discussions of educational problems. And just the other day the writer of this chapter reread the sections in *What Is Faith?* by J. Gresham Machen (1925, pp. 15 ff., pp. 123 ff.) dealing with education. For cool and incisive criticism of the anti-intellectualism and growing idolatry of democracy that thirty years ago were latent in American education, Machen's words are worthy to stand alongside the writing of a Bernard Iddings Bell or

an Arthur Bestor. But among evangelicals, Machen was somewhat of a voice crying in the wilderness of progressive education and his references to education were incidental to his chief concern, which was always theological.

To put it bluntly, only very recently have evangelicals become at all articulate regarding the philosophy and objectives of their kind of education. Sheltered behind the rightness of their cause and convinced of the error of the other side, they were for years content to go their way with little understanding of why they were doing what they were doing. Thus, while public and liberal religious educators were struggling with some of the central problems of philosophy and practice, evangelicalism for the most part withheld its pen if not always its tongue. The years that saw the publication of the enormously influential works of John Dewey and, in the field of religious education, those of George A. Coe, witnessed, with certain exceptions, little writing of a comparable nature among evangelicals. There was, for example, the work of Herman Harrell Horne, Dewey's most able critic, an evangelical at heart, though not generally recognized by the stricter brethren. Likewise, mention should be made of Walter Albion Squires, whose *Educational Movements of Today* (1930) leaves no doubt of the fact that its Presbyterian author saw clearly the extent to which the naturalistic philosophy of Dewey was pervading not only public education but also religious education. Notable also was the point of view expressed by the Christian Reformed Church, a denomination committed to the Calvinism of leading Dutch theologians such as Abraham Kuyper.

For years members of this group have maintained and supported a system of Christian day schools in conjunction with the National Union of Christian Schools. These schools, not parochial but parent-controlled, represent a Protestant effort of long standing and successful experience to maintain for Christian parents God-centered elementary and secondary day schools. Reference to the outreach of this movement through the more recent National Association of Christian Schools will come later in this chapter. The point of interest now is that the Christian Reformed group was one of the first to show a realization of the need for formulating a Christian philosophy of education.

Some thirty years ago, three members of the faculty of Calvin College translated a small book by T. Van Der Kooy, Principal of Dr. A. Kuyper School of Vlaardingen, Netherlands, entitled *The Distinctive Features of the Christian School* (1925). In the light of future developments in evangelical thinking about education, these statements in the translators' preface are noteworthy:

> A book in English, setting forth the distinctive principles of Christian education is, in our opinion, a necessity . . . It is true that our institutions have certain needs in common with every

> school . . . but it is equally true that in addition to, or rather qualifying all similarities between the Christian schools and others, there should be a definite educational consciousness on the part of our people revolving about the 'why' of Christian education . . .
>
> But there is a second consideration. We are in the midst of the stream of Americanization. And just because we have so long stood on the banks, the danger is now greater that we shall be swept along by the current.

The foregoing is doubly interesting; first, because of its clear recognition of the need for spelling out the "why" of Christian education; and second, because of its frank admission of the impetus for doing this. It is the latter that sets apart from most other evangelicals what we may call the Dutch school of educational philosophy. This desire to preserve in their schools the distinctive Calvinism of the Netherlands was a motive that continues today among the Christian Reformed groups; along with the influence of older thinkers like Kuyper and Bavinck, the Dutch strain is still potent among them. An excellent illustration is seen in the recent anthology edited by Cornelius Jaarsma of Calvin College, *Fundamentals in Christian Education: Theory and Practice* (1953); among the sixteen contributors to this book, five are now resident in the Netherlands, the others being Americans of Dutch heritage like Berkhof, Heerema, Jellema, and Van Til. A similar example is *Basic Concepts in Christian Pedagogy,* the Calvin Foundation Lectures for 1954, delivered in Grand Rapids by Jan Waterink of the Free University of Amsterdam (1954). Works like these contain much first-rate thinking about education; in fact, no student of the philosophy of Christian education can afford to neglect them. Yet the significant point is that the impetus behind their writing and publication is closely related to a special theological and national background.

Turning from the Dutch school to the other evangelicals, we find, first, a lag in systematic formulation of educational philosophy, and next a quite different motivation for articulateness. The conservative evangelicalism of recent years has a marked undenominational cast; while it includes institutions under denominational control, some of its strongest representatives have no denominational ties at all. Thus it lacks the theological homogeneity of the Dutch school. Nor, by the same token, is there among the rank and file of evangelicals a continuing national influence. Consequently, the catalyst which has precipitated recent formulations of the philosophy of evangelical education outside the Dutch school must be sought elsewhere than in a unified theology like Calvinism and in a common old-world heritage.

Actually, the catalytic agent in this case contains several elements: reaction against the naturalism of public education on the one hand, and the anti-supernaturalism of the secular college or the modernistic seminary on the other hand; demands of accrediting agencies for written formulation of the aims and objectives of institutions seeking academic recognition; publication of notable studies of educational philosophy, particularly the Harvard Report of 1945, *General Education in a Free Society*.

It is not possible to assess with precision the degree to which each of the foregoing catalytic elements has contributed to the various formulations of the philosophy of evangelical education. As we have already seen, J. Gresham Machen thirty years ago gave pointed expression to the dangers of "progressivism" in education and, as time passed, his strictures were shared by other Christian thinkers, among whom might be mentioned Robert L. Cooke of Wheaton College, whose *Philosophy, Education, and Certainty* (1940) is not only one of the earlier but also one of the most discerning discussions of educational philosophy written by an evangelical. In short, the flooding opposition to the naturalistic bias of progressivism was bound to break through the dam of evangelical inarticulateness.

A second catalytic element leading to the precipitation of evangelical opinion has undoubtedly been the accrediting program of the regional associations, like the Middle States Association of Colleges and Secondary Schools and the North Central Association. The evaluation program, conducted in various parts of the country as a prerequisite to regional accreditation, demands that the school or college furnish the visiting committee a succinct declaration of its philosophy and objectives. Thus more than one institution has been forced for the first time to set down a plain statement of what it is trying to do and how and why it is doing it. Without doubt this too has been an impetus to the study of the philosophy of evangelical education.

Another catalytic element has been the appearance of such books as the widely heralded Harvard Report (1945) and Spencer Leeson's distinguished Bampton Lectures at Oxford (1947), entitled *Christian Education,* which, though published in England, have been widely influential among American evangelicals. The Harvard Report, *General Education in a Free Society,* was directly responsible for the preparation of an important evangelical document; for it was discussion of the Report in the meeting of the Group on Secondary Schools at the 1946 Convention of the National Association of Evangelicals that led to the Convention's authorization of a committee to study the philosophy and practice of education, and this in turn led to the publication of *Christian Education in a Democracy* (1951), a book soon recognized by liberals as well as evangelicals as the most comprehensive and thorough study of education yet made by a conservative group.

Christian Education in a Democracy does not, however, stand alone. It had its predecessors, such as Edwin Rian's able *Christianity and Amer-*

ican Education (1949), to name but one; and it has a growing number of successors. For one thing, a number of the Christian colleges have through faculty study given thorough consideration to the formulation of their philosophies of education. Among such are Wheaton and Houghton Colleges; the Wheaton study, entitled *A Blue Print for Christian Higher Education,* is of book length and is now in process of publication. Significant also is the Winter 1956 Issue of *The Asbury Seminarian,* published by Asbury Theological Seminary and devoted to Christian education with special reference to the Wesleyan tradition.

Other more general treatments of the evangelical philosophy of education include *Abiding Values in Christian Education* by Harold C. Mason (1955), certainly one of the most competent volumes on education yet written by an evangelical; *The Pattern of God's Truth* (1954), which deals with the integration of Christian truth throughout the whole educational program; and the publications of Mark Fakkema, Executive Secretary of the National Association of Christian Schools. Dr. Fakkema's work (cf. *Christian Philosophy: Its Educational Implications*) is important because it has been and continues to be given as special lecture courses in many colleges, seminaries, and churches throughout the country. This unique exposition of Christian philosophy, which reflects strongly the views of the Dutch school, is thus influencing the educational practice of the rank and file of evangelicals.

(2) *An increased consciousness of higher intellectual standards not only as a requirement for accreditation but also as an obligatory accompaniment of Christian education.* This trend, though obvious, is far from insignificant. The day when evangelical schools and colleges were doing little to raise educational standards has passed. Recent decades have seen a deepening concern for accreditation and improved standards on the part of evangelical schools and colleges throughout the nation. Whether or not in some cases this preoccupation with academic standing has in it something of the "have-nots" reaching after accredited status merely for the sake of prestige, the fact remains that by and large this trend has served to elevate evangelical education. Twenty-five years ago, the number of deeply conservative evangelical schools and colleges which had gone beyond state recognition and gained accreditation by the regional bodies was almost non-existent; today a growing company of institutions have achieved regional approval. And to their credit it should be said that they have done this without lowering their doctrinal colors. Despite a minority who insist that the attainment of accreditation entails spiritual compromise, a school or college never has to buy academic standing by selling out its evangelical distinctiveness.

It should be also observed that the drive toward accreditation goes beyond the evangelical secondary schools and liberal arts colleges. Since the foundation in 1943 of the National Association of Evangelicals with its Commission on Education, the Bible institutes and Bible colleges have set up their own accrediting association. This led in 1949 to recognition by the U. S. Office of Education of their criteria as the standard for a new field of accreditation in American higher education—namely, the field, "Bible."

Now there are inevitable corollaries of this drive toward accreditation on the part of evangelicals. Unquestionably it has jolted some schools out of intellectual ruts, opened up new vistas of academic achievement, and hastened the development of essential educational equipment, such as libraries and laboratories, to meet legitimate demands of accrediting agencies. As never before, evangelical education is becoming aware of its responsibility for the maintenance of excellence. No longer can an institution contented with inferior standards take refuge behind the excuse that it is spiritually sound. Of course, any school or college, whether secular or Christian, must begin. It is no disgrace for a new school not to have full recognition. But the constant aim must be for first-rate attainment in the classroom, in the library and laboratory, in extracurricular activities, as well as in the chapel. It is no light thing for a school to declare openly its commitment to Christ and the Bible. Such commitment carries an obligation to do everything possible to achieve excellence—not for pride or prestige, but for God's glory. For evangelicals must never be content to offer a poor education in the Name of God.

(3) *A new consciousness of the relation of Christianity to culture.* Although worthy of separate notice, this trend does not require extended analysis. Actually it is linked closely with the preceding trend. Higher standards have opened up for evangelical education a new appreciation of the best in culture. Moreover, education that takes seriously the principle that all truth is God's truth cannot stand aloof from truth in music, literature, and in art. The question of Tertullian about what Athens has to do with Jerusalem, is not relevant to evangelical education today. As a matter of fact, even the evangelicalism of the Puritans did not insulate itself against true culture, as Percy Scholes and C. S. Lewis have shown in their studies of Puritanism. For evangelicalism to shun culture is not a valid option; according to Emile Cailliet, what is needed is rather a conversation with culture in which evangelicalism stands firmly within "the Biblical landscape of reality" (*The Christian Approach to Culture,* New York, 1953). That this is realized by many an evangelical institution is evidenced, for one thing, by the revival of good music. Never was there more and better music well taught and capably performed in many of our schools and colleges and Bible institutes than today. To be sure, a good deal of the second-rate music too often associated with evangelicalism remains with us. Yet notable progress has been made.

(4) *A penetration of the isolationism of evangelical education through the recognition of values in the educational philosophy and practice of*

Christian groups not commonly associated with evangelicalism. At the Kent Seminar on "The Christian Idea of Education," held at Kent School in Connecticut in November, 1956, and attended by some four hundred educational leaders from coast to coast, the Chairman of the Seminar, Dr. W. G. Pollard, Director of the Oak Ridge Atomic Laboratory, advanced the thesis that we stand today at the beginning of a Christian renaissance. For a long time modern thought and culture have been, he pointed out, in a virtual dark age, during which the Graeco-Roman strain in Western civilization has dominated the Judaeo-Christian strain. But now the climate of opinion is changing. There is a new awareness of the relevance of Christian truth. Under the impact of the present distress of men and nations, we are turning back to biblical categories and supernatural Christianity. The outright evangelical might say that we are entering upon a period of revival. Be that as it may, the fact remains that today Christianity is being taken seriously by many people, including a significant number in academic life, who twenty years ago would not have considered it. Of course, we still have our hard core of naturalists in education like E. F. Chave, Harl Douglass, and Theodore Brameld. But whereas in the past there were very few educational thinkers standing on middle ground between the naturalism of such men as Dewey and Bode, and the biblical supernaturalism of the N.A.E. Report, the mediating position is now to the fore. But "mediating" may not always be an accurate word, because much that is being published on religious education by writers not usually identified with evangelical orthodoxy is clearly on the side of historic, supernatural Christianity. To this statement, however, an exception must at once be made. In nearly every case, writers who represent a return to genuine Christianity in education balk at the high view of Scripture as the inerrant Word of God that is the common premise of the more conservative evangelical schools and colleges. They insist on equating it with theories of mechanical dictation and a pre-critical, slavishly literal outlook simply not held by enlightened evangelicals today.

But let us go on to consider some examples of the mediating position. An illustration of this position with a strong bias toward Bushnell's theory of Christian nurture and the liberalism of George A. Coe is *Protestant Nurture—An Introduction to Christian Education* by Harry C. Munro (1956), in which the author attempts with indifferent success to bring the older liberal views up to date and at the same time hold on to some Christian doctrines. Far more successful and quite crucial in its influence is *Faith and Nurture* by H. Shelton Smith (1941). Theologically neo-orthodox, the book has done much to expose the inadequacy of liberalism in religious education.

In this connection, three other books may be mentioned. *The Mind's Adventure* by Howard Lowry (1950) is a beautifully written discussion of the philosophy and problems of Christian higher education, definitely opposed to secularism and broadly evangelical. Less evangelical and most hostile to "Biblicism," yet making some surprising admissions in advocating for the Christian college much of what conservative evangelical education already practices, is *Christian Faith and Higher Education* by Nels Ferré (1954). Of high significance is *The Teaching Ministry of the Church* by James D. Smart (1954). To a large degree this study takes a thoroughly evangelical position. Much of it is a trenchant analysis of the weakness of modern programs of religious education as deficient in genuine Christianity. Despite misapprehension of the thoroughly conservative view of the Bible, this is an extremely competent discussion that moves far to the right theologically.

Among the most brilliant critics of secular education are some of the Episcopalians, such as James A. Pike, J. Langmead Casserly, Chad Walsh, and Bernard Iddings Bell. These men believe in supernatural Christianity, albeit in a church-centered context. Bell's writings, such as *Crisis in Education* (1949), have been read with approval by many evangelicals. In short, there is in the educational philosophy of Episcopalianism a swing away from liberalism and back to traditional orthodoxy.

The influence of writings such as these has been leading evangelical thought outside the parochialism that has long encompassed it. It has been refreshing and stimulating for earnest proponents of the integration of education with biblical Christianity to realize that there are others besides themselves on the side of the angels. And there are those who hope that, as other Christian thinkers come nearer the position of biblical evangelicalism, the current misunderstanding of what evangelicals mean by the inspiration of the Scriptures will at last be clarified.

(5) *A mounting realization of the need for Christian education on the elementary and secondary levels.* With a few notable exceptions—the Lutherans, the Christian Reformed, and the Mennonites—evangelicals have until recently failed to maintain a proper balance in Christian education. Their chief efforts have been expended upon the upper levels—colleges, Bible institutes, and seminaries. In comparison with these, secondary and elementary schools have been poor relations. The result has been an educational program that may be likened to an inverted pyramid resting upon its apex.

Today, however, there are signs of a change of heart. All over the country, Christian day schools, both elementary and secondary, are springing up in such numbers as to point to a grass-roots movement. In this field the National Association of Christian Schools (an affiliate of N. A. E.), with its clearly-defined philosophy of education, exercises growing influence. It is apparent that when it comes to building lower schools, evangelical parents are reacting constructively against the secularism of public education.

(6) This brings us to the sixth trend—*a concern regarding the secularism dominant in public education.* Such concern finds clear expression in the Christian day school movement. But this movement by no means cancels the responsibility of evangelicals for the American public school. Here is an area where Protestants, from modernists to fundamentalists, stand together against secularism, just as they do against the encroachments of Romanism. Protestant spokesmen of varying convictions are alive to the tendency in public education to elevate democracy to a religious or even semi-religious status. So Henry P. Van Dusen in *God in Education* (1951) sees some of the same problems identified by Leslie R. Marston in his chapter on the public school in *Christian Education in a Democracy* (1951), or by Edward K. Worrell in *Restoring God to Education* (1950).

Regarding the unsatisfactory status of religion in public education, most Protestants agree. But when it comes to solving this stubborn problem, the Gordian knot has yet to be cut. While some, like certain of the Baptists, would ban anything savoring of religion from the public schools on the ground of a strict interpretation of the constitutional principle of separation of church and state, others are quick to point out that such removal of religion from public education teaches by the potent eloquence of silence that religion is unnecessary and God inconsequential. Others press for released time programs, or for Bible reading, and, where the climate of opinion is favorable, as in parts of the South, even for Bible-teaching in the public schools. But whatever be the particular attitude, it is reassuring that many evangelicals are waking up to the spiritual dilemma of the public school. The fact cannot be blinked that public education is a bulwark of our freedom. Evangelicals have a perfect right to support their own schools. But doing this in no way excuses them from the responsibility of assuming their share of support of public education. It is a cardinal teaching of the New Testament that Christians are obligated faithfully to discharge their duties as citizens.

(7) *A growing drive on the part of evangelicalism toward a more articulate and competent scholarship, especially on the graduate and seminary levels.* It was Sir William Ramsay who said, "Christianity is the religion of an educated mind." Through a combination of influences, such as those discussed in the preceding pages, evangelicalism is becoming alert to the truth of Ramsay's statement. This alertness is manifest in what bids fair to be a renaissance of evangelical scholarship. Professors in evangelical colleges, Bible institutes, and seminaries are better trained than before. Academic in-breeding, once a contributing factor to what might have become intellectual and scholarly sterility, is being lessened, so that there is arising a generation of evangelical scholars trained in the great universities, competent in their particular intellectual disciplines, yet holding with enlightened conviction to the faith once deliv-

ered to the saints. Not only that, but these scholars are producing work that compels the respect and attention of a liberalism that has too long assumed that evangelicalism has little to offer from a scholarly point of view. Nor is this renaissance of productive scholarship confined to the Bible and theology. Increasingly, evangelicals of real competence are expressing themselves in such diverse fields as philosophy, psychology, education, archaeology, and science.

Admittedly, there is much land yet to be taken. But an important beginning has been made and evangelicals are producing a growing number of scholarly books. Moreover evangelical scholarship is becoming increasingly self-critical. Studies of biblical and theological views long considered sacrosanct are being made, not in an iconoclastic spirit but with a sincere desire to arrive at the truth as set forth in the Word of God. One does not need to agree with all the conclusions of such studies to recognize in their publication a wholesome symptom of the maturation of evangelical thought.

V. THE UNIFYING CENTER OF EDUCATION

With this survey of trends, we conclude our conspectus of contemporary evangelical thought as it relates to education. If the conspectus has shown us anything, it has revealed the complexity of the tapestry which, in response to present-day needs and tensions, is being woven upon the unchanging framework of Christian truth. Movements in education may come and go. Fashions in the theory and practice of our schooling may change. But there is One who abides unchanging. With the writer of the Epistle to the Hebrews, we may say of the variegated designs upon which we are at work, "they shall all wax old as doth a garment, and as a vesture shalt thou fold them up, and they shall all be changed: but thou art the same, and thy years shall not fail." For the abiding center, the unifying factor that gives meaning and permanence to our education is now, as always, "Jesus Christ the same yesterday, and today, and forever."

PHILOSOPHY OF HISTORY

Earle E. Cairns

Earle E. Cairns holds his Ph.D. degree in history from the University of Nebraska, and once taught New Testament studies at Presbyterian Theological Seminary in Omaha, where he had received theological training. His affiliation with Wheaton College began in 1943, and since 1948 he has been chairman of the history department. He has authored two works, A Blueprint for Christian Higher Education, *and a church history,* Christianity Through the Centuries.

7. *Earle E. Cairns:*

PHILOSOPHY OF HISTORY

EARLY TWENTIETH century men blithely subscribed to the optimistic thought that all was well with the world. The decade of despair which followed the breakdown of international political order with the failure of the League of Nations in the Manchurian crisis in 1932, and the world economic crisis of the depression after 1929, shattered this optimism. Until then progress seemed possible because man was thought to be basically good and perfectible. With science as its tool any achievement seemed possible to the human mind. Pure science opened up vistas of godlike knowledge and power. Applied science through the technology of the continuing Industrial Revolution had created a world of abundance. Men would share this abundance with each other through international democratic organization and world free trade.

I. THE FAILURE OF SCIENTIFIC HISTORY

The promise of scientific history to integrate the material which exhaustive research had created in numerous monographs ruled out any interest in philosophical history of an evangelical variety. The search for ultimate theistic meaning in history was less interesting than the attempt to discover self-evident causation in the descriptive data which the historian had gathered by scientific techniques. Because natural science derived seemingly necessary laws by the scientific technique, it was assumed that history would also yield such laws to the inquirer who made use of the scientific method. At one extreme, the communistic followers of Marx believed that these laws might even be used to build an ideal society.

Historians forgot what most are now recognizing—that history can never be as exact a science as physics or chemistry. The scientist can use the technique of tentative hypothesis, experiment, observation, and verification to provide him with the data to make the inductions which seem to yield necessary natural laws. The historian can be scientific and objective in gathering documents and deriving facts from them, but when he begins to select and interpret those facts in order to arrive at their meaning the subjective element comes into history.

The scientist studies the data of nature, but the historian and his subject, the actions of man in society, are a part of his data. The scientist does not have to cope with the factor of human freedom. His data usually consists of controllable present objects which he can study experimentally in the laboratory, but the historian deals with self-determining dynamic individuals who have left records which were sometimes forged, interpolated, prejudiced, or incomplete. The personal and cultural biases of the historian may also color the meaning he ascribes to his data. Contingency or chance, which may indicate to the evangelical historian the presence of Providence in history, make universal laws questionable. Great men may seize opportunities to control nations and alter the course of history. Natural events, such as the unusually calm English Channel which allowed the British to evacuate their army from Dunkirk in 1940, conspire against the development of uniform laws in history. Historians of all varieties of opinion are beginning to recognize that the application of science to history cannot produce laws that are always and everywhere valid. This constitutes the failure of scientific history to create a science of history.

II. THE CRISIS OF HISTORY

The failure of scientific history leaves the non-Christian historian inadequate to deal with the modern crisis of the twentieth century. The enlargement of the borders of science has seemed only to push God farther into the recesses of the universe, and leave man with a sense of finiteness, ignorance, and aloneness in a universe which often seems hostile with its uncontrollable floods, volcanoes, and earthquakes. Impersonal nature is so vast and powerful that man seems insignificant and weak. This constitutes the *cosmic* crisis of our day.

The average man is still more affected by the *social* crisis which is much more personal to him. The nineteenth century hope that economic interdependence, which the machine has fostered, would be followed by political unification, has been shattered by destructive racial nationalism, class conflict, the depression of the Thirties, two world wars, and the possibility of a third in which bacterial and atomic warfare might annihilate most men and destroy our painfully-created civilization. This crisis is made more terrifying by the demonic forces which have manifested themselves in the cruelty of modern man to his fellows. Genocide, the planned destruction of a nation, is a new term in our vocabulary. The disintegration of personality which modern psychological torture has made possible is more destructive than the most brutal medieval torture. The various ramifications of this social crisis have been ably developed by C. Gregg Singer in an article on the collapse of Western civilization (*The Westminster Theological Journal,* Vol. XV, No. 1, [November, 1952], pp. 125-142).

Modern man is also conscious of a *personal* crisis which has led to the revival of the doctrine of the universality of sin. He is no longer confident that he can cope with the personal and social crises with the resources which he can find within himself or within his culture. The early optimism of H. G. Wells gave way before his death to despair for the future. Men are vitally interested in whether history has any ultimate meaning or an answer to what the future holds. The modern dogma of inevitable, indefinite progress has proved false. This led Oswald Spengler during World War I to adopt a despairing cyclic history in which man is imprisoned until freed by death. Arnold J. Toynbee believes that our civilization may commit suicide, but thinks that there is still hope if we can unify modern civilization politically and economically and develop a universal religion. The evangelical philosopher of history turns from these pessimistic or cautiously optimistic answers to biblical theism as a more realistic answer to crisis.

In crisis a philosophy of history is much more desirable than "scientific" history. The orthodox philosophic *City of God* was Augustine's answer to the crisis of the sack of Rome in 410. The crisis of World War I led Spengler to write his answer in *The Decline of the West.* Man in crisis is concerned with the whence, whither, and why of himself and society. Linear or cyclical views of history replace the optimistic spiral view of history as progress. The linear approach of the Christian interpreter of history involves the belief that our crisis is primarily moral and spiritual. Political and economic crises are merely symptoms of the moral and spiritual disease that afflicts man and his society. The evangelical has a real opportunity to offer the alternative philosophy of history of biblical theism.

III. CAN HISTORY HAVE VALUE IN CRISIS?

If the modern historian had not been so obsessed with the use of science and the cult of progress in historical study, he would have remembered that both the ancient and early Christian historians insisted that history taught practical and moral lessons of value. Classical historians emphasized the political lessons of history; Christian writers stressed the religious and moral lessons of history.

The scientific Greek historian Thucydides believed that history would be useful to men who want to know the past in order to have some idea of what the future might be like (*The History of the Peloponnesian War,* I:22). Polybius thought that history should reveal the reason why what was said or done resulted in success or failure (*Histories,* XII:25b). It should also give methods for dealing with any contingency that might arise (IX:2). Man can reform himself by painful experience or by using the experience of others in history (I:35). The history of the past is the best corrective of conduct, and the lessons of history are the best education for political life (I:1). Livy stated that history provides a vicarious experience so that one can imitate the good and avoid the evil (*Histories,* Bk. I, Preface). Tacitus believed that the knowledge that man's deeds would go down in history was a deterrent to evil deeds and a stimulus to a good life (*Annals,* III:65). Plutarch presented alternate examples of good and bad men so that people would imitate the good (*Lives,* Pericles, II). The modern crisis reminds men that the educative function of history which Paul expressed so clearly was applicable to us "upon whom the ends of the age are come" (Rom. 15:4, I Cor. 10:6,11). In view of this the evangelical historian has the challenge to make philosophy of history again, as in the days of Augustine, relevant to our time.

In view of Paul's conception of the role of history it is surprising that since the days of Augustine until recently evangelicals have had so little to say concerning philosophy of history. Perhaps the feeling that biblical prophecy clearly charts the course of history has caused many evangelicals to feel no need for an organized philosophy of history. They have been so busy proclaiming the Gospel at home and abroad that such studies seemed irrelevant. The liberal idea of the end of history in history by human effort, which was inherent in the social gospel, may have caused others to shrink from this subject. The wide interest of people in a philosophy of history, which is made apparent by the popularity of such works as those of Toynbee, shows that evangelicals should give it more attention. The modern crisis has forced many people to ask whether there is any sense of direction in history or an end to history other than destruction. Is the end destruction or is it perfection by virtue of God's direction of history to its catacylsmic, supernatural conclusion in which the power of evil is ended and the power of good evidenced in the triumph of a perfect order?

An article by E. Harris Harbison (*Church History,* Vol. XII, No. 2 [June, 1952] pp. 97-197) pointed out the increasing interest of neo-orthodox and chastened liberals in the formulation of a Christian philosophy of history, but he mentioned no efforts along this line by recognized evangelicals. While those he mentions have been producing books on this subject, he ignores what little has been done by evangelicals.

Some evangelicals have briefly sketched their concepts of history in developing a philosophy of religion and, in some cases, have given some criticism of other views. Edward J. Carnell in *An Introduction to Christian Apologetics* (1952; pp. 109-111, 292-297) briefly states the major ideas of an evangelical philosophy of history. A short article in *His* by Donald Masters on a Christian interpretation of history (Vol. 13, No. 9 [June, 1953] pp. 4-7) presents some basic principles. James Daane has sketched the outlines of a Reformed philosophy of history (*Calvin Forum,* Vol. XIV, No. 10-12 [May-July, 1949] pp. 209-211, 234-236). In formulating his philosophy of missions, Harold Lindsell briefly developed with some criticism the evangelical and alternative approaches to history in his book, *A Christian Philosophy of Missions* (1949). Gordon H. Clark has given an exposition with some criticism of the ideas of Marx, Spengler, and Toynbee and briefly stated the ideas which he thinks are essential in a Christian philosophy of history in his book, *A Christian View of Men and Things* (1952), but all of this is subordinate to his overall discussion of philosophy of religion. This writer attempted the classification, description, and criticism of alternative philosophies of history and the formulation of a Christian approach in a fairly lengthy article upon which he has drawn for parts of this chapter (*Crisis Christology,* Vol. 5, No. 3 [Spring, 1948] pp. 3ff.). Most of these writers agree on the major points for an evangelical approach to history, and all of them, consciously or unconsciously, draw upon the Augustinian tradition as well as the Bible.

IV. THE NATURE AND MEANING OF HISTORY

Before one can survey the alternatives and the evangelical approach to history, one must consider what history is. *Historia,* from which the word history is derived, meant to the Greeks inquiry, investigation, or research. It refers to the process of gathering historical facts. They later used the term *historikos,* which meant a narrative and referred to the product of historical research, the written reconstruction of the past. The German word *Geschichte* had reference to history as an event or happening. This is the raw stuff of history which happens only once in time and space. Thus history can never repeat itself exactly although the historian may find parallels between different eras. The evangelical historian senses that history as process and product is always relative and that any human answer to the meaning of history can never be absolute. Hence history may be defined as the interpreted reconstruction of man's socially significant past activities which is based on organized data gathered by scientific techniques. This definition means that the historian should give as much attention to the philosophic element in history as he gives to the scientific element.

In the light of this discussion of the nature of history the historian is faced with the necessity of considering how to get at the ultimate meaning of history. He will recognize, as he selects, organizes, and interprets the facts of history, that a subjective element enters into his thinking. No historian can be oblivious to the fact that he will have either an explicit or an implicit, unconsciously-held philosophy of history. This means that any discussion of history cannot stop with the relation of the past to the present in a detached scientific record, but must takc into account the future goal toward which the historical process is moving.

Discussions of the meaning of history fall into two categories. The advocates of a science of history believe that secondary temporal considerations, such as the economic or geographic influences on man, are sufficient causes to exhaust the meaning of history. Though they may not say it or realize it, they are looking for a final causation within the historical process which will give them as valid and universal laws as those of science. Such approaches may be classed as schools of interpretation. The evangelical philosopher can never be content to deal only with such material. He recognizes that history has a vertical dimension which rises above such man-created and non-revelational approaches.

Advocates of a philosophy of history seek to find an ultimate principle which fits all the facts and gives meaning to the whole process of history. They include the origin, course, and future goal of human history in order to see it as a whole. Although the phrase "philosophy of history" did not come into popular use until Voltaire coined it, many have sought a systematic interpretation of history by finding a principle which would unify successive individual events and which would offer an ultimate meaning for these events. Such an approach to the data of history has an appeal for the biblical theist.

Most modern historians have avoided a philosophy of history because they were fearful that an *a priori* hypothesis would lead them to be untrue to the data which they had gathered by scientific techniques. They insisted that history dealt only with empirical facts, but they failed to recognize that any interpretation of history involves philosophizing and that their science of history was based upon an implicit philosophy which they were not conscious that they were holding. Man in crisis cannot be satisfied with a science of history which deals only with the data of time. He wants an interpretation which will give a coherent and unified view of natural, historical and biblical data.

I. SCHOOLS OF INTERPRETATION

Evangelical historians are unable to accept the sweeping claims of the various schools of history because these schools overemphasize the horizontal earthly thrust of history and either ignore or reject its vertical spiritual orientation. They hope to find final meaning in history by linking historical events in a causal chain of inductions which they derive from a study of the descriptive data of history. This is a logical result of the belief in man's basic goodness and perfectibility, which was so common in the eighteenth century, and of the nineteenth century Darwinian principle of development or evolution which was analogically applied to social data. Man or nature apart from God is emphasized by these schools of interpretation.

The Geographic School

The geographical, environmental, or frontier school of interpretation emphasized the role of nature as the causal factor in history. Frederick Jackson Turner's address, "The Significance of the Frontier in American History," before the American Historical Association in Chicago during the World's Fair in 1893, brought this school to birth. Turner reacted against historians who were explaining American institutions merely in terms of our European heritage. He argued that American democratic institutions and ideals, nationalism, energy, and thrift were the result of the influence of the frontier with its free land for settlement. This interpretation, which roots man in nature, did not take into account the fact that democracy existed on the Eastern seaboard and was carried to the frontier by settlers from the East. American democracy, moreover, is derived from English institutions and was brought to the New World by English colonists. Turner and his followers forgot that geography is relatively static and that man is dynamic and able to rise above his geographical limitations. They also rejected any providential element in history.

The School of Economic Determinism

Karl Marx believed that economic techniques of production determined the type of institutions, ideals, and social organization of any age. Economic determinists such as Charles and Mary Beard, though not Marxists, nonetheless borrowed his idea. In his book, *An Economic Interpretation of the Constitution of the United States* (1913) Charles Beard attributed our strong central government largely to the fact that the framers of the Constitution held bonds and currency which were issued during the Revolution and which might become valueless unless a strong Federal government was created. Their many followers agree with the Beards in making the economic factor the key to history. They have done a useful service in pointing out that history must give attention to the fact that making a living is essential to human existence and is as important as battles and politicians. They erred, however, in making it the main causal factor instead of one of several conditioning factors which operate as secondary causes in history. Evangelical historians knew the importance of the economic factor to a full Christian life long before Marx or the Beards (cf. I Thess. 4:11-12).

The "Great Man" School of History

In contrast with those who link man with nature the biographical school emphasizes great men as the causative factor in history. Since World War I Lytton Strachey, Andre Maurois, Stefan Zweig, and others have proclaimed that the great men are the makers of history. The German rise to world power after 1933 is considered to be the result of Hitler's determinative personality. This theory ignores the chaotic postwar conditions in Germany which made it possible for this unscrupulous opportunist to seize power. Men are as much conditioned by historical forces as they are makers of history. These writers erred because they made men the major determining force in history and because they forgot that man is a finite creature whom God has endowed with an eternal spirit.

While it is true that economics and geography influence history, and that great men have been important in history, these schools err by raising a temporal relative factor in history to the point where it becomes a universal absolute. They seem to equate history and nature in order to make their "laws" of history as deterministic as those of nature seem to be. They do not appear to realize that their supposedly empirical causes really have basic underlying naturalistic or humanistic philosophies. They ignore the complexity and plurality of human history and deny the possibility of an ultimate, such as God, transcendent to history but working within the realm of history. They confuse the distinction which can be drawn by the Christian interpreter between secondary or conditioning causes and the primary cause behind the phenomena of history. The evangelical historian recognizes that on the horizontal stage of time how men make a living, their social institutions, their geographical environment, their artistic impulses, their intellectual life, and the influence of great men will be secondary conditioning factors in human history, but that above all these there is the transcendent Creator Who is immanent in history as Lord and Redeemer. The evangelical finds partial answers in history, but believes that the ultimate answer to history cannot be found within the historical process.

II. PHILOSOPHIES OF HISTORY

The distinction between a school of history and a philosophy of history can be presented best in a series of contrasts. The former is based upon descriptive facts gained by empirical techniques, but the latter asks the meaning of these facts in a more subjective deductive approach. The first deals with the partial data of time and space, which a scientific study of human affairs reveals, but the second seeks a wholeness by relating time and space to the eternal and absolute in a synthesis which also includes revelational data. The latter is also a part of history. The main difference is really one of scope rather than essence because schools of history have an implicit unrecognized philosophy. The philosopher of history admits the importance of philosophy in historical study since it will come in the back door if it is denied entrance by the front door. Joseph Pieper in his recent useful little work *The End of Time* (1954) insists that a meaningful synthesis of history can only be found within a philosophic framework.

Some have organized a philosophy of history from the viewpoint of time as cyclic, spiral, and linear or rectilinear. This arrangement is helpful, but Arnold Toynbee combines a cyclic and spiral view which would not fit this pattern. Others suggest that views of history are naturalistic, humanistic, and idealistic, depending upon whether nature, man, or some absolute is the moving force in history. Modern liberal interpretations, however, are humanistic; yet God is brought into history to guarantee progress. Progress, the lack of it, and Providence have been suggested as categories to delimit the various theories, but liberals, such as Shirley Jackson Case and Arthur Munk, link continued progress with Providence. The writer has found that the categories of pessimistic, optimistic, and pessimistic-optimistic philosophies offer the best framework for organizing the various philosophies of history. The different conceptions of time, basic world and life views, progress, and Providence fit readily into this framework.

Pessimistic Philosophies of History

The roots of Oswald Spengler's cyclical view of history are the ideas of classical and oriental thinkers which involved a pessimistic view of human affairs in which progress was impossible. The recurrent day-and-night cycle, the cycle of the seasons, and the regular cyclical movement of the stars in the Great Year of astronomy seemed analogically to suggest this pattern for history. Because they concluded that time was circular rather than linear, they used the symbols of the circle to express the process of history as well as that of nature. Man was thought to be bound to the wheel of time, and his only refuge was flight from the realm of sensation to that of pure being by the exercise of reason. Because they were without hope in time (cf. Eph. 2:12), they were pessimistic and inclined to a deterministic and often fatalistic view of man in history. The movement of a treadmill, a swinging pendulum, or a freespinning wheel serves to symbolize these views. The writer of Ecclesiastes admitted this cyclical determinism in nature, but raised man above it by the operation of divine grace in his historical and moral life (1:1-11, cf. 12:13-14).

Pessimistic philosophies of history share several features. Although they do not include the Christian doctrine of original sin, they emphasize the process of *degeneration* in history. The Greek Hesiod spoke of successive gold, silver, bronze, and iron stages of history. The Golden Age is usually placed at the beginning of each cycle rather than at the end, as is the case with optimistic and pessimistic-optimistic views. The process of degeneration becomes meaningful in time, which is marked by recurrent cyclical *duration*. The deterministic cycles of nature are thought to be reflected in history. There is no freedom for man in time and space. Submission to fate with the hope of eventual redemption from the wheel of time in the meaningful eternal order seems to be the duty of man. This *determinism* contrasts sharply with the emphasis of Christianity upon human responsibility and the origin, course, and consummation of history in time under divine guidance. The pessimist, however, posits degeneration throughout each cycle which goes through the same process.

Plato looked upon the course of time as a series of cycles, each of which begins through the activity of a creative absolute as a Golden Age and deteriorates under the hand of Fate until its destruction takes place and the absolute starts another cycle (*The Laws,* Bk. III:676-678; *Timaeus,* 21-23). Aristotle, noting the circular motion of the firmament (*Meteorologica,* I:3), concluded that the necessary coming-to-be of everything was a circular motion (*De Generatione et Corruptione,* 338a, 5-6, 11, 15-16; see also 337a, 1-9).

Cyclical determinism has not appealed to many modern historians. While Vico (1668-1714) held to a cyclical view of history, he believed that Providence was guiding each cycle so that each subsequent cycle exhibited a higher spiritual level than the one which preceded it. Oswald Spengler, however, in the crash of German ambitions after World War I, published a pessimistic, deterministic, cyclical philosophy of history which shows the influence of the classical pessimists.

Spengler studied science, mathematics, art, and history at the universities of Halle, Munich, and Jena. After completing his doctoral dissertation on Heraclitus, he became a high-school teacher. Some years later he devoted himself to historical study and writing and completed the first draft of *The Decline of the West.* The first World War prevented its publication, and he worked on revising his manuscript. The first volume was published in 1918 and the disillusioned Germans bought fifty thousand copies in four years. The second volume came out in 1922. This heavy work from the pen of the claustrophobic, militaristic Prussian seemed relevant in a world in which progress had been set back rudely by a world war after a century of relative peace. Spengler called his work "a German philosophy" and "the philosophy of our time" which would give a new conception of history (*The Decline of the West,* 2 vols., translated by Charles F. Atkinson, 1946, I:xiv, xv).

Spengler asserted that the basic unit of history is a culture rather than a race or nation (I:21). These entities are natural, self-contained units which recur in history in a given pattern. Biology is applied to history to provide a "morphology" (I:5). Cultures are biological organisms (I:21-22, 104) which go through the same stages of childhood, youth, manhood, and old age as man (I:107). He also used the analogy of the seasons of spring, summer, autumn, and winter to picture their rise and decline (I: Table I). Each of these is a closed unit with no relationship to each other (I:180). He mentions eight cultures, treats only six factually, and discusses in detail only three, the Classical, Arabian, and modern Western cultures. Each of these cultures goes through various comparable stages in its life-cycle (I:27). There is a pre-cultural, primitive, history-less period in which the rural peasant is predominant. This is followed by a culture which becomes a civilization (I:31) marked by a money economy (II:96-98) and democracy in great cities (II:90). Democracy gives way to the wars of states and an era of Caesarism in which a world-dictator takes over. The civilization ends in a history-less period in which a new cycle begins (II:464-465, 506-507).

Each culture, said Spengler, thus goes through this cycle to form a part of the cyclical recurrent pattern of history (I:21-22, 106, 109-110). There is no progress. The deterministic cycle is under blind fate or destiny as much as nature is under the law of causality (I:8, 109-110, II:507). Man cannot guide his destiny. He can only accept it. There is no goal or progress toward which history is guided, because man's history has "no meaning whatsoever" (II:44). Western culture entered its period of civilization about 1789 (I:44-45; II:415-416) and faces the prospect of this money- and democracy-dominated era ending in a dictatorship. War is said to be the only creative force (II:363, 440, 464-465, 507).

The evangelical believes that cultures are not the evolutionary organisms which Spengler thought they were, but are the result of interactions of individuals who in the aggregate form a society. Vital forces are in the individual rather than in the culture. Living societies may also borrow from one another by diffusion, and, far from there being no cultural connection, much of one culture lives on in another as Greek philosophy does in Western culture.

The activistic, buoyant spirit of the young American nation, and a faith that America is an exception to the history of nations, has made Spengler's cyclical theory distasteful to Americans. Perhaps our escape from the destruction of two world wars may help to account for this reaction.

Spengler forgot that love has also influenced the course of history as well as hate and force. Man also has some freedom in the responsible exercise of his will even though nature, his environment, seems to be under fixed laws. Worst of all, Spengler's emphasis upon force led him to adopt a thoroughgoing relativism in truth (I:xiii, 23, 25, 46) and morals (I:315).

Long ago Augustine faced the problem of the cyclic theories of his day and concluded that the "circular maze" (*City of God,* XII:13) of the false doctrines of cyclical interpreters was the only circular thing in history. He took his stand upon the Hebrew-Christian tradition which rejected cycles in history. Both he and the modern evangelical historian accept the Lordship of Christ over and in history and the once-for-all nature of His work upon the Cross. There is no room for a pessimistic cyclical view in this approach.

Optimistic Philosophies of History

While the pessimistic thinkers despair concerning man in history, the optimistic interpreters of history expect too much from man in history. They have a "utopian millenarian" hope of salvation in history which creates a religion of progress. In their desire to make men into angels, the extremists of this school are willing to treat them like brutes. Karl Löwith in *Meaning in History* (1949) makes the point that optimistic interpretations are really perversions of the biblical data. These views may be symbolized by a spiral, by the progressive forward movement brought to a vehicle by the turning of its wheels, or by the jagged upward line of a graph—all of which points to progress to a future golden age.

Such interpreters pervert biblical conceptions of history by making the divine secular, the eternal temporal, and the absolute relative. If God is recognized at all, His transcendence gives way to stress upon His immanence in history. These thinkers emphasize social action as the way to achieve a golden age for man in history. The natural laws of historical progress of the Communists, unaided human effort, or the aid of God are used by these thinkers to guarantee progress. Scientific technology and education are tools which these thinkers would employ in achieving their goal in history. Progress becomes a dogma to them.

The apostles of the cult of progress may be classified as non-theistic and theistic in their approach to history. Communism, which goes back to Karl Marx for inspiration, offers the greatest challenge to evangelical Christianity and its interpretation of history. Marx separated Providence from progress in a militant materialism which he thought was foundational to scientific history. From Hegel he borrowed his idea of the dialectic, a logic of historical progress by conflict and reconciliation of opposing ideas and classes; his materialism from Feuerbach who thought that "Man is what he eats"; from Adam Smith the idea that labor is the only source of value; and from the utopian socialists the ideal society as the goal of history.

By equating history with nature Marx thought that the scientific method, which derived laws from nature to be used in its control, would result when applied to history in social laws which could be used in the management of man in time. Because he thought that reality was only matter in motion, Marx developed an historical materialism by which he explained the social ideas and organization of any era. He argued that the forces of production and distribution in the hands of what he called the exploiting class led to the rich becoming richer and the poor poorer because the surplus profits above the cost of production went to the exploiting class. This led in the modern era to a class struggle between the capitalists and the proletariat which constituted the modern thesis and antithesis of his logic. The conflict would climax in a revolution of the workers in an economic crisis or war, after which there would be a dictatorship of the proletariat. After all capitalists were destroyed, the synthesis, a classless society, would appear. This would constitute his "kingdom on earth." Little wonder that Toynbee looks on Communism as a heresy which perverts Christianity! Modern Communism seems to parody Christianity in several respects, such as the ideal future society of the chosen class. An understanding of this theory of history is important to evangelicals since the leaders of one-third of the world's population fanatically seek to bring still others under its sway.

Marx like Hegel inconsistently stopped his dialectic where he desired. He ignored any force other than the economic in history, and he had no room for any ultimate, such as God, because he thought that religion was an "opiate" used by the ruling class to keep the proletariat content while they exploited them. Despite the word of the Bible to the contrary, Marx believed that in his secularized version of the millennium man can live by bread alone. He was far more deterministic and dogmatic than any of the theologians whom he hated. The facts of history do not fit his thesis because in many democratic countries there has come such a leveling of wealth that the rich have become poorer and the poor richer. Neither Marx nor his modern communistic followers accept the fact of sin nor the sacredness of human personality on which the Christian insists, and they make the state an end rather than a means to aid the individual in achieving development. Some of these criticisms have been set forth in an able evangelical critique of Marxianism by Keith McDonald in *His* (Vol. 7, No. 12 [December, 1947] pp. 6-13, and Vol. 8, No. 1 [January, 1948] pp. 12-14, 32-33).

Other apostles of the cult of progress do not subscribe to the materialistic, atheistic dogmas of the Communists, but they do hold to an evolutionary progress in history. They combine this with a theism which in some cases is very vague, but the divine immanence is looked upon as a guarantee of progress to the goal which is usually an earthly utopia.

Sherwood Eddy in *God in History* (1947) presents a liberal theistic approach to history. The upward progress of the race, he thinks, will come from a synthesis in action of the principles of love and liberty emphasized by the democratic world and those of racial brotherhood and economic justice which he optimistically thought he had found in communist Russia. He asserted that Russia as well as America was serving the purposes of God. The successful synthesis of these principles is guaranteed by Providence working through an evolutionary process which can be accelerated by education. Despite his apparent neo-orthodox dialectic (p. 13), which seems more like Hegelian dialectic, he has a theistic humanitarian optimism based upon an organic evolution and a destructive biblical criticism which is unacceptable to the evangelical historian to whom man is a creation of God and the Bible His inspired Word. Neither can he accept Eddy's species of Socialism which Eddy would use in the process of development of a more perfect order.

Shirley Jackson Case in the midst of the world's most brutal and destructive war also held to a liberal (pp. 161, 169), evolutionary (pp. 142, 213), yet theistic, view of history as progress in the book *The Christian Philosophy of History* (1943). He argued that the moral sense and the intellectual capacity for growth of good men will make them God's instruments as well as His fellow-workers in the eradication of evil from the earth and the shaping of the processes of history in time in an evolutionary development (pp. 180, 186, 216-218). The educatory process of this social evolution will lead to the establishment of the Kingdom of God upon earth (p. 180) and blessed immortality in the hereafter (p. 43). This optimistic postmillennial conception of history has not been at all chastened by the brute facts of history with its display of evil in man in our day. Rather, Case thought that the observed facts of history show progress in all realms (pp. 79-86).

History and God (1952) by Arthur W. Munk contains an interesting philosophy of history which solves the paradox of the persistence of evil in the world and the assertion of progress by applying the concept of a limited God, held by personalists, such as Edgar S. Brightman, to the evolutionary (p. 57) process of history. Munk accepts liberal biblical criticism (pp. 20, 98) and the evolutionary animal origin of man (pp. 75, 94-97, 134). The empirical-rational method (p. 11) of studying history yields five clues to him. The necessity of God is postulated by the fact that He is needed to explain the presence of time, the laws of nature, and personality. Man's intellect, his love of and creation of beauty, and his moral and religious capacity constitute the second clue which can only be explained by theism. The admission of the irrational evil aspect of man's nature is his third clue. The fourth clue is the evolutionary advance to unity and order; the increase of value in history; ideals; moral law and judgment observed in history; Providence seen in the limitation upon evil; Christ; and the Church. The apparent pattern which one can see in history constitutes his fifth clue. The mingling of progress and evil in history leads him to his explanation of the paradoxical nature of his clues by his sixth, rationally-derived clue, the idea of a God Who is limited in power (p. 225) but is still the greatest power in the universe and the "World Ground." Both evil and progress are integrated as this limited God works with man to bring increasing order out of chaos in history. The last clue, immortality, is postulated as the only answer to the question of ultimate doom for the physical universe and to securing for man the justice which he often fails to get in this world. The ecumenical movement, a superior social conscience, and the United Nations are to him signs that the limited God and man are creating international unity and economic justice in the march towards the goal of history (pp. 289-290). While the evangelical historian might accept some of his clues as well-grounded observations from the study of history, the idea of a limited God runs counter to all the biblical documents and is unacceptable to any careful student of the Bible.

Toynbee, the most widely-known philosopher of history today, seems to be theistic in his view that history, despite recurrent patterns, is moving towards the time when earth will become a province of the Kingdom of God. His theism will apparently be a vague syncretism of the four higher religions which claim to have a universal mission. These are Christianity, Islam, Hinduism and Mahayana Buddhism (*Civilization on Trial,* 1948, p. 219). Toynbee's emphasis that the fate of Western civilization depends upon our possible and positive reaction to our political, economic, moral, and religious challenge seems to savor of Pelagianism.

Some think of Toynbee's work as a deductive study of man's history which links classical cyclical views with Augustine's linear conception of history, but the evangelical historian discovers that Toynbee's City of God is only a secularized version of that of Augustine. Toynbee seems to be indebted to Spengler for the clue that the real unit of history is a society which goes through a regular life-cycle. A society is "the smallest unit of historical study" (*ibid.,* 222) which emerges when one attempts to understand the history of one's own land. Society is made up of the interaction of individuals. The study of ancient history by empirical methods led him to the conclusion that one society is contemporaneous with another though separated in time.

A society or civilization *rises*—not by racial superiority nor a favorable environment—but by a successful response to a physical, moral, or spiritual challenge which confronts it. If the society is to develop, the challenge must conform to a golden mean which will stimulate without discouraging creative ability and which will be neither too hard nor too easy. Society rises through the efforts of a creative minority who are imitated by the masses. Although his ten-volume *A Study of History* (1934-1954) is confusing on this point, (cf., IX:419 cf. III:1-2), Toynbee finds twenty-one civilizations which have risen and fallen or are yet alive, five arrested civilizations, and four abortive civilizations. This makes a total of thirty.

A civilization *grows* as the creative minority leads the masses in a process called etherialization, in which the earlier external physical challenge of hard land or climate gives way to an internal moral and spiritual challenge. This process will lead to increasing differentiation, simplification of life, and the freeing of human personality for spiritual struggle (SOH, III:128, 182ff.). The creative minority must withdraw periodically to refresh the springs of creative energy and return to lead the masses in a favorable response to new challenges.

Civilizations suffer *breakdown* when the creative minority becomes proud and idolizes its institutions, techniques, or itself, and when the masses cease to follow it in social mimesis or imitation. Schism then takes place both in the individual soul and society. The creative minority adopts force to hold the masses and thereby becomes a dominant minority which sets up a universal state in which life is standardized. The masses (Toynbee's internal proletariat) cease to imitate the creative minority and seek personal escape by looking to the past, to a future utopia, to monastic withdrawal, or to a religion. The last usually becomes the universal religion of the masses.

In the meantime an external proletariat of barbarians, which lives on the borders of the disintegrating civilization, threatens it and after it it has gone through three routs and rallies during its "Time of Troubles" destroys it in a final rout. Because he holds to a concept of universal sin (COT, pp. 241, 248), Toynbee believes that the breakdown and disintegration of a civilization are not murder by destruction from the outside, but are the result of suicide from within (SOH, IV:120; VIII:527).

Toynbee apparently once thought that the universal religion of the internal proletariat might be the chrysalis of or a bridge to the new civilization (COT, pp. 231-234). His more recent writings suggest that the rise and fall of civilization are essential to the development of a universal religion. This will result in a process of transfiguration by which this world will become a province of the Kingdom of God (COT, pp. 94, 159, 234-236, 263) as a social and spiritual progress is made from generation to generation (SOH, VI: 171-172). Though the history of civilizations is characterized by cyclical recurrence, the history of religion is "a single, continuous, upward line (COT, pp. 235-236; 244-245)." Because of the destructiveness of modern war and class conflict, Toynbee thinks that international unity, an economic compromise between free enterprise and socialism, and the setting of our civilization back on spiritual foundations (COT, pp. 27, 39) are essential for the middle-class creative group. Otherwise Western civilization might perish like its predecessors. Salvation is the transfiguration of the world, the rebellious and sinful province of the heavenly Kingdom, by an irradiation from the Kingdom of God (SOH, VII:558). Learning will come through suffering (COT, pp. 15, 235). Each civilization may be likened to the turn of a chariot wheel which puts one nearer to the goal (SOH IV:33-35; VI:324; VII:423). Toynbee's cycles are not deterministic (COT, 30) but may be changed by a repentant spirit which will unite men in the love of God (SOH, VI:320-321). History becomes a dim and partial vision of God Who manifests Himself in saving deeds to those souls that seek Him in sincerity (SOH, X:1-2).

Though his emphasis on religion may have some appeal for Christians Toynbee cannot be classified as an orthodox Christian because his future religion appears to be a synthesis of existing Christian and non-Christian religions in which there is no place for the unique person, life, and work of Christ. He seems to accept the modern dogmas of evolution (COT, pp. 37, 162, 216) and radical biblical criticism (COT, pp. 235). He holds to progress as the result of creative human effort by which the earth in turn will eventually become a province of the Kingdom of God. The relationship between God and man and God's Kingdom and history is mystical and vague. Such conceptions do violence to the Scriptures.

Why do all these optimistic interpreters of history hold so tenaciously to progress in the present crisis? The evangelical historian recognizes that twentieth century ideas of progress are rooted in the intellectual history of Europe since the Renaissance. Although the men of the Renaissance looked back to the classical past, they discovered in that past an emphasis upon the value of this present life which gave them confidence in the ability of man to solve his problems in history. Bacon shortly after 1600 asserted the value of the scientific method to conquer nature for man's use. Descartes proclaimed the ability of unaided human reason to organize the data of nature which the scientific method gave to man. Condorcet in the late eighteenth century proclaimed that the perfectibility of man was "indefinite." Auguste Comte thought that man had left theology and philosophy behind in his upward development. He believed that the "positive" knowledge of scientific technique would create a hierarchy of sciences in which the social sciences would yield laws which would make social engineering possible in the creation of an ideal society.

Friedrich Hegel's *Philosophy of History* seemed to provide a philosophical foundation for this belief in progress. Hegel believed that history was the purposeful evolutionary development (pp. 18, 24, 26, 57) of the Idea or Absolute in time in the realization of freedom (pp. 10, 13, 19-20, 26, 56, 476) as nature was the development of the Absolute in space (pp. 12, 75). For him reality was mind. The process of development was a dialectic conflict (p. 57). This has led to the description of his ideals as the waltz-step theory of history. Progress is the result of the reconciliation (synthesis) of opposing forces (thesis and antithesis). This continuing process results in the increasing realization of freedom by all men—not just the one or a few (p. 19). This freedom is linked with the state (pp. 40-41, 43, 49), and Hegel rather illogically ends his dialectic with the Prussian, Protestant, monarchial state as the best embodiment of the Absolute (pp. 19, 354) in history. Marx reversed Hegel's view of reality by making matter rather than mind or spirit the only reality, but he borrowed Hegel's dialectical principle and his idea of historical evolution. Thus modern Communism through Marx is indebted to Hegel. Italian Fascism also borrowed Hegel's idea of the importance of the state as a manifestation of the Absolute in time.

The seeming development of scientific proof of the dogma of evolution by Darwin in his *Origin of the Species* (1859) gave a "scientific law of progress" to reinforce Hegel's idea of philosophical evolution. Exponents of Socialism believed that either by democratic evolution or revolution man would be able to create a perfect order on earth in which the Industrial Revolution guaranteed an abundance of goods. Such are the roots of the various views of the twentieth century devotees of progress. Carl F. H. Henry in *Remaking the Modern Mind* (1946) criticizes the dogma of progress from an evangelical viewpoint.

Certain fundamental failures of these ideas of progress seem apparent to the evangelical historian as he turns the searchlight of history and Scripture upon them. Such views, which are based upon speculative reason rather than upon revelation, are man-centered rather than God-centered. There is often contempt for the past with little realization that progress so far has been mainly technological, intellectual, and organizational, and can be perverted to evil ends by man. Little or no attention is given to the data of special revelation in the Bible because God is looked upon as being immanent in nature and history if He is accepted at all. The Bible is considered only as an historical book to be subjected to historical analysis as any other record of history is. The view of sin is Pelagian because the universality of sin is stressed without reference to original sin. War and poverty, which are thought to be the result of ignorance and lack of social organization, will be eliminated by man. They incorrectly believe that the glorious end of history is to come by human effort in history, and the glory of man rather than the glory of God is primary. Not Christ but the historical process is savior, according to them.

Reinhold Niebuhr has correctly pointed out in *The Self and the Dramas of History* (1955, pp. 50-52) that both the pessimistic and optimistic philosophies of history have an element of truth. It is true that there are recurrent parallels to be observed in successive historical situations, but they are not deterministic. The optimistic views of inevitable progress have an element of truth, if we limit progress to technology and social organization, but they are false if we attempt to posit inevitable moral and spiritual progress in the modern world.

Pessimistic-Optimistic Philosophies of History

Exponents of these views accept the failure of man, as do the pessimists, but reject their deterministic cyclical view of history. They are as confident as the optimistic interpreters that the purpose of God for history will be realized, but they do not agree that the end of history is achieved in history by man, the success of whose efforts is guaranteed by belief in inevitable, indefinite progress. Despair of history or undue hope of progress is replaced by a faith which creates love in action in the present and a hope for the future under God. History will be transformed by the transcendent God Who is immanent in it through His Son, the Redeemer. At His catastrophic coming the earth will be made His kingdom. Thus, while asserting the universality of sin because of original sin, they are not unduly pessimistic, nor are they, because of a Pelagian view of sin, unduly optimistic. The transformation of history by human effort leaves most of them pessimistic, but despair with human history is rejected because of faith in God. Most of these general ideas are accepted by the neo-orthodox, the believers in progress under Providence, and the evangelical historians. All turn from spiral or cyclical symbols of history to rectilinear or linear symbols of history as movement in time and space under divine Providence.

The classic expression of this approach to history, which has influenced all three classes of pessimistic-optimistic interpreters, is to be found, next to the Bible, in the *City of God* which Augustine wrote after the sacking of Rome by the Visigoth Alaric in 410. The Romans blamed this catastrophe upon Rome's abandonment of her pagan gods. Marcellinus asked Augustine to refute this charge. In the first five books Augustine demonstrated that worship of pagan gods does not result in temporal prosperity because Rome had suffered just as much under its pagan deities. His Spanish friend Orosius at his request in *Seven Books of History Against the Pagans* documented this thesis by a detailed history of the calamities which have befallen man because of sin. Augustine also pointed out in books five to ten that pagan gods could not bring the blessing of eternal life. Having in this negative historical discussion refuted his opponents' arguments, Augustine builds his positive philosophy of history in books eleven to twenty-two of the *City of God*. In building his system Augustine links reason and Christian faith in a synthesis in which faith is the condition of understanding.

He postulates the *creation* of the historical process in the will of a sovereign transcendent God. His plans in eternity are made possible in time through the work of Christ and effected by the creative activity of the Holy Spirit. Man and his universe are the result of a special creative act of God instead of being the end of an evolutionary process. Man who is both a material and a spiritual being is capable of communion with his Creator.

The *compass* or scope of history for Augustine is universal and unitary. History is the story of the whole human race from Adam—not just that of a city, a nation, a culture, or a class. Because he believed in original sin, Augustine had to divide terrestrial and celestial beings into the City of Earth and the City of God in a temporal dualism. Those of the first city love, live for, and glorify self while those of the latter city love and live for God and His glory (XIV:28). Despite this unitary note Augustine has a real sense of the importance to God of each individual.

Augustine turned from discussion of the origin and scope of history (Bks. XI-XIV) to a description of the *course* of history in books fifteen to eighteen. He opposed the cyclical theories of history in his day (XII: 11-14, 17). While he confessed that when one asked him what time is, he did not know what to that moment he could define (*Confessions, XI: 14*), he broke with the classical idea of time as circular in favor of a linear view of time in which God is active in redemption. Unlike the impersonal disembodied Logos of classicism, Augustine's Christ is personal. Although Augustine accepts technological progress (XXII:24), he does not accept the spiral conception of progress in history through efforts of the Church for human betterment. He divided history into seven ages (XXII:30) of which this age, the sixth, he looked upon as the millennium (XX:7, 9) in which the Church carries on its task in the personal, social, and cosmic struggle of good and evil. He also emphasized for the individual the goal of integration of personality in redemption.

Augustine's temporal dualism is resolved by the *consummation* of history in the return of Christ and the subsequent resurrection and judgment after which the seventh age of the eternal triumphant rule of God will begin. Some amillennial evangelicals disagree with Augustine by rejecting the idea of a millennium entirely, and the premillenarians disagree with his idea that the present age is the millennium.

Both, however, would agree that he has caught the essence of the biblical view of history in which the end and goal of history is supernaturally brought about by Christ's Second Coming.

NEO-ORTHODOX PHILOSOPHIES OF HISTORY

Neo-orthodox interpreters of history claim that they are in the tradition of Paul, Augustine, and Calvin and Luther. Many of them have been influenced by the ideas of Sören Kierkegaard. This frail-bodied emotional individual faced the crises of Denmark's loss of Norway, the failure of the state church and of his own love affair by turning from these mundane inescapable crises to God in a leap of faith. In like manner the crisis of the first World War destroyed the liberalism of Karl Barth, to whom many later neo-orthodox scholars look as the pioneer of this type of thought, and led him to adopt a theology of crisis. The neo-orthodox revolt against reason, the immanental theology of the liberal, and the cult of progress have appealed to many Europeans in crisis. The movement has also become influential in America through the work of Reinhold Niebuhr, Paul Tillich, Otto Piper, and others.

Although they differ on some points among themselves, such as Barth's rejection of Brunner's idea that God is also revealed in natural theology, these thinkers hold certain ideas in common. The unity and continuity of history in time under the Lordship of Christ usually is replaced by dualism in their systems. God as "wholly other" is placed over against sinful depraved man; eternity over against time; and secular history over against the metahistory of Nicolas Berdyaev, or the holy (redemption) history of Otto Piper. God is separated from secular history here and now. Neither the cults of cycles nor progress have any meaning in the light of such dualism.

Escape from these dualisms cannot be found in the temporal order. Only as a man becomes aware of his nakedness before God in the crisis brought about by the above situation and only through the Bible which the Holy Spirit makes God's Word to the soul as he throws himself upon God in act of faith or commitment can a man hope to live. According to the neo-orthodox, the Bible is not an objective historical revelation of God but a book, some part of which may become the revelation of God through the activity of the Holy Spirit.

God only "pierces" history in the Incarnation of Christ. He confronts the individual in his personal soul crisis and in the final fulfillment of history when time is "transfigured" by eternity. Although there are striking exceptions like Niebuhr, many neo-orthodox thinkers have little faith in social action as a means to progress and as a preparation for the end of history in history by human effort. Karl Barth is even credited with the assertion that the care of the world is not the care of the Church. It can only proclaim the Gospel in order that the individual may be confronted by God with his creatureliness and yield the existential response of faith. Man can do nothing to shape the course of history.

Although he differs with the neo-orthodox on some points, Nicolas Berdyaev in his book *The Meaning of History* (1936) illustrates the tendency of this group to distinguish between secular and sacred history. He believed that philosophy of history can lead one to "knowledge of spiritual reality" (p. 14), but that history is basically mysterious and tragic. He thought that the West is in the last stages of a humanistic cultural era which began with the Renaissance and in which the individual will lose his identity in a tide of "impersonal collectivism." The insistence of Renaissance man upon the autonomy of the intellect and the eighteenth century theory of the natural rights of man ruined the unity of man's spiritual life. Man becomes a means instead of an end because he is identified with nature. For this reason temporal history is a story of tragedy and conflict which can only have an end in what he calls metahistory.

Following the German mystics, Berdyaev posited an *Urgrund* which is before being. God emerges to create the world and with a dark abyss in His nature shares the tragedy of the *Urgrund* (pp. 54-56) with man, His creation. Man's history is thus both celestial and terrestrial. With freedom to create and to choose between material and spiritual ends man immersed himself in nature and lost the divine nature. That there is also tragedy and suffering in the interior nature of God is shown by the Cross and the Incarnation in which God shares the tragedy of free yet fallen sinful life (pp. 47-48). In Christ history is pierced by metahistory, and both man in Christ as God's other self and God move in the community of fellowship of the spirit to an eternal eschatological destiny to be revealed outside of history by the supernatural.

Berdyaev believed this to be the only answer to selfish Western individualism or to Eastern impersonal state collectivism. Both time and the world with roots in eternity will end in eternity with the resolution of tragedy (p. 206). Such a mystical approach is more nearly related to the tendency of the Russian and of the Orthodox Church to mysticism than it is to the evangelical understanding of the Scriptures.

In *Faith and History* (1949) Reinhold Niebuhr represents another neo-orthodox approach to history, but he is more inclined to advocate social activity by Christians than most of this group. Both human capacity and man's "cultural achievement and social institutions" are capable of continued development within finite limits because man is creative and a creator of history (pp. 70-74). The meaning of history is disclosed in Christ's life, death, and resurrection, through which God takes man's sin upon Himself. Man is related to God in crisis by a leap of faith as he is confronted with the claims of God to judge him. This act of faith gives unity to history although our lack of understanding forces us to admit the relativism of our historical knowledge and our sin forbids us to claim moral perfection or to solve history by the dogma of progress. Through love made actual in deeds the Christian participates in the limited development of a Christian social order without expecting to make this a perfect order in history. That will come outside history as the act of God (pp. 233, 235) by which time is transfigured into eternity. The present writer questions whether the linking of dualism in history and limited social progress is logical. Neither can he accept Niebuhr's biblical criticism (p. 36), nor his idea that biblical accounts, such as the fall, are only mythical stories which embody historical facts (p. 121).

Both Eric Rust in *The Christian Understanding of History* (1947) and Otto Piper in *God in History* (1939) so separate secular history of the present from sacred history that they have little relation to each other. According to Piper, God covenants with the nation of Israel in which only a remnant finally personified in Christ is the bearer of salvation and the creator of *Heilsgeschichte* (redemption history), which is carefully distinguished from secular history. The Church is now the covenant and has the responsibility to preach repentance, to face men with a crisis in which they exercise existential faith, and to reveal a community of people and ethical good. The Occident may even be saved if the Church does these things, but the end of history is beyond history after continuing present and final judgment. Christ will then supernaturally bring in the Kingdom. Rust's approach is somewhat similar to that of Piper and clearly illustrates the neo-orthodox tendency to liberal biblical criticism (pp. 69-71, 88, 94, 213).

The evangelical is glad for the rediscovery of the universality of sin, the stress on the holiness of God, the emphasis on the insufficiency of reason, and for the repudiation of the modern cult of progress by neo-orthodox thinkers. He takes strong exception, however, to the neo-orthodox denial of the unity and continuity of history under the Lordship of Christ, resulting from the distinction they make between secular history of the textbook variety and the holy history of religion. Although the evangelical agrees that God is transcendent, he can never divorce God from history because He is Creator, Redeemer, and Lord. The relation of the historical Christ to God and to revelation in the ambiguous definition of such men as Barth, Brunner, and Tillich is not biblical. Many neo-orthodox thinkers weaken man's sense of social responsibility to work out the social implications of the Christian law of love. They also depreciate the place of reason in the development of an adequate apologetic to strengthen the faith of the Christian. Because of this their views at times are very subjective and mystical. Their uncritical acceptance of liberal biblical criticism, their idea that biblical realities are less than historical facts, and their tendency to think of the Second Coming and Judgment as symbols of reality rather than reality leave them without a valid objective authority for faith. Their Bible is merely an historical book which presumably becomes God's Word only through the subjective action of the Holy Spirit. The evangelical rejects this because the Bible is to him and those in the orthodox tradition the very Word of God whether or not one believes it. Neo-orthodoxy has revived truths which liberalism obscured and which evangelicals have always proclaimed, but it has not produced a philosophy of history which does full justice to historical and biblical data.

MEDIATING PESSIMISTIC-OPTIMISTIC PHILOSOPHIES

Another group of thinkers seem to take a position concerning philosophy of history between the optimistic liberals and the neo-orthodox school. They accept the neo-orthodox view of biblical criticism and its concept of the universality of sin, but they agree with liberal interpreters in holding to the possibility of social progress through spiritual power until Christ comes to end the age.

Herbert Butterfield, the Methodist professor of modern history at the University of Cambridge, seems to belong to this group. He thinks that scientific, technical, or academic history, which only produces secondary conditioning economic or geographic facts, is not self-explanatory but must be supplemented by a view which integrates these and ultimate facts. The development of the human personality, which exists for the glory of God, is the most important fact of history to him. Human personality is spiritual, according to him, and its spiritual autonomy as an end and its freedom of will must be maintained in a day which puts things above persons (*Christianity and History,* 1950, pp. 29, 67, 112). Freedom of will creates the problem of original and universal sin (pp. 29, 45, 63, 106). Hence no nation is in a position to make moral judgments upon others, for then it becomes a self-righteous sinner (*History and Human Relations,* 1951, p. 109). All are victims as well as agents of history. The dynamic of history is not the state or force but Christ's law of love (HHR, pp. 41-50, 65, 152). Man is free to love because only the world of nature is marked by necessity. Through suffering, his love is perfected (CAH, p. 86). Nations should put this into effect by seeking a balance of power, and, when war is necessary, by fighting limited rather than total wars. Then perhaps an international order might be built up in which progress could take place. Butterfield thinks that Providence has created a world in which man can improve his external conditions despite the presence of evil (CAH, pp. 34, 96-97, 112). Although he mentions the interim judgment of history on nations (p. 66) he has so far said little about the end of history. According to him, the purpose of history is the making and the educating of human souls (p. 76). The evangelical finds much to praise in Butterfield, but regrets that his emphasis on the value of personality and love is not adequately related to the person and work of Christ.

A more clearly defined view of progress within a providential framework is developed by John Baillie in his book *The Belief in Progress* (1950). After an excellent critical sketch of the dogma of progress (pp. 1-154), he states his belief that man can hope to move towards moral and spiritual progress in history in the interim between the present and the coming of Christ and the divine end of history (pp. 190, 214). Because technical and social progress can be used for good or evil and because men are sinful (pp. 176-177), God must be the *a priori* ground for progress. While the end of history is beyond history (p. 183), God will aid Christians by linking their wills with His (p. 186) so that Christ's spirit will be progressively embodied in man and his society (pp. 189-190, 210, 220). Christianity thus gives personal salvation, hope for renewal of all areas of communal life (p. 223), and final salvation at the end of history. Baillie thinks progress is possible because of the power of God, but he does not believe that it is inevitable because man is sinful and free to choose evil.

An even clearer view of progress within the limits of Christ's First Advent and His Second Coming was advanced by Kenneth Scott Latourette in his presidential address to the American Historical Association in December, 1948 (*American Historical Review* Vol. LIV, No. 2, [January, 1949] pp. 259-276). He upheld the sovereignty of God in history over against deterministic cyclical views or ideas of inevitable progress (p. 266), and asserted the value of human personality to God (p. 268). Christianity, according to him, has spread its influence geographically, socially, and morally in such things as the end of slavery and will continue to do so until the apocalyptic end of history (pp. 272-276). He thinks that there is a "strong probability" that God will fully triumph in history (p. 276). Spiritual progress, according to him, occurs through successive eras of spiritual decline and advance, but each advance is higher and each decline less as time goes on.

Jacques Maritain, a Roman Catholic neo-Thomist, also believes that God so controls the historical process that there is progress in the social order through the work of the Church. This, he states, will prepare the way for the coming of the Kingdom of God when, after the transfiguration of society, man's body will also be transformed. These dual goals will be achieved in spite of the culture lag caused by sin, anti-Christian institutions, and Satan.

The views of these men suggest an amillennial but cataclysmic end to history after an era of limited spiritual progress which is the result of the work of the Church. The apparent readying of the world by the

Church for the coming of Christ and progress in history by human effort make these views unpalatable to the evangelical even though he welcomes the giving up of the idea of indefinite progress by these men. Their conception of the role of Christ in history is not at all clear.

AN EVANGELICAL PHILOSOPHY OF HISTORY

The evangelical pessimistic-optimistic historian agrees with the pessimists concerning the presence of evil in history but takes issue with their idea that time is circular. His pessimism is limited to lack of hope that man or the historical process is savior. While this prevents him from being as optimistic concerning the ideal end of history by human effort as the optimists are, he is optimistic concerning history because God is controlling it for His glory and man's good. This self-revealing God by an infallible revelation in the Bible unfolds the origin, course, goal, and purpose of human history to man. The view to be presented is thus in the long orthodox tradition from Paul, Augustine, and the great Reformers. Modern interpreters of history have given up this tradition for the husks of the cult of progress.

Because any view of creation ultimately demands an act of faith, the evangelical believes that the *creation* of the universe is the result of the voluntary act of the will of a transcendent self-existent and self-sufficient personal God in order to display His glory (Ps. 24:1-2; Acts 17:24). God last of all brought man into being as a free, yet responsible, creature (Gen. 1:26-2:25; Ps. 139:14-16; Acts 17:25) to glorify Himself by proper dominion over the works of His creation (Gen. 1:28; Ps. 8:6-8). Technology has given man a large measure of control over nature, but Adam's disobedience to the will of God brought sin into the nature of man, and man, forgetting that he is finite, often has used his power to set himself up as god over his fellows. Small wonder then that the evangelical views history as the result of the creative act of God rather than as a cyclical process or a process of emergent evolution in which man is by his own efforts moving in the direction of a perfect order. Science supports Scripture by revealing the design in nature which points to creation as the act of a supreme intelligence.

Christ is pictured in the Bible as the creative Agent of God's will (Jno. 1:1-3; Col. 1:16; Heb. 1:2). God's Providence in nature is also operative through the Son of God (Col. 1:17; Heb. 1:3). In all this display of Providence in the government of nature one must remember that God is not a part of His creation but is transcendent to it.

The Jews contributed by revelation from God the *compass* or scope of the Christian philosophy of history. Thucydides wrote about his own nation, Marx of the universal class, and Hegel about the Prussian state; but in contrast the biblical view of history is universal and unitary in its inclusion of all men everywhere in one race (Gen. 2, Acts 17:26). All men are the sons of God by physical creation. They have fallen, but they can become actual spiritual sons of God by the new birth. This gives a new dignity and value to human personality which is often forgotten by optimistic exponents of history.

This conception of the unity and solidarity of the human race through the first man is true despite the temporal historical dualism which has been present since Adam sinned in the garden and lost his original innocence (Gen. 3; Rom. 5:12; I Cor. 15:22). Hence the race has been divided into two parts—the redeemed and the lost—since that time. This was what Augustine meant by the two cities. This dualism is seen in the presence in history of the clashing Hellenic and Hebraic traditions. The first pictures man searching for God by reason; the second sees history as God's loving search for lost man. Men perennially try to overcome the disunity and separation within the historical process by the creation of political, social, and economic "new orders." The Scriptures teach that this dualism even has had an adverse effect upon nature (Rom. 8:20-22). Only Judaism, Zoroastrianism, and Christianity hold that this dualism is temporal and will be finally ended by a cataclysmic supernatural intervention of Deity. If men remember this, they will not idolize themselves, their institutions, whether political or ecclesiastical, nor a class. Neither will they try to absolutize the relative nor try to make the temporal eternal.

God's Providence is exerted in many ways in the *course* of history. It is first to be seen in God's control of history. Even pagan nations are said to be under divine control and under the moral laws of God (See Deut. 32:8; Job 12:23; Isa. 10:5-7; Jer. 27:4-8; Dan. 2:21; Amos 9:7; Acts 17:26; Rom. 9:17-18; 22-33). The evangelical recognizes that God's moral laws are absolute in principle but that they are often contingent in their application. The sin of Nineveh called for its destruction, but it was averted by the repentance of the people because of Jonah's preaching. God is indeed Lord of history as well as the God of Nature. We cannot separate God from either His creation or history.

In the second place, God has been active in history in the provision of institutions for the good of man. The family is a divine provision which provides the basic unit of society for the perpetuation of the race and for fellowship (Gen. 1:28; 2:20; Mt. 19:4-6). It also provides a means for the education of the children (Deut. 4:9-10; Eph. 6:4).

The provision of government for the welfare of man is attributed to God by the biblical writers (Rom. 13:1-5; I Peter 2:14). The state is a means under God for the cooperation of man and for the enhancement of his personality. Its laws should embody scriptural principles. One should remember, however, that it is government, not the form of government, that is said to come from God. Sin has brought the aberration of despotism too often into human government.

The existence of sin brought God into history in a third even more intimate way through the Incarnation of Christ. That this was in the mind of God from the beginning seems evident to the writers of Scripture in the use of such phrases as "the fullness of the time" (Gal. 4:4, cf. Acts 2:23; 4:27-28, and I Peter 1:20). With Oscar Cullman in his book *Christ and Time* (trans. by Floyd V. Filson, 1951) the evangelical rejects the classical and, with some exceptions, the neo-orthodox idea of the absolute discontinuity between time and eternity, as well as the modern optimistic conception of time as an upward progressive spiral. Because of his claim that *Olam* in the Old Testament and *Aion* in the New Testament are used in the singular for time and in the plural for eternity, Cullman rather arbitrarily holds that time and eternity are not qualitatively distinct but differ only in that eternity is without beginning and ending while time is limited by creation and the consummation. The evangelical remembers, however, that eternal life in the Bible has ethical, qualitative content, as well as duration, and that the experience of God cannot be limited to temporal experience alone.

The evangelical view of time means that the event of Christ's First Advent is the mid-point of history between creation and consummation. Fulfillment by His First and, subsequently, by His Second Coming is the keynote of the Christian view of history, rather than ideas of progress or recurrence. Matthew in his Gospel frequently uses the phrase "that it might be fulfilled which was written . . ." God comes into the historical process in the Incarnation of Christ (Jno. 1:14, 18) to end the temporal dualism created by sin. The work of the Cross is another *kairos,* a special point in time, in which Christ wins a victory for time and eternity over sin, death, and Satan. The final surrender of Satan is to come at the end of time, but he is provisionally defeated in his plans for the world and actually defeated in the life of the Christian whose faith is in the work of the Cross. The D-day battle of Normandy was a climactic defeat for the Germans, but, although they were beaten from that time, they did not surrender until a year later. So with Satan. Christ is King now in the life of the believer, but the full realization of His Kingdom awaits the end of this age.

Christ's Incarnation, Death, Resurrection, and Ascension are not mere crises in time, but they are historically-verifiable events squarely in what some are pleased to call secular history. The hope of the Jewish people was and is the historic appearance of the Messiah. The Christian Church in the Lord's Supper looks back in faith to Christ's First Advent and forward in hope to His Second Coming (I Cor. 11:25-26).

God's activity in the course of history is seen finally in the existence of the Church, a universal historical community of the redeemed. The

Church even now demonstrates the power and wisdom of God to celestial as well as terrestrial beings (Eph. 3:10) and replaces in the economy of God until Christ's second advent the Jewish nation. That nation has been temporarily given second place in God's dealings in history (Lk. 21: 24; Acts 15:14; Rom. 11:25-26). The true Church, the invisible body of Christ, through the indwelling Christ already shares eternal life. It must, therefore, never idolize itself, but it must work in time because of its love to its Lord.

The proclamation of the Gospel to all men is the first task of the Church in history (Mt. 28:18-20; Acts 1:6-8). It is to be *"light"* as the early medieval Church was when it won the pagan German invaders of the Roman Empire to Christ. While expectantly looking for its Lord's return, the Church will "occupy" by using technological and social progress as means in its proclamation of the Gospel. Conversion then opens up to men the personal goals of present moral and spiritual and future physical likeness to Christ (Rom. 8:28-29; 2 Cor. 3:18; I Jno. 3: 2-3).

Evangelicals must give more attention to the function of the Church to be the *"salt"* of society. The Church should be an active redeemed society which puts into practice the new law of love, the only effective ethical dynamic (Mt. 22:37-40; Rom. 13:8-10). This love must manifest itself in good works—not in order to be saved—but because one has been saved (Gal. 6:10; Eph. 2:10; Titus 3:8). The Christian cannot adopt either an apocalyptic otherworldliness, which ignores the world around it, or a neo-monasticism which retreats from the world. The New Testament teaches participation in the world of human affairs by the application of the Gospel to social life.

The Church should be a critic of the social order by pointing out both evil and the positive corrective application of the Gospel to the evil, but the Church as an organization should avoid involvement in society. The application of Christian principles is rather the work of individual Christians in their various spheres of life. This avoids the assumption of the social gospel that evil is merely environmental and that it can be corrected by social legislation which is to be secured by the Church.

The Christian seeks to permeate his surroundings with Christian values. Christian parents and children will live in the mutual relationship of love so that their home will be a living illustration of the relationship of Christ and His Church (Eph. 5:22 -6:4). The Christian as employer or employee will seek to exemplify the law of love so that his vocation will be a means of glorifying God and rebuking evil (Eph. 6:5-9). His honest work should enable him to be debt-free and independent so that he can help to meet the need of others (I Thess. 4:10-11; Gal. 6:10). He will also render obedience to government, so long as it does not ask him to violate God's law, by the payment of taxes, by respect, and by obedience to and prayer for those in authority (Rom. 13:5-7; I Peter 2:13-14; I Tim. 2:1-2). In democratic countries the Christian has a God-given opportunity to influence human institutions which the New Testament Church did not have under the despotic government.

The *consummation* of history also interested the disciples (Mt. 24:3). This raises the question of the meaning of the phrases, the Kingdom of Heaven and the Kingdom of God. The first, which is used mainly in Matthew's Gospel, seems to refer to Christ's rule in time and history upon earth. Christ's interpreted parables of the wheat and the tares and the good and bad fish reveal that it contains both good and evil in the present era (Mt. 13). It is not synonymous with the Church although the Church is a part both of it and the Kingdom of God. It is not to be identified with the Kingdom of God although a part of it, the Church, is also a part of the Kingdom of God. Scripture teaches that the Kingdom of God is God's eternal rule over those celestial and terrestrial beings who give willing allegiance to Him (Jno. 3:3, 5; 7). The Kingdom of Heaven, which is an historical temporal episode in the eternal realm of God, will be finally merged with it so that God may be all in all.

The course of events making up the consummation of history begins with the return of Christ for the Church and His judgment of it after the First Resurrection (I Thess. 4:13-18; 2 Cor. 5:10). Evil persons (bad fish and tares) will be removed from the Kingdom of Heaven, and Christ with the Church will rule over it for the thousand years of the millennium.† Then the Messianic expectations of the Jews will be fulfilled in the earthly rule of their Messiah over them. Since Satan is bound, there will be no opposition to the rule of Christ during the thousand years (Rev. 20:1-6). When Satan is again allowed his freedom, Christ will be victorious after a short sharp struggle with him and his forces. After the Second Resurrection (Jno. 5:28-29) the wicked dead will be judged and sent away to eternal punishment (Rev. 20:7-15). Then Christ, in whose Kingdom all is finally united (Eph. 1:10), will hand all authority over to God in order that He may be over all and rule eternally (Rom. 11:36; I Cor. 15:27-28). The end of history is catastrophic and intra-historical, but its goal is the extra-temporal final transformation of history in which

† In the interest of objectivity, it should be noted that Professor Cairns' exposition here follows one of three views held by Christians in their attempt to spell out the details of the climax of history: premillennial, postmillennial, and amillennial. The question they raise is whether the Second Advent occurs previous to, subsequent to, or without an earthly reign of Christ. All three views have contemporary exponents. The amillennial view has Augustinian affinities. The premillennial view has both a modern dispensational and an early non-dispensational form which is now undergoing a revival. The strength of the millennial views, exegetical considerations aside, is that they secure the triumph of God's righteous rule within history, which would seem to be implied by a religion of redemption from an historical fall.—ED.

both the Church and Christ will come under the eternal sway of God whose just and righteous will is finally triumphant. This majestic biblical conception of the consummation nerves the Christian to preach and to serve in the present with confidence that the future is in the hands of God.

Neither pessimistic nor optimistic views of history fit the facts of history as adequately as the pessimistic-optimistic approach of the evangelical does. Because of sin in man the evangelical can find no solution for history in history by human effort, but he does not lapse into despairing pessimism because he realizes that God is active in history through His Spirit. He can integrate the secondary economic, social, and other material facts of history with its primary spiritual ground in God. This technique, which Luke used (Lk. 1:1-4) is that of the truly scientific historian who wants to consider all of the data. History has as much practical value in relating man to his past historical environment as science has in giving him understanding of his present physical environment.

Eschatological linear direction rather than cyclical motion or an indefinite spiral of progress characterizes the evangelical approach to history. The glory of God in the present by the life of the Christian and at the end of history by the triumph of Christ is paramount. The evangelical believes with the song-writer Maltie Babcock that, although the wrong often seems so strong, God is still the Ruler. The goal of history beyond history is the ultimate triumph and eternal rule of God. Thus history, studied in the light of such an evangelical interpretation, becomes a revelation of the working in time of the eternal God of Whom, through Whom, and to Whom are all things.

PHILOSOPHY OF RELIGION

Harold B. Kuhn

Harold B. Kuhn received his B.A. from John Fletcher College, and holds the degrees of S.T.M. and Ph.D. from Harvard University. He pursued post-doctoral studies at the University of Munich in 1951 and 1952. He has contributed numerous articles to many theological journals and other publications. At the present time he is professor of philosophy of religion at Asbury Theological Seminary.

8. Harold B. Kuhn:

PHILOSOPHY OF RELIGION

THERE IS no single movement in religious philosophy which, if one should understand it, would afford the clue to the comprehension of the religious thought-situation in America as it existed at the turn of the century. During the nineteenth century, German theology became the theology of Christendom. With its genius for adoption and adaptation, the Anglo-American mentality reached out with a good deal of eagerness to the conclusions of the German theological faculties, chose a great deal, rejected a great deal, and developed out of the imported tradition a general form of religious thought adapted to the Anglo-American scene. This form represents the coalescence of many streams, and was dignified by the broad term of "liberal."

Had one been viewing the American scene in 1900, he might have concluded that the dawning century was to be one dominated by strictly theological presuppositions. The theological vogue, as represented by both major pulpits and major seminaries, was "the new theology." This movement avowed its purpose, not to break with historic Christian thought, but to revise Christian theology to keep it in line with a theistic view of developmentalism. William J. Tucker in his *My Generation* says, "The desire and struggle for progress became the unifying purpose of the generation" (p. 2). Such a dynamic theology required constant revision to meet the kaleidoscopic changes in the thought-world.

I. NEGLECT OF THEOLOGY FOR SPECULATIVE PHILOSOPHY

Had the American philosophical world possessed some type of unity, the theological development might have assumed the form of a unilinear development, remaining more distinctively theological. Actually, theological consideration branched out, the dominant philosophical trends carrying some sector of Church scholarship with it. As a result, much of theology became subordinated to philosophy of religion.

The causes for this situation were by no means simple. First and foremost was the secularization of theology (whether conscious or not does not matter here) in the New Theology. This resulted in a desire, amounting at times almost to a mania, to make religious thought palatable to the general scientific temper. A second factor was the pattern of Church life in America. The religious impulses set in motion by the Protestant Reformation produced a pattern of religious communities differing from those of the Old World. The individualistic spirit of our nation expressed itself in the rise of a number of religious denominations, each one of which had to "sink or swim," depending upon its ability to appeal to the heart and mind of the individual. Each major denomination had its independent institutions of learning, whose source of strength was frequently the presence of a dominant personality, with its own basic philosophy.

Closely associated with individualism was another element which served to shape the American pattern, namely the liberal temper—a spirit which was adventurous, experimental, and self-reliant. Competition, rather than conformity, became a watchword. This, too, favored a subdivision of theology into "Types of Religious Philosophy."

Wieman and Meland, in their *American Philosophies of Religion,* suggest an additional factor which contributed to the growing emphasis of religious philosophy:

> But in an age when the traditional form of religion is not satisfactory, when its basic structure must be re-examined and the abstract essentials distinguished from the passing forms of concrete life, philosophy of religion comes to the front. In such a time the theologians are likely to say that there is no real difference between theology and philosophy of religion. What they mean is that in such a time the work they have to do is really that of philosophy of religion (p. 15).

This raises an issue which is crucial: Was historic orthodoxy unsatisfactory as a message for the twentieth century? The same volume suggests that the factors of social change, of growing sophistication, and of America's peculiar cultural dynamics, rendered it so (pp. 18-32). Now the expanding secularism, with its this-worldly temper and its aversion for other-wordliness, certainly did call historic Christianity into question. The success of modern science in improving the American level of living certainly gave to the questioning quality of the sophisticated mind an aura of intellectual sanctity, and to the attitude of faith the appearance of being fearfully naive.

It may be questioned, however, whether these factors may not themselves be the result of a prior rejection of the historic evangelical emphasis, rather than a reason for their rejection. In other words, a good case can be made for the contention that historic supernaturalism went into eclipse in the first quarter of the twentieth century, not because of any intrinsic deficiency in its message, but for lack of an adequate projection of that message into our national life. This lack of penetration of American thought by historic evangelicalism is not a simple phenomenon. In the first place, orthodoxy in America had not developed a definitive philosophical grounding. A laudable attempt was made by President James McCosh of Princeton. In his *Realistic Philosophy,* McCosh declares:

> The time has come, I believe, for America to declare her independence in philosophy . . . She should require that her philosophy have a character of its own . . . If a genuine American philosophy arises, it must reflect the genius of the people. Now, Yankees are distinguished from most others by their practical observation and invention. They have a pretty clear notion of what a thing is, and, if it is of value, they take steps to secure it. It follows that, if there is to be an American philosophy, it must be Realistic . . . opposed to idealism on the one hand, and to agnosticism on the other. (Vol. I, p. 4).

Whether the reason cited by McCosh here for the adoption of realism as a philosophical basis for our theological thought is the best one, it does remain true that Princeton, with her realistic tradition (imported earlier by John Witherspoon and invigorated by McCosh) persisted longer as a center for maintenance of historic Christianity than did any other of our major universities. Max H. Fisch, in his *Classic American Philosophers* (pp. 329f.) suggests that realism of the Scottish variety served, for a time at least, as a counteracting force to "deism, materialism and skepticism."

A second cause for the failure of historic orthodoxy to retain a guiding role in American religious life in the forepart of the present century was the massiveness of the opposing theological forces. Sweeping changes had occurred in the areas of Old and New Testament scholarship. Old Testament studies in the major seminaries were separated from studies in the New, and were pursued in a so-called scientific spirit, as a branch of the study of the history of religions. The resistance to the reconstructionism in Old Testament interpretation, associated with the names of Astruc, Kuenen, Graf and Wellhausen, was heroic, with the highly-respected William H. Green of Princeton as its leader. Unfortunately, however, trials do not eliminate erroneous teaching; indeed they may strengthen it through publicity. In any case, the documentary theory of the origin of the Hebrew Scriptures became the dominant position of our major seminaries—to remain so until its own inner weaknesses, plus the discoveries of archaeology, compelled its modification.

Trends in New Testament scholarship were seldom of such a sweeping character. However, the anti-supernatural bias of Continental scholarship did not leave American theology untouched. Successively, the Jesus-myth theory of Drews, the socio-historical method of interpretation, and later the form-critical method, added weight to the movement known as theological liberalism.

The weight of these, and of the allied forces of the *Religionsgeschichte* movement and the naturalistic form of the psychological study of religion, was impressive. Orthodox scholarship simply lacked the manpower and the academic resources to meet this multi-front challenge. There were, to be sure, men of stature who championed the cause of historic supernaturalism. One remembers gratefully the work of James Orr, whose *The Christian View of God and the World,* the Kerr lectures for 1890-91, was a classic in respect to its grasp of the forces arrayed against historic Christianity in his day, and as an attempt to meet these forces with philosophical insight. In spite of what may seem like needless concessiveness in a few areas, Orr set an example in the defense of the faith in this work—an example which was too seldom followed in the succeeding decades. Likewise, his volume entitled *The Problem of the Old Testament* went directly to the root of the issues between historic Christian orthodoxy and the newer liberal criticism of the Old Testament. For some reason, this work gathered dust upon the back shelves of the major theological libraries, seldom enjoying a place on the reference shelves.

Mention has already been made of the work of William Henry Green, whose stature and reputation as a scholar are reflected in the fact that he was chairman of the American committee for the Revised Version of the Bible (1901). Outstanding among his works, in addition to his Hebrew grammars, were: *General Introduction to the Old Testament* (1889), *The Unity of the Book of Genesis* (1897), and *The Higher Criticism of the Pentateuch* (1903).

Along with James Orr, another Scotchman made a significant contribution to evangelical scholarship at the turn of the century, Professor Robert Flint. He is best known for his volumes entitled *Theism* and *Agnosticism.* His *History of Dogmatics* is less well known, as is his *Historical Philosophy in France and French Switzerland,* this latter work being the one which gave him status among the masters of the history of thought. Flint's writings combine in rare degree the ability of the scholar with the heart of a Christian. With Orr, he had an unswerving faith in the essential reasonableness of Christianity as that message has been historically understood.

The existence of these men, and the circulation of their writings, undoubtedly did have its effect. At the same time, the major thrust of scholarship moved ahead in relative unconcern for their work and their conclusions. By 1900, the principal institutions for theological training had in their key posts men who, while they differed with respect to which type of religious philosophy they expressed, had for a common denominator the rejection of the authority of the Christian Scriptures, the acceptance of a developmental and social understanding of the Gospel, and a general rejection of Christian supernaturalism. Moreover, the historic circumstances of the day seemed to support a robust optimism with respect to human nature, human good, and human destiny.

II. DOMINANT TYPES OF RELIGIOUS PHILOSOPHY

To understand the present-day status of religious philosophy, and particularly as this relates itself to the contemporary revival of interest in evangelical Christianity, one must have at least a grasp of the basics of the several types of religious philosophy which have been dominant during the first half of the twentieth century. It is the purpose of the next sections to give the reader at least a speaking acquaintance with these forms of thought. It would, of course, require a volume to do justice to the subject, and this survey will include only major principles and prominent names.

Absolute Idealism

The term Idealism is a complex one, and the movements historically associated with the term have been diverse. Certain principles, however, are essential to the idealistic approach to reality, while others are added by those thinkers called "absolute idealists." General essentials to the idealistic understanding of things are these: (1) all that really exists is mind or a state of mind; (2) mind knows only itself, or that which is akin to it; and (3) what is ultimately real is good. To these the absolute idealist would add the doctrine of the Absolute, who is held to be all-perfect, immutable and all-inclusive.

This is mentalistic reductionism, seeking to solve the question of the dualism of *mind* and *matter* by resolving the whole of reality into mind, and further, into one infinite Mind. Arnold S. Nash suggests that until the beginning of World War I, absolute idealism was the dominant philosophy in America (*Protestant Thought in the Twentieth Century*, p. 74), Josiah Royce was the most able exponent of this form of philosophy, his classic work *The World and the Individual* appearing in 1901.

Two factors made his influence significant in the area of religious philosophy: his position in Harvard University gave his system of thought a considerable prestige; and his personal interests crystallized upon the religious bearing of his philosophy between 1900 and 1914. Two works appearing during that period contain his philosophy of religion, *The Philosophy of Loyalty* (1908), and *The Problem of Christianity* (1913).

Royce insisted that the conclusions of the natural sciences could reveal nothing worthy of worship. Religious thought, however, seeks something meriting our devotion by virtue of its goodness. He believed that mind revealed such a reality—an underlying unity which leads to and undergirds perfect goodness. Even experience with evil leads to a grasp of the good: for evil and error are but finite counterparts of an all-inclusive Absolute who embodies supremely goodness and truth.

At first glance it might seem that the Absolute was but a postulate. Royce, however, in his essay, "The Implications of Self-Consciousness," held that belief in the Absolute was the necessary ground for all thought. His Absolute was, he held, composed of individuals, an organism of interrelated selves. He disposed of the charge of pantheism (the doctrine that God is everything) by asserting that each individual within the Absolute shared the freedom which belongs to the Absolute.

The heart of religion, said Royce, was loyalty to that which the individual found to be worthful, beginning with those things nearest to him, and moving outward to higher and more inclusive objects of loyalty until finally loyalty grasps the Universal Community, a moral and spiritual "something" within the Absolute. In religion, therefore, man realizes himself through loyalty to the shared experience of individuals who, viewed collectively, form "the brotherhood of all the loyal."

It is evident that Royce's system is something quite different from historic Christianity. He seizes upon one element in the writings of St. Paul as expressive of the essence of Christianity, and ignores the major factors of the Incarnation of Jesus Christ, the redemptive work on Golgotha, the reality of sin, and the experiential results of personal redemption. In place of personal recognition of the claim of the Almighty upon human life, and instead of a proclamation of a personal relationship between redeemed men and their Lord, he sees as crucial a loyalty to persons of like mind, conceived as participating by nature in the Divine. No use of the vernacular of historic Christianity will render his system acceptable to evangelicals.

William Ernest Hocking, also of Harvard University, continued the tradition of absolute idealism, with modifications. His major religious writing is entitled *The Meaning of God in Human Experience*. His system differs from that of Royce in three important respects: (1) he explores the question of the distinctness of the individual from the Absolute, and in so doing moves in the direction of personalism; (2) he allows to intuition and to will increasingly important roles in religion, thus decreasing the claims of reason as a discoverer of truth; and (3) he shows a profound interest in mysticism, making this in some measure a substitute for the dialectics of Josiah Royce.

In place of Royce's philosophy of "loyalty" as the core of the religious response, Hocking substitutes "man's awareness of the all-inclusive, eternal and perfect reality of the Absolute, or whatever the most inclusive reality may be" (Wieman and Meland, *op. cit.*, p. 111). In clarification of the question of the relation of the individual to the Absolute, he begins with his definition of the divine reality as the changeless, rational Absolute Whole (*Meaning of God in Human Experience,* pp. 183-199). Of this Absolute, thinks he, all men have had some experience, whether by intuition or whether in will-experience. It is, however, the mystic who has experienced "it" the most fully (pp. 336 f.), and it is to him that we must look for the "development of religion" in terms of religious systems.

The weight of Hocking's teaching, so far as religious truth and its attainment is concerned, falls upon two areas. First, he attaches great significance to the claim of the mystic to an immediate intuition of the Absolute, known in terms of "the Other Mind." He says: "Upon this way of reaching the Other Mind, we must make the following comment. That we are still left with only an inference of that Other; a faith, and not a knowledge in experience" (p. 249). The second feature which is prominent, and significant from the evangelical point of view, is his estimate of the role of the will as a "creator" of truth.

Chapter XII is entitled "The Will As a Maker of Truth." Beginning with a consideration of what he believes to be the pilgrimage of "the god-idea," he suggests that every person begins with the whole-idea (p. 142), reacts with initial "resentment," and then enters into a new relationship to reality, in which the individual *will* creates the set of conditions within which the facts of religion can be true. The conclusion which Hocking reaches is as follows: ". . . the universe may . . . be so nicely adjusted (and withal so justly) that each man finds true the things he believes in and wills for . . ." (p. 143). In other words, whether or not a man endures beyond this life depends upon whether he wills it so!

It is clear from the foregoing pronouncement from *The Meaning of God in Human Experience* that a vast gulf exists between the system of Hocking and evangelical Christianity. In place of the sovereignty of God, we have here an astounding assertion of the autonomy of man. In place of fixed truth, we have a radical assertion of the absence of fixities. In place of redemption through the self-offering of the God-man, we find Jesus Christ lamely mentioned as "the founder of a popular religion who held up to the minds of a spell-bound multitude as his own original revelation a God who 'maketh his sun to rise on the evil and the good . . .' " (p. 205); or hear our author say, "We do not quite know what to do with our Holy Writ, or Christ . . ." (p. 357); or again, "There are no deeds more permanent than those of Buddha, of Mohammed, of Jesus" (p. 513).

With respect to his high estimate of mysticism, it needs to be said that Hocking's emphasis upon immediacy renders divine revelation superfluous, and reduces religious truth to, at best, a collation of the finest insights of highly sensitive individuals, and at worst, to the contradictory opinions of religious neurotics. Hocking would insist that "revelation" is unfinished and must be tested for validity by the criterion of its compatibility with the nature of his Absolute.

Religious Pragmatism

Perhaps no thinker stands in the eyes of the world as being more distinctively American than William James. His active academic life may be divided into two periods. The first period, dated approximately from 1880 to 1900, was devoted to psychology, and its high point was the publication of his *Principles of Psychology* in 1890. His international reputation as a psychologist was, therefore, established before he turned his interest primarily to philosophy and to philosophy of religion.

The second period of his life, dating from about 1900 to the time of his death in 1910, found him standing as the chief opponent of Josiah Royce, his colleague at Harvard, and of the system of absolute idealism. Many of his philosophical views were, it is true, developed in his psychological studies; but it was the appearance in 1902 of his *The Varieties of Religious Experience* (Gifford lectures) which brought him into prominence on the American religious scene.

Against all forms of dogmatism (whether religious, philosophical or scientific) James set his view of pragmatism or "empirical theism." His *Pragmatism* (1907) and his *A Pluralistic Universe* (1909) provide a further exposition of his approach. To him, truth was that which served as a good guide to conduct; that is, any belief is to be treated as an hypothesis, and is to be judged true insofar as it enables one to anticipate the course of events. Religious truth must conform to this same test; like "secular" truth, it is never absolute, and is subject to growth as new theories are proposed and confirmed in experience.

There is insufficient space in a discussion of this kind to sketch in detail his theory of mind-matter which he called "radical empiricism." Basically, he holds in this teaching that any thought may be an aspect of both physical and mental entities and an element of more than one consciousness. From his idea of the compounding of consciousnesses, he derived his theory of an ever-expanding series of minds (higher consciousnesses). He rejects, however, Royce's view of a single, all-embracing absolute consciousness, asserting that such an absolute would be responsible alike for good and for evil—and that God should be responsible for moral evil was to him unthinkable.

James's major religious work was his *Varieties of Religious Experience.* He began not only with the rejection of the traditional "proofs" for God, but with a repudiation of the major doctrines of Christianity. Disallowing the claims of the Christian Scriptures to be authoritative, he sought in his massive work to discover evidences for the validity of religion in the experiences of religious men and women. Dean Willard L. Sperry once remarked in the hearing of this writer that another *Varieties* could not be written for centuries, for James had "cut all of the tall timber in this field which had grown up over many centuries." In any case, after the citation of example after example, Christian and non-Christian, he turns to an evaluation of the significance of these "experiences" in the lives of those who have undergone them.

Many of the cases which he cites are of a pathological type. James felt that this fact did not in the least discount their worth as witnesses to the reality of religious experience. Indeed, he suggested that the neurotic may prove more susceptible to "incursions of the divine" than the more tough-minded. He concluded that belief in God made a meaningful difference in the life of the one holding it; it was therefore, by pragmatic definition, a *true* belief. Prayer and mystical experiences, he found, wrought significant changes in personality, the former being especially valuable as serving to refresh and reassure. These facts were held to point not only to the validity of James's pragmatic assumptions, but to his conclusion that there exists, transcending our conscious minds, "a *more* of the same quality which is operative in the universe outside of [us]" (p. 508).

Since he is constitutionally qualified to respond sensitively to incursions from the over-world, the mystic is the medium *par excellence* through whom intimations of religious "truth" can come. James is quick to qualify his approval of the claim of the mystic to have reached normative truth. The mystical state, says he, is, when well developed, authoritative over those who experience it, but has no authority for others which "make it a duty for those who stand outside of them to accept their revelations uncritically" (p. 422).

Applied thoroughly, this proposition would discount the claim of any individual to have written as "moved by the Holy Spirit." James proposes a system of religious individualism which amounts to anarchy. His positive contribution of challenging the dogmatism of the absolute idealists and of the materialists can scarcely outweigh the negative impact upon belief in the validity of the Christian revelation. True, he did seek his "varieties" from among the intellectually "down-and-out," thus challenging the aristocratic monopoly of the genteel tradition in the religious life. He gave to experimental religion a measure of respectability; but even this was in large part neutralized by his leveling of genuine Christian experiences to the common denominator of "religious" states attainable to men who were without the slightest interest in the Redeemer, or in a radical treatment of the element of sin within their lives.

Religious Psychologism

It might seem that the subject of religious psychologism should be included within the discussion of the thought of William James. It is generally agreed, however, that with the possible exception of H. M. Kallen, James left no heir to his major principles. The interest which he showed in the psychology of religion was but a fraction of his total interest; and the train of psychologists of religion who have appeared upon the American scene are in fact indebted to other thinkers for their main emphases.

The subjectivist approach to religious study reached its greatest strength and influence in Europe somewhat earlier than with us. The work of Schleiermacher and of Feuerbach at this point began to bear fruit in America a bit later than the appearance of James's *Varieties.* Schleiermacher's definition of revelation as an original feeling of dependence produced in man by the universe is well known; so too is his location of the essence of religion in the "immediate consciousness of the Deity as He is found in ourselves and in the world" (*On Religion,* p. 101). In him, the theocentric quality of the Christian faith suffered eclipse behind subjectivism. Revelation became not God's self-disclosure, but "any original feeling" evoked in man by his environment. The objective quality of miracles, of faith, or of the Incarnation, evaporated in his anthropocentric doctrine of subjectivity.

Ludwig Feuerbach, an extreme left-wing disciple of G. W. F. Hegel, popularized in Germany the illusionistic approach to theory, asserting that belief in God grew out of wish-thinking. In America, J. H. Leuba, in his *A Psychological Study of Religion* (1912), suggests that man has created his gods (i.e., his god-ideas) as a result of his need for them. In his system, the objective truth of the major doctrines of the Christian faith finds a virtual denial, while their utility as affording "ethical support and affective comfort" and as regulative for human life, is emphasized as the essential of religious faith.

The second and third decades of our century have marked the appearance of a number of religious psychologists, most of whose works represent variations upon the themes announced by the German romanticists. James Bissett Pratt, whose volume *The Religious Consciousness* was published in 1920, laid down the major lines which were pursued by subsequent writers in the field. The chief feature of conversion was not the restoration of right relationships between man and God, but "the unification of character, the achievement of a new self . . ." (p. 123).

While giving recognition to the "striking victory over evil habits of long standing which sometimes comes about through conversion" (p. 162), Pratt locates all of the factors which make for conversion *within the individual himself* (Chs. VIII and IX). He pronounces a funeral oration over mass evangelism, which he feels "is practically gone" (p. 193). One searches his volume in vain for any intimation of a transcendent reality, let alone a personal God operative in the redemption of individual men.

Substantially the same line of reasoning is followed by Francis L. Strickland in his *Psychology of Religious Experience* (1924). His major thesis is stated as follows:

> But a philosophy of religion which emphasizes the divine immanence teaches that the divine power is quite as manifest in the more gradual and familiar processes we call natural as in the unfamiliar processes we call supernatural (p. 125).

He shows no deep concern over the dying out (in some circles) of Christian conversions. In his chapter "The Subconscious" he strikes at the root of the supernatural origin of Christian regeneration, no less than at the reality of divine origin of Scripture.

Professor Frank S. Hickman's *Introduction to the Psychology of Religion* (1926) makes a broader approach to the subject than either Pratt or Strickland. In addition to the method of study of the phenomena of individual religious behavior, he makes extensive use of the social expressions of religion, and explores more widely their role as factors in social life and behavior. His system is, however, more explicit in its recognition of a philosophical basis to his researches. He acknowledges as his own the "scientific claim of the oneness of the universe" with its rejection of the dualism of "natural and supernatural" which underlies the historic Christian view with respect to divine action in the experience of men (p. 536). His attitude toward the classic view of human sinfulness and the consequent universal need for regeneration is contained in his statement:

> Conversion is not the only gateway into religious experience, but for those whose lives have no normal religious development conversion is a necessary means for the inauguration of the religious life (p. 262).

Likewise, he assents to the "newer" view of "God as immanent in the world of nature" (p. 537) and to the sociological understanding of sin, in which "the consciousness of sin seems to be grounded in the natural desire which man has for social approval" (p. 299). Further definitions of sin as "lack of harmony within one's instinctive life" (p. 300), or as inevitably blending into person-to-person relationships (so as to draw the fangs from that theological definition of sin which he dreads), lead the reader to the conclusion that Hickman is hardly moving inductively upon the basis of observed human experience.

Actually, his psychology of religion is basically philosophical. Its major premise is that God and man are essentially *continuous*. His statement of the rationale for the scriptural doctrine of the Incarnation stems from the implicit assumption that Jesus Christ, described as He is in John 1:14 and in I John 1:1, is the end product of the "making concrete [of] the conception of the Divine" which "is really a phase of the anthropomorphic process which enters so strongly into the construction of the belief in God" (p. 425). The author's assumptions concerning human nature are of a piece with the same immanentist philosophy. The application of this serves, in his system, to attenuate the doctrine of the New Birth, so that it has significance only as one of the major adaptations which occur in the normal growing up of the adolescent.

Developing religious psychologism along parallel lines, with the incorporation of newer researches into interpersonal psychology, Paul E. Johnson published in 1940 his work, *Psychology of Religion*. The wife of the writer of this article was a pupil of Dr. Johnson in Boston University at the time the content of the volume was delivered to a class of theological students, and heard not only the written material, but the questions and answers which accompanied its delivery. The heart of the work is, without doubt, the chapter titled "Regenerative Powers."

Dr. Johnson, commenting upon our Lord's conversation with Nicodemus, suggests that "Jesus seems to mean that rebirth is as normal as birth" (p. 92). The developmental metaphysics underlying Johnson's view of religious experience is stated explicitly in terms of C. Lloyd Morgan's view of emergent creativity (p. 95). It is difficult to find any derivative of this type of "rebirth" which is not attainable upon the basis of human natural powers alone. His description of his understanding of the person of Jesus completely lacks a view of the incarnation of the pre-existent Son of God.

The foregoing glimpses of the field of religious psychologism indicate the degree to which its writers are, after all, philosophers of religion. While they may at times seem to be inductive researchers, a closer scrutiny reveals that their systems elaborate deeply-imbedded assumptions. This is not, in itself, a condemnation of their work. It does indicate the necessity for careful exposure of these principles as a means to the assessing of the bearing of this phase of religious study upon historic evangelicalism.

Theistic Naturalism

It was perhaps inevitable that out of the evolutionary movement some specific form of religious philosophy should come. It has been evident from the preceding surveys that the basic assumptions of the evolutionary approach lie beneath most of the forms which have been considered. The factor of immanence rests upon the assumption of continuity; while the general neglect of the supernatural takes for granted the developmental quality of the universe.

The earlier forms of evolutionary dogma were oriented in biology. Its rationale rested successively upon Darwin's theory of "survival of the fittest," the assumption of the inheritance of acquired characteristics (usually associated with the name of Lamarck), and the phenomenon of mutation (usually associated with the name of DeVries). As these were progressively weighed and found wanting, the major areas of the learned world sought to place the doctrine of evolution beyond the reach of experimental endeavor—that is, to ground it in metaphysics. This does not mean that no speculative work had been done in this area previously; for Hegel had in the nineteenth century proposed a grandiose system of dynamic rationalism. His general emphasis upon *process* as more basic than structure, and his dogma of *continuity* were powerfully instrumental in preparing the mind of the age for what was to come.

The philosophical application of the evolutionary principle to religious philosophy began earlier in Great Britain than in America. Its pioneer was Samuel Alexander, whose Gifford lectures *Space, Time and Deity* appeared in 1920. Less specifically interested in religion were two other Gifford lecturers: C. Lloyd Morgan, author of *Emergent Evolution* and *Life, Mind and Spirit;* and Henri Bergson, whose *Creative Evolution* had a large impact upon the world of religious philosophy prior to the appearance of his *The Two Sources of Religion and Morality*.

The movement in religious philosophy which stemmed in America from these antecedents is variously known as theistic naturalism, naturalistic theism, cosmic theism, and (in some of its aspects) religious realism. Its pioneer on this continent was Alfred North Whitehead, whose Gifford lectures, *Process and Reality,* were delivered in Edinburgh in 1927-28, appearing in print in 1929. This is a work so massive that any adequate survey of it would require a lengthy chapter. The most that can be done here is to trace its major principles, and to suggest their influence upon other writers.

Whitehead seeks, first of all, to create a new set of terms and categories, for he believes that our customary modes of expression are hopelessly involved with a static universe. This novel vocabulary renders his writings abstruse. Certain tenets of his system are, however, relatively apparent. First is his basic assumption that process and not structure is basic in the universe. In this, he revives—and in the grand manner—the ancient thesis of Heraclitus. His cosmology is basically Platonic: he asserts three basic formative elements, "creativity" (which he substitutes for Plato's indeterminate "matter"), "eternal objects" capable of being exemplified in actual objects, and a "primordial actual entity" which he identifies with God (pp. 127-147).

"God" is to him a postulate of his dynamic theory of "reality" as a "growing together" of the "occasions" or actual entities (pp. 31ff.). With respect to the nature of God, he distinguishes between the "primordial" and the "consequent" natures of God. By the "primordial" nature, he means two things: it is "a factor in God, deficient in actuality" (p. 50), and it is "the concrescence of an unity of conceptual feelings, including among their data all eternal objects" (p. 134). By this latter he seems to mean the world of Platonic "forms" which serve as a primordial limitation upon the creative process.

By the "consequent" nature of God, Whitehead seems to mean the manifestation of His work as "principle of concretion" so that the eternal objects comprising His primordial nature are operative in the world of temporal events so that there is "a reaction of the world on God," so that there is a "completion of God's nature into a fullness of physical feeling" which is derived from "the objectification of the world in God" (p. 523, cf. also *Religion in the Making,* p. 90).

Religious philosophy was not the primary concern of Whitehead. His *Religion in the Making* (1926) reveals the more specific rootage of his "theological" views. It is his analysis of creativity which yields his postulate of God (p. 90ff.). Likewise, in his *Science and the Modern World* (1925) he sets forth what is fundamentally a cosmological argument for God's existence (pp. 248-250). This does not mean that his "god" is personal, for in *Religion in the Making* he specifically repudiates belief in a personal God Who transcends the universe (pp. 60ff.).

The impact of Whitehead's philosophy upon the philosophy of religion has been almost wholly in the direction of the rejection of the biblical view of a personal God, and a total repudiation of historical revelation and the doctrines of Christianity which rest upon historical events. While accepting the idea of the love of God (he professes in this connection a fondness for the Gospel of St. John), he has no place for either human redemption from outside man, nor for morality as obedience to a revealed will of a personal God. Moreover, his view of reality, namely that that which is completely real is *process,* is actively hostile to the view that in the beginning "God created the heavens and the earth."

More basic still is his rejection of the dualism, natural-supernatural, and his substitution of the twin dogmas of immanence and continuity. This leaves no basis for the intervention (in redemption and in providence) of a transcendent God into the life of the world. So far as "redemption" goes, he sees this in societal terms, and insisted that *ideas* (chiefly the Platonic idea of soul) transform society and conserve human gains (cf. Morris R. Cohen, *American Thought,* pp. 58f.). After all, if we are to regard God Himself as *growing* and in the second "phase" of His "dipolar" nature undergoing inner transformation, it is difficult to see how He could manifest Himself in any manner beyond that of vague cosmic activity (cf. William H. Werkmeister, "The Philosophy of Whitehead" in his *Philosophical Ideas in America,* pp. 343-366).

The major impact of Whitehead's thought upon religious philosophy in America came through his pupil, Henry Nelson Wieman. The fidelity with which Wieman follows his master is clear from the section, "Alfred N. Whitehead," in Wieman and Meland, *American Philosophies of Religion* (pp. 229-231), a section which is probably from his own pen. Wieman's major writings are these: *Religious Experience and Scientific Method* (1926), *The Wrestle of Religion With Truth* (1927), and *The Source of Human Good* (1946).

Earlier, Wieman was concerned lest Whitehead should yield to theological pressure and commit himself to belief in a personal God. In *Religious Experience and Scientific Method,* he neither affirms nor denies belief in God's personality. In *The Source of Human Good* he virtually repudiates such a belief when he says, "The only creative God we recognize is the creative event itself" (p. 7). In the same breath, he denies to God even the measure of "transcendent" quality which might be implied in the primordial antecedents of creativity, suggesting that "the order or structure of the creative event is not imposed upon it but is intrinsic to the very nature of such an event" *(loc. cit.).* Thus, in his latest work he disavows the last shred of belief in either a personal or a transcendent God!

Because of space limitations it is not possible here to show the manner in which Wieman transforms historic Christian doctrines, in accordance with his assumptions, until such terms as faith, salvation, grace and the like are left with little or no resemblance to their meaning in Scripture.

One is tempted to ask whether such a system is really "theistic" at all. Certainly its "god" did not create (in the usual sense of the term) the universe; certainly "he" is at best in but partial "control" of it. It is difficult to see how such a "god" could inspire reverence and worship, or how he could elicit even the "loyalty" which Whitehead mentions, to say nothing of making the claim which historic Christianity has understood the Lord of Heaven and Earth to lay upon the lives of men.

Religious Humanism

If in the matter of relinquishing the basic historic concepts of Christianity, the theistic naturalists have chastised historic evangelicalism with whips, another group, the religious humanists, have chastised it with scorpions. This group of thinkers includes many shades of belief with respect to the denial of objective reality in religion: a few are frankly atheistic, believing that the historic belief in the existence of God is not only absurd, but that it has a baneful influence upon those holding it, in that it has diverted their attention from useful areas of human endeavor. Others are more fairly described as agnostic: their contention is that the existence of God is incapable of any form of demonstration, and that belief in such existence represents a hold-over from a childish stage of human culture in which the unexplained was referred to the activity of a deity or of deities. In the interest of human betterment, the belief should be abandoned.

Basic to this type of "religious" outlook is the Kantian contention that the human reason has no capacity for penetrating into the nature of reality. Knowledge is thus confined to a knowledge of phenomena; sense experience gives us all that we can know concerning the nature of reality. So far as religion is concerned, man's religious experiences yield no evidence of the reality of their own objects. John Dewey, in his doctoral thesis on the thought of Kant, made it clear that he believed that the sage of Königsberg was the founder of true philosophic method (Herbert W. Schneider, *A History of American Philosophy,* pp. 476ff.).

Dewey agreed with James that there is a "religious" quality in experience which is independent of the beliefs of institutionalized religions. In his *A Common Faith,* he says: "The opposition between religious values as I conceive them and religions is not to be bridged" (p. 28). His attitude toward the religion which should prevail in our society is as follows:

> He regards religious faith as something that men can and should have in common, uniting them in their basic enterprise of relating what together they hold to be ideal. God as the symbol for this union of believers and as the name for the partial union of actuality and ideality, is an object for loyalty rather than of affirmation. (Schneider, *op. cit.,* p. 560).

Significant for this study is the list of denials which proceed from the religious humanists' repudiation of the possibility of any knowledge of the unseen and the transcendental. Revelation, in any significant sense of the term, is ruled out at one stroke. The existence of a personal God is either ruled out, or else relegated to the limbo of the undisclosed (*cf.,* J. A. C. F. Auer, *Humanism States Its Case,* Chapter IV). The eternity of matter is taken for granted, and creation thus treated as a scientific absurdity (Corliss Lamont, *Humanism As a Philosophy,* p. 195). A transcendent God is held to be a useless absurdity (Auer, *op. cit.,* p. 90). Any conception of good and evil as being rooted in a realm above nature is held to be invalid and unscientific; "values" represent the accumulated and funded experience of the race (cf. John Dewey, "The Construction of Good" in Max H. Fisch (ed.) *Classic American Philosophers,* pp. 360ff.).

A little thought will reveal that religious humanism is in reality an extension of the principles of some other systems in which these principles are pursued fearlessly to their conclusions. This writer recalls hearing his tutor Dr. Auer mention this fact in his lectures; Dr. Auer frequently asserted that he carried the basics of much of so-called liberal theology or "modernism" to their logical end, and that in so doing he was simply more honest than the religious liberals. While they sought to cling to some of the terminology of theism, they were nevertheless giving implicit assent to the contention of the humanist, that the qualities which men traditionally worship in God are actually human qualities worthy of worship where they are most easily found—in man (Auer, *op. cit.*, pp. 98ff.). A consideration of religious humanism is likewise instructive for the understanding of less radical forms of anti-supernaturalism, in that humanists frankly admit the relativity of their principles and their anti-theistic biases. Their system is admittedly a "way of thinking," derived from a recognized independence of historic Christianity. Much of so-called "liberal" theology should be more forthright at this point. (For a discussion of "Religious Humanism As a Way of Thinking" the writer mentions his own doctoral dissertation, *An Inquiry Into the Problem of Human Self-Transcendence in Contemporary Religious Philosophy*, submitted to Harvard University, 1944, pp. 171ff.)

In spite of its affinities with the contemporary scientific spirit, religious humanism is not fulfilling the expectations of its formulators by becoming the religion of the future. As Dean Willard L. Sperry once said in the writer's hearing, the religion of the mid-century is not the bland humanism of President Lowell, but the evangelicalism of the Pentecostal sects.

Personal Idealism

There is a form of religious philosophy which to the casual observer seems to have much in common with historic evangelicalism. It is that system first formulated in America by Borden Parker Bowne, and developed by Albert C. Knudson, Ralph Tyler Flewelling, and Edgar Sheffield Brightman. It has been called variously personal idealism, personalism, and personal realism.

Ralph T. Flewelling states the basic thesis of personal idealism as follows:

> It holds that all reality is in some sense personal; that there are only persons and what they create; that personality is self-conscious and self-directive both in finite individuals and in a supreme creative Intelligence which is the world-ground and source of all reality ("Personalism," in D. D. Runes [ed.] *Twentieth Century Philosophy*, p. 324).

Borden Parker Bowne returned from his studies in Göttingen to a professorship at Boston University thoroughly committed to the principles held by his tutor, Hermann Lotze. In the development of his own system he reacted especially against the thought of Herbert Spencer, who, it seemed to Bowne, carried the sensationalism of Locke to a point which resulted in the destruction of the self. Spencer and William James seemed to him to have carried the organization of experience to a point which lost sight of the "self" which did the organizing.

Bowne insisted that reality was of the nature of *idea*. "He considered the forces in the objective universe to be the expression of ideas. The material world is realized idea—idea which has somehow had force put into it" (Joseph L. Blau, *Men and Movements in American Philosophy*,

p. 201). His "transcendental empiricism" had for its basis the belief that conscious experience is the only reality. Space and time are for us "principles of thought or principles immanent in our mental operation" (Bowne, *Personalism,* p. 128).

His insistence upon the integrity of the self, and upon the root-idea that all reality is in some sense personal, leads to a conclusion in terms of a personal pluralism—which might indicate an anarchy of finite selves. He solves this problem by suggesting an interaction of these individuals, who are in constant dependence upon "one all embracing being, which is the unity of the many, and in whose unity an interacting plurality first becomes possible" (Bowne, *Metaphysics,* p. 126).

The obvious conclusion which proceeds from this is that what appears to be empirically the manifestation of a plurality of individuals is actually a manifestation of the immanent action of one infinite and absolute Being. Finite selves manifest this Absolute, who is present in them all as their underlying ground (cf. Flewelling, *Creative Personality,* pp. 268-270). While personalism considers nature as a part of God, yet insists that selves by contrast are creatures other than God, both realities seem to reduce, in this formulation, to empirical manifestations of the Absolute.

The bearing of this upon historic Christian theism is clear: God is fundamentally immanent in the world-process and in men. Creation was not something which occurred "in the beginning"; rather, the universe is the objectification of the nature of God, Who, as immanent in it, is still creating. Process becomes more fundamental than structure; the regularities of nature express His activity at its best.

No consideration of personal idealism is complete without at least a brief statement concerning the question of the absoluteness of God. While Bowne differed fundamentally with the absolute idealism of Royce, he did insist upon God's infinity. He and his pupil Knudson insisted that God was "one absolute personality" (Wieman and Meland, *op. cit.,* 136). Any limitations upon Him are self-imposed (Flewelling, *op. cit.,* p. 267; cf. also his *The Reason in Faith,* p. 232). Within the group of men known as personal idealists, however, is one who found the idea of an infinite God increasingly unsatisfactory. Edgar Sheffield Brightman, pupil of A. C. Knudson, struck out on somewhat independent lines, while at the same time managing to inherit the title of major exponent of personal idealism.

Brightman adduces five major objections to theistic idealism, which "taken together, render it a highly improbable view" (*A Philosophy of Religion,* p. 309): it rests upon an appeal to ignorance; it ascribes "surd evil" to the divine will; it tends to make good and evil indistinguishable; it tends to cut the nerve of moral endeavor; and it is unempirical in character. His conclusion is that while God may be infinite in "will to good," He is limited by evil, which under the euphemism "The Given" is held to be a part of His own nature.

The major differences between the presuppositions of personal idealism and those of historic evangelicalism may now be mentioned. While personal idealism insists that all reality is of the nature of mind or idea, most evangelicals have taken for granted that the universe manifests two orders of reality, mind (or spirit) and matter. Personal idealists consider God to be immanent in an existential sense in all of nature; evangelicals insist that God is in essence transcendent to the universe, and that He is immanent only by way of personal presence and operation. Personal idealists deny the dualism of nature and grace; evangelicals in the historic tradition recognize as not only valid but essential the dualism of nature and grace, seeing in it the philosophical basis for distinguishing the natural from the supernatural. In addition, between finitistic personalism and evangelicalism a vast gulf is fixed: Brightman's view, which places evil within the nature of God, is supremely distasteful to one holding the biblical understanding of God. As Julius S. Bixler (a humanist) frequently said in his Harvard lectures in the philosophy of religion, "Would such a God be God at all?"

Albert C. Knudson once remarked in the presence of this writer, "My pupil's [Dr. Brightman's] religious philosophy is a baptized naturalism in which the waters of baptism have not effected any significant regeneration." It may be asked whether any system of religious thought which begins with the assumption that the physical universe is an objectification of the divine experience will ever escape the danger of degenerating into naturalism.

Wieman and Meland comment that "When one reads the works of Borden P. Bowne today one is amazed to see how fully they express the generally accepted liberal view among Christian people of our time" (*op. cit.*, p. 139). This does not mean, however, that all who claim adherence to a personalist religious philosophy are themselves by that fact to be considered in the liberal theological tradition. Some have accepted the basics of personalism for lack of something better, and adjust it to meet the claims of historic Christianity. The issue of realism versus idealism aside, the notion that nature is a part of God is a serious error, and the personalist handling of special revelation is equally objectionable. A careful study of the literature of the personal idealists might lead those who appeal to it to wonder whether this philosophy of religion can contribute much that is stable to their theology, or whether in reality their theology must carry their philosophy.

Religious Existentialism

The existential movement in Europe, in interaction with political and economic events of a revolutionary character, ushered in what was termed "The Theology of Crisis" or "The Dialectical Theology." This theological movement, spearheaded by the publication of Karl Barth's *Epistle to the Romans,* and developed by Barth in subsequent writings, and by Emil Brunner, made itself felt in American religious thought through the instrumentality of several men who came as temporary or permanent immigrants, notably Wilhelm Pauck and Josef Hromádka. It found, however, its most powerful native expression in the work of the German-trained Reinhold Niebuhr and his brother Richard. Somewhat later Paul Tillich, an immigrant from Germany, began to make his influence felt on the American scene. Tillich is at present one of the most significant figures in American religious philosophy.

The dialectical theology was in part a protest against the philosophizing of theology; its early thrust was against the principle of continuity in general, and against the supposed continuity of reason in faith in particular. As such, it might have seemed to promise a cancellation of religious philosophy; actually and practically, it did nothing of the sort, but it involved in its spread the elaboration of a religious philosophy of its own.

Theologically, this movement stressed an uncompromising transcendentalism. God was declared to be the Wholly Other; He is the Sovereign of the world, who breaks into the stream of our common life "perpendicularly from above" in revelation. God is held, further, to be radically discontinuous with our total experience, including our thought-experience. He demands an unconditional response to His Word, whose central reality is Christ, Who speaks the divine message with finality and certainty. The Incarnation, asserted by the crisis theologians, is not a doctrine to be comprehended and defended rationally, but an inscrutable deed, revealing God through His redeeming grace.

On the human side, this form of theological thought implied God's confronting of the individual with an absolute crisis. "This ultimate crisis is the necessity of deciding for God or against God" (Wieman and Meland, *op. cit.,* p. 86). This decision must be made in the absence of rational understanding of God or of His ways; man can only know God (and hence repose faith in Him) through the "Word spoken in Christ." This Word must not, insist the crisis theologians, be identified with the Bible, nor can Christ be identified, in an absolute sense, with the man Jesus. To explain these things, these thinkers resort to the expediencies of myth and paradox. (Cf. H. Shelton Smith, *Changing Conceptions of Original Sin,* p. 209.)

The question of the nature of man brought the existential type of religious philosophy into sharp focus. Its fullest contemporary expression is found in the works of Reinhold Niebuhr and Paul Tillich. Niebuhr belonged to the so-called "social gospel" school in the days of his pastorate in Detroit. As was the case with the earlier thinker, Walter Rauschenbusch, he was brought to his "realistic" view of human nature, with its innately evil quality, through his reflections upon the social structure. "Perceiving how will-to-power, pride, and other forms of egocentrism characterized every type of existing group, large or small, he was impelled to conclude that modern liberal culture's optimistic estimate of human nature was fatuous" (Smith, *op. cit.,* p. 208).

The bearing of the existential revolt in philosophy upon Niebuhr is not easy to pinpoint. Certain of its themes recur in his writings: The homelessness of the human spirit, emphasized by existentialists, is akin to Niebuhr's description of "the sense of security" (*The Nature and Destiny of Man,* I, pp. 190f.). His anxiety resembles the state of mind engendered as man senses himself to be guilty, but does not understand precisely the nature of the charges against him (*ibid.,* I, pp. 168; 182-186). Again, Niebuhr's approach reflects a common quality of existentialism, in that the questions he raises are considered to be more basic than the answers he offers. This very absence of a system is an indication of affinity.

Both Niebuhr and Tillich show their relationship to the irrational approach in connection with the question of propositional revelation in the Christian Scriptures, by their emphasis upon the role of *myth* in theology. Niebuhr distinguishes between the "primitive" and the "permanent" myth, the former being pre-scientific, the latter "suprascientific" ("The Truth in Myths" in *The Nature of Religious Experience,* pp. 118f.). He uses his analysis of myth to explain his departure from traditional Christian doctrine, which he holds to be full of "literalistic errors." Tillich, in the first volume of his *Systematic Theology,* finds theological thought to be encased in myth (p. 16); he holds that "reason in existence" expresses itself in "myth and cult" in matters which lie beyond possible expression in rational form (p. 81f.). Nels F. S. Ferré, in his "Where Do We Go From Here in Theology?" in *Religion in Life* (Winter, 1955-56), suggests that Tillich has "rejected classical Christian supernaturalism as impossible in the face of a century of science" (p. 9).

The first volume of Tillich's *Systematic Theology* dealt with the questions of Revelation and God; the second has not yet been published. H. Shelton Smith, who had access to notes taken from lectures which embody the material of Volume Two, indicates that it will continue and extend Tillich's view of myth as applied to the fall of man and the nature of human moral history (*op. cit.,* pp. 218ff.). Following his "correlational" method, Tillich finds his "answers" to rest upon previously formulated questions. These questions reflect his deeper philosophical presuppositions. Ferré foresees the future of Tillich's system: "Existentialism is . . . more flexible than a faith based on a given external revelation . . . As a matter of fact, Tillich can make self-criticism the very 'Principle of Protestantism' " (*op. cit.,* p. 10).

The bearing of religious existentialism upon evangelicalism is relatively clear. The factuality of the biblical is ruled out upon the basis of its allegedly "unscientific" character. The Kantian agnosticism with reference to the basic elements of Christian truth is supported by an appeal to the element of myth, which is held to be the only valid manner of expressing the "suprascientific" propositions of religion in general, and of Christianity in particular. The classic understanding of God, of Creation, of the Fall, of the Incarnation, of Redemption, and of the final triumph of Jesus Christ, will be treated no more kindly by theological existentialism than they have been under the other forms of sub-evangelical religious philosophy which we have investigated.

Ferré sums up the effect of this type of philosophy of religion upon historic Christianity as follows:

> Is classical supernatural Christianity dead for those who are both honest and competent? If Tillich is right, the objective faith of the apostles and of the great company of Christian witnesses throughout the ages was wrong, and he plainly tells us so. Their "original" rather than "objective" faith was then in the power of love to unite life and to resist nonbeing. There is, for Tillich, no personal God who *objectively is,* who rules the nations and our lives, and who has judged us and saved us in Christ Jesus by his own coming into the world, being crucified, and being raised from the grave. Nor is there, for him, any life after death for us all, and thus no eventual solution of the tragedies of our existence. (Review of *Biblical Religion and the Search for Ultimate Reality* by Tillich, in *The Christian Century,* November 2, 1955, p. 1273).

This evaluation is the more meaningful for evangelicals, for it comes not only from one who speaks for an "ecumenical theology," but from one who has in the past and does at present disavow fundamentalism. If the dangers in religious existentialism are apparent to him, surely none can accuse evangelicals of seeing ghosts when they perceive these same perils.

Each of the types of religious philosophy surveyed in the course of the preceding pages, excepting only religious existentialism, subordinated religious thought in spirit to general speculative philosophy. This assumption, taken in combination with the adventurous and experimental temper of the "liberal" mind, resulted in a secularization of theology, which in turn issued in a loss of the distinctively Christian character of most of contemporary theology. In consequence, the major sectors of American Protestant thought are today submerged in the secular patterns of modernity.

III. REVIVAL OF EVANGELICAL RELIGIOUS PHILOSPOHY

The opening section of this chapter dealt with the thought-situation in the American religious world at the beginning of the present century. In that section, it was noted that the major theological writers and institutions were not only committed to a developmental and social understanding of the Gospel, but that most of them were frankly negative in their relation to Christian supernaturalism. They were thus susceptible to being influenced by the variety of philosophical approaches, both those current and those on the horizon. In large measure, philosophy of religion became a substitute for systematic theology.

Evangelical scholarship during the first half of the twentieth century was, logically enough, less directly interested in religious philosophy than in systematic theology and in biblical studies. This does not mean that no conservative writers understood philosophy, nor that the bearing of philosophical speculation upon theology was becoming increasingly great. It was largely a matter of emphasis.

Three men dominate the area of the scholarly defense of the historic evangelical position from 1900 to 1930, Benjamin Breckinridge Warfield, Robert Dick Wilson, and J. Gresham Machen. Of these, Machen is occasionally recognized in such volumes as Wieman and Meland, *American Philosophies of Religion* (four brief references); in D. C. Macintosh's *The Problem of Religious Knowledge* (one reference); and in Arnold S. Nash's *Protestant Thought in the Twentieth Century* (one reference). Warfield and Wilson are ignored, while F. L. Patton and F. A. Mullin are mentioned once in Wieman and Meland's volume.

Evangelicals will do well to remember that even this grudging recognition is indirect witness to the intrinsic ability of the men and the worth of their writings. After all, the principles for which these men stood, seemed, in the current trend, hopelessly quaint during the years just prior to World War I, when Walter Rauschenbusch announced that the major areas of American life, including politics, the home and education, were already Christianized, and that "The swiftness of evolution in our own country proves the immense latent perfectibility in human nature" (*Christianity and the Social Crisis,* p. 422). When such leaders of American theological thought, we say, felt that "The largest and hardest part of the work of Christianizing the social order has been done . . ." (*Christianizing the Social Order,* p. 124), one would not expect a warm reception to be accorded those men who dared to assert the biblical principles of human sinfulness and the divine plan of redemption.

B. B. Warfield's study, "Christian Supernaturalism," in his *Studies in Theology,* emphasizes in clearest fashion the centrality of the dualism of nature-supernature to the Christian understanding of things. This dualism is rooted, of course, in the doctrine of the transcendence of God (pp. 31f.), and finds expression in the doctrine of creation "by which nature itself and all its laws were brought into existence" (p. 35). He looks to the root of the anti-supernaturalism of his day; it is an attempt to "explain away" redemption by seeking "to evaporate it into a set of platitudes about the guiding hand of God in history . . ." (p. 41).

The implications for Christian doctrine of the replacement of divine transcendence by divine immanence seem most clear in relation to the doctrine of redemption, seen by Warfield against the background of the assertion in Scripture of the attributes which portray God as distinct from the world in general, and the world of sinful men in particular (pp. 110f.). The sweeping significance of the question of the supernatural appears in a number of connections in Warfield's other writings. Its meaning for the understanding of the nature of Jesus Christ is set forth in *The Lord of Glory* (pp. 33ff.) and especially in his article on "The Person of Christ" in *The International Standard Bible Encyclopedia* (Vol. 4, pp. 2338-2348).

A reading of the writings of Warfield reveals that while his major interest was theological, he came to his work with a philosophical mind. Behind the newer criticism of the Bible, he saw the controlling force of philosophical presuppositions. He indicated, for example, that the doctrine of the "two natures in Christ" is not a synthesis of several strands of New Testament teaching concerning Christ, but the presupposition underlying each of these strands (*The Person and Work of Christ,* p. 237). The role of presuppositions in critical study of the question of revelation is likewise recognized in his article "The Real Problem of Inspiration" (*ibid.,* pp. 169-226), and in "Recent Christological Speculation" in *Christology and Criticism* (pp. 259-310).

The contribution of Robert Dick Wilson to the apologetic of the period under study belongs to the chapter dealing with Old Testament studies, since his work was primarily philological and exegetical. More directly philosophical was the contribution of J. Gresham Machen.

Machen's volume *Christianity and Liberalism* embodies the major features of his own philosophy of religion, setting them in sharp contrast to the presuppositions of the liberal-modernist tradition. Against both Kantian agnosticism and "the theology of feeling" he opposes that "the knowledge of God is the very basis of religion" (p. 55). Against the immanentism to which modern liberalism clings, he opposed the doctrine of divine transcendence as describing the "one attribute of God which is absolutely fundamental . . ." (p. 62).

His treatment of the question of the supernatural (pp. 99-102) is likewise philosophical, involving as its basis a belief in the dualism of natural-supernatural. This rests in turn upon a theistic conception of God, as distinguished from both extreme transcendence (Deism) and Pantheism. (Machen rightly observes that while modern liberalism may not be explicitly pantheistic, it is pantheizing in tendency.) Thus, his world-outlook is basically that of the creationist-realist, with a recognition that after creation, there existed in the universe God, plus the products of His creative energy, the latter enjoying a conferred existence separate from God, and being subject to His providential care.

With reference to the nature of religious truth, Machen accepts as evident the view that truth is one, and that there is validity in that which man may learn concerning God from a study of nature (*God Transcendent,* pp. 20f.). Theology rests upon facts; its truth is of a kind with the truth which forms the basis for scientific endeavor (*What Is Faith?*, pp. 32ff.). Thus, "our knowledge of God on the basis of His revelation of Himself is, we hold, true as far as it goes" (*ibid.*, p. 52).

Machen's opposition to such dualism as that of Plato appears in connection with his treatment of the question of sin (*The Christian View of Man,* pp. 210ff.). He rejects the position that sin is "the triumph of the lower part of man's nature over the higher part . . ." or that any of God's creation is to be considered evil *per se.* Nor is sin to be considered to be "conduct opposed to self-interest" and as such a "trifling matter" which a genial God may treat in terms of "let bygones be bygones" (*Christianity and Liberalism,* p. 129).

In short, Machen's religious philosophy continues the realistic trend for which Princeton has been historically famous. His understanding of religious truth is exceedingly significant. In his *The Christian Faith in the Modern World,* he says:

> A good many people seem to think that every generation lives in a sort of intellectual water-tight compartment, without much chance of converse with other generations. Every generation has its own thought form, and cannot by any chance use the thought forms of any other generation (p. 9).

This view he terms "nonsense"; in his critique of it, he lays a finger upon a sensitive spot in contemporary liberalism, which not only acknowledges that it represents a deviation from historic Christianity, but glories in the supposed fact that Christianity is a "dynamic" religion, which *ought* to be formulated anew by each generation.

In his *The Origin of Paul's Religion,* Machen penetrates deeply into the philosophical implications of the Christian faith. He notes the dissimilarity between Christian and pagan thought (pp. 293f.); he sees that philosophy not only undermined the traditional Greek religious pattern (p. 219), but also failed miserably to fill the void which this undermining left in the Greek mind (p. 224). More important still, he sees in this volume, as in *Christianity and Liberalism,* the profound implications of supernaturalism for the whole thrust of the Christian Evangel, particularly for the doctrine of redemption (pp. 288ff.).

It is interesting and significant that evangelicals have paid relatively little attention to the study of religious psychology, or at least have done little writing in this field. No systematic reply to William James's *Varieties of Religious Experience* appeared for over three decades. In 1937,

Sverre Norborg published a volume under title *Varieties of Christian Experience,* in which he defends the thesis that a psychological uniqueness attaches to Christian experience. This is in reply to James's thesis that the psychic quality of all religious experiences is the same (p. 10). While recognizing James's general contribution as a pioneer, and as a reporter of religious data (p. 27), he protests mere description as a methodology (pp. 23f.), and shows that James does in reality defend a theory of his own. Norborg insists that Christian experience has its own laws and its own structure (p. 29), and that its pursuit leads to certainty with respect to God's existence (p. 91). He utters a strong protest against the materialistic dogmatism of Freud and others (p. 65), absolute or identificationist mysticism (p. 80), and insists that modern psychologists have no eyes to comprehend Christian conversion (p. 169).

While Norborg's volume is less readable than that of James, it merits serious consideration in evangelical circles. His work was ahead of its time in its recognition of the character of existentialism, and of its probable future role (p. 61).

Edgar Young Mullins was another significant figure in the area of religious philosophy. In his volume *Freedom and Authority in Religion,* he touched upon the vital areas of difference between modern liberalism and evangelical Christianity. In Chapter IV, entitled "The Unstable Equilibrium of Philosophy," he saw both the proper function and the limitations of philosophy in relation to the comprehension of Christianity. In his *Christianity at the Crossroads,* he proposes a type of "religious realism" and defends the position of the knowability of God as religious Object (p. 45). He sets in contrast historic Christianity and the so-called "religion of science" (pp. 75ff.) and insists that the heart of the contrast is to be found in the difference between Christianity's dualism of nature-grace on the one hand, and liberalism's insistence upon *continuity* in the universe: that "God" is continuous with the world, the spiritual order is continuous with the natural order, and religion is continuous with the whole of man's grasp of natural processes. Seldom has the contrast between supernaturalism and naturalism been more penetratingly stated (cf. especially pp. 113ff., pp. 201ff.).

While Mullins' *Why Is Christianity True?* is less directly philosophical in its apologetic, it contains valuable philosophical insights. Here Mullins emphasizes the concrete quality of Christian truth, as against the view that doctrine is merely "idealistic" or symbolic (p. 305), and criticizes with penetration the reductionism of both the pantheist and the materialist, which makes unity the major goal of philosophical endeavor, and in which the basic dualities underlying historic Christianity are lost (pp. 26-29; 33-40). He insists upon the integrity of both mind and matter (pp. 43f.) and exhibits the implicit omniscience of the agnostic position (pp. 48-57).

In his *The Christian Religion in Its Doctrinal Expression* he extends his critique of agnosticism (pp. 108f.) for its profession of omniscience, its narrow view of human knowledge, and its destructive implication for morality and for the religious life.

In the same chapter, he offers a critique of idealism, observing its major point of strength (namely, its opposition to materialism) and its basic weakness of inability to explain the differences between thought and things (pp. 111f.). His personal philosophy is, as he indicates in the course of his discussion, a type of person-centered realism. In his *Christianity at the Crossroads,* he states as the major postulate of biblical supernaturalism the reality of personality and of freedom in God and in man (p. 123).

With regard to religious truth, Mullins insists upon the propositional content of religious truth (*Freedom and Authority in Religion,* pp. 272ff.), and sees Christian experience as the bridge between the two "worlds" of Kant (p. 281). He faces the liberals with the contention that we can comprehend neither the natural nor the supernatural *in toto* (CC, p. 181), and protests the contention that a supernatural event lies outside the realm of historical research (p. 182). He alleges that liberals reject supernatural events as historical, not on historical grounds, but upon the basis of *a priori* principles (p. 196).

Leander S. Keyser gave to the evangelical world two valuable volumes, *Contending for the Faith* and *A Philosophy of Christianity.* The former of these is chiefly an analysis of the conclusions of critics, rather than an analysis of their presuppositions. Yet even here he has a section upon ontology (the philosophy of *being*) as it is related to the person of our Lord (pp. 257ff.), and another in which he takes liberals to task for their failure to have even a speaking acquaintance with the major conservative works in philosophical apologetics (pp. 277f.).

As one would expect from the title, *A Philosophy of Christianity* is more distinctly philosophical. The heart of the work in this regard is the chapter, "Some Basic Problems of Philosophy," in which he surveys, more briefly than we would wish, the questions of metaphysics, psychology, epistemology and ethics. Underlying these discussions, as well as Keyser's consideration of human nature, is the basic "common sense" type of realism, which accepts the dualisms of mind-matter, subject-object, and Creator-created. His section, "The Christian View of Man" rejects psychological monisms (p. 167) as well as biological determinisms. Keyser's works, while simply written, are penetrating. He expounds a point of view designed to make the understanding of Christianity in terms of a realistic philosophy intellectually defensible.

It will be observed that most of the religious philosophy which challenged classic liberalism during the first three decades of the present century was of the realistic variety. It continued the earlier tradition of Princeton, which was for decades the stronghold of the realism which issued from the Scottish universities. Not all evangelical scholars will share the writer's opinion at this point, but to him it is not surprising that a type of realism formed the basis of America's most effective apologetic.† Philosophical idealism has been the underlying thought-factor in liberal theology since the days of Horace Bushnell.

The same approach is characteristic of several other volumes which have appeared more recently. Samuel G. Craig's *Christianity Rightly So Called* has as its primary task the offering of an evangelical definition of Christianity, rather than a philosophical elaboration of it. Warren C. Young in his *A Christian Approach to Philosophy* indicates his belief that a disciplined form of realism is most nearly compatible with the Christian message. He develops this in Chapter XII of his work, under title "The Christian Realistic World View."

Another work which merits consideration in a discussion of evangelical religious philosophy is Cornelius Van Til's *The New Modernism*. The thesis of this volume is that despite superficial similarities (chiefly in terminology) between the dialectical theology of Barth and Brunner and historic Christianity, there is a radical difference between them at every significant point of doctrine. The first half of the volume, which incidentally is not easy reading, traces the indebtedness of both liberalism and the "new supernaturalism" to the critical epistemology of Kant. Van Til shows that both are grounded in "the idea of the autonomous man." The sources of the systems of both the liberals and the dialecticians are shown to be: Kant's dualism, Hegel's dialectic, Overbeck's motif of "primal history" and Heidegger's *Existenz Philosophie*.

As a result, the dialectical theology is deeply involved with precisely those aspects of liberalism which are most hostile to historic orthodoxy. Its interpretation of the very doctrines which it proposes to hold in common with historic Christianity are radically reinterpreted, so as to deprive them of their basic thrust. Thus, the "new orthodoxy" is shown to be a blood cousin to liberalism. This volume may be criticized in that it rests its analyses upon the earlier works of Barth and Brunner. However, the one who criticizes it thus must himself show that the later writings of these men indicate an abandonment of the basic assumptions which motivated their earlier works. To date, no one has done this, and we can assume that Van Til's work is still fundamentally sound in its critique.

Two volumes must be mentioned here, although they belong properly

† Evangelical writers, in fact, have developed Christian philosophy along the lines both of realism and of objective idealism, avoiding, of course, the errors which characterize those views in their speculative forms. Floyd E. Hamilton is doubtless right in his assertion that "the vast majority of Christians either consciously or unconsciously" take a realistic view of the universe (*The Basis of Christian Faith*, p. 40). He adds: "Either Christian realism, or personal pluralistic idealism is in harmony with the Bible, but the Bible directly teaches neither theory" (p. 42)—ED.

to the chapter on apologetics. They are Gordon H. Clark's *A Christian View of Men and Things,* and Edward John Carnell's *An Introduction to Christian Apologetics.* This chapter closes with mention of Carnell's *A Philosophy of the Christian Religion* and of two volumes by Carl F. H. Henry, *Remaking the Modern Mind* and *The Drift of Western Thought.*

Carnell's *An Introduction to Christian Apologetics* analyzes the rational grounds upon which the case for the acceptance of the Christian world-view rests. In his *A Philosophy of the Christian Religion,* the appeal is two-fold: to the axiological (pertaining to *values)* consistency of Christianity, and to the aesthetically satisfying quality of its message. Defining a value as "simply anything which we prize or esteem" (p. 16) he explores the factors by which values are graded, and because of which they are ultimately sought or bypassed. He shows the axiological inconsistency of non-theistic systems, particularly philosophical absolutism, Marxist materialism and scientific positivism.

Carnell's concern with the question of religious truth indicates the role of the aesthetic in his religious philosophy. While assenting in general to the "test of coherence" as a criterion for truth, he recognizes that so long as we prophesy in part, the test can be but partially and incompletely applied. As an additional factor he proposes the aesthetic —that is, the appeal of Christianity to the whole man, including his imagination, his emotions, and so forth. Says he, "The heart knows a depth of insight which, *while it may never be separated from rational consistency,* is yet not univocally identified with such consistency" p. 39).

With reference to the demonstration of the validity of Christianity, Carnell's method is that of reducing the number of live options, until he establishes "a dialectic of despair as the alternative to the Christian option" (p. 45). Reason is not ruled out as an instrument for the comprehension of life (pp. 184ff.); it becomes a false leader only when it professes to speak for the whole man (p. 213). There is "an apex in the pyramid of knowledge" which centers basically in the dimension of fellowship with God; this is basically a knowledge of God by acquaintance, which as an axiological fact goes far beyond knowledge by mere inference, as in the case of knowledge derived from speculative theism (pp. 179ff.).

Carnell offers an excellent survey of "the revolt against reason" of Kierkegaard and existentialism in general (pp. 455ff.) and indicates that the retreat into irrationalism is a station near the end of the line of modern man's dialectic of despair. Our author makes a good case, then, for his thesis that the rejection of the Christian world-view is supremely foolish, because it is supremely destructive of man's highest values, and because it impoverishes the whole man by neglecting or denying the claims of the deeper areas of his need.

Carl F. H. Henry in his *Remaking of the Modern Mind* offers a similar critique of modernity, if based upon slightly different grounds. He traces the manner in which the major presuppositions of the "modern man" have been challenged, and even undermined, by the events of the twentieth century, and indicates that the net result is an *impasse*. His "gods" are dead; and at the same time he has been rather effectively preconditioned against a return to the older foundations of Western civilization through his "denial of rationality anywhere" (p. 261). Henry shows that recovery from the frustration and pessimism which mark modern man's present mood must be preceded by a recapture of certain controlling ideas. In other words, there must be restored to both philosophy and science "a revelational context" (p. 278).

This volume is highly significant in terms of its survey of the role of Christian presuppositions—the principles of a Christian philosophy, if you will—in human culture. Thus, the supreme hope of the West is to be found in a message which is held by a relatively small group of humble people. In their hands lies the key to the rebuilding of what the cankerworm of a so-called modernity has destroyed. In his *The Drift of Western Thought* Henry pursues this idea further. He traces the cultural impact of the reception or abandonment of the Christian world-view, showing the final alternatives to be: Christian supernaturalism or thoroughgoing naturalism. Our author indicates the crux of Christian supernaturalism to be found in its claim to a special and final revelation.

It remains true for our century, as for centuries preceding, that Christianity implies for its followers a distinctive and characteristic way of viewing things—a distinctive philosophy of life, and of men, and of their origin and their destinies, and of the larger context which governs these, centering in God and His ways toward the world and toward men.

> The evangelical compulsion to view Christianity, and its Founder, and redemption, and the Bible, in this special way, derives not from a philosophy of nature, but from *the living God who has spoken, who has inscripturated His revelation, and enters into personal relations with men* (*op. cit.*, p. 158).

This is a scandal to the "modern mind," which charges that this claim is impossible, that it is superfluous, that it is basically immoral, and that it expresses a hopeless and damaging bigotry (pp. 85ff.). Against these objections, Henry suggests the fundamental grounds upon which the Christian revelation-claim rests, and presents it in terms of a live option. He makes clear that the real *issue* is one of "starting points" or presuppositions, and shows that between the presuppositions of historic evangelicalism and those of the classic liberalism were differences of the most profound sort. To understand these differences is to comprehend the major task and the direction of the major effective thrust of evangelical religious philosophy today.

SCIENCE AND RELIGION

Carl F. H. Henry

Carl F. H. Henry holds a Ph. D. degree from Boston University, and a Th.D. degree from Northern Baptist Theological Seminary. He has served as professor of philosophy of religion at Northern Baptist Seminary (1942-47) and since then as professor of systematic theology and Christian philosophy at Fuller Theological Seminary. He is currently on leave as editor of the Protestant fortnightly magazine, Christianity Today. *The latest of more than a dozen books which he has authored was recently published by William B. Eerdmans Publishing Company under the title* Christian Personal Ethics.

9. *Carl F. H. Henry:*

SCIENCE AND RELIGION

THE CLEAVAGE between science and religion is one of the defacing characteristics of our culture. Even casual observers must detect its ugly scar upon our world of thought.

Certainly there is no need to argue the fact of this cleavage. For it is the conflict between science and religion which supplies modern life with one of its most evident tensions. Secular publications allude to the situation with monotonous regularity. *Fortune* magazine reports that forty-five per cent of the younger American scientists of distinction now lean toward agnosticism. The impressive articles published periodically by *Life* since December 8, 1952, on the origin of the universe, of man, of religion and of civilization, contribute no rapprochement with historic Christianity. Despite the widespread acknowledgment that a renewed interest prevails in religious realities, that the need for a theological answer to totalitarianism is more firmly sensed, and also that democracy founders without a spiritual basis, the cleavage of science and religion remain nonetheless a patent fact of our era.

Anyone who faces this condition with a sense of cultural concern must move inevitably to thoughts of pathos, of peril, of prospect and of program. The pathos of perpetuating the cleft, the peril of compromising the cleft, the prospect of transcending the cleft, the program for repairing the cleft—such considerations obtrude irresistibly into view.

Like human beings generally, the prime contenders in this conflict are indisposed to ready an inventory of their own liabilities. The scientist is prone to think only of the cost to religion if the warfare is prolonged. And the theologian meditates on the cost to a scientific age if the tensions remain unsurmounted. The price of continuing this controversy, equally to science and to religion, and beyond that, to modern life and culture, and, in truth to the whole human enterprise, is more staggering than the multitudes discern.

I. THE PATHOS OF PERPETUATING THE CLEAVAGE

Beyond doubt, religion has suffered most from this modern conflict. Everywhere *the dissolving effect of science upon religion* may be detected.

Religious life no longer supplies the strategic center of our cultural pattern. In fact, today the life of religion is not regarded as an indispensable element of cultural completeness and integration.

The achievements of religious faith, consequently, are dismissed as irrelevant by scientifically enlightened men. The prevailing tendency is to classify faith along with the irrational and emotive aspects of life. Religious experience is viewed, therefore, as a special problem requiring justification to the modern outlook. Full-orbed religious commitment is not only ignored, but in many circles is regarded as an oddity. The refusal to assign a determinate role to religion is no longer confined to extremists like Marx and Nietzsche. Many Anglo-Saxon leaders, while repudiating a barbarian way of life, today devaluate religion as catering only to human weakness.

From such considerations the enormous cost of this cleavage to the religious side of life is painfully clear; science rules the center of our culture while religion survives as a displaced refugee. The form in which the religious question is put today already salutes this state of things: "What is the relevance of religion in a scientific age?" Even an evangelical work like Bernard Ramm's implies a certain priority by its title: *"The Christian View of Science and . . ."* The benefits science bequeaths the modern world; its embarrassment to religion; the futility of prolonging this cleavage: these emphases supply the primary orientation of the current debate.

The modern era tends to ignore, therefore, *the loss accruing to science if the cleavage with religion is not repaired.* Only recent glimpses of a world wavering in all its spiritual loyalties have brought into anxious purview this settled indifference to religion.

The very foundations of the scientific enterprise are imperiled by the cleavage with Hebrew-Christian monotheism. The Christian religion, referring reality as a whole to one ultimate, rational, sovereign principle of explanation, was historically the source of the scientific confidence in the unity of the universe. Christianity provided the climate of conviction which stimulated the rise of science and then guided its growth. Science originated in the West, not in the Orient; in the West, moreover, it sprang from the Christian view of nature, not from Greek philosophy. Science without Christianity is metaphysically vagabond.

The readiness to invoke a plurality of explanatory principles in accounting for phenomena amounts to a sophisticated return to polytheistic divinities, and ultimately will deprive science of confidence in a single ultimate rationale.

Furthermore, Western European civilization, the highest yet achieved by the human race, gained its main inspiration from the Hebrew-Christian religion. The weakening of ties to biblical religion started and sped the decline of Western culture. Dismissal of the traditional world-life view as scientifically untenable is a main ground in the cultural breakdown, since all attempts to perpetuate Christian morality in the absence of Christian metaphysics have crumbled.

The integrity of human experience is also threatened. The modern man is torn psychologically by irresolvable tensions and inner frustrations. He finds himself irremediably religious by nature, yet he is unable to correlate the scientific claim and the spiritual-moral claim. The resulting scientific-religious conflict, productive of a divided self, has impaired the intellectual and practical vigor of multitudes. An unintegrated personality is forerunner to a disintegrated personality. Since no satisfactory integration of the scientific and the sacred is achieved within the same mind and heart, the unresolved division in the self easily leads either to the scientific demon-spirit or to the anti-scientific religious zealot.

Science itself can provide neither ethical sanctions nor ethical norms, and therefore lacks the power to strengthen our civilization morally. For experimental science deals only with the *is,* with the descriptive; it cannot determine the *ought,* the normative. The modern segregation of science from religion leaves the scientific temper devoid of final standards. This neglect of theological and moral realities has shorn our generation of moral restraints and has escorted society to the verge of a shameful collapse.

The totalitarian state, moreover, stands before us today as the incarnation of scientific power detached from a superior religio-moral claim. Loosed from ethical imperatives, the whole atomic age has been placed at the disposal of the demonic in and through the moral prodigality of its scientific parenthood.

These far-reaching effects mirror the pathos of prolonging this cleavage. Whether measured by its price to the religious enterprise, or by its price to the scientific, it can no longer be doubted that the opposition of religion and science has already escorted modern culture to the hazardous brink of bankruptcy.

From this sad situation, in what direction may modern man go? Without question, from the predicament sketched in this preamble, men today turn in hundreds of diverse directions. Tens of thousands of individuals, no doubt, seek subjective mystical solutions. Like most home-made remedies, these offer no promise of social antidote, and are not really intended for retail to others. We are concerned especially over the evangelical turn, which dare not, if it aims to be culturally significant, lead down some private lane, inaccessible to the multitudes.

Whoever would orphan either theology or science at this stage of world affairs contributes to the delinquency of the whole human family. The scientist bears, therefore, a proper obligation to guard any projected treaty from dismantling his empire of assured results; the theologian is rightly concerned that the essential requirements of religion be not disregarded nor minimized.

Is there a solution which mixes fully both with science and with theology? Is there a program which preserves the requirements of general and of special revelation alike, harmonizing God's activity both in nature and in redemption? Can significance any longer be saved for the cherished Hebrew-Christian conviction that God's speech is translated both into the word of power in nature, and into the Hebrew and Greek of the Bible?

II. THE PERIL OF COMPROMISING THE CLEAVAGE

The younger evangelicals today are deeply distressed over the tragic bifurcation in our culture. Quite understandably, they long for the swift reconciliation of theology and science. For science seems to win all the practical battles, while theology is left only with the impractical disputes. Any working compromise might therefore seem better than none, provided only that it gains a hearing in scientific circles for the religion of redemption, by casting evangelical theology in scientifically respectable molds.

It would be unfair to imply that, in such hands, the evangelical philosophy of science ventures to accommodate as much evolutionary theory as can be thrust into the biblical silences. Yet certain dangers seem to this writer to attend some recent efforts to bridge the gap between Christianity and science. Such attempts to reconcile biblical theology and contemporary science frequently run the risk of needless concession. If they do not actually fail to grasp the essential contrast between creation and evolution, they imply, perhaps unwittingly, an acceptance of principles hostile to biblical theism.

Especially is this the case in the espousal of concepts like "progressive creationism" and "threshold evolution" as acceptable categories of a Christian and evangelical doctrine of origins. The difficulty is that these phrases contribute to a verbal illusion which attracts the interest of the contemporary evolutionist somewhat under false pretenses, and his enthusiasm over their surface impression can only embarrass the evangelical overture. For creation, in its biblical sense, is something quite distinct from what the scientist insists is "progressively" knit into the warp and woof of reality, while "threshold evolution" can hardly be a part purchase of the developmental rationale if it presumes to be biblical. In other words, while Christian theism leaves room for progression of a sort, it repudiates the notion of a continuing, advancing divine creation; while it insists on thresholds, it does not abandon any sphere of reality to what the developmentalist means by evolution. Little can be gained, and much lost, by a failure to clarify from the outset the distinctive components of the biblical doctrine of origins. The Bible doctrine of origins admits of no merger, even at the secondary level, of theistic and non-theistic categories of explanation.

The important fact is that two competitive doctrines of origins are contending for the primacy today. In the history of ideas, the terms evolution and creation have developed independently, and communicate distinct concepts of origin. Until their essential differences are brought into view, it is futile to tour the horizon in search of concord between them. From the standpoint of mediating apologetics it may seem strategic to identify theistic origins with "threshold evolution" or with "progressive creation." But have the terms "evolution" and "progressive creation" a right to biblical sanction unless and until we are assured that current usage does not interpret such concepts by principles destructive of Hebrew-Christian doctrine?

Essential to the biblical idea of creation are three elements: (1) a sovereign mind and will, (2) origination by fiat command, (3) fixed grades of being and life. Whatever additional appendages attach to the Hebrew-Christian doctrine of origins, these are its primary and definitive components.†

Essential to the speculative idea of evolution are three contrastive

† Some modern expositors of Genesis dispute the presence in the creation account of the second and third elements, i.e., instantaneous creation and graded orders of life. They argue that fiat creation cannot be exegetically sustained, since *bara* is not used simply of *ex nihilo* creation (cf. Gen. 1:7 and 1:21, as well as 1:1 and 2:4, where the sense of *ex nihilo* creation is confirmed by Hebrews 11:3). But the essential point is that creation involves a unique divine activity, whether with or without the agency of secondary causes; quite obviously, after Gen. 1:1, the narrative deals with mediate creation. *Bara* may indeed sometimes be used interchangeably with *asah, yatsar,* etc., in the use of which the factor of divine transcendence is not always conspicuous. But God's transcendent relation to the universe is an essential biblical idea, and it is especially significant for the Hebrew-Christian doctrine of creation. Throughout the Old Testament the sacred writers who knew their own language best carry creation back to God's Word as well as His Will. During the ministry of Jesus it was especially His performance of miracles "by a word" which readily suggested His deity. Moreover, the idea of fixed orders of life is adduced not only by the creation account, but in the Noahic gathering of the kinds of life into the ark, and in the resurrection theme that "all flesh is not the same flesh: but there is one flesh of men, and another flesh of beasts, and another flesh of birds, and another of fishes" (I Cor. 15:39), as well as in the permanent divine assumption of human nature in the incarnation. What could the phrase "after their kind" mean in the Genesis account, if it does not imply graded orders of being?

elements: (1) an endowed or unactualized primitive entity, (2) temporal development, (3) progressive acquisition of new capacities. Whatever else may be added to the formula of evolution, these elements are its warp and woof.

The fundamental contrast between the Hebrew-Christian doctrine of creation and the Greek-modern doctrine of evolution is therefore crystal-clear. The Genesis creation account depicts a personal supernatural agent calling into existence graded levels of life by transcendent power. The Greek-modern theory depicts a simple primitive reality temporally differentiated by immanent activity into increasingly complex entities that retain this capacity for future development.

In the evolutionary approach the principle of *becoming* is metaphysically determinative. Time is not merely the actualizer of new forms, but it originates them. Reality is intrinsically developmental.

This representation of evolution may be protested as narrow and unimaginative. For do not numbers of influential evolutionists today repudiate such an exposition of origins as over-simplified? Certainly this is not what Christian theistic evolutionists at the turn of the century proposed as a bridge between Christianity and science. Nor, admittedly, is this what our evangelical apologists intend today by threshold evolution and progressive creation. Edward John Carnell, as the exponent of threshold evolution, specifically repudiates "total evolution" (*An Introduction to Christian Apologetics,* p. 239); Bernard Ramm, while supporting progressive creation, insists that the processes actualize nothing but the "master forms" in the mind of God anterior to creation (*The Christian View of Science and Scripture,* p. 116). Certainly no friend of theism intends to import a chunk of naturalism into his system.

But every such protest overlooks an important semantic consideration. The terminology of debate today is largely fixed not by the theological endeavor but by the scientific enterprise, especially by the secular philosophy of science which today holds the ideological initiative. The employment of conventional phrases with a contrary intention therefore runs needless apologetic hazards. What does "evolution" signify today to the man of science, and especially to the current philosophy of science, to which our overtures for reconciliation are extended? What does "progression" imply in the atmosphere of contemporary debate?

For background in answering these questions let us recall the outlines of the modern controversy over origins. For this will bring into focus the debate over immanence and transcendence toward which evangelical criticism was specially directed.

Evolutionary theory took its rise in a century in which Christian intellectual loyalties had already turned lukewarm. The Hegelian philosophy had excluded a transcendent Deity, and already viewed development as the essence of things by supporting the thesis of the unity, and indeed the identity, of mental and material processes. The speculative pantheistic dogma that the universe is a logical evolution of the Absolute lurked in the background of the Darwinian thesis that man and the other forms of life are a biological evolution from the inorganic. Hegel stressed reason and appealed to philosophy; Darwin stressed sensation and appealed to science. Both disallowed transcendent miracles. Darwin derived all the complex forms of life by natural development, slow, gradual, almost imperceptible, from simpler forms.

But the closing paragraph of *The Origin of Species* offered a sop to the Christian tradition. There Darwin admits the possibility of a divine origination of the first living cells from whence all else came. The storm of criticism which this concession aroused can be appreciated only by those mindful of the history of ideas, wherein evolution enthrones *becoming* or space-time process as the ultimate explanatory principle. What made Darwin an evolutionist was not his tolerance of a deity of sorts at the beginning of the process, but rather the insistence that all the forms of life are fluid, emerging by temporal process from an unendowed primitive original.

The evangelical controversy with Darwin centered especially in the questions of divine transcendence and immanence. Darwin's confinement of divine activity to the primal beginning of things was too deistic; champions of speculative pantheism and of traditional biblical theism both decried the view. And on each side, pantheistic and theistic, evolutionists arose to insist that the developmental process itself must be traced to an immanent activity of God. The pantheistic wing disallowed any role for fiat miracle, and many theists likewise, while defending some measure of supernatural transcendence, abandoned the traditional emphasis on miraculous creative acts divinely interspersed through the process. The devout scientist and theistic evolutionists were content to refer natural selection and evolutionary process to supernatural design, and to insist on this ground that the mechanical explanation had not crowded out the teleological.

In this shift the teleological argument—from design and purpose in nature to an intelligent architect of the universe—underwent an obvious but important change. Paley's *Natural Theology* (1802) and evangelical works of a similar nature expounded the Creator's method by the analogy of the watchmaker and the watch. Emphasis fell on God's operation from without. The post-evolutionary statement, to the contrary, placed the emphasis on God's immanent activity. Given the new role of geological time and gradual evolution, the moderns could tolerate only a deity whose continuous association with this process was assured. Traditional representations of God's operation from without now appeared objectionably deistic.

In this dispute, a rigid antithesis was in the making. Whereas Christian theology wore the insignia of fiat creation, modern science raised the banner of a leisurely evolution. Christian theism (whatever else it entailed) implied external design, design from without; whatever shaped itself from within had no need of a Creator. Evolution, however, implied immanent design. These two conceptions drew further and further apart as modern thought banished the miraculous, and their divorce was virtually guaranteed by the additional revolt against every last vestige of supernatural transcendence.

The evangelicals soon divorced God from the idea of a temporal process gradually actualizing new forms. The evolutionists divorced God from the idea of divine miracle calling fixed forms into being.

To the evolutionist, biblical theism implied deism; to the biblical theist, evolution implied atheism.

Both these judgments, of course, were radical. Biblical theism was not deistic in temper. And many evolutionists were professed theists of one sort or another.

Actually, the religion of incarnation champions God not as transcendent Creator only, but as the immanent Preserver of the space-time world as well, to Whose sovereign will its providential development is continually referred. Biblical theology relates all God's works, from the moment of their origin, to a continuing providential preservation, development and control. In the face of this Hebrew-Christian insistence on divine immanence, the modern indictment of biblical theism as deistic has no justification. But the fact that modern philosophies of science tend to be pantheistic or idealistic in tone, rather than theistic, encourages such a bias. For these speculative viewpoints reject the doctrine that the divine creative activity has ceased, and they refuse to refer the present universe simply to divine control and providential development.

Yet it is significant that evangelical theologians like Charles Hodge rebuffed the evolutionary attempt to ascribe natural selection to divine immanence. Simply to call evolution the "divine method of origins" was hardly an evangelical solution. Hodge pointed to Darwin's own emphasis that while the selective process might appear to be divinely ordered, in actual fact it is not; natural selection for Darwin was a self-sufficient principle of development.

The real question, as evangelical theology saw it, was not whether natural selection should be supplemented by considerations of genetics and mutations, and then referred to God, but whether the evolutionary principle itself adequately expresses the cosmic revelation of divine purpose and activity. The new theory of immanent teleology, asserted by the evolutionary gradualists, worked against the traditional doctrines of miracle, of a primal creation, and of fixed kinds of life. It encouraged instead the notion that "creation," "miracle," and novelty permanently characterize the whole space-time process.

Since the second decade of this century, secular philosophies of science have bolstered this emphasis on continuing creation and miracle through controlling ideas presumed to shed light on the ultimate mystery of origins. The tendency to regard the whole of reality as incipient mind is now in vogue. The philosophy of modern science is stated more and more in the framework of panpsychic, or of personalistic or quasi-pantheistic theories of reality. Consequently, the distinction between the non-mental and the mental, and between the inorganic and the organic is viewed as relative. A second and related tendency is the widening approval of a doctrine of continuous evolution. On the basis of ongoing creativity, the scientist is regarded as possessing a standpoint from which he can make pronouncements about the ultimate organization of the universe and the origin of its forms of life. A revelation of the ultimate mystery of creation is sought, therefore, within the speculative notions that distinctions between all creaturely forms are relative, and that new forms continue to appear.

That new forms originate as continuing temporal events is a central plank in the modern evolutionary platform. Whether by the methodology of Darwinian gradualism or by the leaps and bounds asserted by the emergent view, the prospect of new forms continues. Evolutionary theory, whatever scope it may allow an immanent God, is predicated still, and in some circles even more deliberately than a century ago, upon a denial of the origination of fixed kinds of life by divine fiat. Hence evolutionary hostility to the concept of a transcendent Creator is sharp. Where God is invoked as the dynamic surge of the developmental process, He is not superior to the principle of becoming, but rather represents instead the divinization of that principle.

It is tempting at this point to show that this hostility to a transcendent God already obstructs the religion of sin and redemption, and to labor the point that a compromise on secondary positions which tolerates a fatal concession at this level is not worth the investment of Christian energies. The alternatives are no less staggering and important if the issues of sin and redemption are ignored for the moment, and if only the Christian doctrine of creation be kept in view. The consequences of a theory which pictures the origination of new kinds of life as ongoing are far-reaching. An open, indeterminate universe arises in which increasingly complex and increasingly significant forms must be anticipated. Consequently the uniqueness and supremacy of man in the  creature world is thrown into doubt, since the process may be expected sooner or later to transcend him. Moreover, if movement and fluidity be ultimate, science is stripped of all ability to predict the novel and striking evolutionary emergents which hold the key to the future. Indeed, when spun out philosophically, the ultimacy of becoming involves also the irreconcilability of the fixed concepts of human reason to the flow of reality. The reigning importance of the idea of a predetermined goal toward which the whole process is teleologically directed is likewise jeopardized.

The biblical doctrine of the creation "rest" of God, on the other hand, asserts (1) that the creation of new *kinds* reached its climax and completion in the originally graded orders of being and life, (2) that fixed laws and limits govern the creation, (3) that the law of stability is now more fundamental in the space-time universe than that of changing forms, (4) that man bears a permanent dignity and supremacy among the animals.

Whoever seeks a reconciliation between biblical theism and evolution must clarify these differences at once. Otherwise, he either compromises Christian theology or he gains merely a verbal truce, the value of which is only that of "a scrap of paper." The apologist who scurrilizes the evangelical churches for not accepting evolution, and thinks thereby to make orthodox Christianity relevant to scientific circles, strikes the same hard bargain as the scientist who insists that he will give fair hearing to the Christian doctrine of the Creator-Redeemer only if the dogma of evolution be first exalted. No scientist, before he will consider the evidences for theism, has the right to exact in advance from the Christian theologian an assent to the doctrine of evolution, for the result can only be some speculative monster, a hyphenated form of creationism-evolutionism, whose future is without hope either in this world or in the next. If the scientist demands a verdict for evolution as such, before discussing the case for biblical theism, he should expect resistance from those who are unwilling to worship process as a god. The doctrine of creation is capable only of superficial connections with the philosophy of evolution. How can declarations about development, as part and parcel of an explanation of reality which conceives the emergence of new kinds of life as an ongoing process, be grafted on an explanation of origins which insists upon graded and fixed levels of existence?

The Christian must indeed concede, and insist upon, the reality of process and of providential development, but only as secondary and not as primary facts of the cosmos. Acceptance of the dogma of change, without clarifying the fundamental principle of created fixity, gives the modern mind unnecessary and undeserved leverage against the Christian view. If Christianity be true, not one spark of life can be explained by the advancing complexity of immanent process, but the whole movement of space-time existence rests rather on the principle of providential development within created bounds.

These considerations attest the perils of apologetic mediation. If Christian theism holds hope for spanning the chasm between science and religion, it requires something more than the adjustment of biblical theism to evolutionary philosophy. Not even on the level of secondary interaction can their differences be advantageously ignored, for here two competitive metaphysical ultimates contend for the mastery, and one must concede to the other.

The one involves a universe essentially predictable and foreseeable by man, except for divine miracles, and even these the sovereign Creator-Redeemer may disclose prophetically. The other involves a universe foreseeable only at secondary levels, one in which the forms of life and existence ascend ever higher through the latent dynamic surge of the universe. The former belongs to the Hebrew-Christian view, from which the scientific enterprise actually took its rise; the latter is part and parcel of the Greek-modern theory, which threatens the integrative competence of the scientific task.

III. THE PROSPECT OF TRANSCENDING THE CLEAVAGE

Having dwelt so long upon the pathos of perpetuating, and the peril of compromising, the cleavage, the evangelical reader may despairingly conclude that he is foredoomed in this debate to an existence between nostalgia for the past and apprehension over tomorrow. Nonetheless, the hopeful prospect of transcending this cleavage brightens our perspective.

Reconciliation between science and religion will come, as every reconciliation, only through repentance and faith. The conflict runs deeper than a divergence over the interpretation of objective facts. The facts indeed exist, and men transfer them from one perspective to another, without essentially changing or altering them. But they are interpreted and colored, and in this process of reconstitution not even the data of natural science can be isolated from the danger of misconstruction by the operation of volitional and emotional as well as intellectual factors.

Repentance is not a need confined simply to one or the other of the contenders; it is due from both theologians and scientists.

The present readiness of both groups to re-examine their entrenched dogmatisms is one of the signs of hope in the search for mutual understanding.

On the side of evangelical theology, greater humility and caution prevail today in defining the content of the scriptural revelation in its bearing upon science.

This observation requires careful analysis and comment. It would be false to the facts to imply that evangelical theology has weakened in its assurance of an inspired biblical revelation. Evangelical theology holds fast to the reality of special divine revelation, of the propositional and verbal nature of that revelation, of the identity of Scripture with special revelation. Moreover, it generally defends the reliability of the Genesis creation account as an exposition of historical-empirical origins.

But the evangelical movement is increasingly aware that it, no less than non-evangelical thought, is exposed to the danger of subjective bias in the exposition of biblical teaching. The risk of unjustifiable dogmatism is always near.

No one feels as keenly as evangelical scholarship the embarrassment brought to the Christian cause by earnest contemporaries, all treasuring the Bible as the revealed Word of God, yet dogmatically fissuring over competing interpretations. The evangelical cause runs the risk of bankruptcy by such widespread assignment of divine sanction to erroneous speculations. Arbitrary identification of the chronology of creation with the date 4004 B.C., of the specially created "kinds" with the "species" of modern science, of the creation-days with six successive twenty-four-hour periods, has reduced respect for Christianity as an authoritarian religion, and has multiplied doubt over its unique knowledge of origins. Contemporary evangelical theology is more determined not to speak beyond the bounds of exegesis in such areas of controversy and to stress the normative character of the biblical narrative even over against evangelical interpretations of that record.

Today, fortunately, dogmatic insistence upon the gap theory of Genesis or a literal six-day creation, or the age theory, or some other exclusive alternative, is not requisite to a reverent regard for the creation narrative. Alert to large gaps in the biblical revelation, evangelical theology today marshals the data of Scripture primarily for its special relevance to redemption, rather than to answer all the questions of concern to history and to the sciences. There are many biblical gaps—gaps in history, gaps in genealogy, as well as gaps in the creation story; whoever ventures to prepare an exhaustive index to the events of history or to the behavior of nature exclusively from the Bible undertakes the impossible.

Virile centers of evangelical theology today find in the creation account abundant room for the antiquity of the earth, room for a staggering aggregate of intermediary species and varieties between the specially created "kinds" of life; room even for a greater remoteness for primal man in the genealogies of Genesis; room alongside the transcendent fiat acts of God for the providential development of novel space-time forms of life by an immanent divine operation. In fact, evangelical thought reveals a growing impatience with those who, in the name of infallible exegesis, disallow such correlations in the Genesis narrative.

It would be incorrect, however, to imply that contemporary evangelical thought shares in common no assured truths on the basis of the Genesis creation narrative. That a sovereign, personal, ethical God is the voluntary creator of the space-time universe; that God created *ex nihilo* by divine fiat; that the stages of creation reflect an orderly rational sequence; that there are divinely graded levels of life; that man is distinguished from the animals by a superior origin and dignity; that the human race is a unity in Adam; that man was divinely assigned the vocation of conforming the created world to the service of the will of God; that the whole creation is a providential and teleological order: the whole front of evangelical theology finds these irreducible truths of revelation in the Genesis creation account. That the word of creation is no mere instrumental word, but rather a personal Word, the Logos, who is the divine agent in creation; that this Logos permanently assumed human nature in Jesus Christ; that the God of creation and of revelation and of redemption and of sanctification and of judgment is one and the same God: these staggering truths evangelical theology unanimously supports on the basis of the larger New Testament disclosure.

The importance of these evangelical unanimities is apparent. Not one of these affirmations can be discarded without fundamental violence to biblical theism. Some bare form of theism may still be salvaged in the absence of these convictions, but it will be speculative in temper, moving far outside the range of the Hebrew-Christian revelation, and needlessly concessive to the modern spirit. For precisely these affirmations supply the characteristic marks of Hebrew-Christian theism, distinguishing it from the modern scientific world view. They constitute primary emphases within which Christian reconciliation must be ventured; any concord on secondary issues, indifferent to these foundational tenets, demeans the distinctives of evangelical thought.

If a new humility and caution may be detected in evangelical scientific pronouncements, the prevalent philosophy of science also reveals today a changing conception of the bearing of scientific realities upon the concerns of religion.

To overstate this change would be easy, but unjustifiable. The newer theories in physics and biology do not signify a restoration of what, by evangelical theology, might be designated as Christian physics or Christian biology, *i.e.,* science which proceeds consciously and deliberately from the standpoint of Christian theism. Such evaluations represent more of a romantic hope than of concrete actuality.

Nonetheless, the changes in the scientific temper during our generation are nothing short of remarkable. In 1929, the world of thought was being catechized in the thesis that only scientific illiterates any longer believed in the supernatural. Not only Russia but Anglo-Saxon intellectuals pronounced this charge; not only the followers of totalitarian Karl Marx, but those of democracy—befriending John Dewey as well; not in a naturalistic setting but rather in that supplied by the Gifford lectures; not by someone on the fringe of American thought but by the prime mover at the very base of contemporary secular philosophy of education was belief in the supernatural discounted as naive and untenable. Less than the span of one generation has brought tremendous change. Although bitter attacks upon supernaturalism in the name of science are still found (cf. Oscar Riddle's *The Unleashing of Evolutionary Thought*), the speculative character of such assaults is more widely detected today.

Several developments within science account for the new tolerance of religion. Development of powerful instruments adequate for international and perhaps even global destruction, alongside widening confession of science's inability to provide absolute moral guidance, has provoked spiritual concern. Even great scientific centers like M.I.T. have introduced courses in religion. Summer conferences for scientists now consider the place of religion in modern life. Foundation grants are multiplying seminars and conferences on the subject of science and the spiritual.

The unsettling of evolutionary theory is another significant sign. While science today looks to the evolutionary framework as its profoundest organizing principle, the scientific *ipse dixit* is conspicuously more mellow. Even a contributor to the *Hibbert Journal* (October, 1955) ventures the words: "I do not suppose that anyone would argue that, say, a Darwinian, or neo-Darwinian, theory of evolution is finally 'proved.' But at any rate it is respectably thought out and in many ways is borne out by observation" (L. Arnaud Reid, "Religion, Science, and Other Modes of Knowledge"). The evolution of evolutionary theory itself and the widening front of debate by competent representatives of diverse viewpoints, have aided this transition. The signs of disorder are now conspicuous among evolutionary claims; consequently, some scholars prefer to speak of "conservative hypotheses based on facts" rather than of "the fact of evolution," since the nature of this fact is so much in debate today. Derivation of new forms first from inherited characteristics, then from environmental influence; paucity of missing links to confirm the rise of species by minute intermediate transformations; repudiation by scholars like T. Dobzhansky of sudden derivation of new species by gene mutation; growing readiness to attribute new forms to inexplicable emergence: these reflect the unending revision in science today. Criticisms of evolutionary theory similar to those offered a generation ago in the ablest evangelical circles, but then swiftly countered as the backwash of religious ignorance and of an anti-scientific temper, are now openly voiced in evolutionary circles.

To the evangelical observer, the most striking evidence of a changed mood among scientists is their revolt against the mechanical, deterministic view of nature prevalent at the turn of the century. Its reduction of reality to iron-clad causal uniformity had ruled out in advance the very possibility of miracle and hence assailed the credibility of incarnational religion. Today that view is almost everywhere in disfavor. That an absolutely uniform causal connection prevails between all events, thus excluding all miraculous exceptions, whether in the history of the Hebrews or in the life of Jesus Christ, is now recognized for what evangelical theology declared it to be, namely, a speculative dogma arbitrarily imposed on the data of nature. The newer interpretations of the universe—Heisenberg's role for indeterminacy in nuclear physics, Planck's quantum physics representing the energy of nature as discrete rather than as continuous, the rising favor especially in biology of theories of emergent evolution—all worked against the mechanical view.

The new sufferance of religion, the new debate over a superscientific (and perhaps even supernatural) sanction and source of morality, the new reserve in the statements of evolutionary theory, the new indeterministic approach to nature, are signal evidences of a shift in scientific perspective.

To claim, however, that this changed outlook involves the scientist actually in a mood of repentance is to interpose a category which to the contemporary scientist seems irrelevant. Since tentativity is the essence of his methodology, the scientist tends to justify every doubt and revision. The sense of ultimate responsibility, of a verdict in the presence of the sacred in nature, is all but gone. Yet it is ill-becoming for the evangelical theologian to broadcast the scientist's flight from contrition. For while a new and welcome reserve breathes through the finest evangelical theology, academic repentance, or contrition in the presence of excessive dogmatisms, which perchance have contributed to an unfortunate scientific misunderstanding of the biblical claim, is nowhere a conspicuous virtue.

Reconciliation between science and theology, we have said, will come only through the avenue of repentance and faith. Evidence of today's more favorable interaction of theology and science is heartening. Neither theologian nor scientist, however, yet welcomes that personal humiliation and contrition commensurate with his professional responsibility for the cultural cleavage. Rightly might their prayer of confession read, "Almighty God, Maker of all things, Judge of all men; we [theologians] [scientists] acknowledge and confess our manifold sins which we most grievously have committed by thought, word and deed. We have failed to think Thy thoughts after Thee, yea we have exalted our own words as the word of revelation, and we have broadcast speculations that have needlessly provoked the [scientists] [theologians] and misled the common people. We do earnestly repent, being heartily sorry for these our misdoings. The remembrance of them is grievous unto us. Have mercy upon us, have mercy upon us, merciful Father. For the Redeemer's sake forgive us all that is past. Grant us future service pleasing to Thee, and enable us to proclaim Thy revelation in nature and in Scripture. Amen." Yet such a prayer moves far above the realities of the present hour; indeed it gains an air of artificiality from the climate of the times. Yet only from mutual contrition is a new spirit of liaison likely to arise.

The prospect of transcending the current cleavage depends not only upon repentance but, as already indicated, upon faith as well—the faith which grasps the Living God revealed both in nature and in Scripture.

With faith, the problem is not whether to exercise faith or not to exercise it; rather, the real issue is whether faith be turned to the right, or to the wrong. Christian monotheism subsumed nature rationally under a single principle of explanation, that of ethico-rational will. The neglect of incarnational religion resulted in a failure to understand reality in relation to personal categories. The scientific appraisal of ultimate reality only by the sub-personal categories of weight, measurement and mathematical formulae led finally to relativity. For confidence in an orderly universe, and in the interdependence of all the forces of nature, declined swiftly when detached from a supernatural religious basis.

Yet even the modern scientist could not operate without faith (even if detached from supernaturalism and biblical religion) Science continually works within undemonstrable postulates; without them, the scientific enterprise itself would collapse. At point after point, the scientist *believes* in order to *know*. He believes in the continuity of personal identity; in the evidence of his senses; in the reliability of the laws of thought; in the value of honesty in research; in the dependability of the laws he charts. These beliefs make demonstration possible, yet they are not demonstrable beliefs.

The scientist is faith-qualified, for all men by nature are prone to faith. The difference between scientist and non-scientist therefore lies not in their disposition to worship, but rather in the object of worship. The reverence paid to false gods distinguishes the unbelieving scientist and philosopher from the devout believer. Science will bolster its undergirding principles somehow; if not by an appeal to Christian theism, it will lean upon some non-Christian metaphysics. The scientist who cuts himself off from the changeless norms of Hebrew-Christian ethics, sooner or later will smuggle in absolutes and idolatrous value judgments on his own. No sooner does the scientist glory in deliverance from the worship of a personal God than he is tempted to bow down and worship the $\sqrt{-1}$, or Einstein's $E=mc^2$.

Nowhere is the scientific proneness to faith-postulates more obvious than in the modern devotion to the undemonstrable principle of the uniformity of nature. Nothing in the regularities of nature today actually dictates the certainty of regularities tomorrow. The present events of nature may accord with uniform principles, or future events (if any) may prove totally dissimilar; or, intermediate to these extremes, a whole range of combinations of regularity and irregularity is possible. No scientist, on the basis merely of a century of observation, can pronounce an absolute verdict. Given a dozen centuries, or were he a contemporary of Jesus Christ, his judgment might, indeed, be radically different from that ventured from the twentieth century stance alone.

The influence of the faith-factor in science can be detected still, despite the current withdrawal of science from its earlier commitment to an absolute uniformitarianism. Recent scientific interpretations are gravitating already, perhaps even unconsciously, into a new hostility to the Hebrew-Christian view of the universe. This judgment conflicts, no doubt, with a growing readiness to hail contemporary views as hospitable to orthodoxy.

The scientist's acknowledgment of indeterminacy in nature, or at least of a measure of scientific unpredictability, has encouraged many hurried and excessive theological claims by voices friendly to Christian orthodoxy. Both evangelical scientists and evangelical ministers have joined the eager chorus of hopeful vindication.

This kind of apologetics, however, is headed for disappointment. To share the contemporary scientist's questionable premise that Christian miracle depends one-sidedly upon the activity of nature chartable in the twentieth century, or worse yet, upon the scientist's confession of momentary gaps in knowledge, really depreciates credible evidence for historical actualities in the prophetic and apostolic eras. Evangelical theology does not suspend its confidence in miracle upon the relativities of modern scientific experiment, but rests rather upon the accomplished purpose of God in biblical times. Evangelicals who have found ideal weather in recent scientific climate might have discovered a basis for caution in the direction given the new winds of thought in scientific circles. For the indeterminacy of nature is now widely interpreted in a manner unfriendly to the biblical conception of creation, of the fixity of kinds, and of miracle.

Current scientific theory no longer regards its plotting of nature as unveiling an absolutely uniform network of causal necessity. Rather, its index to nature is likened to statistical averages which, like life insurance figures, are reliable as a general summary of events but useless for anticipating particular instances with certainty. Moreover, instead of considering the scientist as the passive observer of an objectively-given causal order, emphasis is now placed on the scientist's own creative contribution to his charting of nature. Some circles tend, in fact, to depict nature objectively considered as haphazard contingency.

Obviously, any theory which conceives novelty as part of the structure of nature can hardly attach absolute significance to an irregular event at any one time and place. A theory which makes exceptions the rule no more supplies a biblical basis for miracle than does a theory which rules out exceptions. The current scientific doctrine of contingency in nature must not be misread, therefore, as a return to the biblical doctrine that the Creator-Redeemer publishes His redemptive revelation by a series of once-for-all acts in nature and history, greatest of which is the Incarnation of Jesus Christ.

Recent scientific favor for the doctrine of continuous creation should also bespeak the fact that the new views of nature are being ranged antagonistically against the Hebrew-Christian concept of creation. According to the continuing creation theory, new forms of being and life perpetually exist on the horizon of nature. The possibility of novel and unpredictable emergents is thus permanently sustained. This conception is consistent with the essential idea of evolution, namely, that space-time realities are actualized by resident forces into increasingly complex forms. But the theory is inconsistent with the essential idea of creation, that the limits of life originally established fix the spheres within which development takes place. The emergent theory involves essentially the unforeknowability of the new forms of space-time reality at the strategic future levels of advance. The biblical view, on the other hand, involves the idea of a fixed and permanently predictable order containing a providentially bracketed realm of change within established kinds.

These considerations supply evidence that contemporary philosophy of science continues to defer to metaphysical faith-constructs, especially to the important dogma that *all pronouncements about the nature of ultimate reality must be vindicated to present scientific observation and experience*. The philosophy of science wants no doctrine of creation unless it can vindicate creation *today*. It wants no doctrine of miracle unless it can vindicate miracle *today*. It suspects the doctrine of *Incarnation* unless the Logos will enter the virgin's womb *today*. The only conceptions of creation and miracle it will tolerate are those patterned after the field of experience *today*.

It is obvious, therefore, that the dogma of uniformity still shapes contemporary speculations, more than one might be led to expect from the scientific admission of indeterminism and its defense of emergent evolution. The contemporary philosophy of science retains its basic hostility to transcendent divine activity. Whatever range it assigns to the idea of novelty, it is committed still to the bias of uniformity.

This faith in uniformity promotes the main plateaus of conflict between science and Christianity. True as it may be, and is, that without a prevailing uniformity science would be impossible, it is equally true that the confidence in uniformity which Christianity inculcated has been transformed into a fetish which is now invoked against Christianity in an endeavor to discredit it. Wherever modern science falters in the presence of Christian claims—the unique creation of man, the virgin birth, the bodily resurrection, and so on—it is always faith in uniformity as an idolatrous principle to which the scientist pays his vows. This mocking of the miraculous in the name of absolute uniformity is not modern; the Bible is already aware of it, and repudiates it. In 2 Peter 3:3-6, the sacred writer challenges skepticism over the final divine judgment of history on the part of those who appeal to the regularity of events: "In the last days mockers shall come with mockery . . . saying,

Where is the promise of his coming? for, from the day that the fathers fell asleep, all things continue as they were from the beginning of the creation." The God of Hebrew-Christian revelation makes possible the scientific enterprise, yet He casts down the idol of uniformity. He is the God of anthropology, fashioning man uniquely in His image; the God of biology, entering human history by the virgin; the God of astronomy, guiding the wise men of old by Bethlehem's star; the God of physics, raising the Redeemer from the dead; the God of history, planting the Cross at its midpoint and climaxing the long sweep of events. An original creation distinct from the providential development of the graded kinds of life; an Incarnation distinct from all human births; a resurrection contradicting all human deaths; a future supernatural judgment of history distinct from all human catacylsms—such is the miracle-fibre of which Hebrew-Christian theism is loomed.

The scientist stands already in the place of theological decision at this crossroads of uniformity and miracle; he is already involved in a theological verdict at the juncture of evolution and creation. Whoever declares that *becoming* or process is the ultimate metaphysical principle, whoever declares that miracle is impossible, simultaneously defies the Logos revealed in nature. This negative spiritual verdict inevitably extends the distance between the scientist and the Logos become flesh. The faith to which the scientist resorts may range him in determinate opposition to the God of redemption and sanctification. While Christian theism supplies the field and conditions which make science possible, the modern scientist nibbles readily at the bait of false gods, and shows himself prone to worship cosmic idols. And this revolt against the God of creation provides him leverage for the revolt against the God of redemption.

The present situation in the religio-scientific cleavage is therefore highly ambiguous. There exists, on the one hand, a new mellowness on the part of both scientists and evangelical theologians, manifest in the readiness to appraise critically the inherited dogmatisms, the former group in the light of nature's revelation, and the latter in the light of biblical revelation. But this does not imply, on the other hand, that fluidity has completely displaced fixity of thought, for the areas of re-investigation are limited by each group. The evangelical retains the historic Christian confidence that the God of nature has also revealed himself authoritatively in Scripture; the scientist retains the confidence that the contemporary behavior of nature supplies the master key to nature's possibilities and implications for our generation. Beyond the new amiableness of current theory stands the scientific tendency, already discernible, to list away from biblical theism and toward secular reconstructions of nature.

The prospect of transcending the cultural cleavage seems therefore, even at this highly opportune moment, to be slipping away from us. Indeed, it may even seem as if evangelical Christianity has no effective point of contact with scientific theory in this strategic hour of scientific re-examination, revision and restatement.

But the situation is not so unpromising and hopeless as this. For the twentieth century scientist has ample evidence for the truth of the Christian view of nature. No scientist is justified in a non-theistic or an agnostic conclusion about reality. The scientific enterprise must deal with the Christian insistence that the evidences for theism are accessible to the scientist.

On some of the most troublesome and vexing questions which remain for contemporary science—*e.g.*, the origin of life, the origin of kinds, and specifically the origin of man—the Hebrew-Christian account of creation clearly enunciates a principle of explanation, referring all inquiries to the transcendent activity of the Living God.

Yet the internal inadequacies and difficulties in contemporary scientific theory hardly constitute the only ground on which the Christian alternative is to be pressed.

The evidence for biblical theism, according to Hebrew-Christian theology, is unambiguous. The scientific data are not so ambivalent that the scientist requires special revelation and regeneration to reach a theistic conclusion. The inference to God is the most natural and the most consistent inference from his field of daily experience. That the scientist is faced continually with evidence for the Living God in nature is the consistent emphasis of the Bible. This is the message of the Old Testament, wherein the Davidic psalms assert that "the heavens declare the glory of God and the firmament showeth his handiwork" (Ps. 19:1), and of the New, wherein the Pauline letters contend that "the invisible things of God since the creation of the world are clearly seen, being perceived through the things that are made, even his everlasting power and divinity" (Rom. 1:20). The underlying premise is that all the space-time evidence which confronts the scientist in his examination of nature and man is at one and the same time evidence for the Living God.

IV. THE PROGRAM FOR REPAIRING THE CLEAVAGE

Contemporary evangelical scholarship has not as yet produced a full-fledged Christian philosophy of science. But it is grappling earnestly with the basic related issues, namely, the unity of truth, the validity of the divine revelation in the universe, the nature of evidence and of knowledge, the question of common ground, and the connection between common grace and restorative grace. These subjects enter unavoidably into any serious discussion of the connection between theology and physics, biology, anthropology, psychology and the other sciences. No program for repairing the cleft between Christianity and science dare long ignore them.

In dealing with the cultural conflict, evangelical theology appeals to more than the divine general revelation in nature; it exhibits also the special divine revelation in Scripture. The cosmic witness of nature does not abide alone; the redemptive witness of the Bible stands written alongside it. God is no terrestrial cadaver, stretched taut upon the racks of the constellations and awaiting scientific autopsy. He is alive, a living Mind and Voice and Will. What He thinks and says and does is part of the field of human experience. His active purpose embraces both the plan of creation and the plan of redemption. The concord and unity of His revelation in nature and in the Incarnation, as a disclosure of the Creator-Redeemer, is a basic premise of Hebrew-Christian theology. The scientist is therefore confronted by two revelations of God in relation to nature: the general revelation given through the created universe, and the special revelation given in the inspired Scripture.

If God spoke in Scripture only about redemption, and not about nature, no conflict of science and Scripture would be conceivable; no verdict of science could in that event trespass against the biblical revelation. But because nature is a divine creation, and because the Creator-Redeemer works out his purposes in nature and history, incarnational religion dare not disjoin science and theology.

The Bible presents, above all else, a theology; its primary doctrine is of the Creator, its primary message religious and ethical. But it is not on that account disinterested in man and nature. It cannot be dismissed either as disinterested in scientific concerns, or as unscientific.

Admittedly the data of Scripture lack scientific form of systematic arrangement, but this is true of its theological and ethical content also. Admittedly the writers use popular or common language, rather than a technical scientific vocabulary, but this actually confers a permanent and universal intelligibility upon their words, since intricate scientific constructs are often grasped only by highly trained minds, and, moreover, frequently are retired as antiquated by the next generation. Admittedly the writers use phenomenal conceptions, employing the language of appearance rather than detailed scientific formulas. But it cannot be argued that because of this use of language of appearance, the Bible nowhere postulates the actual order of the universe.

The mediating theology of the late nineteenth century often resorted to this view, that biblical statements about the universe are merely phenomenal, whereas modern science defines the inner constitution of nature. Ramm's volume, *The Christian View of Science and Scripture,* assumes this contrast, although he insists that biblical statements do not cease to be factual because they are phenomenal rather than postulational. Apart from his awkward contrast of the factual and the structural or postulational, Ramm apparently attributes to science a competence in defining objective reality which leading philosophers of science have more and more disowned, among them John Dewey, E. Mach and P. W. Bridgman. The present drift of scientific theory, regarding the "laws of nature" merely as statistical averages of high utility, rather than as an absolute index to nature, actually suggests that science (rather than the Bible) is confined to a phenomenal account of nature. And on what ground can it be argued, on the other hand, that the Hebrew-Christian Scriptures, when they deal with specific events in nature and history, do not intend to be understood categorically?

The prime issue between the Bible and science, therefore, is not whether or not the Hebrew-Christian Scriptures make postulational statements, but whether any of its postulational statements touching science are demonstrably false. In assessing this question, what the Bible itself says must be carefully discriminated from what has been attributed to it second-hand, by theologians and scientists alike.

No claim is made that the sacred writers, as individuals, were personally exempt from the naive world-view of their own day, nor that their writings articulate a classified and systematized science involving general laws. What is claimed is that, as the messengers of holy revelation, they were lifted beyond their own capacities, and that their declarations bearing upon nature and upon man are as reliable as their teaching about God and His activity. To free the discussion of the Bible and science from those tense emotional overtones which the subject has inherited in our century may be difficult, but theologian and scientist alike can further the cause of truth only by a spirit of scholarly objectivity in this dispute. The facts and mere hearsay can be as different in dealing with the Bible as when dealing with the universe. It is one matter to reject the biblical teaching on science as inevitably culture-bound, and consequently to dismiss its outlook as pre-Copernican and pre-Ptolemaic; it is quite another to realize that the Bible nowhere specifically asserts that the earth is the astronomical center of the universe (even if Turretin thought he had vindicated the sun's movement around the earth, against Copernicus, on biblical grounds), but only that it is the moral and spiritual center of the redemptive drama; and it is still another to assume that modern astronomy has given us a fixed and final cosmology.

In evaluating biblical teaching of scientific relevance, three types of content call insistently for fair and just appraisal: the use of figurative and poetic language; the categoric assertion of events in nature and history which are intrinsic to the theistic view of incarnational religion; the remarkable absence, from the opening of Genesis to the close of Revelation, of time-bound speculative notions about the universe by which the biblical writers were everywhere surrounded in the cultures of their day.

Evangelical theology, if it is to make a major contribution to synthesis, must propound a Christian philosophy of science tracing the implications of the sovereignty of God for all the branches of science. The only real alternative to the segregation of science and theology is their integration. This is guarded by the evangelical emphasis that evidence constantly confronts the scientist in support of a unitary principle of creation, of redemption, of sanctification, and of judgment. The God who regenerates and sanctifies men by the Spirit is the same God who creates and preserves the space-time universe and all creaturely life, and who came in the flesh of Jesus of Nazareth to accomplish redemptive atonement in history. The power which awes the astronomer and which intrigues the physicist has been disclosed in Jesus Christ as the power of righteousness and of love.

The evasive handling of the cleft between theology and science, which assigns each to separate and inviolate compartments, characteristic of Protestant liberalism influenced by Kant and Ritschl, and perpetuated by the dialectical theologians Karl Barth and Emil Brunner, inevitably does violence to incarnational religion. For it implies falsely that redemptive religion can be maintained in all essentials although the inherited theistic belief in creation and miracle be suppressed. It eliminates the conflict between Christianity and science by depriving Christianity of the right to speak with scientific and historical relevance.

Since no category other than Jesus Christ is vast enough for comprehending the space-time process, and since the cleft between science and religion can be transcended only by latching the cause of science and theology alike to the revelation of the Creator-Redeemer God, what common ground exists between theologian and scientist for grasping the universe as the revelation of the God who is Logos, Lord, Light and Love? Science has tended to seek the meaning of the universe through impersonal categories, while Hebrew-Christian theology defends a special avenue of knowledge over and above the scientific method of experiment and observation. What solid ground exists, therefore, for hope of a mutual relating of all existence and experience to the God of creation and preservation, of redemption and sanctification, of judgment and glorification? What proposals are offered for reconciling the knowledge of created reality adduced respectively by modern science and by Christian faith?

Evangelical scholars are devoting careful attention to this issue. For all evangelical theology it is consequential that the modern man is a sinner; even his evaluation of nature cannot be divorced from this fact. The noetic effect of sin, or the negating and distortive consequences of spiritual rebellion in the comprehension of God and His creation, enters into the discussion of the cultural cleft. But the implications for faith and knowledge are worked out in various ways, and some brief mention of these representative positions is relevant.

The widest emphasis on the antithesis between Christian and secular (regenerate and unregenerate) knowledge is found in Cornelius Van Til's writings. The antithesis is contingent, and provisional, and not ultimate and absolute; that is, it has been introduced into human experience as a consequence of the fall of the race in Adam, and is due therefore to man's predicament in sin. The unregenerate man interprets all facts from his own perspective of moral revolt; the regenerate man aspires to God-interpreted experience. Hence the man of faith and the unbeliever have no common ground. Regeneration alone supplies the methodological standpoint which provides a common ground between Christian and non-Christian scientists. Van Til allows all men a surviving point-of-contact with the truth of general revelation on the basis of the *imago Dei,* but the unregenerate man gives this no principal significance. And he grants that regenerate men do not consistently apply the standpoint of revelation, and hence an accidental point-of-contact exists with the unregenerate perspective also. The *imago* preserves the truth in all men, but sin deflects it; regeneration restores the truth, but the remnants of sin blunt it. The virtue of this view is that it does not ignore the relation between the mind and the will, between interpretation and morality; its weakness is that it attaches the hope of reconciliation between science and religion too onesidedly to the requirement of regeneration. If the gulf between Christianity and contemporary science can be narrowed only by the regeneration of the scientist, the prospects are meager; if the revelation of nature is addressed to man as man, biased scientific theory may be repudiated for what it is, and the Christian view vindicated.

Gordon H. Clark bluntly challenges the validity of the empirical method in science. There is no denial, of course, that science is highly useful—but "however *useful* scientific laws are, they cannot be *true*" (*A Christian View of Men and Things,* p. 209). The argument emphasizes the creative contribution of the scientist to his data, the selective and revisionary nature of descriptive scientific theory, the disagreement of scientists over methods, the disavowal of faith and choice by some scientists while science itself acts within such categories. Clark's conclusion is that science is "incapable of arriving at any truth whatever" (*ibid.,* p. 227), but supplies only highly respected opinion constantly subject to revision. The reply to Clark that scientific empiricism supplies its own corrective, so that science becomes "more and more true," presupposes what Clark denies, that truth is in process of "becoming" (*i.e.,* that truth is not absolute but relative) and forgets that all scientific verdicts, tomorrow's as well as yesterday's, are inherently tentative.

Science by nature is always forced to a premature verdict on the basis of less than complete evidence. If scientific conclusions are correlated with revealed doctrines on a single plateau of truth, either the truths of revelation are demeaned to the status of tentative and revisable judgments, or the verdicts of science are absolutized beyond the rights of the empirical method.

Edward John Carnell protests that this view exaggerates the disjunction between revelation-truth and scientific truth. The truths of revelation have a probability side, and the probabilities of science have a legitimate truth status, Carnell contends. Even in the handling of divine revelation, certainty is psychological and subjective; the logical evidences upon which belief rests never rise above probability, even in the sphere of revelation. Carnell is a champion of common ground at the level of scientific knowledge; regenerate men of faith and unregenerate scientists hold this realm of impersonal description of objects in common. While there assuredly is a Christian theology and a Christian ethics, it is as inane to speak of a Christian physics as to speak of a Christian monkey-wrench. But when metaphysical judgments enter they color this neutral ground by divergent systems of interpretation (*An Introduction to Christian Apologetics,* p. 213ff.). Yet even here Carnell rejects an absolute antithesis, due to the *imago Dei* which survives in all men. Critics have asked whether this defense of a neutral block of information in regenerate and unregenerate thought minimizes the noetic effect of sin in human experience, and also the scope of the restorative work of the Holy Spirit. Carnell's insistence that the coherence of Christian evidences never exceeds probability does not, moreover, constitute a reply to Clark's argument that empirical science cannot lead to truth, whereas revelation, and revelation alone, can. Granted that all certainty is subjective, and that all rational coherence is less than absolute, are the declarations of revelation and experimental verdicts thereby leveled to the same plane? And must we ignore the conviction that it is the Spirit who carries the ego, and not the ego the Spirit, in every theology worthy of the name Christian?

Henry Stob is less than happy with any representation of Christianity "as a total commitment that embraces the whole of life, and nevertheless believes that certain of the sciences cannot be qualified as Christian" (*The Reformed Journal,* Vol. V, No. 4 [April, 1955], p. 2). To hold that certain of the sciences are not amenable to religious qualification, he contends, is a needless concession to dichotomal thinking. The Christian and secular researcher may use the same methods and arrive at the same conclusions in the investigative phases. But science is always in the service of some principle of faith and value, proceeding within the framework either of true or false faith. Hence a Christian physics, mathematics and logic are as requisite as a Christian theology. This does not mean that Christianity supplies novel laws of thought nor that it alters the data of the various sciences; rather, it contributes a different perspective within each of the sciences. A verdict can be given for or against Christian mathematics no less than in philosophy.

Bernard Ramm refuses to trace the modern cleft primarily to the fact that the scientific outlook is forged by unregenerate scholars. Rather, he ascribes it to a neglect of the limitations of their respective methodologies by theologian and scientist alike. He promotes a truce by the subtraction from Scripture of the right to speak scientifically, and by its restriction, insofar as it maintains scientific relevance, to assertions of phenomenal fact. While Ramm contends that the inspired writers were safeguarded from the grotesque and mythological, he disallows them any transcendence, in scientific matters, of the cultural standpoint of their day. Thus we are left with an awkward view of inspiration, which expunges error without communicating scientific truth. Is not such a view, we may ask, precluded from exhibiting a Christian philosophy of science? And does it not tend uncritically to invest the current view of nature with an excessive and sacred authority?

Perhaps the most hopeful sign in these diverse efforts, despite their intra-mural differences, is that many evangelical scholars are now grappling vigorously with the essential outlines of a Christian philosophy of science, in the interest of rapprochement. They reflect, moreover, a unanimous confidence in the unity of truth—and thereby avoid the fatal concession to the dualism of science and theology made by many liberal Protestants and perpetuated by the dialectical theology. They hold firm to the essential clarity of the created universe as revelatory of God's existence and purposes, and hence reject the dialectical-existential disjunction of God-truth and world-truth. The loss of confidence in the universe as a revelation of God has abetted modern doubt that a unitary science and rationale exist, and that the whole of reality and experience can be comprehended in a unified world-life view, and has weakened belief also in an orderly universe. The evangelical temper resists this widening despair over the ultimate significance of the devout reason.

In addition, evangelicals regard scientific empiricism and scriptural revelation as legitimate approaches to truth, although they resist the attachment of finality to scientific verdicts and also the demotion of biblical revelation to the same plateau as experimental tentatives. While experimental science is not permitted to fix the content of the biblical revelation of nature, it is welcomed as a negative check against false exegesis, and as a complement and supplement to the biblical data. Moreover, evangelical theology insists that God speaks in nature as well as in Scripture. Its hope of harmony between science and religion is tied to this emphasis on this twofold revelation of the Creator. The Hebrew-Christian view, indeed, is that the scriptural revelation is contingent (a redemptive supplement because of sin), and hence will be unnecessary in man's final state of glorification, whereas the natural revelation will continue while the universe endures.

We have emphasized that science and Christianity share the standpoint of knowledge in the context of faith. But the evangelical failure to articulate a Christian philosophy of science is a distressing fact, for its absence deprived the scientific movement of an external written stimulus to the biblical view. An obligation rests on evangelical Protestantism to state the biblical view of science with contemporary force. The venture of the American Scientific Affiliation, *Modern Science and Christian Faith* (F. Alton Everest, ed., 1948) represents a commendable beginning, but its effort is conspicuously weak in the discussion of philosophy of science. If the physical universe is not to be comprehended exhaustively in terms of weight, measurement and mathematical formulas, but rather as a commentary on the Logos, the implications of this must be spelled out. This is a task which the science and philosophy departments of our Christian colleges neglect at great disservice to the evangelical enterprise. Yet the basic blame for scientific unbelief must not be imputed to the evangelical movement. The invasion of Protestant theology by secular philosophy encouraged the illusion that prevailing scientific attitudes were Christian long after they had defected to rationalism. The Christian contribution to science cannot be narrowed to the shadowland idealistic observations that space-time realities constitute a cosmos, that the universe yields verifiable results to sustained investigation, that the marks of intelligence are inscribed upon all its processes—although biblical theology indubitably sustains these emphases. The contemporary scientist does not bow before the sacred in nature; his passion is to conquer and exploit; his standpoint is that of utility and control. He cares not a hoot about the *why,* but only the *how;* not an iota about the *who,* but only the *what.* His search of nature is tapered to his own arbitrary limits. Things—their weight, measurement, regularity or irregularity—become the object of his devoted concern.

The unqualified thrust of Old and New Testament alike is that the Living *God* is revealed in nature, not merely above it. Scripture does not assert that *nature* behaves thus and so, but rather that an eternal power and divinity are disclosed in and through nature. Nowhere does the Bible soften its stress that the space-time world confronts the scientist continually with evidence sufficient for the acknowledgment of the Living God. The Bible does not supply technical knowledge and general laws about the universe, but leaves this to the revisionary judgments of science. The question of general revelation, as G. C. Berkouwer notes, "is never one of the knowledge of nature as such (itself), but it is a question of the glory of God, or what Paul calls 'His eternal power and divinity' " (*General Revelation,* p. 290).

The revelation in nature therefore includes much more than is disclosed by laboratory experiments. Christian theology, in its appeal to special biblical revelation, admittedly includes much which falls outside the scope of direct observation, but the cosmic Christ already confronts the scientist in his day-to-day interaction with the created universe.

The general revelation, moreover, does not stop with this divine confrontation of man (the scientist included) in external nature. The scientist is faced not only by light from the outside, but by an inner light; the Logos is manifested in the conscience and mind of man, not simply in nature and history. And this inner and outer revelation interact and agitate each other constantly, supplying the silent background of all human thought and action. Even before the scientist comes to decision about nature and God, he is enmeshed in inner spiritual tension as a responsible moral agent. No scientist ever reaches his verdict about nature and nature's God without a previous spiritual case history—indeed, a history of moral revolt against God. The scientist is a sinner in revolt against light, both the interior and exterior light of the Logos. This doctrine of universal moral revolt is as fundamental to Hebrew-Christian theology as that the Living God is revealed in nature.

The effect of sin upon human thought and volition provides, therefore, an important consideration in the Christian evaluation of scientific theory about God. The effect of sin upon the mind and will promotes the scientist's disposition to settle for less than, and for other than, the true and Living God revealed in nature.

But while man as sinner distorts the natural revelation of God in handling it, he is unable to destroy it. Hence its essential original function, to light the way to fellowship with the Creator, yields to an accidental or condemnatory function: it renders man guilty, adding new and longer chapters of culpability to his biography of moral revolt.

The scientist's verdict passed upon nature, therefore, is no mere logical-rational verdict; it is a religious, an ethico-spiritual verdict, which he passes equally upon himself. For he is constantly bracketed, even in the twentieth century, by multiple evidences—for an almighty mind and will, in nature; for a sovereign good, in conscience; for a gracious Redeemer, in the Bible; and for a divine renewer of the souls of fallen men, in the living witness of the regenerate. If he turns aside from these—from the proclamation of the Church, from the Book of redemption, from the witness of conscience which hales men constantly to moral judgment, and from the anthem of the stars in their courses and of the earth and its movements of life, then the twentieth century scientist will stand inevitably in an adverse relationship to nature and to nature's God. In Christ's day, "not many wise, not many mighty, not many noble" read the glories of nature aright, and hailed the Redeemer as the incarnate Creator. But the company of the regenerate, though ignorant, ignoble and impotent in the world's eyes, became the moral leaders in a pagan age; they dared to turn a self-destroying world upside down, and their descendants saw the proud Roman empire crumble into that same dust of earth which had already powdered the ruins of the worldly-wise civilizations of ancient Babylon, Assyria, Persia, Syria, Phoenicia, and Greece.

That the final cause of redemption is also the final cause of nature, that the universe is a revelation of the righteousness and love of God as well as of the power and wisdom of God, indeed that the meaning of creation which manifests the invisible Logos is inseparable from the manifestation-in-flesh of the Logos as the Redeemer of fallen man—these great Christian beliefs maintain their vital relevance to our confused century. They bear relentless testimony to a unitary principle of creation, of redemption, of sanctification, of judgment.

From the foregoing considerations, it is obvious that the discussion of Christianity and science involves much more than debate over the opening chapters of Genesis. Yet the creation account is, nonetheless, the *locus classicus* of the Hebrew-Christian doctrine, and, in contrast with the speculative philosophical accounts of ancient times, it maintains a permanent interest, even in secular scientific circles. W. F. Albright has commented on its "sequence of creative phases so rational that modern science cannot improve on it, given the same language and the same range of ideas in which to state its conclusions. In fact, modern scientific cosmogonies show a disconcerting tendency to be short-lived and it may be seriously doubted whether science has yet caught up with the biblical story" (in *Old Testament Commentary* [Alleman and Flack, ed.]: "The Old Testament and Archaeology," 135).

The danger of all attempts to reconcile Genesis and science, from the standpoint of revealed theology, is the troublesome assumption that prevailing scientific theory has achieved finality. Those who, like A. H. Strong in his *Systematic Theology,* correlated the Mosaic narrative with the then-popular nebular hypothesis, contributed unwittingly to the impression that Genesis was superseded when that scientific view was no longer prevalent.

Yet, if the Genesis account purposes to touch the sphere of empirical, historical origins, its comparison with scientific theory is inevitable and necessary. For by their living interaction, revelation and science best stimulate each other.

When one surveys the diverse interpretations of the creation account by theologians, the growing emphasis that the biblical narrative holds a normative significance over and against all interpreters and interpretations appears timely indeed. Speculative ideas about Genesis have provoked the Bible and science conflict no less than speculative ideas about nature.

The conflict with science is removed, of course, though at an exorbitant theological price, by those theories which deprive the creation narrative of all relevance to empirical-historical origins.

The ancient view, of a *meta-historical* creation, which depicts the present historical world as fallen, has been revived in our century by Nicolas Berdyaev and Karl Heim. The Genesis account, however, regards God as Creator of the concrete historical world, and gives no comfort to the theory that the historical is intrinsically sinful.

The *mythico-historical* view has been popularized by Emil Brunner and the existential theologians, who regard the creation account as a literary expression of the psychological tension between man's predicament in sin and his status on the basis of creation. But the view can supply no consistent reason, on its own premises, for not dismissing the biblical narrative *in toto* as significant only psychologically and not historically. Moreover, it presupposes a dualistic theory of knowledge, highly objectionable to incarnational religion, since it disjoins scientific theory from all responsibility to the content of revelation, while denying to revelation the right of pronouncements relevant to science.

The older liberal Protestant view dismissed Genesis as scientifically irrelevant, while prizing it as a reliable source of eternally *valid spiritual principles* (cf. Theodore Haering, *The Christian Faith,* I, 377). But the sacred writers made no such distinction between their trustworthiness in spiritual and in scientific-historical matters; indeed, the two are often inextricably inter-woven. The so-called neo-orthodox theology moves to the left of this inconsistency, by repudiating all revealed doctrine, theological and ethical, no less than scientific-historical truths. Neither view deals earnestly with biblical pronouncements which, in the interest of the religion of incarnation, bear directly upon natural and historical events.

The question of concord between Genesis and science arises only where the creation narrative holds its relevance for the empirical-historical origins of the universe. A transition theory is the pictorial-revelation view, which has been defended recently by Ramm. The pictorial-revelation theory finds in Genesis a description of six days of revelation-activity, rather than of creation-activity (P. J. Wiseman, *Creation Revealed in Six Days,* 1948). The importance of the creation account is theological, emphasizing that God is Creator, but it does not disclose the specific order of creation. Ramm supplements the view, curiously, with an appeal to "moderate concordism," pointing out the fact that the sequence of Genesis and that of modern scientific theory is comfortably similar. One weakness of the theory is that exegesis will not sustain the substitution of the notion that "God showed" (or revealed) for the reading "God made." Moreover, the narrator implies that a chronological significance attaches to the creation narrative (Gen. 2:4).

Indeed, this view seems to make vulnerable concessions to the objectionable spiritual-truth theory, and to deprive the biblical revelation needlessly of statements of scientific relevance.

The creation of the universe in *six literal and successive days* is supported in Louis Berkhof's *Systematic Theology* (3rd rev. ed., 1946). This theory calls forth many elaborate attempts to account for scientific evidence for the antiquity of fossils. It is widely correlated with argument for a world-wide Noahic flood, especially under the influence of George McCready Price (*The New Geology,* 1923) carried forward by Byron Nelson (*The Deluge Story in Stone,* 1931) and A. M. Rehwinkel (*The Flood,* 1951). The theory is confronted, however, by lack of persuasive archaeological evidence for a global flood, and by the insistence of scientists that the geological and paleontological data resulted not from a single catastrophe but from a plurality of temporally distributed forces.

An alternate theory by which some scholars have attempted to correlate a literal six-day view with geological claims is the gap theory, which finds in Genesis 1:2, "the earth was without form and void," the judicial desolation of an original creation, and refers the subsequent account to the subsequent rehabilitation of a portion of the present earth in six days. The Scofield Reference Bible popularized this view. Its difficulties are multiple: the theory deprives Hebrew-Christian religion (except for the bare opening words of Genesis) of a revealed account of the original creation; it artificially wrenches the continuity of the creation account; it finds no explicit confirmation elsewhere in Scripture; it offers no theistic standpoint for interpreting the actual geological data.

The age-theory of Genesis interprets the creation-days as successive epochs rather than literal days. Exegetes point out that the term is used even in the creation account in several senses. By assigning the Hebrew word *yom* the metaphysical sense it sometimes bears in the Bible, time is provided for the geological ages. Most of the evangelical scientists in the American Scientific Affiliation today favor this view. It differs from theistic evolution in that the major kinds of life are referred to a transcendent divine activity, rather than simply to a power of development immanent in nature. Its difficulties are that, even when regarded as epochs, the Genesis days do not harmonize fully with the chronology proposed by modern science; that its enumeration of the forms of life is incomplete alongside contemporary schemes of classification; and that the literal sense of *yom* seems exegetically more natural (although cf. Psalm 90:4, in a prayer which the Hebrew tradition ascribes to Moses).

The *transcendent-activity view* supplies a novel bridge between the day and age theories. It does not deny the vast antiquity of origins, nor the slow providential development of new forms, yet it finds in the Genesis account the divine fiat acts which punctuate this process at dramatic intervals. The days of Genesis are miracle-days, not necessarily contiguous; they represent the fiat divine acts which control the whole movement of origins (Peter Stoner, *Science Speaks,* 1953). The Bible often discloses a foreshortening of prophetic perspective (as when it links the First and Second Advents); here it reflects a foreshortening of pre-history. One difficulty of this view is that Genesis does not distinguish the antiquity of the world from the creation days, by explicitly wedging special periods between the days. Moreover, the view inherits the same difficulties of chronological harmony as the age-theory, with the added burden that man and all the animal forms on this theory would presumably be created simultaneously.

The competition between these several views and yet the further fact that several seem to have a certain merit, provokes an observation about the nature of the biblical revelation. The biblical history is selective. Its data are organized especially with a view to the divine interest in and redemption of man. Even this redemptive history is excerptive. The Gospels supply us no complete biography of Jesus Christ; they hasten over the eternal hinterland, barely touch the youth and early manhood, concentrate on the three-year public ministry. John's Gospel, indeed, is mostly preoccupied with Passion Week. Important as the excerptive chronological standpoint is, even it is sacrificed at times to topical arrangement. These facts are not without a certain parallel in Genesis. The book hastens over the pre-Mosaic history, with most attention to the participants in the Abrahamic covenant; it moves swiftly from pre-history to the story of man as its central interest. Genesis One allows the topical arrangement to dominate; even plants and trees and animals are called into existence in relation to man. But already in Genesis Two the topical intrudes into the chronological, and even the chronological is selective and incomplete. Indeed, we may well ask ourselves, since divine revelation has not provided us with a complete history of the Incarnation, do we have reason to expect from the Genesis account a complete history of the creation? The striking absence of any reference in the creation account to the angels, elsewhere in biblical theology an important element, serves to emphasize the concentration on man; only on the periphery of the temptation and the Fall, implicitly in the account of the temptation, explicitly at the gates of Eden from which rebellious man is excluded, are such creatures even recognized.

Yet there can be little doubt, once the incompleteness of the history and its occasional deviation to topical arrangements are acknowledged, that a certain chronological intention persists in the creation account. Yet it is surely not the purpose of the author to supply us with a geological time-table. The primary thrust of the Genesis account is teleological rather than chronological. The days of creation, indeed, are enumerated in sequence; they begin, succeed each other, and end, giving place to the divine rest. But another category dominates the Genesis account, persevering through the first two chapters, and then through the entire book, and the Bible as a whole. That is the category of moral purpose. The sequences of creation are punctuated with the divine verdict: "and God saw that it was good" (1:4, 12, 18, etc.), intensified as a crescendo after the creation of man to "and God saw everything that he had made, and behold, it was very good" (1:31). The climax of the account is therefore that a creature bearing the divine character is called into being. Man is made, like his Maker, for an existence in social relations; it is "not good" that he should dwell alone (2:18). The moral purpose of God in creation dominates the account. The fall of man introduces a tragic rupture of relations, and redemption aims to restore man to his lost holiness. The day of creation becomes the background for the day of redemption. The interest in the historical and chronological is never merely secular.

Yet the secular reconstruction of the past is regarded as normative by the modern mind. The question of concord arises therefore at levels of secondary concern to the biblical record. The problems are not simple, and about some of them we may be confident that neither theology nor science has yet come up with the last word. The origin of life, the origin of man, the antiquity of man, are as vigorously debated today as a century ago. The question of animal suffering—has the scope for "tooth and claw" in nature a theological explanation (is it an aspect of the curse upon sin?), or is it an element in the created structure of things?—comes again to the fore with the expanding emphasis on the natural ideal of adjustment to environment, rather than competition, in plant life. The origin of culture and the origin of language raise similar problems. The modern view is that language was differentiated through man's geographical distribution; the biblical view is that it was differentitiated through divine judgment—its perspective is theological, not secular.

The antiquity of man and its bearing on the unity and solidarity of the human race in Adam supply at present the crucial pivot of debate. That the race is a unity in Adam is a central Bible doctrine; its implications for Hebrew-Christian theology are far more fundamental than the question of the antiquity of man. The loss of the biblical view that man is a unique creation at the apex of the sequence of earthly life, and the substitution of an evolutionary view of his development, has gnawed away at confidence in man's dignity and destiny. Nietzsche wrote off the bulk of mankind as insignificant; only superman has permanent significance. Thus, through prophecies about the future, Nietzsche assailed the doctrine of the essential unity of mankind. Current evolutionary theory weakens the doctrine by its reconstructions of man's past.

There is no disagreement over the relative recency of the human race, nor the recency of culture. That the preponderance of human forms have existed in the last six thousand years, that the present generation represents a fifth or sixth of all human beings who ever lived, that civilization dates back less than seven or eight thousand years—on all these issues there is virtual unanimity. The much-lampooned date of 4004 B.C., which Ussher speculatively attached—and the best scholarship of his day with him—to primal origins, as Arnold J. Toynbee notes, "approximately marks the first appearance of representatives of the species of human society called civilization" (*The Atlantic Monthly*: "Civilization on Trial," Vol. 179 [June, 1942], p. 35). Sir Arthur Keith would trace the beginning of "the era of man the tamer of nature who ushered in the present world of human history" to "only about 9,000, or perhaps 10,000 years ago" (*A New Theory of Human Evolution*, pp. 267ff.). Not before 6,000 B.C. in the Neolithic age, according to most current scientific calculations, does man appear in the biblical role of the domesticator of nature.

The correlation of this time-span with the Genesis account has presented no great problem. John Urquhardt has shown from within the narratives that a strict chronology is not preserved in the genealogies, but that they are selective, so that the spiritual representative of a family or line, rather than the first-born son, is sometimes obviously given (*How Old Is Man?*, 1904). Warfield argued that the genealogies are carried forward toward the Messiah through tribal connections and representative persons, rather than by a strict line of father-son descent, but it is difficult to prove that only representative individuals appear. The representative or abbreviated character of the genealogies is supported by Edward J. Young (*An Introduction to the Old Testament*, p. 414) and Merrill F. Unger (*Archaeology and the Old Testament*, p. 339). Thus a date for the beginning of civilized man reaching back eight or ten thousand years is a distinct biblical possibility.

The center of debate, however, is the relation of the *Homo-like* animate forms, and whether they are in fact to be regarded as human, sub-human or non-human species. Contemporary evolutionary thought catalogues these forms as human, on the premise that anatomical similarity implies physical descent, and dates them not merely ten, but hundreds of thousands of years ago. The new method of carbon-dating the past has steadily dissolved evangelical reservations over the antiquity of such forms, and many evangelical anthropologists today no longer regard the antiquity of man, as long as 200,000 to 500,000 years ago, an unproved assumption.

The projection of a pre-Adamic human race, to reconcile these manlike forms with the biblical account, faces difficulties. The catastrophe theory is unconvincing as an exposition of Genesis 1:1-2, and in the matter of fossil forms it provides no solution of the problem of where the supposed first race ends and the second begins. But the theory of a pre-Adamic race is not dependent upon catastrophism. The pre-Adamic *Homo*-forms, it has been argued, bear a structural relationship to Adam, but not an ethico-spiritual relationship. Anthropologists reply that creatures skeletally similar to modern man utilized crude stone implements at least 500,000 years ago; that at the time of Neanderthal man (100,000 years ago) there is evidence of burial of the dead; that by 30,000 or 40,000 years ago these creatures produced fairly detailed drawings. Their continuity with the biblical Adam is therefore argued on the ground of physical form, skills and customs.

Among these early manlike-forms, mutational subspecies or variants—and hence several types of *Homo*—are said to have existed. The current classification distinguishes *Homo erectus* from *Homo sapiens,* in view of the latter's enlarged brain capacity, absence of brow ridges, presence of chin projection, and these in turn from *Homo sapiens sapiens,* or modern man. The critical point in the naturalistic transition of animal forms to the genus *Homo* is now thought to be the abandonment of the forelegs for locomotion.

Yet evolutionary theory in recent years has evidenced increasing interest in the theory that the human species, and other orders of life, originated suddenly. R. Goldschmidt declares that "the large step from species to species is neither demonstrable nor conceivable on the basis of accumulated micromutations" (*The Material Basis of Evolution,* p. 199). G. G. Simpson calls attention to the "regular absence of transitional forms" (*Tempo and Mode in Evolution,* p. 107). The whole discussion of evolution today is more amenable to the acknowledgment of gaps or discontinuities existing objectively in nature, rather than existing merely in the observation and evidence of the scientist.

Alongside this new readiness to bow to mystery in the presence of these gaps one may detect, at least in some quarters, an uneasiness over the dogmatic dating of human history hundreds of thousands of years in the past. Ruth Moore tells us that "since 1950 the scientific evidence has pointed inescapably to one conclusion: man did not evolve either in the time or in the way that Darwin and the modern evolutionists thought most probable. The physicists and geologists by 1950 had clearly shown that the world is older and man is younger than anyone had dared to estimate before" (*Man, Time and Fossils,* p. 391). She contends that fluorine-dating now indicates that "humans who had the requisite intelligence to be called man did not reach that high status until about 50,000 years ago. . . . And if our 50,000-year tenure of earth must be adjusted, the chances are that it will be shortened" (*ibid.,* p. 403). It must not be forgotten that geo-chronology is among the youngest of the sciences, and that progress remains to be made in its imposition of concise time-scales upon the distant pre-historic past.

The biblical record does not settle the uniqueness, antiquity, and unity of the human race by a central appeal to morphological considerations. The disjunction between man and the animals, of the sub-Adamic forms and the Adam form of life, in Genesis, takes place with the formation of a creature under moral command. Man's basic distinction is that he is divinely endowed with the *imago Dei,* through the specially inbreathed breath of life. The Bible knows man as from the beginning intended for fellowship with God, for rational-moral-spiritual discrimination, for social responsibility, for dominion over the earth and the animals. The record moves swiftly, in biblical theology, from the primal Adam, who is already a "cultured gentleman," to the beginnings of society and civilization. And here it must not be ignored that the study of the origin of religion discloses that religion is as old as man; no primitive tribe is without a form of religious life and activity.

Perhaps we are not to rule out dogmatically the possibility that the "dust" of man's origin may have been animated, since the animals before man appear to have been fashioned from the earth (Gen. 1:24). The Bible does not explicate man's physical origin in detail. The fact that, after Genesis 1:1 the narrator deals with a mediate creation, which involves the actualizing of potentialities latent in the original creation, should caution us against the one-sided invocation of divine transcendence. The new levels of being arise with quite obvious dependence on the lower in the creation account. Yet man's disjunction from the animals appears specific enough, especially since fiat beginning is an essential idea in the Hebrew-Christian revelation of origins, and since Eve, while deriving her body from an anatomical form, gains it from Adam in distinction from the lower forms.

Be that as it may, it is the ethico-religious fact about man which marks him off most conspicuously from the animals. Only an age secular in spirit could concentrate its interest in *Homo* on morphological structure, seeking to understand man's origin and nature by focusing solely on prehuman and sub-human forms, then naming man for the brute, and finding his *imago* at last among the beasts. From the Hebrew-Christian viewpoint this course, by which man in a scientific age makes bestiality self-respecting, is but another chapter in his sophisticated revolt against God. If the cleft between Christianity and science is to be repaired, the theology of revelation will not ascribe to nature and nature's God any course disputed by the assured results of science, nor will science find man's dignity, and its own renown also, in anything inferior to thinking the Creator's thoughts after Him.

EVANGELISM AND PREACHING

Andrew W. Blackwood

Andrew Watterson Blackwood was born in Kansas, reared in Ohio, and educated at Franklin College, Harvard University, Princeton Seminary and Xenia Seminary. He pastored churches, mainly in educational centers, for seventeen years. His teaching career includes the posts of professor of Bible, Louisville Presbyterian Seminary (1925-30); professor of homiletics, Princeton Seminary (1930-50); professor of preaching, Temple University School of Theology (1950-). He is the author of eighteen books, nine of them Pulpit Book Club selections, and another, Doctrinal Preaching for Today, *distributed by Evangelical Books.*

10. Andrew W. Blackwood:

EVANGELISM AND PREACHING

SINCE THE outbreak of World War II we all have witnessed a renewal of concern about evangelism and preaching. These two forms of Christian activity belong together, but here we shall deal with them separately. First we shall think about evangelism, with special reference to the pulpit. We may think of an evangelistic sermon as one that brings a group or a throng of people face to face with Jesus Christ as the Son of God, voicing the truths of God so that the unsaved or unchurched hearer will accept Christ as the Son of God, and unite with the local church. In almost every preaching situation more than a few auditors have already accepted Christ as Redeemer, and are actively engaged in His service. Still we ought to think of the pulpit evangelist as aiming primarily to win for Christ and the local church every hearer not yet a believer in Christ and a worker for the Kingdom.

This widespread concern about evangelism shows a remarkable reversal of opinion and practice. After the outbreak of World War I, the large majority of church leaders here in the United States seem to have agreed that the era of mass evangelism had passed, never to return. So they sought to discover or devise other methods than this one brought down from New Testament days. During that period of disbelief in mass evangelism, Walter A. Maier started the Lutheran Radio Hour, which he continued from 1930 until his death in 1950. Maier and his ways of presenting the Gospel did not appeal to many who loved the Lord and His Church, but still he is said to have addressed over the radio more persons than any other speaker of his day. During the period since World War I, Charles E. Fuller and others have shown over the radio that the so-called demise of mass evangelism had been exaggerated. On the other hand, group evangelism did to a large extent disappear from many a local church, where such activity ought to center.

I. A REDISCOVERY OF EVANGELISM

In our time Billy Graham has again brought mass evangelism to the fore. Starting in 1949, at the age of twenty-nine, he has conducted soul-winning campaigns in city after city, here in the homeland, over in Great Britain, on the continent of Europe, and even in Asia. The end is not yet. William Franklin Graham has his critics, mainly among those who have neither met him in person, nor listened to his preaching. In South America, notably in Argentina, Tommy Hicks is said to have been equally effective in appealing to hosts of eager listeners. About him and his work I know little except that he has shown the possibilities of making a religious appeal to men en masse.

At the same time evangelistic activity has increased among nearly all branches of the Church. For convenience we shall think only about bodies other than Catholic. The Missouri Lutherans, to whom Maier belonged, have continued their Radio Hour. They have also done pioneer work over television, a field that the Protestant Church in general has yet to capture and employ for the winning of souls. Other bodies of Lutherans have shown that it is possible for a Church with liturgical forms of worship to engage actively in soul winning from the pulpit, as well as by personal work, and by catechetical classes.

In more than a few places the Protestant Episcopal Church, also, has held preaching missions. Coming over from England at times, Bryan Green has charmed hosts of Anglicans and others, both ministers and laymen. By winsome presentation of the Gospel he has won many recruits for Christ and the Church. His book, *The Practice of Evangelism* (1951), has commended the cause to many who have not heard him speak. His ways differ from those in other churches, but he impresses many of us favorably. He stresses the worship and the work of the local church and its minister. He promotes evangelism in the spirit of worship, and in an atmosphere of reverence. All the while he gives a commanding place to marriage and the Christian home.

Among church bodies not liturgical, group evangelism seems to have been flourishing. In many circles the Disciples of Christ have never ceased their endeavors to win recruits through preaching in the local church, mainly by the pastor. The same has held true of the "new" Evangelical United Brethren Church, and of Baptist churches, especially in the South. There the growth in membership through confessions of faith is said to be larger from year to year than in any other branch of Protestantism. At the Baptist Theological Seminary in New Orleans, third largest in size among Southern Baptists, the professors and students engage in evangelistic work every weekend, and at other times. They have set as a seminary goal the winning to Christ of enough persons to start a new Baptist congregation every week of the year.

So does the vast Methodist Church show increased activity in group evangelism. Without ceasing to stress personal work, visitation evangelism, and the winning of a family for Christ, such leaders as Bishop Arthur J. Moore keep promoting evangelism of the sort once associated with Wesley and Whitefield. On the denominational Board of Evangelism, Harry Denman—a layman formerly associated with Bishop Moore—works with Henry Williams and G. Ernest Thomas, a man with a pastor's heart, and the author of devotional books most helpful. These leaders, and others, strive to promote the kind of soul winning long associated with Ocean Grove.

Space does not permit me to mention other "old-line" denominations which report activity and progress in group evangelism. As a Presbyterian I hail with joy every token that our leaders are striving to restore the old-time emphasis on public soul winning. According to more than one capable historian, there was a time in Scotland when Presbyterianism stood for a record of almost continuous revivals. Out of the old Free Church in those days came the majority of my own missionary heroes and heroines. I do not mean that the Church of my forebears held mass meetings, as we Americans often do, but that they exalted the winning of souls, not least through preaching the Gospel, in the atmosphere of prayer.

Much the same spirit of evangelism obtains among what are known, inaccurately, as "newer churches." In many respects the Free Methodists, the Nazarenes, the Christian and Missionary Alliance, the Church of God (with headquarters at Anderson, Indiana), and other bodies not usually listed among major denominations, put the rest of us to shame by their diligence, their gifts of money, and their ways of appealing to common people. Their beliefs and practices differ at times from those to which we have become accustomed. Even so, the work of these friends should appear in any account of present-day evangelism. We ought to pray for the blessing of God on their labors. Please note that the list does not include such sects as Jehovah's Witnesses and the followers of Father Divine.

Whatever the denomination or group, the work of soul winning today does not escape criticism. Sometimes the pulpit appeal may seem to be narrow, as though the hearer did not have a body, and did not live in a world filled with problems. At other times the appeal may seem so broad that it confuses a simple-minded hearer, much as Paul and Silas would have confused the Philippian jailer if they had talked to him about the ethics he would learn after he became a follower of Christ. At other times the doctrinal foundations may seem to be shaky or insecure. But if the Apostle could rejoice over the way other men preached the Gospel, however imperfectly (Phil. 1:14-18), much more should we rejoice to witness in our day a widespread increase of public evangelism.

How the picture has changed! In 1936, at a gathering of Christian leaders representing major denominations, one of our foremost "religious statesmen" declared: "You can divide the ministers and congregations of our country into two groups—those that believe in evangelism, and those that do not believe." He seemed to think, perhaps mistakenly, that one group was as large as the other. At least he ranged himself and his congregation on the side of those who did not believe. Today in a group of that sort such a statement would call forth this reply: "So can you divide the ministers and congregations of our land into two groups—those that believe in the New Testament and those that do not believe."

A Return to the New Testament

The wisest leaders of evangelism today get their ideals from the New Testament. In a helpful discussion of such pulpit work, Bryan Green starts with the book, *Apostolic Preaching and Its Developments,* by Charles H. Dodd of Cambridge University. Without understanding or accepting what this New Testament scholar writes about "realized eschatology," I rejoice in the facts that Dodd presents about apostolic preaching. These facts any well-trained minister can verify by a firsthand study of Greek New Testament words and sayings about the *kerygma.* Dodd's book first appeared in 1936. Since then it has gone through various printings. The following excerpts come from the 1949 edition:

> "It pleased God," says Paul, "by the foolishness of the preaching to save them that believe." The word here translated "preaching," *kerygma,* signifies not the action of the preacher, but that which he preaches, his "message," as we sometimes say.
>
> The New Testament draws a clear distinction between preaching and teaching . . . Much of our preaching in church at the present day would not have been recognized by the early Christians as *kerygma* . . . It was by *kerygma,* says Paul, not by *didachē* (pulpit teaching), that it pleased God to save men (pp. 1-2).

With this teaching of C. H. Dodd about the *kerygma,* other New Testament scholars agree. How could they escape the conclusion he has stated so clearly after an exhaustive study of the facts? Dodd also makes clear that the New Testament contains a wealth of "teaching" and exhortation, addressed to believers. The epistles "expound and defend the implications of the Gospel rather than proclaim it. . . . Paul was well aware that what gave authority to his teaching was the Gospel which underlay it all" (pp. 9-10). The fact remains, as Dodd abundantly shows, that in the New Testament the word preaching uniformly refers to evangelism. In many a local church, until recently, such pulpit work had either disappeared or else assumed an inconspicuous place.

For a scholarly study of New Testament preaching we are indebted to Jesse B. Weatherspoon, professor of homiletics in the Southern Baptist Theological Seminary at Louisville. Under the title, *Sent Forth to Preach* (1954), he has given us a Christian philosophy that deserves more attention than it has received. While he stresses the facts about the *kerygma,* rather than the practical application to the pulpit now, he would agree with other students of the New Testament that a minister today ought to deal at times with the *didachē,* but that the main stress ought to fall on the *kerygma.* Herein lies the most heartening fact about present-day evangelism: it bases practical counsels on New Testament doctrines, and tends to fill the local pastor with New Testament ideals. This in turn should mean being filled with the Holy Spirit.

In other days Baptists wrote most of our American books about the history of preaching. I refer to John A. Broadus, *Lectures on the History of Preaching;* T. Harwood Pattison, *The History of Christian Preaching;* and Edwin C. Dargan, *A History of Preaching,* in two volumes. Some admirer of Broadus, the scholar, ought to carry Dargan's work into a third volume, bringing it up to date, with added stress on evangelism. Better still, someone ought to write a history of evangelism, starting in the Old Testament, with its record of declensions and revivals. We have capable histories of missions, worship, and many things else, but no one has written about the rise and progress, as well as the decline, of evangelism.

Meanwhile we have books about various aspects of the subject, viewed historically. For instance, Frank G. Beardsley has written about *The History of American Revival* (1904). James Burns has given us an abler book, perhaps our best discussion of the subject, except the Bible. In *Revivals, Their Laws and Leaders* (1909), he has dealt with the matter biographically. Starting with Francis of Assisi, and ending with John Wesley, Burns has led us to think of the Reformation as a revival sent from God, and based solidly on Bible doctrine. Without reference to this volume, which has gone out of print, present-day writers have begun again to stress the theological foundations of evangelism.

Three such works deserve more than a passing glance. T. A. Kantonen, a Lutheran who was born in Finland and educated in our country, has written *The Theology of Evangelism* (1954). This book has four chapters, each with direct reference to evangelism: "Theology and Evangelism," "God the Creator," "God the Redeemer," and "God the Sanctifier." Kantonen does not write popularly or practically, but he sets forth truths that we practical folk need to ponder. He does not incur the criticism of our foremost liberal philosophical theologian, Paul Tillich, who insists that many evangelical writers have permitted the Second Person of the Trinity to obscure the First Person.

Vincent Taylor, an English Wesleyan, has written about *Doctrine and Evangelism* (1953); and Julian Hartt of Yale, *Toward a Theology of Evangelism* (1955). From a point of view more liberal than that of Kantonen, these men write popularly. They bring out much that should help to correct the faults of evangelistic preaching in the States. The following excerpt from Taylor's book pleases me in every way except one: he seems to say that we men preach en masse. Where Jowett wrote about *The Preacher, His Life and Work* (1912), Taylor resorts to the present-day fashion of stressing the weak plural. The following excerpts come from the beginning of the little volume, and from the end:

> [Congregations] want to know what the faith is, and it is the business of preachers to tell them, plainly, tersely, effectively . . . We are too anecdotal, too peripheral, too limited in our range . . . How different it might be if we would preach the faith! (pp. 8-9)
>
> [By prayer and meditation] doctrine must be part of ourselves. . . . Doctrines become dead if they do not touch mind, feeling, and will. When they are living they colour our ways of thinking and determine our relationships with others; they become mighty themes for preaching and evangelism; they set the course of history and shape the lives of men (p. 87).

The subjects of the various chapters show that the author feels much concern about theology proper. In a small volume he can not deal with any subject exhaustively. Perhaps he attempts too much. Even so, the list of his chapter headings affords any pastor a way of checking up on his pulpit work. During the past year how many of these Bible truths have sounded out? "Doctrine in Evangelism," "Why We Believe in God," "Authority and Belief," "The Divine Image in Man," "Sin," "Salvation," "Grace," "Jesus," "The Son of God," "The Atonement," "Faith in Christ," "Justification by Faith," "Sanctification," "The Holy Spirit," "The Exalted Christ," "The Church and the Ministry," "Baptism," "The Lord's Supper," and "The Life Everlasting." Personally, I should omit some of these, even though important, in order to include "The Final Return of Our Lord," and "The Certainty of the Judgment Day."

When a scholar of tomorrow writes about the history of evangelism, he may think of the nineteenth century in terms of Charles G. Finney's well-known *Lectures on Revivals of Religion* (1835). Today the emphasis has changed. May the historian feel able to describe our era as one in which churchmen rediscovered the doctrinal foundations of evangelism. For example, take the Bible teaching about sin. Partly because of World War II, and more because of possible World War III—with the accompanying dread of the hydrogen cobalt bomb—many clergymen have begun to face frankly the fact of sin. Harry Emerson Fosdick seems not to have returned to all the old-fashioned Baptist doctrines in which he was reared, but in his last book of sermons, though not his ablest, he declares:

> I am much more realistic about man than I used to be. Man is a sinner; there is truth in that old doctrine of original sin—something fundamentally wrong in us from which we desperately need to be saved, and from which science alone can not save us, nor education alone, nor any automatic evolution, only what the New Testament calls the grace of God, forgiveness, spiritual rebirth, being inwardly transformed by the renewing of our minds (pp. 179-180).

In many circles today there has been a trend toward New Testament thinking about such matters as conversion. It has again begun to seem intellectually respectable to believe in conversion, even in adult conversion, with no upper age limit on the power of grace to redeem and transform. We now understand what we might long ago have learned from the Book of the Acts, that the new birth may be painful, even excruciating, and that it may not. The resulting conversion may come suddenly and violently, as with Saul of Tarsus and the Philippian jailer. The change of heart and life may begin more quietly and inconspicuously, as with the Ethiopian eunuch and Lydia, the business woman. In any case the proof of the new birth is the new life. As Moody used to insist, the only way to get into God's Kingdom is to be born into it. But the ways of being born do not always conform with theories of "non-theologically-minded" high-pressure revivalists here in the States. So let us resolve to take our evangelism from the Scriptures, and to base it on Christian doctrine.

The Weaknesses of American Revivalism

I believe in the best American revivals, such as those under Moody and Sankey, and the earlier one in 1857-58. I believe still more in the sort of continuous revival that seems to have marked the work of Spurgeon in his London Tabernacle, and George W. Truett in the First Baptist Church of Dallas. I believe that the work of revival, under God, depends mainly on the local church, and that it depends chiefly on the pastor, as the leader of Christian men and women who engage actively in personal work. I believe, too, that we ought to study the revivalism of other times here in the United States, so as to learn what we should avoid. Here I used the term "revivalism" to indicate unwholesome aspects of revivals. Technically, I often think of revivals in terms of the Old Testament, and of evangelistic work in terms of the New. Here I am not writing technically. Neither am I sitting in judgment on anyone except myself.

American revivalism has often ignored or minimized the God-given relation between the sermon and other parts of public worship. On a street corner in a city, as in some parts of South America, an evangelist may wisely determine to do nothing but preach. In a situation far more common, a man finds it possible also to have singing and prayer. If so, the singing and prayer should all be addressed to God. I believe in the best of Gospel songs, not a few in number. I also feel strongly that whenever we engage in public worship we ought to sing and pray to God, in Christ, through the Spirit. In the United States Senate a beloved chaplain felt justified in using a prayer to warn solons about stomach ulcers, but in an evangelistic service let no man "get something across to people" by way of the mercy seat. Whenever thou prayest, pray, and do not preach!

I might enumerate still other reasons why the revivalism of other days alienated many persons whom we longed to reach. They would not have objected to innocent horseplay among boys in a barn, but the critics of revivals saw no connection between the stunts that often preceded a "soul-winning" sermon and the spirit of the message itself. When the man in the pulpit wishes the one in the pew to fall down on his knees and give himself into the hands of God, as young Isaiah did in the Temple, all the steps that lead up to a decision ought to be in harmony with the holiness of the occasion. This does not mean that any part of an evangelistic service ought to resemble an old-time funeral, full of grief and despair. Neither does it mean that a man ordained of God to pray and preach ought to compete with a vaudeville show of the coarser sort. "Let all things be done decently and in order."

Other objections have to do with the prominence of human factors. New Testament evangelism stressed the presence of the Living Christ, with His pierced hands, and the power of the Holy Spirit. The human agents relied chiefly on prayer, preaching, and personal work. They did not strive for the glory of the workers, many of whom we do not know by name. In America at times the stress of revivalism has fallen on men, money, and machinery. Such activities properly call for expenditure of money on no Lilliputian scale. There must also be organization, with skilled leaders. But in the thinking of pastor and people, things spiritual ought to bulk larger than anything human. In these respects Billy Graham seems to have kept his record as clear as that of Dwight L. Moody. He never was accused of letting men, money, and machinery overshadow prayer, preaching, and personal work. Moody put the first things first!

Criticisms of another sort have to do with what we loosely term social psychology. Current writers have added little to the indictment of Frederick M. Davenport, a sociologist, in a searching book, *Primitive Traits in Religious Revivals* (1905), and of Sinclair Lewis, a novelist, abetted by a clergyman dupe, in a revolting caricature, *Elmer Gantry* (1927). Both Davenport and Lewis had more than a little basis for their "findings." Everyone who knows the facts about the Kentucky Revival of 1800, and rural life in Ohio and Kansas a hundred years later, must deplore revivalism that employed mob psychology, appealed to primitive emotions, apart from a stable basis in doctrine, and aroused the baser passions. Who can wonder that a stigma still attaches to the good old biblical word, revival?

Especially unfortunate were certain methods of recruiting boys and girls. In Pittsburgh years ago hundreds of children at the age of ten and twelve were entertained by an exciting display of imported flags, culminating with a proper salute to Old Glory. To all of this no one could object, but after the patriotic display the boys and girls were herded up front and without explanation were asked to sign their names to certain cards. Later the parents learned that their sons and daughters had publicly professed faith in Christ, and had indicated which churches they wished to join. Of all this the boys and girls themselves, most of them, were unaware. No believer in child evangelism can justify or condone such ways of securing young recruits for Christ and His Church.

The evangelism of our day has shuffled off many of those earlier excesses, which were usually due to untrained and irresponsible leadership. On the other hand, with our "improved methods," we may have lost the fervor, the zeal, the passion, whatever we call the outworking of the Spirit in the life of a believer who wishes to share his peace and joy with everyone who does not yet believe and rejoice. If we wish to recover "the lost radiance of the Christian Church," we can find it where we lost it, in the Old Book, with its doctrines of grace to redeem and transform. These doctrines all center in the Christ of the *kerygma:* the Christ of yesterday, who died to redeem us from sin; the Christ of today, who dwells in our hearts by His Spirit; the Christ of tomorrow, who is coming in glory, to complete His work of redemption and transformation.

The Prospects for Evangelism

The outlook for evangelism seems brighter today than at any time in our century. Men and women of middle age, many of them, have tried all sorts of substitutes for the Gospel of redemption. Now they are ready for the real thing. Countless young people, victims of what Pitirim A. Sorokin calls a "sensate civilization," seem to be ready now for a faith that will lead them to look up and be set free from their baser selves. Hosts of boys and girls all about us are growing up with needs and aspirations that only Christ can satisfy. Whatever the age group, or the community, people all about us, unchurched and unsaved, keep groping after what we have to give them in the Gospel. To whom shall we turn for leadership in such evangelism?

"The professional evangelist," to use an unfortunate term, still has a place and a mission. Among such leaders whom I have seen and heard, I thank God especially for Dwight L. Moody, J. Wilbur Chapman, Gipsy Smith, Sr., Gipsy Smith, Jr., and Billy Graham. Friends whose judgment I honor would add to the list Billy Sunday, Reuben A. Torrey, and a score of others, including more than a few still at work. Almost every one of these men would have agreed with what J. Wilbur Chapman used to tell us, lovingly: "The professional evangelist seems to me good in his place; the pastoral evangelist, better in his way; the personal evangelist, best of all." He referred to a dedicated layman who volunteered to do "individual work for individuals," one by one.

Present-day writers, such as A. E. Kernahan and Dawson C. Bryan, encourage visitation evangelism, by teams of two. These authors quote such a text as Mark 6:7: "He called the twelve, and began to send them forth two by two." Yes, but He sent them forth to preach and heal. In New Testament personal work, as a rule, one man deals with another man (John 1:35-51 and Acts 8:26-40). Really the New Testament does not stress the number of workers, but the method each of them employs. Current ways of personal work sometimes lead only to church membership, with no visible evidence of conversion. In apostolic times, after a person such as Saul of Tarsus, Lydia, or the Philippian jailer confessed faith in Christ, that person began at once to do something for Him.

Whatever the reason, many church members today give no visible evidences of having been born again. In New Jersey a church bulletin recently compared the statistics of the home congregation with those of fifty years before. With a resident church membership practically twice as large as half a century ago, attendance at morning worship averages less than half the attendance fifty years ago; attendance at the church school has fallen off still more; there is at present no evening service, and no mid-week meeting, whereas such gatherings were formerly well attended, as such things went in that older time. Meanwhile, what has taken place? Year after year, the congregation has welcomed many new members, including boys and girls of proper age. Few of these boys and girls have formed the habit of attending their own church. And yet this congregation has helped to swell the official statistics that lead Protestants to boast that the number of our church members has kept increasing by leaps and bounds!

The experience in the New Jersey church seems not to be unique. Writing in *Theology Today* (July, 1953), an enthusiastic advocate of present-day evangelism, Elmer G. Homrighausen, reported the findings of a survey in Ohio, among the local churches of an evangelical denomination which he did not name. Twenty per cent of the members never prayed; twenty-five per cent never read the Bible, thirty per cent never attended church, forty per cent never gave through the home church, fifty per cent never attended the church school, ninety per cent never had family prayers, ninety-five per cent never gave the tithe, ninety-five per cent never invited a person to become a Christian. These last three items no doubt largely referred to the same men and women. If a nurseryman had such an orchard, he would sharpen his pruning shears and his saw. Before he applied them rigorously, he would try all the approved methods of nurture. But he would not tolerate in a tree or an orchard a single dead branch. Neither would he judge the value of his orchard by the number and size of the unpruned trees.

In that same year an Episcopal professor of theology, William N. Pittinger, wrote for *Christian Century* (September 2, 1953) his conclusions after a survey of church conditions across the country: "One can hardly offer statistics on a matter of the sort, but it would not be far wrong to say that perhaps five per cent of the 70 or 80 million church members among the 150 million Americans have some real grasp of what their faith means; and that appears to be a generous estimate." "A generous estimate"! From a point of view quite different, I estimate that ten per cent of our Protestant church members are reasonably well informed, and that twenty-five per cent are living up to their limited light. But "what are these among so many?" Even with my more optimistic surmise, where does it leave a typical local church? As at Laodicea of old (Rev. 3:14-19), in need of a revival, and of pastoral nurture!

No minister has a right to sit in judgment and determine the state of any man's soul except his own. Among the members of a local church, who but the divine "Reader of human hearts" can tell how many and which ones have had a personal experience of redeeming grace, and now live in vital union with the Head of the Church? Even so, that minister in Jersey, like those pastors in Ohio, no doubt feels this way: "Not only do countless other people in this community need the Gospel; the members of this congregation need it too, and need it desperately." Alas, it proves doubly difficult to win for Christ and real church membership a person or a family already enrolled, 'in good and regular standing,' despite lack of 'fruit,' 'more fruit,' 'much fruit,' such as the Lord expects from every vine He has planted (John 15:1-8). Getting these persons to attend their own church and to read the Bible at home would not guarantee their change of heart, but would expose them to the influences of the Spirit, who alone can bring about a birth from above (John 3:8).

With the work of evangelism, hand in hand, ought to go the most careful Christian nurture, especially by the pastor. Why else did the Apostle keep writing "letters to young churches?" Guided by the Holy Spirit, Paul knew that the *didachē* ought to follow the *kerygma*. In the Jersey congregation, as among the Ohio churches, a study of the facts would show that the falling off in church attendance, and in other visible signs of invisible grace, came during a period when the local minister felt too busy to do pastoral work, either by home visitation or by counseling at the church. Since 1925, when I ceased to serve as a full-time pastor, I have ministered as a pulpit supply in all sorts of churches, except among multimillionaires. I have come to know the feelings of many laymen, loyal to their ministers and zealous for the Kingdom. Again and again I have come home with the conviction that our noblest laymen wish the dominie would quit doing many other things not wrong in themselves, and begin to take loving care of the home flock, especially the weaker sheep and the little lambs.

At times I have found laymen eager also for more frequent opportunities to worship God at the home church. In a certain congregation there had been only one service on the Lord's Day, year after year. When the pulpit recently became vacant the lay officers asked me to help them start an evening service. They wished an hour of worship less formal than in the morning, and with pulpit guidance on how to read and enjoy the Bible today. Little did they know how strongly I believed in making the "second service" informative, with stress at times on how to read the Bible, preferably by books, and at other times on what Christians ought to believe in the way of Bible doctrine. Local conditions may call for some different procedure, but any normal congregation would profit from two different sorts of public worship every Lord's Day. Then there would be time for both the *kerygma* and the *didachē,* with the main stress on the former.

Another factor enters into the local scene. The decline in church attendance, when compared with church membership, seems to have begun during the careless days when we quit encouraging fathers and mothers to bring to morning worship boys and girls of school age, so that the members of a family could worship together in a familiar pew. In the beauty of life's morning, boys and girls form the habit of attending church, and of enjoying public worship. Or else they fall into the habit of not attending and not enjoying anything religious, unless it is especially prepared for them alone. Meanwhile we have experimented with the junior church, which may work well in a large congregation, with the requisite leadership, equipment, and constituency. In most places the junior sermon fits better, and renders a useful service, especially if boys and girls sit with their parents and remain for the entire service. Otherwise they may never witness the baptism of adults, or the celebration of the Lord's Supper.

Best of all, many of us believe with former Bishop John H. Vincent, a staunch conservative, and the late Dean Willard L. Sperry, a pronounced liberal, that the most important hour of the week, religiously, for any growing boy or girl, is the time set apart for morning worship in the main sanctuary, under the leadership of the pastor. According to my reading of biography, from such church-attending boys and girls—and almost only from them—have come our ablest ministers and missionaries. All of this has much to do with "child evangelism," a term I never use. I think of "children" as too young for church membership, which normally begins at about twelve years of age, when lads and lasses prefer to be called boys and girls. All the while the smallest ones need loving Christian nurture.

A minister of the right sort can lead in public worship and preach so as to interest and help a growing boy or girl. For the morning service he may deliberately plan that every portion of worship will have something of interest, value, and uplift for a normal lad or lass. In the pulpit he can winsomely present the claims of Christ as Saviour. After an ingathering he can guide new church members into paths of Christian service and growth. But not if they have formed the habit of "absent treatment."

Evangelistically, every congregation needs more than an occasional visit from a professional evangelist, and a yearly series of union meetings lasting a week. Such gatherings have their place and their limitations. During my seventeen years in the pastorate I encouraged the people to take part in union meetings under evangelical auspices. Only once did we fail to unite, and that time I feel that we acted unwisely. But on looking back I can see that each congregation where I served accomplished more when we did our share of the Lord's work our own way, and asked for God's blessing on neighboring churches at work in ways quite different. I also feel that we accomplished most by what the Westminster Shorter Catechism calls "the diligent use of the outward and ordinary means of grace" than when we resorted to special methods. Why should not every congregation have more or less of a continuous revival?

Through the years I have learned much about all these things by watching Baptist pastors at work. I thank God for a book of yesterday, *The Evangelistic Church* (1927) by Frederick E. Taylor. As a Baptist pastor for years in Indianapolis, he held only a few special meetings, at irregular intervals, not charted in advance. Near the close of public worship, morning or evening, he always felt free to extend an invitation to the unsaved, but for weeks at a time he did no such thing. In all these matters he sought and followed the guidance of the Holy Spirit, who never let him lose sight of the unsaved, or fall into any stereotyped way of asking for decisions. All the while, under God, he depended more on lay workers than on himself. He took delight in serving as leader of an "evangelistic congregation." By this he meant something easy to understand, and hard to attain:

> A church which from pulpit to primary [department] is permeated by a desire to see a constant succession of people who have come to know Christ as Saviour and Lord, and who in turn are seeking to lead others to the same experience (pp. 36-7).

Here and there through the years I have known such pastors and churches. Without exception I have found the minister happy with his people, and the laymen delighted with their pastor. I have also found the church free from serious problems about money for benevolences and current expenses. People who love the Lord, and keep striving to win others for Christ, grow in knowledge and in grace. All of this assumes that they have as minister a man of God who devotes himself to evangelism and to Christian nurture. So it seems that the best way to prevent congregational ills, and to deal with them when they break out, is to lead in making and fostering an "evangelistic church." In other words, have a present-day example of a Christian congregation, according to the ideals set before us in the Book of the Acts.

Sometimes we at a distance wonder about the growth of Southern Baptists as a denomination. At Birmingham recently, and at Memphis a little later, I found in each city and its suburbs approximately a hundred congregations. Each one had a Bible school, morning worship, an evening service, and a mid-week meeting—the year around! When I reported these facts to a seminary professor who knows his denomination at large, he told me: "I never heard of a Southern Baptist congregation that did not have all four services every week." Those brethren believe in evangelism and in preaching. They also believe in higher education, and are making it increasingly available to the ministers of tomorrow. All the while the fathers and mothers pray that with the "new" book learning, their sons who preach will not lose their zeal for winning souls, and for loving care of every sheep in the fold.

It still pleases God to save men and women, boys and girls, one by one, through the preaching of the Gospel. And yet it would be hard to find any first-class book, except the Bible, about the content and form of an evangelistic sermon. While in seminary I fell in love with a little volume by Henry Clay Trumbull, *Individual Work for Individuals* (1903). More recently I have read many other good books about evangelism. Why can we not have something equally inspiring about the evangelistic sermon? What then are the marks, ideally?

1. Both in content and in spirit a soul-winning sermon should be biblical. If ministers now do not preach this way often enough, the reason may lie in their way of approaching the Scriptures. If so, the seminary graduates of tomorrow ought to do better when they become pastors. In an up-to-date school of theology a student now does not spend the major portion of his time, biblically, trying to follow surmises of deceased German scholars about who did or did not write various parts of Holy Writ. With nothing more than such "biblical learning," how would Philip have known what to tell a distinguished stranger about the meaning of Isaiah 53? Today a worth-while seminary lays more

stress on what P. T. Forsyth termed *Positive Preaching and the Modern Mind* (1907).

2. An evangelistic sermon ought to be doctrinal. Perhaps not directly doctrinal, because it may prove hard to teach the meaning of grace, or faith, while pleading with a hearer to accept Christ as Saviour. Still every soul-winning discourse ought to have at its core a doctrine taken from the Scriptures, and so presented that the hearer will understand. "He that received the seed into the good ground is he that heareth the word, and understandeth it" (Matt. 13:23). As a safeguard against sheer emotionalism, and as a remedy for excessive anecdotage, a young pulpit evangelist should determine never to prepare a soul-winning sermon without having at its heart some vital portion of the *kerygma*. "I am not ashamed of the Gospel, for it is the power of God unto salvation unto everyone that believeth" (Rom. 1:16). In terms of today, the super-atomic power of God, released from the pulpit, and received by faith!

3. A soul-winning message is personal. Perhaps I should have started here, for a sermon born of God often begins, consciously, with a desire to meet the heart needs of a certain person, or group of persons, as bond slaves of sin. In the Bible there is nothing impersonal about sin or salvation. Especially as it draws towards the end, a soul-winning sermon becomes more and more a matter between the Lord and one hearer, one of many. However large the assembly, the heart of the speaker yearns for the salvation of these persons, one by one. God does not redeem sinners by the dozen or the gross. While John 3:16 begins with God's love for the world, revealed supremely in the Cross, this golden text of the Bible leads to belief on the part of one person, "whosoever." Anyone who believes finds life, here and hereafter.

4. Strange as the fact may seem to an outsider, an evangelistic sermon worthy of its high calling is hard to prepare. A man with a glib tongue can easily make an impromptu talk about religion in general, and relate a number of childish stories taken from a book that ought to be entitled "Stale Mush for Immature Ministers." But who finds it easy, in a sermon of moderate length, to explain clearly and winsomely what a pastor means when he says: "Believe on the Lord Jesus Christ, and thou shalt be saved, and thy house" (Acts 16:31)? In the seminary, when I used to assign the text and hear the sermon, I would get here a discourse about what it did not mean to believe, and what it did not mean to be saved. Where did those young men full of zeal learn to use cheap negations as an easy way of dodging the difficult? As their teachers and pastors, we older men must have encouraged them to deal with a positive subject negatively, which may show how a man refuses to think.

Fortunately, our students now seldom resort to "simple simplicity" as a substitute for a soul-winning sermon. One time in September a young man came back to the seminary for his senior year. During the preceding fifteen months he had served an internship as the interim supply of a rural church. "I preached an evangelistic sermon about once a month." "Why not oftener?" "Because it took me at least a month to get ready, and even at that I had to work hard." To his amazement he found those soul-winning messages the most effective of all his pulpit work. They led the saints to recall former experiences of redeeming grace, and to thank God for a young man who dared to preach that way at the morning service. The sermons also led to conversions. So he resolved that when he became a pastor he would give soul-winning sermons a major place in every year's program.

While in the seminary many a young man begins to think about planning his work for the pulpit. From Dr. William Osler the future pastor may have learned about two sorts of physicians, both full of zeal. One plans his work, and does it well. The other does not plan his work, and before long gets lost in confusion. In the ministry today, with all its demands on time and attention, the pastor who wishes to give evangelism the pulpit attention it deserves must look ahead and plan, even if it be broadly, by the year. This line of thought suggests that we now turn to preaching in general. Instead of thinking about soul-winning sermons as though they stood alone, let us consider the larger background known as Christian Preaching.

II. THE REDISCOVERY OF PREACHING

"The rediscovery of the significance of preaching" is probably the most central and distinctive trend in contemporary Christian theology. So declared Herbert H. Farmer in a thought-provoking book about preaching, *The Servant of the Word* (1942). As a professor of theology, now the successor to Charles H. Dodd at Cambridge University, Farmer knows the doctrinal thinking of our day, both in Britain and on the Continent, as well as in the United States, where he used to teach at Hartford. While Barthian in spots, his book contains much that all of us ought to know. Indeed, the whole Barthian movement calls for study by every non-Barthian who wishes to preach in the latter half of our century. Emil Brunner, while not a Barthian, belongs to much the same school. His current book of sermons, *The Great Invitation* (1955), falls in line with the ideals of Farmer's book.

In a chapter about "Preaching as Personal Encounter," Farmer advises:

> Be very sparing of quotations. These . . . come between the preacher and the hearer . . . Preaching is *you* speaking to a man's heart and will—not Milton, or Shakespeare, or anybody else, however great his name . . . A sermon too full of literary quotation or allusion is like a vessel with a thousand and one little leaks, each one negligible, but taken together they may

> drain it nearly empty . . . Do not be afraid to use the pronoun *you,* which is our common usage for *thou* . . . It would be wearisome to speak thus in the second person through the sermon . . . Used too persistently and in the wrong way, it might give the impression of nagging or browbeating, and of the preacher setting himself up on a pedestal . . . If there is no point where you can say *you,* it is strongly to be suspected that your discourse is not a sermon, but an essay, or a lecture (pp. 62-4).

Surely a change has come over the theological world in its attitude towards preaching! The "new" attitude appears in such a survey as *What Present-Day Theologians Are Thinking* (1952), by Daniel D. Williams, or as in *A Layman's Guide to Protestant Theology* (1955), by William Hordern, a young neo-orthodox author who strives to deal with everyone fairly, however orthodox. Much the same concern about doctrine appears in a current issue of the *Pulpit Digest,* where the able young review editor writes appreciatively about a new book on religious values in the Psalms. The reviewer closes with a note of regret: "Whatever the genesis of preaching, it should come before it is through to the *kerygma* of New Testament proclamation. This note is weakly sounded." In like manner the gifted young book reviewer of the *Christian Century* recently wrote much of good about a new book on evangelism, but closed with the sad comment that the volume contained almost everything worthy except the Gospel.

The change appears even more vividly in theological seminaries. In more than a few strong schools of theology every professor feels that he ought to help train young men who can preach and pray. The professor of Old Testament joins with the man in New Testament, the teacher of Church history, and the guide to theology, in feeling that he ought to present the subject with reference to the preaching and pastoral ministry of the future graduate. I do not mean that this professor should quit dealing with his own subject, and begin teaching homiletics, but that up-to-date seminary teachers now know why the Church founded theological schools. Before World War II, if many teachers of these four basic disciplines were trying to help prepare pastor-preachers, the professors carefully concealed their intentions. The same comment applies to many of their books.

You can judge a seminary fairly well by the books in the library, and by their distribution. Rarely can you find a theological library with an adequate collection of books about preaching and evangelism. By a good working library in such practical theology I do not refer to inspirational manuals made up out of other manuals, many of which resemble an old-fashioned Mother Hubbard gown, "covering everything and touching nothing." I refer to a representative collection of books with a serious purpose, including representative sermons from yesterday and the day before. How can a professor of preaching, evangelism, worship, counseling, or anything else in the practical field, deal with the subject adequately unless he and the students have easy access to source books for study of the matter historically? However far we fall short, this is the ideal that many of us practical men cherish for the training of future preachers, and future teachers.

The University of California Press is now issuing in ten large handsome volumes, superbly edited, the sermons of John Donne (d. 1631). Other publishers, notably in Grand Rapids, have been sending out reprints of preaching classics, most of them carefully edited and well printed. The list, which keeps growing, includes works from P. T. Forsyth, who dealt strongly with the doctrinal content of preaching; and sermons from the following: Lancelot Andrewes (d. 1626), *Sermons on the Nativity;* John Calvin; Charles Simeon (d. 1836); William Jay (d. 1853); Charles H. Spurgeon; Dwight L. Moody; F. B. Meyer; and G. Campbell Morgan. These men, and others like them, have much to show us about the content of preaching and the primacy of the pulpit. Without exception they would have rejoiced in the present-day concern about pulpit use of the *kerygma.*

Everywhere among local churches and laymen I note a strong desire for good sermons. Especially among ministers who have been ordained since World War II, I note a growing concern about the work of the pulpit, and increasing uneasiness because other things push theological reading and sermon preparation into a secondary place; in some cases, a forty-secondary niche! Herein lies the chief cause of mental unrest in the hearts of young men who ten years ago entered schools of theology because they felt called of God to preach the Gospel. Now they feel that they must spend much of their time doing things not directly in line with their loftiest ideals. Even so, many signs indicate that the ministers of tomorrow will set themselves free from bondage to mistaken customs carried over from yesterday.

Recent Substitutes for Preaching

During the period between the two World Wars, many church leaders seem to have kept searching after substitutes for preaching as a main concern of the local church and its pastor. One extremist even called for "a moratorium on preaching." With most of the substitutes I have a good deal of sympathy, especially with the first two I shall list. In those earlier days church leaders felt the need for larger emphasis on religious education, which I prefer to call "Christian education," and on the improvement of public worship, especially the prayers. Still others pleaded for extensive use of audio-visual methods, most of them good in their place, which is by no means small.

Other changes had more to do with the content of preaching. In Victorian days, among both conservatives and liberals, the stress often fell on truth and duty as they concerned one person, one of many. Then a succession of able men began to advocate and promote the "social gospel." While I do not care for that term, I believe that the pulpit today ought to follow the prophets and the apostles in proclaiming both doctrine and ethics. Like the prophets, a minister ought to make clear what the Bible says about the social order; like the apostles, he may stress truth and duty as they relate to one person. In all these matters it is hard for a man in the pulpit to keep the New Testament proportion between the *kerygma* and the *didachē*. In the preaching of Bible doctrine and ethics, it is hard to preserve the balance between the welfare of the individual hearer and the message to society. A study of the New Testament will show that the apostles gave the priority to the *kerygma,* and application to one hearer.

After World War I, many an able man in the pulpit practically ignored the Bible truth of individual salvation, and the resulting service. In 1923 at the Ohio State University Summer School for Pastors, mainly rural, a distinguished advocate of the social gospel delivered ten strong addresses about the teachings of our Lord. I had supposed that Christ taught a good deal of doctrine about the Kingdom, and that He usually spoke in terms of application to one hearer, one of many. After the closing address, able and charming, came a time for questions from the floor. Speaking kindly, to a lecturer whom I liked, I asked: "Do you agree with Professor Francis G. Peabody, of Harvard, that in the social teachings of our Lord the main stress falls on the individual?" The question related to the best-written book in its field, *Jesus Christ and the Social Question* (1900). The lecturer thought for a little while, and then replied: "Yes, I agree." And yet, in the fashion of that day, no one of the ten addresses had touched on any truth or duty as it related to one person. In addressing rural preachers the lecturer had been busy telling about non-Christian conditions in the packing plants of Chicago, and in the steel mills of Pittsburgh. There was nothing about the lost soul of a farmer in Ohio.

Today this tendency to "far-sightedness" is being corrected. Partly because of the "new" stress on pastoral counseling, and more because of a return to Bible ways of presenting truth and duty, many a pastor has rediscovered the importance of the one man for whom the Redeemer died. But another tendency still prevails, especially among pastors who look to distinguished metropolitan divines as exemplars of what to preach. These famous men sometimes use psychology as a substitute for theology, or as an alternative. Much as many of us believe in pastoral counseling, we feel that it should proceed on Christian principles. So we deplore the spread of what has become known as "the cult of reassurance." It stresses the individual, but does not often lead him to bow down before God.

A still more sweeping change has to do with the practical philosophy of preaching. Prior to 1914, and back through the centuries, pulpit masters as a rule preached about truth and duty with primary reference to the Bible. That older preaching was deductive. Search history and see. After World War I, able men began to advocate "inductive preaching." The preaching fathers, most of them, began with certain "constants," such as the authority of God, and of His revelation through Holy Scripture, centering in Christ, the Living Word. In other terms, the *kerygma!* Inductive pulpit work takes nothing for granted, other than the fact of human experience. "The whole spirit and method of thought in our day is inductive, and if we are to win the men of today to the truths of faith we must use the method by which they find truth in other fields." So declared Joseph Fort Newton, an eloquent advocate of *The New Preaching* (1930, p. 139).

In able and careful hands the "new preaching" brings out more than a little truth revealed of God, but the stress falls on human "discovery" rather than on divine revelation. In the years following World War II, the official representative of Protestantism used to speak over the radio at five o'clock on Sunday afternoon. He insisted that "the old authoritarian preaching" had died. At six o'clock the official spokesman of the Roman Church, Fulton J. Sheen, engaged in authoritative sermonizing of a sort that refused to remain buried.

The "new" idea of pulpit work appeared in the leading article of *Harper's Magazine,* July, 1928. In nine pages of lucid and moving prose Harry Emerson Fosdick answered the question, "What Is the Matter with Preaching?" Since his kind of "problem preaching" has prevailed in many pulpits during our generation, the article affords any pastor a mirror in which he can look with profit for himself and his people. After a searching critique of pulpit work in 1928, the writer presents his thesis: "Every sermon should have for its main business the solving of some problem—a vital, important problem, puzzling minds, burdening consciences, distracting lives." This kind of pulpit work becomes a "co-operative enterprise between the preacher and his congregation. A sermon, then, is an engineering operation, by which a chasm is spanned so that spiritual goods on one side are actually transported into personal lives upon the other."

This theory contains much of value, but tends to make preaching seem horizontal. One of Fosdick's ablest sermons, homiletically, deals with "Six Ways to Tell Right from Wrong." In class, I often use this discourse as an example of sturdy structure that stands out, of factual content about persons, and of stress on a single hearer. In each of the six divisions the preacher begins with a sentence like this: "If a man is sincerely perplexed about a question of right and wrong, he may well submit it to the test of common sense." Other key sentences, practically the same, point to sportsmanship, his best self, publicity, his most admired personality, and foresight. The sermon appears in what I consider the ablest book of Fosdick's sermons, *The Hope of the World* (1933, pp. 126-35). My students point out that the six ways, all valid, have little to do with such old-fashioned means of grace as reading the Bible, prayer, coming to church, talking things over with a Christian counselor, doing the known will of God, and waiting on Him for more light. Of course no one but a master would dare to treat six answers in one discourse, and then he would need all of the thirty-five minutes that Fosdick set apart for a sermon in church.

In many of his other sermons, especially of late, Fosdick uses the Bible freely. In the *Pulpit* (May, 1950) one of his ardent admirers states the relevant facts correctly in an article: "How Dr. Fosdick Uses the Bible in Preaching." After a careful study of sermons in various books the admirer reports: "He has used the Bible to a surprising degree. While he quotes from Shakespeare, Emerson, Lincoln, Shaw, Stevenson, Karl Marx, and others, the quotations from all combined would not approach the extent of space that he gives to quoting the Bible . . . In no case did I notice that he used the Bible authoritatively . . . When he quotes from the Bible he does not assume that these quotations have authority because of their source, but because the principle is true and its truth is demonstrable in life now." In terms of the classroom, the basis of authority here is subjective, not objective.

For a fuller statement of much the same philosophy read Fosdick's earlier lectures at Yale, *The Modern Use of the Bible* (1924). To this book I feel indebted, because it opened my eyes to the meaning of currents that influenced many thinking ministers after World War I. Since 1924 Fosdick seems to have changed some of his ideas, often for the better, but he has not changed his practical philosophy of preaching. For the *New York Times* one of his best-informed admirers wrote an article entitled "Dr. Fosdick at 75—Still a Rebel" (May 24, 1953). Personally I do not believe in attacking him from the pulpit, partly because some of the hearers today do not even know his name; also because they need a more positive presentation of revealed truth. On the other hand, I believe that every young minister, on his knees, ought to decide whether or not to accept this horizontal theory of pulpit work.

Wherein lies the basis of authority for a preacher? In God, who has revealed Himself supremely in Christ as the Living Word, and in the Bible as the written Word. This was the doctrine of the early Church, and of the reformers. "Thus saith the Lord!" So it grieves me when our ablest philosophical theologian, Paul Tillich, in his work on *Systematic Theology* (Vol. I., 1951), devotes the first third of his space to reason, before he turns to revelation. This volume is unexpectedly easy for anyone to read, but not easy for me to understand. Why should a son of the Reformation not start with revelation, as it speaks to reason?

"Come now, let us reason together, saith the Lord" (Isa. 1:18). "Think on these things," writes the Apostle (Phil. 4:8). Paul believed that "these things" had been revealed to him from God.

After World War I, able preachers resorted to the "life-situation sermon," the case method, and other supposedly new ways of presenting truth and duty. As with the "problem approach," most of these methods are new only in name. In His parables, and often elsewhere, our Lord employed the "problem approach," the case system, and the "life-situation method." In recent years Clarence E. Macartney has published more than one volume of orthodox "life-situation sermons." As in his other pulpit work, he strives to meet the needs of the hearers today. Preaching topically, he uses "modern methods" of presenting truth as he finds it in Holy Writ. So do many other conservative ministers use portions of Holy Writ in meeting the needs of sinners and saints. Sometimes, alas, the stress falls on the human being with his fears, his worries, or his doubts, not on the Lord God with His revelation of the truth that sets a man free from sin and every disorder in the soul.

The Weaknesses of Evangelical Preaching

There must have been a reason for the changes in the philosophy of preaching. Why did evangelical pulpit work suffer a partial eclipse after 1914? Why did we young dunces sometimes preach the man-made "Gospel of Progress," declaring that every day and in every way the world would keep on growing better and better? Looking back I can see that we were tempted to turn aside from older ways of preaching because we felt that they had become outmoded. We also felt that the fault lay partly with the teaching of homiletics, which often seemed wooden. Brethren, pray for us who try to train preachers for tomorrow!

In my day as a student, a typical school of theology exalted the pulpit orator. More recently an able student of preaching delivered to seminary men a series of lectures on *Six Kings of the American Pulpit* (1939). Most of the hearers were going out to serve in states largely agricultural; not one student in a score could hope ever to become a pulpit orator, after the oldtime "grand manner." And yet five of the six chosen exemplars had achieved their fame as pulpit orators, and only one had even tried to excel as a pastor. Personally, as a student I did not aspire to become a Beecher or a Talmage. I wanted to become a sermonizer, with Alexander Maclaren as my homiletical hero. Now I learn from Baptist friends, who know the facts about Maclaren in Manchester, that he labored there in Union Chapel forty-five years, and yet made no lasting impression on the religious life of the city. Perhaps because he did not engage in pastoral work, he did not in the pulpit show much concern about the needs of the hearers. By example he encouraged us younger men to make preaching from the Bible an end in itself, not a means of grace.

Partly because of such examples, and such teachings, our early expository sermons tended to seem impractical and uninteresting. Our doctrinal messages became heavy and futile, especially when we set up men of straw and then knocked them down. Our evangelistic appeals often sounded hollow and unreal. Our ethical discourses, and our pastoral sermons, were more hortatory and denunciatory than edifying. If all of this seems far-fetched, remember that I am speaking out of my early experiences and observations. In those days writers as diverse as Booker T. Washington and George A. Gordon told about early exposure to orthodox sermons with no more reference to human needs than the quacking of ducks on a mill pond.

The ministers now in view prided themselves on speaking extemporaneously. They may not have heard the saying of old Charles Hodge at Princeton, that the best preaching, and the worst, was extemporaneous. By the latter he meant that a man in the pulpit "went everywhere preaching the Gospel," and that the resulting effusion seemed to be "without form and void." For many such reasons, in a charming autobiography, *I Was Made a Minister* (1943), the late Bishop Edwin H. Hughes warned young clergymen against "the peril of extemporaneousness." He meant that no man ought to enter the pulpit without a message from God, and that no one ought to misrepresent the Lord of all truth and grace by making Him seem dull, dreary, and drab. A few years ago one of our leading churches had to go outside our country to secure an evangelical minister who could conduct an hour of worship without making grammatical blunders. At the same time more than a few liberal preachers excelled in giving every sermon a dress fit to adorn a daughter of the King.

In view of such facts I have long since decided that as a teacher I can learn much from able liberals about making a sermon interesting and clear. Believing in the Bible as the written Word of God, I do not think that any educated minister ought ever to preach from it so as to make it seem dull and muddy. I see no reason why the most orthodox interpreter should ever unintentionally misrepresent Christ by making Him seem unable to interest strong men who think in terms of the problem approach, case studies, and other present-day methods of security, variety, clarity, and interest. From up-to-date conservatives I learn that it is possible to use such means in a sermon with biblical substance, doctrinal form, and popular appeal. How otherwise did John Bunyan "preach" to the men of his day?

The Outlook for Tomorrow

By way of summary let us think about prospects for the pulpit of tomorrow. To me they look bright. In our country all sorts of people have been buying copies of Holy Scripture. In a recent year, says the American Bible Society, almost 10,000,000 persons here at home secured new Bibles. These men and women have also been buying and reading many other books about religion, so much so that they now feel confused. The door stands open wide for a pastor who loves the Lord, knows his Bible, and preaches theology,—all always with charm, clarity, and "sweet reasonableness." In order to save time let me simply list a number of other elements that enter into a hopeful view of tomorrow. Among them I shall include a few obstacles that need be surmounted.

1. *The central importance of the local church.* Many a pastor and his people now see that in a large sense evangelism, Christian nurture, missions, world brotherhood, and all other things relating to human aspects of the Kingdom, depend on the spiritual health of the home church.

2. *The pivotal importance of the local pastor.* Under God, the progress of His work here at home and beyond the seven seas depends on the local pastor or missionary more than on anyone else here below. We who teach, and those who administer, have places of importance and influence, but the pastor at home, like the missionary elsewhere, does the basic work of the Kingdom. For some such reasons, when Chrysostom stood at the pinnacle of his fame as the world's most eloquent preacher, he went out of his way publicly to laud ministers of small and struggling churches in outlying rural districts.

3. *The strategic importance of preaching.* Ideally, the minister of a local church excels as a pastor, as a preacher, and as a leader in the other parts of public worship. These three belong together, and nothing else than Christian character stands on the same high level. In the life and work of a man called to the ministry, nothing should bulk so large as preaching, in the spirit of prayer and praise, to people who love their pastor, and eagerly await the bread of life that he loves to break.

4. *The call for a full-length sermon.* In our commendable zeal for improvement of public worship, some of us have been allowing less and less time for the sermon. With a lively fancy and a glib tongue a pulpiteer can deliver in ten or fifteen minutes a bright little semi-religious "pep talk." Only a master would undertake to preach a doctrinal or an expository sermon in much less than twenty-five. On the other hand, only an exceptional man these days can wisely keep on for thirty-five, as Fosdick did regularly at the Riverside Church. I think of twenty-five minutes as enough, with thirty as the upper limit. "Let your moderation be known unto all men" (Phil. 4:5). In the history of the pulpit so far, every man who has made his mark has done so by preaching something other than little "pink tea sermonettes."

5. *The opportunity to preach oftener.* Beecher taught himself how to preach by a careful study of sermons, and by preaching often. So did Spurgeon. Even if a minister now can thrive with a restricted pulpit schedule, every normal congregation needs on the Lord's Day more than one opportunity to engage in the public worship of God (which of course includes a message from the pulpit). In the history of the Chris-

tian Church, when has a one-hour-a-week pulpit schedule ever developed among the members a knowledge of the Bible, a habit of prayer, a delight in soul winning, and a hope for the hereafter? Herein lies a test of our pulpit schedules: "By their fruits ye shall know them."

6. *The arrangement for boys and girls to worship in the main sanctuary every Lord's Day, under the leadership of their pastor and friend.* If on every Sunday morning the man of God preaches and prays so as to interest and help boys and girls of ten or twelve years, he also interests and helps their parents and grandparents. Like his Lord, the Ideal Preacher, the friend in view can be simple without seeming shallow. Such simplicity calls for much more ability, and much more time in the study, than if a man uses the sort of complicated pulpit jargon he finds in erudite volumes written by pundits who never have learned how to draw their English words from wells of living water, pure and undefiled.

7. *The wisdom of letting a mature minister continue to serve God as a pastor.* In some circles of late the craze for youth in the pulpit, with its consequent inexperience, has been giving way to more sober counsels. Recently I moderated a congregational meeting where the people had enjoyed in succession the ministry of three young men, each of them with ability and promise. In speaking about their desires for a successor, those laymen mentioned only one detail: they wanted a man fifty years of age, with a little leeway in either direction. As for ability to interest and help young people, that does not depend on a minister's age, but on his personality, and his love for the young. In a typical congregation, a glance over the gray heads of those present next Lord's Day will show that during the years when we have stressed youth in the pulpit we have lost young folk from the pews. By all means let us give inexperienced ministers every opportunity to grow by using their God-given powers. But let us not put any forward-looking man of mature powers on the shelf before he has given his best years to the service of God. "Youth shows but half; trust God, see all, nor be afraid."

8. *A larger sphere for laymen.* In the local church of tomorrow, let us hope, laymen will become as numerous, as active, and as zealous as laywomen. Knowing that the minister needs time and energy for the kind of spiritual ministry the Lord has committed to him alone, the "men of the church" will take over the practical work, under his leadership, as laymen did under Brooks in Boston and Spurgeon in London. Fortunately, a congregation need not be large and famous, or have a well-known pastor, before the laymen can set him free from duties and tasks the Lord intended for other hands.

9. *A renewed dedication of the pastor to the service of God.* "For their sakes I sanctify myself" (Jn. 17:19). In a free paraphrase this means: For the sake of the people committed to his care, the pastor makes the most of all his God-given powers. In the pulpit and out among people,

his usefulness and his influence, under God, depend on his personality. With the passing of every year, he becomes a better shepherd of souls, or else a worse; a better leader in prayer, or a poorer; a better preacher of the Gospel, or a weaker. Especially during the years between forty and fifty he must in a sense catch his second wind, or else start casting about for a vacant shelf, there to scan the distant heavens, looking for stars that have ceased to shine.

10. *A better sort of theological training.* Here I refer only to the preparation of a future pastor-preacher who can pray. Long ago I learned by my own experience that a student of theology thrives best under a professor of ability who has served as a pastor, and still has the heart of a shepherd. In his *Memoirs* (1947) the late President of the Southern Baptist Seminary in Louisville, John R. Sampey, shows why through the years that school of the prophets has sent out a succession of strong pastors who can preach and pray: "With the possible exception of four men, all the members of the faculty from 1859 to 1945 have been primarily preachers . . . Broadus [professor of New Testament] went so far as to say that no one was qualified to be a professor in a seminary unless he preferred to preach" (p. 284).

After a number of years in the pastorate, a man who would teach homiletics, or anything else in the practical field, ought to secure special training, with an earned doctor's degree. This training, I believe, ought to include a mastery of church history as it relates to his chosen specialty. The history of preaching begins with the Old Testament and the New, each of which the teacher of future ministers ought to know as a master. If the laymen who give bountifully for the development of theological seminaries knew the facts about the paucity of opportunities for graduate study in the history of preaching, they would make it possible for any professor-elect to secure as complete and adequate a training as he could secure in his field if he were planning to teach the Old Testament or theology. When a professor of homiletics takes a sabbatical year, where can he find the right sort of postgraduate training either at home or abroad?

Now let me turn again to the young minister for whose training the fathers and mothers established the theological seminary. We may think of a newly-ordained minister in charge of a relatively small church, with time to read, to think, to pray, and to grow. Let me suggest that he should draw up a homemade creed, for no other eyes than his own. The one that follows is subject to no restrictions about use in private.

The Creed of a Pastor-Preacher

I BELIEVE:

. . .in this congregation as for me the most important agency of the Kingdom on earth, except the Christian home.

. . .in the public worship of God as the most important activity of this congregation, or of any other that loves God in Christ supremely.

. . .in the reading of the Scriptures and the preaching of the Gospel as the most important parts of public worship, except the celebration of the sacraments or the observance of the ordinances.

. . .in making ready for leadership in worship, and for preaching the Gospel, as my most important work from week to week.

. . .in the meeting of human needs here at home as the guiding purpose in every hour of public worship, and in every sermon.

. . .in prayer for the leading of the Holy Spirit that I may sense the needs of the people in this community, and make ready to meet their needs through the prayers of the sanctuary, and through the preaching of God's Word.

. . .in using the Bible as the main source of materials for meeting the needs of men and women, boys and girls, whom I know well and love much as their pastor and friend.

. . .in preparing every sermon so that both in content and in form it will worthily represent the King from whom all truth and beauty flow.

. . .in delivering each message so that the hearer will accept the truth in it, and resolve to do the will of God, instead of merely praising me and my sermon.

. . .in trusting the Lord to follow every sermon with His blessing according to His promise about the faithful use of His revealed truth (Isa. 55:10, 11).

A SELECTIVE BIBLIOGRAPHY

OLD TESTAMENT

Oswald T. Allis, *The Five Books of Moses.* Philadelphia: Presbyterian and Reformed Publishing Co., 1949.

———, *The Unity of Isaiah.* Philadelphia: Presbyterian and Reformed Publishing Co., 1950.

Alexander Heidel, *The Babylonian Genesis.* Chicago: University of Chicago Press, 1951.

C. F. Keil and F. Delitzsch, *Biblical Commentary on the Old Testament.*

Merrill T. Unger, *Archaeology and the Old Testament.* Grand Rapids: Zondervan Publishing House, 1954.

Edward Joseph Young, *An Introduction to the Old Testament.* Grand Rapids. William B. Eerdmans Publishing Company, 1949.

NEW TESTAMENT

J. Gresham Machen, *The Origin of Paul's Religion.* New York: The Macmillan Company, 1923.

W. M. Ramsay, *The Bearing of Recent Discovery on the Trustworthiness of the New Testament.* London: Hodder and Stoughton, 1915.

A. T. Robertson, *A Grammar of the Greek New Testament in the Light of Historical Research.* New York: George H. Doran Co., 1914.

Henry C. Thiessen, *Introduction to the New Testament.* Grand Rapids: William B. Eerdmans Publishing Company, 1943.

Geerhardus Vos, *The Self-Disclosure of Jesus.* New York: George H. Doran Co., 1926.

THEOLOGY

Louis Berkhof, *Recent Trends in Theology.* Grand Rapids: William B. Eerdmans Publishing Company, 1944.

———, *Reformed Dogmatics,* 4 vols. Grand Rapids: William B. Eerdmans Publishing Company.

G. C. Berkouwer, *Studies in Dogmatics,* 17 vols. Grand Rapids: William B. Eerdmans Publishing Company.

Carl F. H. Henry, *Fifty Years of Protestant Theology.* Boston: W. A. Wilde Company, 1950.

———, *The Protestant Dilemma.* Grand Rapids: William B. Eerdmans Publishing Company, 1949.

Lawton, J. S., *Conflict in Christology*. London: Society for the Propagation of Christian Knowledge, 1947.

John MacLeod, *Scottish Theology in Relation to Church History Since the Reformation*. Edinburgh: Free Church of Scotland, 1943.

B. B. Warfield, *Revelation and Inspiration*. New York: Oxford University Press, 1927.

———, *Christology and Criticism*. New York: Oxford University Press, 1929.

ETHICS

Clarence Bouma and others, *God-Centered Living* (A Symposium). Grand Rapids: Baker Book House, 1951.

Gordon H. Clark, *A Christian View of Men and Things*. Grand Rapids: William B. Eerdmans Publishing Company, 1952.

Carl F. H. Henry, *The Uneasy Conscience of Modern Fundamentalism*. Grand Rapids: William B. Eerdmans Publishing Company, 1947.

———, *Christian Personal Ethics*. Grand Rapids: William B. Eerdmans Publishing Company, 1957.

John Murray, *Aspects of Biblical Ethics*. Grand Rapids: William B. Eerdmans Publishing Company, 1957.

H. J. Stob and others, *The Secularization of Modern Life* (A Symposium). Montpellier, France: Societe Calviniste de France, 1953.

APOLOGETICS

Edward John Carnell, *An Introduction to Christian Apologetics*. Grand Rapids: William B. Eerdmans Publishing Company, 1948 (5th ed., 1956).

Gordon H. Clark, *A Christian View of Men and Things*. Grand Rapids: William B. Eerdmans Publishing Company, 1952.

Herman Dooyeweerd, *A New Critique of Theoretical Thought*. Philadelphia: The Presbyterian and Reformed Publishing Co., 1953.

Floyd E. Hamilton, *The Basis of Christian Faith*. New York: Harper and Brothers, 1946 (3rd ed.).

Carl F. H. Henry, *Remaking the Modern Mind*. Grand Rapids: William B. Eerdmans Publishing Company, 1946 (2nd ed., 1948).

J. Gresham Machen, *Christianity and Liberalism*. New York: The Macmillan Company, 1925.

———, *What Is Faith?* New York: The Macmillan Company, 1923.

Samuel Thompson, *A Modern Philosophy of Religion*. Chicago: Henry Regnery Co., 1955.

Cornelius Van Til, *The Defense of the Faith*. Philadelphia: The Presbyterian and Reformed Publishing Co., 1955.

CHRISTIAN EDUCATION

Mark Fakkema, *Christian Philosophy: Its Educational Implications*. Chicago: National Association of Christian Schools, n.d.

Frank E. Gaebelein, *Christian Education in a Democracy* (Report of the National Association of Evangelicals). New York: Oxford University Press, 1951.

Spenser Leeson, *Christian Education* (Bampton Lectures). London: Longmans, Green and Co., 1947.

Howard Lowry, *The Mind's Adventure*. Philadelphia: Westminster Press, 1950.

Harold C. Mason, *Abiding Values in Christian Education*. Westwood, N. J.: Fleming H. Revell Co., 1955.

James D. Smart, *The Teaching Ministry of the Church*. Philadelphia: Westminster Press, 1954.

Jan Waterink, *Basic Concepts in Christian Pedagogy* (Calvin Foundation Lectures). Grand Rapids: Wm. B. Eerdmans Publishing Company, 1954.

PHILOSOPHY OF RELIGION

Edward John Carnell, *A Philosophy of the Christian Religion*. Grand Rapids: William B. Eerdmans Publishing Company, 1952.

Carl F. H. Henry, *The Drift of Western Thought*. Grand Rapids: William B. Eerdmans Publishing Company, 1951.

Leander S. Keyser, *A Philosophy of Christianity*. Burlington, Ia.: The Lutheran Literary Board, 1948.

E. Y. Mullins, *Christianity at the Crossroads*. New York: George H. Doran Company, 1924.

Cornelius Van Til, *The New Modernism*. Philadelphia: Presbyterian and Reformed Publishing Co., 1947.

Warren G. Young, *A Christian Approach to Philosophy*. Wheaton, Ill.: Van Kampen Press, 1954.

SCIENCE AND RELIGION

G. C. Berkouwer, *General Revelation*. Grand Rapids: William B. Eerdmans Publishing Company, 1955.

F. Alton Everest, ed., *Modern Science and Christian Faith*. Wheaton, Ill.: Van Kampen Press, 1948.

Theodore Graebner, *God and the Cosmos*. Grand Rapids: William B. Eerdmans Publishing Company, 1943 (2nd ed.).

C. S. Lewis, *Miracles*. New York: The Macmillan Company, 1947.

Bernard Ramm, *The Christian View of Science and Scripture*. Grand Rapids: William B. Eerdmans Publishing Company, 1954.

PHILOSOPHY OF HISTORY*

John Baillie, *What Is Christian Civilization?* New York: Charles Scribner's Sons, 1948.

Herbert Butterfield, *Christianity and History*. London: George Bell & Sons, Ltd., 1949.

Otto Piper, *God in History*. New York: The Macmillan Company, 1939.

Eric C. Rust, *The Christian Understanding of History*. London: Letterworth Press, 1947.

Arnold J. Toynbee, *Civilization on Trial*. New York: Oxford University Press, 1948.

(*) In lieu of a satisfactory Evangelical bibliography in Philosophy of History, the above volumes, representative of diverse viewpoints, are included to suggest important contemporary literature in this field.

EVANGELISM AND PREACHING

Andrew W. Blackwood, *The Fine Art of Preaching*. New York: The Macmillan Company, 1937.

———, *Doctrinal Preaching for Today*. New York: Abingdon Press, 1956.

John A. Broadus, *A Treatise on the Preparation and Delivery of Sermons*. New York: A. C. Armstrong and Son, 1902.

Edwin C. Dargan, *A History of Preaching*. Grand Rapids: Baker Book House, 1954 (Reprint of 1904 edition).

Bryan Green, *The Practice of Evangelism*. New York: Charles Scribner's Sons, 1951.

Clarence Edward Macartney, *Preaching Without Notes*. New York: Abingdon-Cokesbury Press, 1946.

AUTHOR INDEX